Voice Assistants in Action-oriented Mediation Practice

ŁÓDŹ STUDIES IN LANGUAGE

Edited by Barbara Lewandowska-Tomaszczyk and Łukasz Bogucki

Volume 76

Klaudia Gajewska

Voice Assistants in Action-oriented Mediation Practice

Insights from Polish Learners of English as a Foreign Language

PETER LANG

Berlin - Bruxelles - Chennai - Lausanne - New York - Oxford

Bibliographic Information published by the Deutsche Nationalbibliothek
The Deutsche Nationalbibliothek lists this publication in the Deutsche Nationalbibliografie; detailed bibliographic data is available in the internet at http://dnb.d-nb.de.

Library of Congress Cataloging-in-Publication Data
Names: Gajewska, Klaudia, 1994- author
Title: Voice assistants in action-oriented mediation practice : insights from Polish learners of English as a foreign language / Klaudia Gajewska.
Description: Oxford ; New York : Peter Lang, 2025. | Series: Beiträge zur Germanistik und angewandten Linguistik / Contributions to German studies and applied linguistics, 2196-3649 ; 16
Identifiers: LCCN 2025004120 (print) | LCCN 2025004121 (ebook) | ISBN 9783631907917 hardback | ISBN 9783631912638 ebook | ISBN 9783631912645 epub
Subjects: LCSH: English language--Study and teaching (Secondary)--Polish speakers | English language--Computer-assisted instruction | Mobile-assisted language learning | Intelligent personal assistants (Computer software) | Communicative competence--Study and teaching | Task analysis in education
Classification: LCC PE1128.3 .G35 2025 (print) | LCC PE1128.3 (ebook) | DDC 428.0078/56454--dc23/eng/20250409
LC record available at https://lccn.loc.gov/2025004120
LC ebook record available at https://lccn.loc.gov/2025004121

The cover image courtesy of Benjamin Ben Chaim
This publication was financially supported by Maria Curie-Skłodowska University, Poland.

ISSN 2196-3649
ISBN 978-3-631-90791-7 (Print)
E-ISBN 978-3-631-91263-8 (E-PDF)
E-ISBN 978-3-631-91264-5 (E-PUB)
DOI 10.3726/b22798

Published by Peter Lang GmbH, Berlin (Germany)

info@peterlang.com

This publication has been peer reviewed.

www.peterlang.com

Table of Contents

List of figures and tables

List of abbreviations

AI	Artificial intelligence
ALM	Audiolingual Method
ALTE	Association for Language Testers in Europe
AOA	Action-oriented approach
BENJA	Badanie efektywności nauczania języka angielskiego w szkole podstawowej (Research on the effectiveness of English language teaching in primary schools)
BUNJO	Badanie uczenia się i nauczania języków obcych w gimnazjum (Research on the effectiveness of foreign language learning and teaching in middle schools)
CA	Conversational agent
CALI	Computer-Assisted Language Instruction
CALL	Computer-Assisted Language Learning
CEFR	Common European Framework of Reference for Languages: Learning, teaching, assessment
CKE	Centralna Komisja Egzaminacyjna (Central Examination Board)
CLT	Communicative Language Teaching
CoE	Council of Europe
CRQ	Central research question
CtrlG	Control group
CV	Companion volume
DS	Dialogue system
DV	Dependent variable
EALTA	European Association for Language Testing and Assessment
EFL	English as a foreign language
ESL	English as a second language
ESLC	European Survey of Language Competences
ESOKJ	Europejski System Opisu Kształcenia Językowego: Uczenie się, nauczanie, ocenianie (Common European Framework of Reference for Languages: Learning, teaching, assessment)

EU	European Union
ExG	Experimental group
FL	Foreign language
FLT	Foreign language teaching
FL1/FL2	First/Second foreign language
GTM	Grammar-Translation Method
HCI	Human-computer interaction
HHC	Human-human interaction
HMC	Human-machine communication
ICALL	Intelligent Computer-Assisted Language Learning
ICT	Information and communication technology
ILTS	Intelligent language tutoring system
IMALL	Intelligent Mobile-Assisted Language Learning
IPA	Intelligent personal assistant
ISCED	International Standard Classification of Education
IV	Independent variable
IVA	Intelligent virtual assistant
L1/L2	First/second language
MALL	Mobile-Assisted Language Learning
MM	Mixed-methods design
MPC	Multimedia personal computer
MVS	Maximum variation sampling
NA	Needs analysis
NLG	Natural language generation
NLP	Natural language processing
NLU	Natural language understanding
OECD	Organisation for Economic Cooperation and Development
OKE	Okręgowa Komisja Egzaminacyjna (Regional Examination Board)
PC	Personal computer
PDA	Personal digital assistant

PISA	Programme for International Student Assessment
PLATO	Programmed Logic for Automatic Teaching Operations
POLPAN	Polskie Badanie Panelowe (Polish Panel Research)
PPP	Presentation-practice-production
SAMR	Substitution, augmentation, modification, and redefinition
SLA	Second language acquisition
SSI	Semi-structured interview
TAM	Technology Acceptance Model
TBLT/TBLL	Task-based language teaching/Task-based language learning
TELL	Technology-Enhanced Language Learning
TFOH	Technology-facilitated oral homework
TL	Target language
TODS	Task-oriented dialogue system
TPR	Total Physical Response
TSLT	Task-Supported Language Learning
VA	Voice assistant
WELL	Web-Enhanced Language Learning

Introduction

Developments in linguistics and psychology taking place in the last decades of the 20th century have redefined the notion of language education. A period of unsuccessful foreign language teaching associated with the controversial Age of Methods (Decoo, 2001; Sheen, 1994) created the anti-method movement (Richards, 1990), signalling the emergence of the Post-Method Era (Kumaradivelu, 1994) in the 1990s. The symbolic "death of method" (Kumaradivelu, 2006) started an accelerating trend towards internalisation of the teaching process (Salmani-Nodoushan, 2006), as reflected in the shift away from method- to teacher-based approaches (Richards & Rodgers, 2014) and from teacher- to learner-centredness (Freeman & Richards, 1993).

At the same time, advancements in information and communication technologies have further revolutionised the field of language education. Technological progress, which contributed to a massive upsurge in computers and electronic devices, led to the creation of entirely new teaching and learning environments. The earliest room-size mainframes inherent to the Behaviourist phase of Computer-Assisted Language Learning were superseded by smaller yet more powerful personal and multimedia computers (Davies et al., 2013). The subsequent transfer of their functions to increasingly sophisticated portable devices encouraged the use of the latter in in-class and out-of-class English as a second and foreign language learning contexts (Kukulska-Hulme & Shield, 2008; Stockwell & Hubbard, 2013), opening up a new field that came to be known as Mobile-Assisted Language Learning (Chinnery, 2006; Kukulska-Hulme, 2019).

The proliferation of sophisticated portables facilitated informal any-time-and-anywhere language learning (Miangah & Nezarat, 2012). Despite their early technological constraints, mobile devices (including smartphones in particular) increased in prominence both in personal and educational domains due to their low cost, small size, and user-friendliness. As a matter of fact, these devices can be used nowadays in a variety of ways and for a variety of purposes, with apps available through various stores further increasing their technological capabilities (Miller, 2012; Stockwell, 2022; Yang, 2013).

Even though foreign language students can receive additional support in their target language reception and production outside instructed settings thanks to their interactions with instructors, friends, and family members, only the most privileged of pupils can in fact enjoy such luxury given the high cost of private tuition and monolingual social backgrounds of the vast majority of them. The problem related to students' limited interaction in the target language not only in out-of-class settings, but also on-site took on greater significance in the wake of the SARS-CoV-2 outbreak and the implementation of e-learning techniques, which to a greater or lesser extent paralysed (language) education systems across the globe. In view of the above, the prospect of a competent and tireless human-like device which can provide unrestricted and immediate access to personal assistance has become enormously appealing in foreign language instructed settings (Kukulska-Hulme & Lee, 2016).

Since the first use of the term in the 1950s (Benko & Lanyi, 2009), artificially intelligent machines, or those that thanks to natural language processing, machine learning, and information retrieval think and act like human beings (Chamberlain, 2017), have become omnipresent, from systems underlying financial technologies, through e-commerce and marketing, to manufacturing (Pokrivcakowa, 2019). The application of concepts from the field of artificial intelligence in language education led to the development of Intelligent Computer-Assisted Language Learning (Gamper & Knapp, 2002). Interactions therein have been categorised into tutorial and non-tutorial (Levy, 2009), each of which taking place through the medium of intelligent language tutoring systems and dialogue systems respectively (Schulze & Heift, 2012).

In the 21st century, task-oriented dialogue systems, also known as voice assistants, commonly found on smartphones, smart home devices, and in some cars and wearables (e.g., watches, glasses, and clothes) (Kukulska-Hulme, 2019) might become one way to support the demanding (and once impossible to fulfill) requirement concerning the provision of non-stop personal assistance in informal language learning. The availability of intelligent machines has attracted greater public attention relatively recently, that is after the launch of the first intelligent virtual assistants (e.g., *Siri*, *Google Assistant*, *Alexa*) on mainstream smartphones in the 2010s (Arif, 2018; Kukulska-Hulme, 2019). Human-computer interactions involving natural language can be accomplished by intelligent virtual assistants anytime and anywhere through the performance of everyday electronic tasks, such as setting alarms, drawing up shopping and to-do lists, and finding answers to factual questions (Goksel-Canbek & Mutlu, 2016).

The influence that modern and increasingly intelligent computer technologies, such as voice assistants, have on English as a second and foreign language learning has generated considerable research interest. The findings from the empirical studies revealed a positive impact of this technology on language- and psychology-related aspects of learning (Chen et al., 2020; Daniels & Iwago, 2017; Dizon, 2017, 2020; Dizon & Tang, 2019, 2020; Moussalli & Cardoso, 2016, 2017, 2019; Tai & Chen, 2020, 2022; Underwood, 2017). The preliminary research, however, has suffered from several methodological limitations, such as small sample size, short duration, and insufficient number of instruments of data collection. Furthermore, a critical analysis of the available studies does not allow for an objective evaluation of voice assistance in view of the gaps in the research and conflicting findings. This thus creates a pressing need for further examination of the phenomenon in language education.

Given its research and pragmatic value, the design and implementation of voice assistance in foreign language educational settings is more than justified. To fill in the gap in the CALL research, the book *Voice assistants in action-oriented mediation practice: Insights from Polish learners of English as a foreign language* aims to provide a better understanding of the novel phenomenon of task-oriented Intelligent Mobile-Assisted Language Learning. In this discussion, it stands for voice assistance implementation within the area of English as a foreign language smartphone-based self-instructed learning of text mediation by Polish adolescents. To be more precise, the objective of the research is to find out if enriching regular English as a foreign language action-oriented self-instruction with a voice assistant, here Amazon's *Alexa*, will have a positive impact on Polish teenage learners' ability to mediate a text. Both text mediation and mediation in general have assumed greater importance in Poland in the wake of the *Common European Framework of Reference for Languages: Learning, teaching, assessment. Companion volume with new descriptors* (CoE, 2018) online publication and have been therefore selected and operationalised for the purpose of the current investigation. Furthermore, the strengths and weaknesses of task-oriented Intelligent Mobile-Assisted Language Learning in providing mediation practice will be identified based on the learners' evaluation of the experimental intervention.

In light of the aforementioned research objectives, the study will attempt to answer two central research questions:

1. How does the VA-supported task performance affect intralinguistic text mediation of the Polish learners of English?
2. How do the Polish learners of English evaluate the VA?

For the purpose of the current study, a mixed-methods design involving experimental and descriptive research will be adopted to evaluate the treatment in a natural out-of-class learning context. It will allow the collection and analysis of data of different formats and origins to ensure greater validity and to facilitate further investigation. An eight-month research procedure including the technology-mediated needs analysis, selection of target tasks, design of instructional treatment for experimental and control group students, pilot testing, main study, and programme evaluation will guide the process of quantitative and qualitative data collection and analysis.

The book consists of five chapters. Each of them plays an equally important role in the presentation of the theoretical and methodological background to the research project.

The first chapter focuses on the presentation of the trends in European policies and practices for developing foreign language learners' communicative competence. It begins with the introduction of the communicative competence construct. Next, it discusses the significance of the action-oriented approach developed within the Council of Europe's seminal documents. Lastly, it offers a joint theoretical and practical perspective on the latest concept of mediation in the context of language education in Europe.

The second chapter addresses the problem of English as a foreign language learning, teaching, and assessment in post-war Poland. It presents the selected education reforms implemented by the Polish government before and after the 1989 transformations effected by the fall of communism and discusses the administration of English as a foreign language secondary school exit examinations from both European and Polish perspectives. Finally, it identifies the challenges underlying the development of communicative competence by foreign language learners in Poland.

The third chapter forms a historical background for the educational use of voice assistants by overviewing the application of computer technologies in language instruction since the 1960s. It underlines the growing mobility of computers and discusses implications involved in their implementation in foreign language teaching. Next, it overviews technological advancements facilitating the emergence of Intelligent Mobile-Assisted Language Learning and the basic tenets underlying this young subfield of Computer- and Mobile-Assisted Language Learning. Chapter Three also introduces and describes the novel concept of task-oriented Intelligent Mobile-Assisted Language Learning which has been developed by the present author for the purpose of the current discussion. Next, it presents the research trends and locates the sources of limitations of the selected empirical studies investigating the phenomenon of voice assistance.

The fourth chapter focuses on the presentation of the methodology underlying the research project that was carried out among the Polish secondary school students. It specifies the research problem, aims, questions, and hypotheses. Next, it describes a mixed-methods approach to research design and provides basic information about the population and sample. The six-stage research procedure involving the needs analysis, target task selection, instructional treatment design, pilot testing, the study proper, and programme evaluation is then presented. The chapter ends with a section on ethical considerations.

The fifth chapter reports the results of the current quasi-experimental research study. It discusses the findings of the quantitative and qualitative data analysis obtained from the main study and programme evaluation. In addition, the chapter deals with the pedagogical implications and conclusions that follow from the data presented therein. Lastly, it presents limitations to the study and puts forward suggestions for future research.

Chapter 1
Developing foreign language learners' communicative competence: Trends in European policies and practices

1.0 Outline

The primary objective of Chapter One is to offer a general overview of the trends in European policies and practices for developing foreign language (FL) learners' communicative competence that have emerged in the field of language education in the last century. The chapter is divided into three subchapters for this purpose. The first subchapter forms a historical and theoretical background of communicative competence and discusses the construct in the context of its different models and the relationship that different methods have to the growth of the Communicative Language Teaching (CLT) paradigm. The second subchapter introduces the action-oriented vision of communicative competence within the conceptual model promoted by the *Common European Framework of Reference for Languages: Learning, teaching, assessment* (2001) and its supplementary documents published in 2018 and 2020. The third subchapter brings mediation to the centre of the current discussion in the context of the update of the framework through the publication of the companion volumes. The final subchapter offers a joint theoretical and practical perspective of the concept by investigating the origins and definitions of the term in the field of foreign language teaching (FLT) and beyond, and exploring the issues involved in the implementation of mediation tasks in language instruction.

1.1 Communicative competence in language education

1.1.1 Theoretical and historical background of the communicative competence construct

1.1.1.1 Teaching traditions in the Pre-Method Era: From the Classical to Direct Method

The beginnings of FL education can be traced back hundreds of years to the time of Confucius, the Chinese philosopher called the father of teaching (Salmani-Nodoushan, 2006). Until the end of the 19th century, FLT had consistently relied on commonsensible teaching techniques uninformed by any scientifically established theories of language and learning (Kelly, 1969). This tendency was clearly reflected in pronunciation instruction which was limited to the use of mimicry (Celce-Murcia et al., 1996). This period of intuitive FL education came to be known as the Pre-Method Era as it was referred to by Louis Kelly (1969) in his publication *25 centuries of language teaching.*

Given the high status of Latin in education, philosophy, commerce, religion, and government in the 1500s, students' mastery of reading and writing in this classical language was identified as the primary objective of language instruction not only at that time, but also in the centuries to come (Richards & Rodgers, 2014). Classroom procedures implemented to teach Latin in the 16th and 17th century were referred to as the Classical Method (Brown, 1994; Jin & Cortazzi, 2011). This method relied on deductive teaching of grammar and students' rote-learning of vocabulary lists. Learners' theoretical knowledge of grammatical rules, lexis, declensions, and conjugations was to enable them to perform written translation-based exercises (Richards & Rodgers, 2014). The continual preoccupation with the study of literary texts in the classroom led to the exhaustive investigation of written language to the disadvantage of oracy (Brown & Yule, 1983).

Even though Latin gradually declined in importance as a lingua franca to the advantage of European vernaculars, such as French, Italian, and English (Richards & Rodgers, 2014), the Classical Method was still applied to the teaching of the modern languages in the 18th and 19th century (Brown, 2000). It was referred to as the Traditional Method (Sierra, 1995) and the Grammar-Translation Method (GTM) (Richards & Rodgers, 2014). In the GTM, the skill of reading and the ability to translate literary texts were also considered superior to oracy (Larsen-Freeman, 1986). The primary aim of language instruction in the GTM was the mastery of literacy closely associated with education and philosophy. Brown (2001) pointed out that "languages were not being taught primarily to learn oral/aural communication, but to learn for the sake of being 'scholarly' or, in some instances, for gaining a reading proficiency in a foreign language" (p. 18). Teachers usually began lessons with the presentation of a grammatical rule and the introduction of the list of vocabulary translated into students' first language (L1) to further continue with translation exercises (Stern, 1983). Several disadvantages to the GTM were retrospectively identified in the literature. They included frequently inaccurate word-by-word translations, overemphasis on rule memorisation, and tenuous connection with out-of-class language use (Roulet, 1972). The utter negligence of teaching oracy and the use of students' mother tongue as a means of instruction did not allow language learners to develop their ability to speak (Patel & Jain, 2008).

A ground-breaking moment in the history of FL education emerged in the 19th century, when the study of spoken language began with powerful opposition to traditional teaching approaches, known as the Reform Movement (Richards & Rodgers, 2014). In 1886, the International Phonetic Association was founded to improve FLT by applying the principles underlying the process of L1 learning to FLT. It designed the International Phonetic Alphabet, which allowed for an exact representation of speech sounds in a given language by means of written symbols. The establishment of phonetics as a formal and scientific study of speech sounds revolutionised the ways in which oral language was perceived, with phoneticians underlining the prominence of speaking and marginalising the role of written language (Celce-Murcia et al., 1996).

Late 19th-century instructed settings witnessed a radical change in the attitudes towards FLT by popularising naturalistic language learning principles through the use of pantomime, demonstrations, props, and visuals in the language classroom (Harmer, 1991; Richards & Rodgers, 2014). With the development of the Series Method by Francois Gouin, language instruction started to be organised in such a way so as to resemble the L1 acquisition process (Liu & Shi, 2007; Brown, 2000). In the Series Method, language was presented to learners as a series of simple actions (Gouin, 1892). The teacher began with orally introducing and miming several short statements, each of which containing concrete action verbs and using the same tense and person, namely "I walk towards the door. I draw near to the door. I draw nearer to the door. I stop at the door" (Brown, 2001, p. 20). The class first performed the actions and then repeated the sentences after the teacher while performing the actions. The students first chorused the sentences and later practised them individually (*Using the Gouin series in the foreign language classroom*, n.d.). Neither L1 translations nor grammatical rules were explicitly given in the classroom (Celce-Murcia et al., 1996).

At the turn of the 19th and 20th century, Gouin's method gave place to one of the most renowned of the natural methods, the Direct Method (Brown, 2000), or the Berlitz Method as it was referred to by its founders Lambert Sauveur and Maximilian Berlitz (Richards & Rodgers, 2014). The method was developed to facilitate target language (TL) learning in the most natural and interactive manner. Similarly to the Series Method, it promoted the use of a FL; emphasis, however, was placed on student-student and teacher-student interaction (Liu & Shi, 2007). The Direct Method laid the groundwork for a more communicative approach to FLT (Kępczyński, 2015), which was best reflected in its cardinal principles including the exclusive use of the TL, emphasis on everyday vocabulary and phrases, question-and-answer-based nature of interaction between teachers and students, oral introduction of new material, and inductive grammar teaching (Richards &

Rodgers, 2014). The use of the Direct Method facilitated students' understanding of the TL through the introduction of audio-visual aids and implementation of the learning-by-doing principle (Patel & Jain, 2008). Despite this, the Direct Method was most often criticised for the obligatory participation of a native instructor and the lack of basis in applied linguistics theory, as demonstrated by Richards and Rodgers' (2014) critique that compared this method to "the product of enlightened amateurism" (p. 13) and suffered a decline because of a number of practical problems relating to its implementation, such as overcrowded classrooms and limited education budget (Brown, 2000).

In the 20th century, the field of FL education fell under profound influences from outside the language classroom. With the growth in interest in linguistics and psychology, theories of language and language learning began to inform the work of second language (L2) and FL practitioners. They combined with the social, economic, and political events of the 20th century continued to exert a massive impact on FLT classroom practices.

1.1.1.2 The Age of Methods in FL education: From Audiolingual to Designer Methods

The adoption of scientific approaches to language instruction led to the emergence of the concept of a method. In this discussion, a method stands for "a systematic set of teaching practices based on a particular theory of language and language learning" (Rodgers, 2001, para. 1). The term, however, has been a source of controversy in FL education. Many did recognise positive aspects of using methods in FLT, one of the most important of which was the creation of the direct link between theory and practice in the language classroom (Sierra, 1995). On the other hand, the idea was faced with a barrage of criticism, with the opponents pointing out to the extremely confusing (Pennycook, 1989), politically-motivated, prescriptive (Brown, 2002), and unsuccessful (Sheen, 1994) character of the concept.

Despite this, the search for yet more effective (?) methods became a major preoccupation, or as Brown (2002) put it obsession, for language teaching specialists in the period between the 1950s and 1980s, defined as the so-called Age of Methods (Rodgers, 2001) and also disparagingly referred to in the literature as the Dark Ages of FLT (Brown, 2002). Throughout this Method Era (Kelly, 1969), theoreticians and practitioners embarked on the continuing quest for the one method that could ensure the success of teaching and learning. Each of the FLT methods, however, rose to short-lived fame as "common to each [of them] is the belief that the teaching practices it supports provide a more effective and theoretically sound basis for teaching than the methods that preceded it" (Richards &

Rodgers, 2014, p. 4). This meant that the methods frequently gained in popularity and fell into oblivion only to later become reincarnated into a new set of teaching practices (Kelly, 1969).

In addition to theoretical considerations from the emerging fields of linguistics and psychology, circumstances from outside the educational context combined with practical experiences, intuition, and inventiveness of the applied linguist affected the development of the method concept (Liu & Shi, 2007). A good example illustrating how a global socio-political issue had direct impact on the field of FLT is the Army Specialised Training Programme, or an oral-based programme involving an intensive study of a FL through memorisation, mimicry, and repetition (Sierra, 1995). The programme was implemented by the American government in response to the growing need for speakers of different languages in the wake of the outbreak of World War II (Savignon, 2018).

Moving forward in time, the growing prominence of behavioural psychology in tandem with the descriptive, contrastive, and structural influences from linguistics contributed to the development of a new method on both sides of the Atlantic. It was the British Oral Approach in the 1920s, which approximately three decades later evolved into Situational Language Teaching (Richards & Rodgers, 2014) and its American counterpart, the Audio-Lingual Method (ALM) whose beginnings date back to the outbreak of the Second World War (Alemi & Tavakoli, 2016; Celce-Murcia et al., 1996).

Language instruction within Situational Language Teaching and ALM could be characterised by the following features. The fundamental principle of the two was the situational practice of a language manifested through the use of objects and realia. Classroom teaching was based on two concepts: the separation of four language skills (i.e., listening, speaking, reading, writing) and the superiority of audio-lingual over graphic skills (Liu & Shi, 2007). It was therefore a commonly implemented procedure to teach vocabulary and grammar items inductively via dialogues (Mart, 2013). Another feature included the provision of explicit instruction within the Presentation-Practice-Production (PPP) pedagogic procedure, which was to guarantee the proceduralisation of declarative knowledge and the subsequent automatisation of procedural knowledge (Gower et al., 1983).

Furthermore, drawing heavily from behaviourism, the methods presupposed that the process of language learning was a matter of habit formation which takes place through positive reinforcement (Harmer, 2007; Simensen, 1999). A lot of attention was thus paid to oral language practice through dialogues and drills, which were memorised and frequently repeated by students to eliminate errors in line with the concept of overlearning (Moulton, 1963).

Linguistic structuralism also established a powerful FL classroom tradition in that period. The so-called 'focus on forms' defined language as "a system of structurally related elements for the encoding of meaning, the elements being phonemes, morphemes, words, structures, and sentence types" (Richards & Rodgers, 2001, p. 55). This concept lent itself to the interventionist perspective that views teaching and learning as a process of dividing language into smaller and more manageable linguistic units, known as building blocks (Liu & Shi, 2007).

The Direct Method and ALM principles evolved over time into the Callan Method established in England in 1960 by Robin Callan (Hrehovcik, 2003; Kępczyński, 2015; Nowosielska, 2018). On the one hand, the method shared close affinity to the Direct Method, as evidenced in inductive grammar teaching and oracy development through question-and-answer guided conversations between teachers and students. On the other hand, an audiolingual perspective on teaching was adopted therein through the comparison of language acquisition and language to the process of mechanical drilling and the concept of structures respectively (Kępczyński, 2015). The main goal of the Callan Method, also known as the Conversational Method, was to develop students' TL oracy thanks to high speed, repetition, and error correction (Hrehovcik, 2003; Nowosielska, 2018). The typical Callan Method lesson had a fixed structure organised into three steps. Step One began with listening and speaking practice involving question- and answer-based work. Step Two involved the revision and assimilation of the new learning material. Step Three introduced reading- and dictation-based activities (*What is the Callan method?*, n.d.).

Despite the popularity of Skinner's behaviourism in the mid-20th century, the challenge to the ALM came with the *Theory of syntax* publication by Noam Chomsky (1965). The scholar introduced the figure of an ideal speaker-hearer, whose inherent predisposition to understand and produce an infinite number of written and spoken utterances was based solely on their innate knowledge of language rules. Equally importantly, the process of language development remained unaffected by the external influences and the psychophysical limitations of an individual. The innatist view contradicted the assumptions posited by behaviourism. According to Chomsky (1965), human language development was a much more creative process which could not be explained in the context of operant conditioning. The scholar made a distinction between context-free and context-dependant language use by formulating the terms 'competence' and 'performance'. He defined the former as a child's inherent ability to appropriately construct and successfully comprehend spoken and written messages. The latter was used by Chomsky to describe the actual use of language, or the by-product of linguistic competence (Janowska, 2015).

Soon, the effectiveness of the synthetic approaches to FLT in developing learners' ability to communicate in a FL was further called into question. Corder (1967) formulated the built-in syllabus concept to suggest that the process of language learning does not take place in a linear fashion because the structures taught in the classroom are not immediately internalised by learners unless students reach an appropriate developmental stage. Also, Selinker's (1972) Interlanguage Theory pointed to the unconscious and autonomous character of interlanguage, that is the version of the linguistic system that learners rely on to produce the TL in meaningful communication (Frith, 1978). Moreover, having addressed the problem of fossilisation[1], Selinker (1972) challenged the behaviourist perspective associated with the ALM, which prescribed that language learning was only a matter of conditioning and habit formation. Further, research findings conflicted with the principles underlying the structuralist method. One of the scholars to provide such empirical evidence was Sandra Savignon (1972). The results of her comparative research study conducted with three groups of adult beginner French learners indicated that encouraging students to establish spontaneous communication during classroom practice where lexico-grammatical and pronunciation errors were allowed did not result in the participants' loss of grammatical accuracy.

The developments concerning Chomsky's (1965) innatist view on language acquisition and development, together with the influential work in cognitive psychology and applied linguistics associated with Caroll (1966) and Chastain (1971) yet again modified the perception of how the process of instructed FL learning ought to take place. This was manifested in the classroom adoption of the Cognitive Code Learning approach in the 1960s. It was described by Hinkel (2012) as "an updated variety of the traditional grammar-translation method, with an attendant goal of overcoming the shortfalls of the audio-lingual approach" (p. 625), and it revived interest in GTM practices. The idea of habit formation was abandoned therein for the sake of the conscious study and explicit learning of grammar, vocabulary, and sounds (Celce-Murcia et al., 1996).

The innatist view on language acquisition did not escape criticism either. The fundamental weakness of Chomsky's (1965) linguistic theory, as identified by the field, was that it neglected pragmatic aspects of language development. One of the outspoken opponents of linguistic competence who, as reported by Savignon

1 The phenomenon of fossilisation manifests through phonological, morphological, and syntactic deviations; namely, native language transfer, overgeneralisation, and transfer of training. They occur under the influence of psycholinguistic processes that take place during learners' TL production. Fossilisation is said to prevent FL students from reaching a native-like level of language proficiency (Tarone, 2014).

(2018) made an important contribution to initiating the communicative period in language education, was Dell Hymes (1967, 1972). He used the term of communicative competence to provide a much broader (i.e., social and functional) view of language use. Paradoxically, the scholar did not diminish the significance of linguistic competence since, as he argued, "a normal child acquires knowledge of sentences, not only as grammatical, but also as appropriate" (p. 277). Hymes (1972) isolated four questions in regard to which language performances can be judged: 1) whether (and if yes, to what degree) exchanges are formally possible (or grammatically correct), 2) whether they are feasible (or apt for implementation), 3) whether appropriate (or fitting for a given context), and 4) whether delivered (or what consequences they carry in real-life situations). Hymes' (1972) understanding of communicative competence shed a new light on the process of language development. By combining both linguistic and sociolinguistic competence, the scholar put into the background a mental view of language acquisition associated with Chomsky's (1965) linguistic competence in exchange for a broader perspective of the process that considers "when to speak, when not, and as to what to talk about with whom, when, where, in what manner" (Hymes, 1972, p. 277). Competence was thus no longer perceived as an inborn ability, but rather as an ability acquired through social interactions.

In view of the generally accepted theories of language and language learning from structural linguistics and behavioural psychology, Hymes' (1972) communicative competence formulated at the beginning of the 1970s was regarded as nothing short of revolutionary (Savignon, 2018). At the same time, however, it was given great prominence in L2/FL education as applied linguists used it extensively to justify and support the emerging CLT paradigm in the late 1970s and early 1980s (see section 1.1.2).

Additionally, the period between 1960s and 1980s deserves attention because of the unprecedented significance of L2/FL learning (Brown, 2001). The concentration of researchers' efforts on investigating how the process of FL learning takes place led to the development of innovative methods, referred to as Alternative Approaches and Methods (Rodgers, 1986, p. 83) and Designer Methods (Nunan, 1989, p. 97). As presented below, they aimed to simulate the L1 acquisition process by placing emphasis on affective and cognitive factors and the development of early language skills (i.e., listening, speaking).

Calleb Gattegno, founder of the Silent Way, promoted the idea of limiting teacher talk in favour of student-student interaction. Language teachers were therefore expected to remain silent and use gestures to communicate with learners (Gattegno, 1963). Exceptionally rare instances of the former's verbal participation

in classroom activities involved the implementation of discovery learning and creative problem-solving techniques (Harmer, 2007). A characteristic feature of the Silent Way was the use of the Cuisenaire rods (or coloured wooden sticks), wall charts with functional vocabulary, and sound charts (also known as Fidel charts) whose function was to draw students' attention to the TL (Abu-Rmaileh, 2018). Even though the method was designed to support the development of learner autonomy (Budiharto, 2018), it came under strong criticism, with Brown (2001) pointing out that it "was too harsh [...], and the teacher too distant, to encourage communicative atmosphere" (p. 29).

Based on the psychological theory of trace learning (Brown, 2001), James Asher's (1965) Total Physical Response (TPR) built upon motor action to reinforce students' retention of the TL. According to Asher (1965), "essence of the approach was for the learners to be silent, listen to a [...] command, then along with the instructor as a model, obey the command by acting it out" (p. 291). Since in the TPR it was assumed that a FL is internalised through code breaking, the Silent Period, which stands for the long listening period prior to speech production, was allowed to take place (Talley & Tu, 2016). However, due to its imperative-based language teaching, Asher's method was regarded as very successful only in the initial stages of language learning (Martin, 1996).

Georgi Lozanov stressed the importance of affect in language learning. To refer to his method, he used the term Suggestopedia, which was "derived from suggestion and pedagogy" and aimed at accelerated learning (Rustipa, 2011, p. 2). To minimise students' psychological barriers and facilitate peripheral (and effortless) learning (Harmer, 2007), a relaxed atmosphere and home-like environment were to be created by the choice of a new identity by learners, Baroque music, visual images, and positive suggestion in the language classroom (Talley & Tu, 2016). However, Lozanov's claims that learners have to be relaxed, interested, and positive to learn were not empirically validated and Suggestopedia was relegated to pseudo-science (Martin, 1996).

As evident above, the field of FL education had gone through different phases since the beginning of the 20th century, with continuous educational innovations and conflicting teaching ideologies dominating the scene of FLT (Alemi & Daftarifard, 2010). Radical shifts from the GTM to the Direct Method, from Audiolingualism to Cognitive Code Learning, and from Designer Methods to CLT (see section 1.1.2.2) took place in the previous century (Richards & Rogers, 2014; Sierra, 1995). Teachers' and learners' dissatisfaction with language teaching and learning outcomes (Decoo, 2001), historic events (Savignon, 2018), and changes in the educational objectives motivated by the developments in linguistics and psychology (Richards & Rodgers, 2014) put the 20th century FL education into a state of flux.

1.1.2 Evolution and legacy of the communicative competence construct

1.1.2.1 Models of communicative competence: Towards the CLT paradigm

Different models of communicative competence were designed in the last three decades of the 20th century. According to Folse (2010), one of the first researchers to adapt the aforementioned concept to the educational context was Christina Paulston (1974), who emphasised the meaning-oriented use of language. Paulston (1974) drew heavily from Chomsky (1965) and Hymes (1972), as evident in the concepts of linguistic competence, linguistic performance, and communicative competence underlying her model of language teaching. Nonetheless, she introduced a new component referred to as communicative performance, which as she explained "carries no distinctive social significance" (p. 40). This allows students to communicate freely in the FL classroom via the so-called communicative activities, which "lack specific deep structures of social meaning" (p. 40). In her model presented in Figure 1.1, Paulston (1992) accentuates the role of learners' linguistic and communicative performance in developing their linguistic and communicative competence.

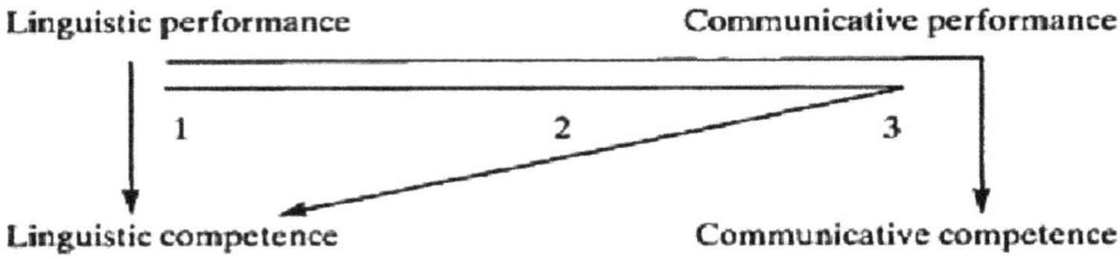

Fig. 1.1: *Paulston's model of language teaching (Paulston, 1992, p. 40)*

Also, the researcher raised awareness on the importance of the socio-cultural aspects of communication in language teaching (Paulston, 1992). She argued in favour of organising language practice allowing students to use language in different contexts to help them establish the close connection between the context of a situation and the appropriacy of register, style, and small talk. This is best reflected in the following description of a language teaching process: "when we teach 'How do you do' in the first lesson, we better also teach that it is only used in face to face encounters, and when we later do telephone conversations we can easily contrast the 'Hello, this is John Doe' with 'How do you do, I am John Doe'" (Paulston, 1992, p. 44).

One of the most popular models of communicative competence was designed by Michael Canale and Merrill Swain (1980) and presented in their influential article *Theoretical bases of communicative approaches to second language teaching and testing*. The researchers designated three components of their model. The first one, grammatical competence, stands for speakers' knowledge of language subsystems (i.e., lexis, morphology, syntax, grammar, phonology). Sociolinguistic competence denotes learners' knowledge of sociocultural rules, or those which enable them to produce socially and culturally appropriate utterances. Strategic competence helps speakers compensate for deficiencies in their performance caused either by their poor grammatical and/or sociolinguistic competence or the disruptions connected with the process of communication (or both). The last component (discourse competence) was introduced by Canale (1983). It refers to learners' ability to construct logically organised (i.e., coherent and concise) and generally acceptable utterances. The two models can be found in Figure 1.2.

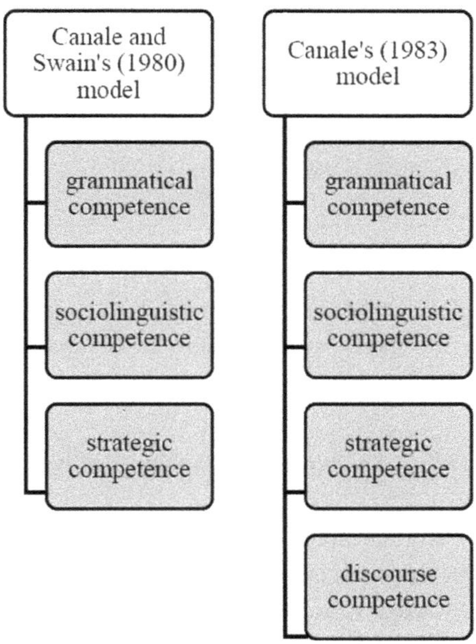

Fig. 1.2: *Models of communicative competence developed by Canale and Swain (1980) and Canale (1983)*

Each of the components of the two models was believed to hold an equally important role in developing students' communicative competence. Although the principles behind the Communicative Approach were established amid a growing conviction expressing a subordinate role of grammatical form over communicative purposes of language use, Canale and Swain (1980) clearly promoted their equality in language instruction.

A slightly different approach to the conceptualisation of communicative competence that originated in the field of language assessment was adopted by Lyle Bachman (1990). In what he called the communicative language ability framework (see Figure 1.3), the scholar isolated five elements that affect learners' ability to communicate: strategic competence, psychophysiological mechanisms, context of situation, knowledge structures, and language competence.

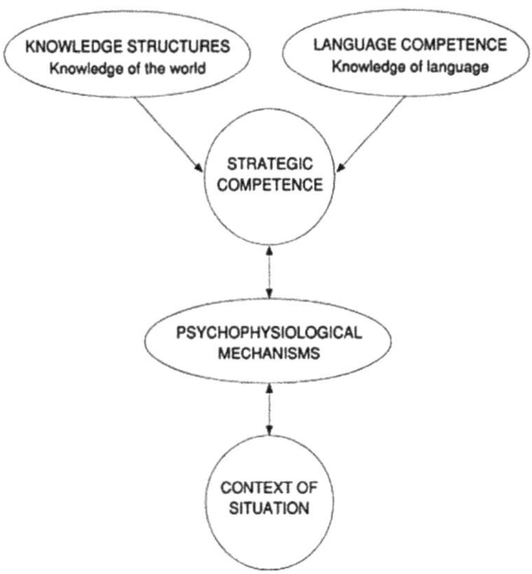

Fig. 1.3: *Bachman's (1990, p. 85) framework of communicative language ability*

Bachman (1990) demonstrated the inter-relationship between the five components of his framework. According to the researcher, learners' language competence and knowledge structures determine the choice of strategies. Strategic competence is affected by (and affects) psychophysiological mechanisms, whereas psychophysiological mechanisms, as illustrated above, not only remain under the influence of the context of a situation, but also influence it. Bachman's

(1990) classification of the two components of his framework, language and strategic competence, seems to bear a close resemblance to Canale and Swain's (1980) model, in which the scholars also highlighted the role of language and strategies, that is grammatical and strategic competence respectively. In contrast, however, Bachman (1990) elaborated at length on the previous model and provided a hierarchical organisation of the added elements. He divided language competence into two types: the ability to (de)construct grammatically correct sentences (i.e., organisational competence) and to (de)code linguistic signals with reference to other people, objects, and phenomena (i.e., pragmatic competence). The two were in turn further categorised into grammatical and textual competence, and illocutionary and sociolinguistic competence respectively (see Figure 1.4).

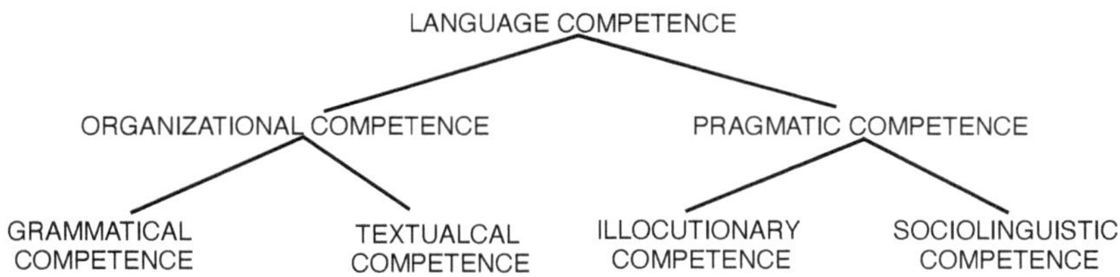

Fig. 1.4: *Components of language competence in the communicative language ability framework (Bachman, 1990, p. 87)*

A major advantage of the framework over the three previously mentioned models pertains to its minuteness in isolating the components of the ability to communicate. In contrast to Paulston's (1974), Canale and Swain's (1980), and Swain's (1983) models, Bachman's (1990) classification offered a more comprehensive account of the concept. Equally importantly, it also considered the influence of speakers' world knowledge and the psychophysiological aspects on strategic competence.

A model of communicative competence specifically designed for classroom teaching, referred to as pedagogical framework of communicative competence, was proposed by Marianne Celce-Murcia, Zotán Dörnyei, and Sarah Thurrell in 1993. The researchers generated their schematic representation of the construct as "a pyramid enclosing a circle and surrounded by another circle" (Celce-Murcia et al., 1993, p. 16). As presented in Figure 1.5, the smallest circle within the pyramid, which is at the same time the central component of the model, stands for discourse competence. Each of the three angles of the triangle denotes sociolinguistic, linguistic, and actional competence respectively. The circle surrounding the pyramid represents strategic competence, which enables a non-native language user to compensate for deficiencies in any of the remaining competencies.

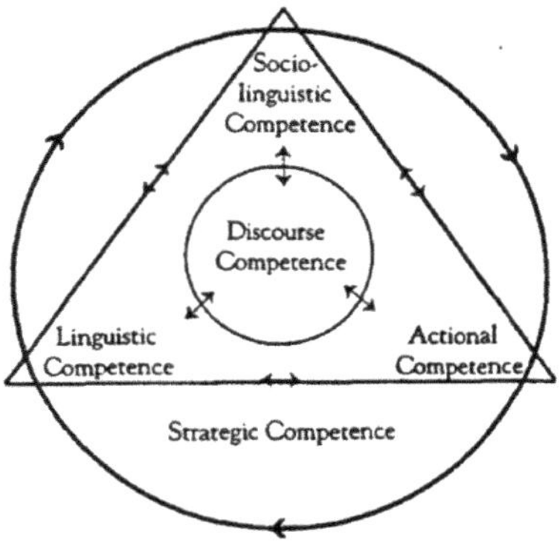

Fig. 1.5: *Pedagogical framework of communicative competence (Celce-Murcia et al., 1993, p. 16)*

Celce-Murcia et al.'s (1993) conceptualisation of the communicative competence construct varied from those discussed above. A noteworthy difference between the pedagogical framework of communicative competence and its likes discussed above lies in the isolation of actional competence by the researchers. This subtype of competence is said to help students perform speech acts, or utterances that can be described in relation to speaker's intentions and the effects they have on their partners (e.g., directives, such as commands, commissives, such as promises, and expressives, such as apologies) (Crystal, 2008).

Regardless of terminological and conceptual differences between them, the advent of the communicative competence models, some of which have been summarised for the purpose of the current discussion, provided impetus for the movement away from grammatically correct towards socio-culturally appropriate language use in communication, as best reflected in the shift away from interventionist to non-interventionist perspectives on FLT, or in other words from teaching synthetic to analytic syllabi (Celce-Murcia, 2007).

1.1.2.2 From communicative to task-based language teaching

In addition to criticism against structuralist methods voiced by Chomsky (1965) and the formulation of the communicative competence construct by Hymes

(1972), other developments did facilitate the growth of CLT. Most noteworthy, Wilkins' (1974) concept of the notional-functional syllabus, which derived from functional linguistics, put to the front the context of a situation in understanding language systems and language use. Equally importantly, a powerful triad of second language acquisition (SLA) theories redefined the role of contextualised language input, negotiation of meaning, and learners' language output in FL acquisition. It comprised Krashen's (1981) Monitor Model, Long's (1981, 1983) Interaction Hypothesis, and Swain's (1985) Comprehensible Output Hypothesis.

Stephen Krashen's (1981) Monitor Model underlined the cognitive, subconscious, and affective character of a language learning process, which as an input-driven and context-embedded phenomenon, occurs when learners are able to understand written and spoken language samples. Krashen's (1981) construct laid the foundations for the Natural Approach. Developed in collaboration with Tracy Terrell, the approach was based on the naturalistic view of language acquisition (Krashen & Terrell, 1983). In other words, it stressed the role of FL reception, authenticity, and interaction, thus promoting the analytic approach to language teaching.

Long (1981, 1983) also claimed that comprehensible input contributes to FL acquisition. Nevertheless, the scholar argued that language can be made comprehensible by "modifying not the input itself, but the interactional structure of conversation through such devices as self- and other-repetition, confirmation and comprehension checks and clarification requests" (Long, 1983, p. 100). Negotiation of meaning, which implies learners' involvement in interaction aiming to solve communication problems, is said to direct their focus not only to challenging linguistic aspects, but also to commonalities and dissimilarities between their language and the language of their interaction partners.

In addition, Swain (1985) suggested that FL students cannot learn the language unless they notice gaps in their knowledge. She explained that output, rather than input, facilitates FL acquisition as the former performs noticing-triggering, hypothesis-testing, and metalinguistic (also known as reflective) functions in the language classroom (Swain, 2005). Any failure in language production is thus said to promote learning given the fact that students are "pushed to use alternative means to get across ... the message ... precisely, coherently, and appropriately" (Swain, 1985, p. 248-249).

Under the influence of the interventionist and non-interventionist perspectives, CLT branched out into two directions (Littlewood, 1981). Weak CLT did not differ much from the earlier methods in that it shared a lot of similarities with the Type A approach to syllabus development (White, 1988), according to which learning and teaching objectives dictating what should be learned and taught were established a priori any considerations of students' needs. In addition to receiving explicit instruction in the language structures, learners were taught notions (e.g., time, space, quantity) and functions (e.g., apologising, inviting, ordering). Given its non-interventionist and holistic character, strong CLT allowed for language teaching through rather than for communication to take on greater significance (Prabhu, 1987). It could thus be compared to the Type B approach to syllabus design, in which both teachers and learners were equally important decision-makers. Influenced by Chomskian (1965) innatist view on language acquisition and Krashen's (1985) Input Hypothesis, strong CLT forsook formal instruction in exchange for implicit learning. The study of language occupied a subordinate role in the analytic approach as teachers' efforts were centred on providing comprehensible input to learners and engaging them in meaningful communication.

Even if the Communicative Approach offered a welcomed diversion to synthetic syllabi, some accusations were levelled against its introduction to the language classroom. The most frequent ones concerned the disregard towards learners' accuracy, problems with implementation in big groups, and the problematic nature of the adoption of teachers' and learners' roles (especially in Asian cultures) (Komorowska & Krajka, 2020). Despite the fact that CLT tasks were introduced with the intention of giving students a chance to communicate, they did not serve a purpose other than communication itself. The critics of CLT also demonstrated that the overemphasis on fluency did not lead to the development of learners' ability to speak, with learners' inadequate knowledge of FL grammar making their speech appear fluent yet hardly comprehensible (Hinkel, 2006).

At the turn of the 1980s and 1990s, weak and strong CLT laid a foundation for task-supported (TSLT) and task-based (TBLT) language teaching. TSLT provided a bridge between traditional and communicative language practice. The use of tasks in TSLT gave learners a chance to use linguistic structures in the contextualised practice within the PPP cycle (Gower et al., 1983). In contrast, given the implementation of the deep-end strategy (Johnson, 1982), that is the PPP upside-down cycle (Willis, 1994, as cited in Harmer, 1996), TBLT involved language learners in task performance rather than focus on forms and language modelling. Learners were expected to complete a task and discuss the language crucial for the activity to be performed. This not only allowed to shift language users' focus towards meaning during task performance, but it also helped isolate problematic aspects of language to be worked on in the consecutive stages of the lesson (Komorowska & Krajka, 2020).

The role of tasks was also open to conflicting interpretations, as evident in the principles underlying strong and weak TBLT (Nunan, 2004; Skehan, 1996a). The former viewed tasks as a learning and teaching tool, or "the necessary and sufficient condition of successful second language acquisition" (Nunan, 2004, p. 21). It stressed a real-life character of language use, which was to ensure unconscious process of language acquisition to take place (Krashen & Terrell, 1983). The latter, on the other hand, treated tasks as an essential element of teaching, yet it restricted their potential to pedagogic contexts in that "they (…) may be preceded by focused instruction, and after use, may be followed by focused instruction" (Skehan, 1996a, p. 266).

Despite increasing the authenticity of language learning, TBLT did not always bring definite advantages. The most frequent criticism was targeted at its unsuitability for low-level students, excessive emphasis on task-related vocabulary, and a demotivating (especially for adult learners) procedure which forces language users to produce imperfect samples of a FL at the beginning of each lesson (Komorowska & Krajka, 2020).

All in all, decades of singularly ineffective FLT associated with the controversial Age of Methods (Decoo, 2001; Sheen, 1994) led to the development of the anti-method movement (Richards, 1990), which heralded the beginning of the Post-Method Era (Kumaradivelu, 1994) in the 1990s. Manifested by the transition away from top-down (or method-based) to bottom-up (or teacher-based) approaches (Richards & Rodgers, 2014) and from teacher- to learner-centredness (Freeman & Richards, 1993), the symbolic Death of Method (Kumaradivelu, 2006) reflected an increasing trend towards internalisation (Salmani-Nodoushan, 2006). Thus the shift in the view from the curriculum developer towards the teacher and from the teacher towards the learner could be observed, which was clearly reflected in the principles underlying the post-method pedagogy (i.e., particularity, possibility, practicality) that were brought to the forefront by Kumaravadivelu (2006) with an intention of encouraging practitioners to adapt their teaching practices to the needs of increasingly diverse language classrooms.

1.2 Action-oriented perspective on communicative competence in the *Common European Framework of Reference for Languages*

1.2.1 Introduction to the CEFR

1.2.1.1 Development and reception of the framework

A growing need for isolating a set of broad and practical guidelines on curriculum planning and assessment providing an international standard for FL instructors and learners and encouraging cooperation between different institutions across

Europe contributed to the publication of the *Common European Framework of Reference for Languages: Learning, teaching, assessment* (CEFR). The document was issued by the Language Policy Division of the Council of Europe (CoE) first in two draft versions and then in the final English and French versions in 2001 (*Historical overview of the development of the CEFR*, n.d.). The Polish translation by Waldemar Martyniuk *Europejski system opisu kształcenia językowego: Uczenie się, nauczanie, ocenianie* (ESOKJ) was published by the Central Teacher Training Centre (Centralny Ośrodek Doskonalenia Nauczycieli, CODN) in 2003 (Martyniuk, 2021).

The document was divided into nine chapters accompanied by four appendices (CoE, 2001). It opened with the presentation of CEFR's objectives and functions (Chapter 1) and the introduction to the action-oriented approach (AOA) as its conceptual model (Chapter 2). This was followed by the description of the common reference level labels (A1-C2) and descriptors (also referred to as can-do statements and illustrative scales) standing for the vertical and horizontal dimensions of the descriptive scheme respectively (Chapters 3-5), and the discussion of language learning, teaching, and assessment within the approach (Chapters 6-9). Appendices A-D were attached to provide information on the descriptors development.

Soon after its publication, the CEFR acquired the status of a standard point of reference for FL learning, teaching, and proficiency assessment (Little, 2006). Translated into over forty European and non-European languages (as of April 2022) (*Common European Framework of Reference for Languages: Learning, teaching, assessment. Companion volume*, n.d.), the framework has caught worldwide interest. As reported by Runnels and Runnels (2017), the number of publications with the CEFR as a keyword grew steadily from 1,000 in 2009, to over 3,000 in 2016. The document has supported decision makers, curriculum planners, syllabus designers, course developers, and language testers by suggesting comprehensive (yet not exhaustive) lists of descriptors which specify what learners are able to do at different levels of language proficiency (Alexiou & Stathopoulou, 2021).

The history of the CEFR is inextricably intertwined with the Council of Europe, the organisation founded in 1949 to defend human rights, develop mutual respect, promote cooperation, and strengthen parliamentary democracy in its member states (Little, 2006; Trim, 2010). Virtually from its beginning, the CoE actively supported modern language teaching and learning in Europe. In 1954, the European Cultural Convention was passed to facilitate innovation in language and teacher education, support international cooperation, and promote a learner-centred approach to FLT based on common principles (Trim, 2001).

In the early 1970s, the Committee for Out-of-School Education agreed to investigate the proposal for the European unit-credit scheme for language teaching in adult education. It resulted in the development of the Threshold Level based on notional-functional concepts of language use introduced by Jan van Ek in 1975. The specifications described everyday linguistic challenges of migrants and guest workers living in a foreign country (van Ek, 1975). Following the success of the Threshold Level, other ones, such as Breakthrough, Waystage, and Vantage descriptors, were subsequently published (Komorowska, 2016).

The CEFR incorporated the previously established specifications, such as Waystage (A2), Threshold (B1), and Vantage (B2). In the framework, they were supplemented with additional reference level labels, A1, C1, and C2 (Trim, 2010), and arranged into three bands: basic (A1-A2), independent (B1-B2), and proficient user (C1-C2) (see Figure 1.6).

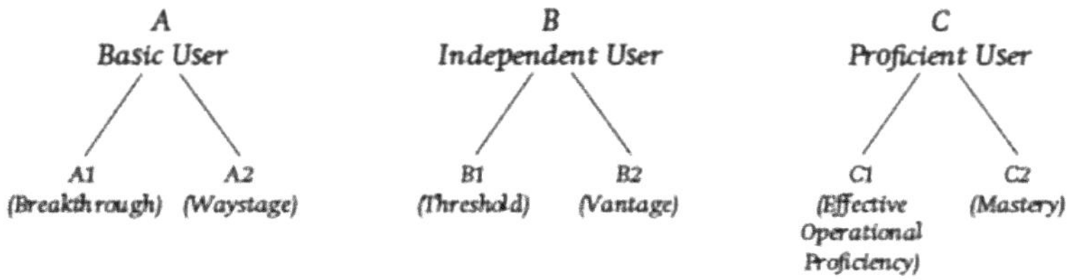

Fig. 1.6: *Division of the common reference level labels in the CEFR (CoE, 2001, p. 23)*

The CEFR is well-known for its bands and level labels (Schneider, 2020). Soon after the publication of the framework, they were widely adopted by different stakeholders, which helped to unify the presentation of language learning and teaching objectives, targets, and outcomes in Europe and beyond (Figueras, 2012). For example, the CEFR labels were used to report the results of the European Survey on Language Competences (ESLC) administered in 2011 by SurveyLang on the initiative of the European Commission (*About the survey*, n.d.).

Also, the reference level descriptors have been a major innovation introduced in the CoE's document (Figueras, 2012). Their origins go back to the DIALANG and Association of Language Testers in Europe (ALTE) can-do projects conducted during the period of the CEFR preparation (CoE, 2001). The illustrative scales were developed for aural and written reception, spoken and written production, and spoken and written interaction. They were user-oriented and positively worded in that they described language learners' communicative behaviours, competences, and strategies in terms of what the former can do in a FL (Little, 2006).

In addition to creating universal metalanguage to define language proficiency in educational systems across different countries (CoE, 2001), the CEFR triggered a paradigm shift with its forward-looking approach to language and language learning (North, 2021; Piccardo, 2010). Its flagship concept of action orientation provided "a complex but operational definition of language that embodied the work of many decades" (Figueras, 2012, p. 478), with the communicative competence and the learner seen as social agents moving the field of language education beyond CLT (Piccardo, 2014; Piccardo & North, 2019). The descriptive scheme replaced the traditional division of language skills with four modes of communication (i.e., reception, production, interaction, mediation) to reflect the situated and integrated nature of language use within the AOA (Piccardo et al., 2019) (for further discussion, see section 1.2.2).

The mass appeal of the CEFR is attributable to the fact that it supported plurilingual and pluricultural communities. The document promoted cultural and linguistic diversity (Little, 2006) and applied the principles established by the CoE, such as learner autonomy, equal rights, and social justice (Alexiou & Stathapoulou, 2021). Since its commercial publication in the European Year of Languages, the framework has inspired a number of initiatives further illustrating and promoting the plurilingual approach (Martyniuk, 2021). One of the CEFR-inspired projects is the Platform of Resources and References for Plurilingual and Intercultural Education[2]. It enables the member states to develop programmes related to language teaching by offering "an open and dynamic resource with systems of definitions, points of reference, descriptions and descriptors, studies and good practices" (*Platform of resources and references for plurilingual and intercultural education*, n.d., para. 2).

The CEFR has been the focus of numerous recommendations provided by the CoE. In accordance with the principles that the Committee of Ministers formulated within the CM/Rec(2008)7 on the use of the CEFR and the promotion of plurilingualism, different stakeholders were encouraged to "adopt a learner-focused, action-oriented, competence-based approach; take into consideration the social and cultural dimensions of language learning; [and] situate their efforts concerning language teaching in relation to the CEFR in a transparent way" (CoE, 2008, p. 3). Further, the CM/Rec(2014)5 recommendation stressed the importance of developing competences in the language(s) of schooling to ensure both equity and quality in education to bring learners' future educational success (CoE, 2014).

2 https://www.coe.int/en/web/language-policy/platform

The framework has stimulated several projects supporting international collaboration in the field of FLT and beyond (Alexiou & Stathapoulu, 2021). Testing has seen impressive impact through this collaboration, as evident in CEFTrain[3], or the Dutch CEFR construct project, and the creation of European Association for Language Testing and Assessment (EALTA). The field of teacher training also took advantage from the CEFR publication. Activities initiated by the European Centre for Modern Languages contributed to the development of the European Portfolio for Student Teachers of Languages (Newby et al., n.d.). Another example is EUROPASS[4], the European Union's initiative whose objective is to ensure the transparency of European citizens' qualifications.

Once the CEFR achieved international recognition, it also came under rigorous scrutiny. Even though its authors never claimed the framework to be perfect and complete (North, 2014), the document received moderate criticism. Scientific critique often focused on the common reference level descriptors. Some researchers questioned why plurilingualism received little attention in the scales (e.g., Krumm, 2007). Others pointed to the marginalised position of mediation as no validated and calibrated descriptors were designed for that communicative language activity (North, 2007). McNamara (2014) expressed doubt over the adoption of the out-of-date perspective of the native speaker. Moreover, Alderson (2007) underlined the vague wording of some descriptors. A major challenge was the descriptors' usefulness in assessment since the meaning of such phrases as "long", "short", and "familiar" was not disambiguated in the document, as evident in the illustrative scales presented in Table 1.1.

Tab. 1.1: *Common reference level descriptors for overall reading comprehension (CoE, 2001, p. 69)*

C2	Can understand and interpret critically virtually all forms of the written language including abstract, structurally complex, or highly colloquial literary and non-literary writings. Can understand a wide range of long and complex texts, appreciating subtle distinctions of style and implicit as well as explicit meaning.
C1	Can understand in detail lengthy, complex texts, whether or not they relate to his/her own area of specialty, provided he/she can reread difficult sections.

3 https://blogs.helsinki.fi/ceftrain/
4 https://europa.eu/europass/en

B2	Can read with a large degree of independence, adapting style and speed of reading to different texts and purposes, and using appropriate reference sources selectively. Has a broad active reading vocabulary, but may experience some difficulty with low-frequency idioms.
B1	Can read straightforward factual texts on subjects related to his/her field and interest with a satisfactory level of comprehension.
A2	Can understand short, simple texts on familiar matters of a concrete type which consist of high frequency everyday or job-related language Can understand short, simple texts containing the highest frequency vocabulary, including a proportion of shared international vocabulary items.
A1	Can understand very short, simple texts a single phrase at a time, picking up familiar names, words and basic phrases and rereading as required.

The field of SLA has been very critical of the CEFR's descriptors. In his seminal article *The shaky ground beneath the CEFR: Quantitative and qualitative dimensions of language proficiency*, Jan Hulstijn (2007) called into question the two pillars of the illustrative scales: the quantity dimension, or what a learner can do in a language, and the quality dimension, how well they can do it (p. 2). According to the researcher, there was no empirical evidence supporting the assumption that learners' development of oral language proficiency takes place sequentially from the lowest (A1) to the highest (C2) levels. No proof was also given that learners are able to perform all the tasks associated with the lower levels of language proficiency. The claim that their vocabulary range, grammatical accuracy, and phonological control are at the same level as their oral language proficiency was not empirically validated either.

Another criticised aspect related to the misuses of the document. As evidenced by Martyniuk and Noijons' (2007) summary of the survey on the use of the CEFR in the thirty CoE member states, the framework was widely used at all education levels. Even though it was developed to support adult FL learning in Europe, it was introduced to primary, secondary, and upper secondary schools, and tertiary education settings.

Despite several inadequacies, some of which have been referred to above, the CEFR has risen in status to become an internationally recognised reference material in language education (Komorowska, 2016). First, the framework fostered innovation through its descriptive scheme (North, 1997). Second, its labels and descriptors provided a solution to the long-standing problem of the Tower of Babel (North, 2014): in the pre-CEFR era, "a teacher of Spanish in a secondary school in southern France, a teacher of French to Polish adults and a teacher of English to German businessmen would have taken ten to twenty minutes to establish any common ground for a discussion" (North, 2014, p. 229). The CEFR tackled the above-mentioned issue by facilitating international cooperation and communication between educational institutions.

1.2.1.2 Publication of the CEFR companion volume

Increasing migration, population mobility, and the rapid development of information and communication technologies (ICTs) have continued to stimulate the growth of increasingly multilingual and multicultural societies. As a consequence, regular contacts between groups from diverse socio-cultural, linguistic, and ethnic backgrounds have gradually become the rule rather than the exception (Stathopoulou, 2021). In view of the all-encompassing globalisation-driven changes, the update of the CEFR was not only welcome, but necessary. The decision was reached in Strasbourg, France, in 2013 to update the framework (North & Piccardo, 2019). The objectives of the project were conceptual and technical: they aimed to provide additional comments on mediation and plurilingualism overlooked to the advantage of the remaining components of communicative competence and supplement the scales missing in the 2001 edition (Martyniuk, 2021).

The years 2013-2017 marked the process of designing, validating, and calibrating the scales within the project managed by Brian North from the Eurocentres Foundation (Gadomska, 2019). The results of the four-year project were presented during the conference *Building inclusive societies through enriching plurilingual and pluricultural education at a grassroots level: The role of the CEFR companion volume* held in the CoE's headquarters in Strasbourg in 2018 (North & Piccardo, 2019). The provisional version of the document was titled the *CEFR companion volume with new descriptors* (CV) in 2018 (CoE, 2018). Two years later, the CV was edited and officially released by the CoE under the title the *Common European Framework of Reference for Languages: Learning, teaching, assessment – Companion volume* (CV) (CoE, 2020).

The CVs (CoE, 2018, 2020) aimed to expand the 2001 edition of the framework (Deygers, 2021). For example, the previous version did not include online interaction, which as a matter of fact achieved exponential growth in the field of language learning over the last twenty years (Abbate, 2021). The illustrative scales for mediation were missing in the 2001 publication (North, 2007). The plurilingual and pluricultural competence, or the ability of an individual to "draw upon all of their linguistic and cultural resources and experiences in order to fully participate in social and educational contexts, achieving mutual understanding, gaining access to knowledge (…)" (CoE, 2018, p. 157), was not elaborated upon either. The CV updated previously existing scales and included the new ones (Alexiou

& Stathopoulou, 2021). The document provided descriptors for those communicative language activities that were not included in the CEFR, namely online interaction and mediation. It presented new plus levels, pre-A1 levels, and C levels (Gadomska, 2019). The CV also focused on plurilingualism and broadened the understanding of mediation which was hailed as the key mode of communication (see section 1.3). The new illustrative descriptors for young learners and sign language users were another important addition to the framework (Deygers, 2021). The extension of the CEFR illustrative descriptors to include mediation, plurilingual/pluricultural competence, and sign language was to "contribute to the quality inclusive education for all, and the promotion of plurilingualism and pluriculturalism" (CoE, 2018, p. 22).

Nonetheless, Deygers (2021) expressed a certain degree of scepticism about the CEFR update. The researcher pointed out the dual nature of the framework as both a policy document and a quasi-scientific text. It was justified from the policy perspective that the CV did not radically depart from the CEFR. The value of the CV as a quasi-scientific publication, however, was not entirely obvious. Not only did many criticised aspects of the framework remain unchanged, but also the document received little empirical backing, which was disqualifying from a scientific perspective, as argued by Deygers (2021).

Despite these weaknesses, the CV publication marked an important milestone in the history of the framework, moving it beyond language teaching, learning, and assessment. Due to change in the understanding of the role of education in learners' life, through the presentation of a school as the place supporting the development of both communicative language competences and general competences, the CV provides the basis not only for FLT, but also for the organisation of education in general (Martyniuk, 2021).

It is hard to disagree that both the CEFR and CVs have continued to affect the field of language education worldwide. Even though the framework was subjected to examination in Europe in the majority of cases, 25% of the studies were conducted in Asia, North America, and Oceania (Runnels & Runnels, 2017), with the CoE's documents having been in use in different countries in Europe and beyond, for example, in Poland (e.g., Kucharczyk, 2013), Turkey (e.g., Tosun & Glover, 2020), Malaysia (e.g., Kok & Aziz, 2019), Vietnam (e.g., Nhung, 2019), and Uzbekistan (e.g., Musoeva, 2019). The CEFR also enjoyed great popularity in Japan, where the European framework was adapted to the Japanese context and published under the name of *CEFR-J* in 2011 (Negishi et al., 2013). The need for universal metalanguage in FLT, emphasis on positive behaviours in can-do statements, and the importance of the scales in increasing the clarity in testing were primary reasons behind the global uptake of the CEFR (Figueras, 2012).

1.2.2 Action orientation in FL learning

1.2.2.1 Basic assumptions of the action-oriented approach

The AOA introduced within the 2001 edition of the CEFR provided a detailed elaboration of the problem of language use in the context of actions. The CoE's (2001) conceptual model generated discussions on the implications it carried with regard to the roles of learners and the perception of teaching and learning. The complex nature of action orientation was best encapsulated in the CoE's quotation:

> Language use, embracing language learning, comprises the actions performed by persons who as individuals and as social agents develop a range of **competences**, both **general** and in particular **communicative language competences**. They draw on the competences at their disposal in various contexts under various **conditions** and under various **constraints** to engage in **language activities** involving **language processes** to produce and/or receive **texts** in relation to **themes** in specific **domains**, activating those **strategies** which seem most appropriate for carrying out the **tasks** to be accomplished. The monitoring of these actions by the participants leads to the reinforcement or modification of their competences. (CoE, 2001, p. 9)

In the AOA, L2/FL learners are treated as language users who operate in a given learning context within a specific community (Piccardo, 2010) by taking language- and non-language-related actions, or performing tasks by implementing strategies and demonstrating appropriate competences (Delibas & Gunday, 2016). In line with the action-oriented language use, the learners act as individuals and social agents who focus on personal construction and knowledge sharing (Piccardo et al., 2011). Through the vision of a language user as a social agent, the CEFR emphasised the "constant movement between the individual and social level in language learning (CoE, 2018, p. 33). These individual and social aspects of language acquisition laid the foundations for collaborative learning and language mediation, as evident in the latest buzzword called languaging. Defined as "the process of making meaning and shaping knowledge and experience through language" by Swain (2006, p. 98), it successfully underlines the role of private and dialogic speech in facilitating language learning.

What allows language users to deal with the above-mentioned duality of language learning is the use of strategies (Piccardo et al., 2011). A strategy is defined in the 2001 CEFR as "any organised, purposeful, and regulated line of action chosen by an individual to carry out a task which he or she sets for himself or herself or with which he or she is confronted" (p. 10). The implementation of strategies helps language users complete tasks successfully and as a consequence become more effective learners.

In addition to strategies, learners are expected to activate their competences to accomplish a task within the AOA. In the CEFR, competence stands for "the sum of knowledge, skills and characteristics that allow a person to perform actions" (CoE, 2001, p. 9). In the document, the distinction was made between general competences (i.e., knowledge, know-how skills, existential competence, ability to learn) and communicative language competences (i.e., linguistic, sociolinguistic, pragmatic). As demonstrated in Table 1.2, the two combined with strategies (i.e., reception, production, interaction, mediation) are crucial for a language user to perform communicative language activities (i.e., reception, production, interaction, mediation) and thus successfully accomplish a task (CoE, 2018, 2020).

Tab. 1.2: *Components of overall language proficiency in the CV (CoE, 2018, 2020)*

Overall language proficiency			
General competences	**Communicative language competences**	**Communicative language activities**	**Communicative language strategies**
Knowledge Know-how skill Existential competence Ability to learn	Linguistic Sociolinguistic Pragmatic	Reception Production Interaction Mediation	Reception Production Interaction Mediation

Any task performance requires the use of both competences and strategies. The two are in turn further developed and improved through that experience, that is task completion to be precise (CoE, 2001).

The idea for extending the notion of competences by adding plurilingual and pluricultural dimensions has its roots in plurilingualism promoted by the framework. As opposed to multiculturalism, the plurilingual approach acknowledges the close inter-relation between users' languages and cultures during task performance (CoE, 2001). The ability to build on and comprehend plurilingual/pluricultural repertoire allows learners to express sensitivity to linguistic and cultural heterogeneity, deal with ambiguity caused by cross-cultural differences, and, if necessary, use different languages interchangeably (CoE, 2018, 2020).

As already stated, language users engage in actions under the guise of tasks which referred to as "federative tools" are said to occupy a central role in action orientation by making "learning tangible, palpable, and meaningful" (Piccardo, 2014, p. 27). Experiential learning (Dewey, 1938, as cited in Norris, 2009) is an important theoretical construct in the AOA as it stresses the importance of activities around which learning is organised. Action-oriented learning, also known as learning by doing, allows the contextualisation of learning and teaching by transporting it outside the confines of the language classroom and diminishing the likelihood of language being practised for its own sake (CoE, 2001).

The AOA has therefore helped to extend the views on language learning and teaching from communication to a social action (Delibas & Gunday, 2016), with this shift being an answer to recent changes in the perception of the role of education systems. The function of schools is to prepare learners for a future professional and social life rather than to blindly transmit theoretical knowledge (Piccardo, 2010). FLs are therefore considered not as subjects to teach, but as resources that learners can use outside the language classroom (Abbate, 2021).

In so far as claims were made that the term social agents introduced within the AOA began a new era in FL didactics (Bourguignon, 2006, as cited Janowska, 2011), the CEFR's descriptive scheme is as a matter of fact an essential step forward in the evolution of the field (Janowska, 2008, 2011, 2012, 2014; Piccardo, North & Goodier, 2019). Van Lier (2007) argued that despite obvious differences in their objectives, principles, and practices, the AOA bears resemblance to task-based, content-based, project-based, exploratory, and experiential teaching in that they all conceptualise a learner as an active person rather than "a copier of behaviours, a receptive input receiver, or a rote memoriser of facts" (p. 48). Also, the AOA shows affinity to its methodological predecessor, TBLT, in yet another respect. The latter, an offshoot of strong CLT, popularised the use of real-life tasks in the FL classroom as early as in the 1980s and 1990s (Baran, 2015).

At this point, it is thus justified to underline the fact that the AOA encouraged much-needed improvements rather than offered a radical departure from FLT traditions. By adding the third component, action, to language and communication, as reflected in Bourguignon's (2006, as cited in Piccardo, 2010, p. 28) notion "communicaction", the action-oriented vision of language use can fully comply with the requirements of the 21st century language classroom.

1.2.2.2 Terminological problems in Polish

Both tasks and actions provide the cornerstone for the AOA. Nevertheless, the former performs a subordinate role in the CEFR's conceptual model as it only functions as a medium for an action to be undertaken by language users (CoE,

2001). Despite critical importance of the aforementioned distinction in the framework, certain inconsistencies with regard to the terminology underlying the AOA can be identified in the Polish version of the CoE's document, ESOKJ (CODN, 2003).

As demonstrated in Table 1.3, ESOKJ causes considerable terminological confusion in the field. The Polish translation of AOA, *podejście zadaniowe*, means exactly the same as *task-based learning* in English, *approche par taches* in French, and *aufgabenorientierter Ansatz* in German.

Tab. 1.3: *Concepts of task, task-based learning, action, and action-oriented approach in the English, French, German, and Polish translations of the CEFR (Janowska, 2011, p. 79)*

English	French	German	Polish
task	tâche	Aufgabe	zadanie
task-based learning	approche par tâches	aufgabenorientiert-er Ansatz	podejście zadaniowe
action	action	Handlung	działanie
action-oriented approach	approche actionnelle	handlungsorien-tierter Ansatz	podejście zadaniowe

The Polish translation of the term *podejście zadaniowe* proves somewhat controversial in view of the fact that the concept of action, rather than the task, is foregrounded in English, French, and German. The problem has remained largely unnoticed although it has been addressed by the pioneers of action orientation in Poland, such as Gębal (2010), Janowska (2011), and Miodunka (2013). More importantly, however, the use of *podejście zadaniowe* in exchange for an exact translation of the AOA, *podejście działaniowe* (or, alternatively, *podejście ukierunkowane/zorientowane na działanie*), has erroneously strengthened the association of the CEFR's philosophy with task- and project-based teaching (Janowska, 2011; Miodunka, 2013).

The general terminological trend that emerged with the publication of ESOKJ in 2003 has greatly reinforced the position of TBLT to the disadvantage of the AOA in Polish glottodidactics. Given the fact that *podejście zadaniowe* is used instead of (or interchangeably with) *podejście działaniowe*, it is far from clear which approach is adopted. This problem was identified by Miodunka (2013), who referred to Janowska's (2011) *Podejście zadaniowe do nauczania i uczenia się języków obcych. Na przykładzie języka polskiego jako obcego*[5] and Niemiec-Knaś' (2011) *Metoda projektów w nauczaniu języków obcych*[6] to prove that without a careful study of the publications and readers' basic knowledge of the history of the CEFR's AOA, it is hardly possible to discern their action-oriented character. A similar tendency can also be noticed in Baran's (2015) article in which the scholar used the terms task-based and action-oriented learning interchangeably.

Interestingly, the lack of the proper terminological distinction is far from accidental. Given a close resemblance between the AOA and TBLT, the introduction of the term *podejście zadaniowe* in exchange for *podejście działaniowe* was probably an intentional act performed by the author of ESOKJ with an intention of revealing the similarity between the two (Janowska, 2011). Since the AOA can be defined as another rung in the evolutionary ladder of FLT, or put simply a continuation of previous methodological and SLA traditions (e.g., Figueras, 2012), it is justified to use the two terms (TBLT and the AOA) interchangeably to emphasise the direct connection between the assumptions of the CEFR's approach and the achievements in FLT covering the second half of the 20th century. Furthermore, there is no denying the fact that despite the great prominence of an action as a central component of task performance in the AOA, it is still the concept of a task around which learning, teaching, and assessment are organised (Gębal. 2010). Therefore, once the focus has been shifted from language actions towards task performance as reflected in ESOKJ, the idea of *podejście zadaniowe*, or TBLT, used with reference to *podejście działaniowe*, or the AOA, seems entirely appropriate (Gębal, 2010).

In view of the disputable nature of the Polish translation of the AOA in ESOKJ, there is a real practical necessity to popularise the concept *podejście działaniowe* and *podejście zorientowane/ukierunkowe na działanie* (AOA) as a superordinate term to *podejście zadaniowe* (TBLT) in Poland (Miodunka, 2013). This could help first better reflect the social dimension of the philosophy developed in the CEFR (Delibas & Gunday, 2016) and second clear up the unnecessary confusion caused by the use of TBLT in relation to the AOA in Polish glottodidactics.

5 *Task-based approach to language teaching and learning on the example of Polish as a foreign language*

6 *Method-based projects in foreign language teaching*

1.3 Conceptualising mediation in foreign language teaching

1.3.1 Presentation of the concept

1.3.1.1 Origins and definitions of mediation

The etymology of the term mediation reveals that it had its beginnings several centuries ago. The first uses of the word in the English language can be traced back to the time of Geoffrey Chaucer, the prominent 14th century English poet, philosopher, and diplomat. According to Raymond Williams (1983), who overviewed the development of the term in his publication *Keywords. A vocabulary of culture and society*, it is possible to identify three examples of the meaning of mediation: "interceding between adversaries, with a strong sense of reconciling them", "a means of transmission, or agency as a medium", and "division or halving" (p. 204). While the third sense of mediation was rendered obsolete, the first two became commonly applied in religious and political contexts to denote the act of Jesus Christ's intercession before God, reconciliation between enemies, and the intermediate agency of material objects and mental acts (Williams, 1983).

Even before the term had been created, mediation underlay the traditions of ancient societies (Janowska & Plak, 2021). This practice was for example deeply rooted in the ethical code system in China 2,500 years ago, where the risk of litigation was perceived as a flagrant violation of social norms of Confucianism and had to be avoided at any cost with the help of mediators (Kordasiewicz, 2018). In the Phoenician civilisation, mediation was commonly adopted in the trade negotiations of purchase and sale (Stathopoulou, 2015). In contrast, in Asian, African, and South-American communities, the process of mediation was reserved for diplomatic purposes and was used to describe the communication process between a representative of a given society, usually its senior and knowledgeable member, with people from the outside (Dendrinos, 2006).

Mediation also became a standard technique implemented by European rules and monarchs to resolve conflicts. According to Janowska and Plak (2021), the earliest surviving example of mediation dates back to the 9th century, which was when King Louis the German acted as an intermediary between Charlemagne's successors. In medieval Europe, the Church played an important role in promoting mediation, with papal legates taking on the role of mediators to settle feuds between nobles and magnates (Janowska & Plak, 2021).

In the next centuries, mediation took on a greater social significance. It became professionalised in Italy in the 16th century, when towns began to pay mediators a salary for solving economic disputes (Kordasiewicz, 2018). The status of mediation had a significant rise in 1856: the Declaration of Paris was issued then by the plenipotentiaries of Great Britain, France, Austria, Russia, Sardinia, and Turkey, who approved the following recommendation: "states between which any misunderstanding might arise should, before appealing to arms, have recourse so far as circumstances might allow [...] to the good offices of a friendly power" (Crackanthorpe, 1911, para. 1).

The development of institutionalised and professionalised mediation received impetus in the United States in the second half of the 20th century. Strikes, which highlighted the necessity to restore relations between employers and employees, and the crisis in the judiciary system, which was overcome by mediators giving American citizens access to legal assistance, allowed the modernisation of the conceptual understanding of mediation (Janowska & Plak, 2021).

The success of mediation programmes in the United States provided a model for initiatives promoting amicable settlements of conflicts on the European continent (Kordasiewicz, 2018). The first attempt was made by the CoE in the early 1980s, when the Committee of Ministers published the CM/Rec (81)7, according to which "[m]easures should be taken to facilitate or encourage, where appropriate, the conciliation of the parties and the amicable settlement of disputes before any court proceedings have been instituted or in the course of proceedings" (CoE, 1981, p. 2). The application of mediation was further extended in the late 1990s when the Committee of Ministers put forward recommendations supporting, among other uses, family mediation (CoE, 1998).

The conceptualisation of mediation has evolved significantly in the last century. At the beginning of the 20th century, mediation was limited to "the intervention of a third power, on the invitation or with the consent of two other powers, for the purpose of arranging differences between the latter without recourse to war" as defined by Montague Crackanthorpe (1911). Based on the contemporary definition provided in the Cambridge dictionary (n.d.), its meaning has been broadened nowadays to include "the process of talking to two separate people or groups involved in a disagreement to try to help them to agree or find a solution to their problems".

Even though in the common understanding mediation is most often associated with correcting misunderstandings and reducing the tension (Gadomska, 2019; Gee-Milan & Gee, 2020), there is little agreement on the meaning of the concept in the literature. As a nomadic notion, it can be applied with reference to a myriad of situations, therefore depending on the field and discipline in which it is used, it might be open to multiple interpretations (Lenoir, 1996, as cited in North & Piccardo, 2016).

Mediation has its roots in the 19th-century philosophy (North & Piccardo (2016). Georg Hegel, a German philosopher and the chief exponent of idealism, equated mediation with a thought, which conceptualised as an abstract operation was believed to underlie the process of knowledge acquisition (Janowska & Plak, 2021). A pair of German philosophers, Karl Marx and Friedrich Engels, extended Hegel's cognitive views on mediation in their philosophical approach called dialectal materialism. They added a social dimension to the concept by arguing that mediation describes the relationship between the opposites in the society (North & Piccardo, 2016).

The cognitive and social perspectives on mediation were, as reported by Creanga (2020), transferred from philosophy to the emerging field of psychology by Lev Vygotsky, a Russian psychologist, at the beginning of the 20th century. He claimed that humans do not interact with their environments in a direct way. Mediation (or a mediated action) was used by Vygotsky (1978) with reference to social interaction, which is always facilitated, or mediated to use a precise term, through cultural tools, both those symbolic (i.e., language) and physical (i.e., objects, such as a spade).

The mediated action notion laid a foundation for what later came to be known as the first generation of the Cultural Historical Activity Theory (CHAT). CHAT was developed to account for the fact that humans learn by doing and employing tools of different kinds in a collective environment (Kaptelinin & Nardi, 2006).

As a reaction against the then dominant Skinnerian behaviourism and Piagetian psychological theory, Vygotsky's idea of mediation, which viewed the process from the individual's perspective, was extended to consider the influence of social rules, community relations, and division of labour on the performance of mediated action (Igira & Gregory, 2009). This marked the development of the second generation of CHAT, according to which collective effort underlay mediation (Engeström, 1987).

In the wake of the increased population mobility, the mediated action was further extended in the current (third) generation of CHAT. Two interacting activity systems that share an object (i.e., work on an issue) were included in the third-generational model by Engeström (1987) to account for the conflicting traditions, views, and perspectives of different community members. The understanding of mediated action evolved throughout the 20th century, as evident in the models developed in three generations of CHAT. They presented mediation as an activity initially taking place in isolation and, subsequently, through a collective action in an increasingly diverse community.

Sujecka-Zając (2016) examined the phenomenon of mediation in the context of education. She used the term double mediation to explicate the process of learning and teaching. The scholar made a distinction between, what she called, didactic/external mediation, or teaching, which is said to facilitate cognitive/

internal mediation, or learning. Specifically, Sujecka-Zając (2016) identified the social versus individual aspect of mediation, yet she accentuated the primarily learner-centred character of the educational process. In her view, it is the learner who takes on the role of the cognitive mediator and shoulders the responsibility for their learning.

The concept has also been applied in social communication and media studies (Janowska & Plak, 2021), where it was subjected to conflicting interpretations. Silverstone (2002), for example, limited his definition of mediation to the process of information transmission that takes place via "institutionalised media of communication", such as the press, radio, television, and the Internet (p. 3). In contrast, in his definition, Couldry (2008) extended the meaning of mediation, describing it as the influence of media on contemporary societies.

For the purpose of this discussion, however, we adopt a social and pragmatic perspective on language mediation popularised by the CEFR (CoE, 2001) and CVs (CoE, 2018, 2020). The concept is therefore defined here as a set of everyday linguistic practices that provide a bridge between individuals in public, personal, occupational, and educational domains (North & Piccardo, 2016; Stathopoulou 2015). To be specific, language mediation stands for the "process which connects the social and the individual" (Swain et al., 2015, p. 151) and arises from the need to make information accessible to somebody who has various types of difficulties (i.e., linguistic, cultural, semantic, technical) in accessing it (CoE, 2018, 2020; Stathopoulou 2015). It is a procedure based on cooperation and interaction which is implemented by an individual to ensure successful communication (Abbate, 2021). In other words, mediation stands here for any language activity in which the language learner assumes the role of an intermediary to facilitate (mutual) understanding (CoE, 2018, 2020). Therefore, the development of the ability to mediate improves communication in general (Rysak, 2010).

The purpose of mediation is to provide an individual with access to a text, concept, and communication that they cannot understand. In this respect, mediation can be conceptualised as a two-step process (Dendrinos, 2006). It involves firstly the comprehension of meanings articulated in a source text, which serves as a source of information for mediators (Hayes, 1996) and secondly, the creation of new meanings through clarifying, interpreting, summarising, reformulating, selecting information, switching from oral to written expression (and vice versa), and transferring numerical information into verbal description, to mention some of the most popular source text modifications (Coste & Cavalli, 2015; Stathopoulou, 2015).

Mediation is a complex process which requires linguistic and conceptual modifications of the source text to be made in response to the needs of interlocutors, the specificity of the situation, and the objective of the communication process (Andrzejewska, 2011). To be able to do that, mediators, referred to as meaning negotiators and meaning-making agents by Dendrinos (2013), are expected to gain a number of sub-competencies (i.e., linguistic, intercultural, interpersonal) (Howell, 2017) and possess a high emotional intelligence to demonstrate sufficient empathy for the needs of the party (parties) involved in a communicative situation (Creanga, 2020).

In mediation, as opposed to translation, emphasis is placed on the adequacy of the target text rather than its equivalence (Howell, 2017). Mediators should therefore be concerned more with the ideas and needs of others than their own ones (CoE, 2018, 2020). To cater to those needs, they are expected to adapt the final product of mediation by either condensing or expanding the amount of information from the source text (Howell, 2017) and changing its genre, mode, register, and style (Stathapoulou, 2015).

1.3.1.2 Mediation in the 2001 CEFR and 2018 CEFR CV

In the late 1990s, the draft version of the CEFR, *Modern languages: Learning, teaching, assessment* (CoE, 1997), pioneered the introduction of the mediation term to language education (Janowska & Plak, 2021). It was presented therein as one of the four modes of communication along with reception, production, and interaction. Mediation, however, was described to be more complex than the remaining three (North, 2019). As demonstrated in Figure 1.7, it usually combines all of them; it functions as the prolongation of interaction, which is in turn a combination of receptive and productive modes of communication.

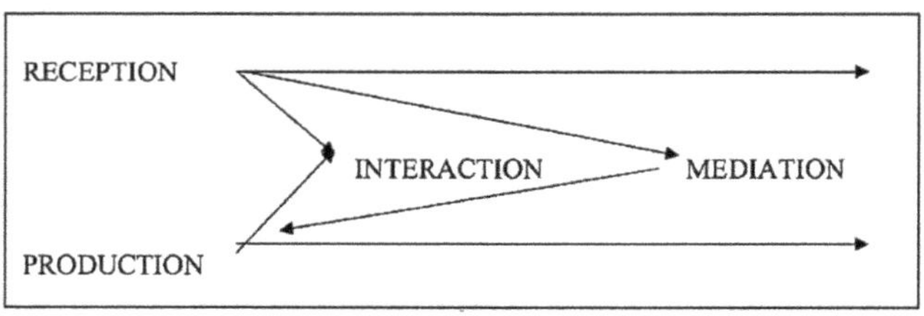

Fig. 1.7: *Schematic representation of the role of mediation in the 1998 draft version of the CEFR (CoE, 1998, p. 15)*

The diagram, however, was not included in the official 2001 CEFR publication and mediation lost its significance that was originally expressed in the draft document (Martyniuk, 2021), with the concept being severely limited to two types of activities: oral mediation (including simultaneous, consecutive, and informal interpretation) and written mediation (standing for exact and literary translation, summary, paraphrase, and record) (CoE, 2001). Also, general conviction restricting the understanding of mediation to cross-lingual mediation was strengthened for no apparent reason in the wake of the CEFR publication (North & Piccardo, 2016). The fact is that the framework did not confine the meaning of the concept to cross-linguistic mediation. It instead equally promoted both intra- (i.e., within one language) and inter- (i.e., between languages) lingual mediation, as clearly reflected in the following citations: "language user (…) is to act as an intermediary between interlocutors who are unable to understand each other directly, normally (but not exclusively) speakers of different languages" (CoE, 2011, p. 87) and "[b]oth input and output texts may be spoken or written and in L1 or L2" (CoE, 2001, p. 99). In addition, despite a substantial difference between the two, there was a tendency to treat translation and mediation synonymously (Janowska & Plak, 2021). In contrast to translation, the act of mediation requires the adaptation of the content and structure of the source text to the context of a communicative situation rather than the exact transmission of information (Andrzejewska, 2011). As opposed to translators, who are allowed neither to add explanatory comments nor omit pieces of information from the original text (Dendrinos, 2006, 2013), mediator is a "visible and active participant in the interaction" with other interlocutors (Howell, 2017, p. 150).

Even though officially introduced as a mode of communication and a communicative language activity, mediation received little attention in the CEFR. Fifty-three descriptors were developed for reception, production, and interaction (Martyniuk, 2021). By contrast, there were no illustrative scales suggested for the ability to mediate (North, 2007, 2011). This disproportion marginalised mediation practice in the language classroom (Creanga, 2020). As reported by Howell (2017) and Piccardo et al. (2019), the exception to this unfortunate tendency were German, Swiss, and Greek FL education systems, where cross-linguistic mediation started appearing in language curricula and examinations in the early 2000s (for the discussion of the Polish education system, see Chapter Two).

In the next several dozen years, mediation received increasing attention in the European educational initiatives. Two CoE's projects performed a decisive role in raising once lowly status of mediation. In *Education, mobility, otherness. The mediation functions of schools*, Daniel Coste and Marisa Cavalli (2015) described mediation as the key concept both in the CEFR's updated conceptual model and in education in general. In their publication, they called mediation "a reducer of distance" (p. 27), explaining that "the aim of the mediation process (…) is to reduce the gap between two poles that are distant from or in tension with each other" (p. 12). Coste and Cavalli (2015) differentiated between two types of distance: cognitive and relational. To deal with the former, a series of mental operations underlying the transmission of knowledge, known as cognitive mediation, is required. To cope with the latter, the management of social interactions, referred to as relational mediation, is needed to improve cooperation and mutual understanding between individuals.

Developing illustrative descriptors of aspects of mediation by Brian North and Enrica Piccardo (2016) filled in the gap relating to the missing mediation descriptors in the CEFR. The project involved three phases (North & Piccardo, 2016). Phase One was mainly intuitive as experts formulated the descriptors based on their knowledge and experience. In Phase Two, they focused on the qualitative aspects of the descriptors. Phase Three involved the quantitative analyses conducted to calibrate the best scales with a view to assessing the appropriateness of a particular scale with reference to the level for which it had been designed.

The two publications substantially contributed to the update of the CEFR (Janowska & Plak, 2021). The typologies published by Coste and Cavalli (2015) and North and Piccardo (2016) were adopted in the document *CEFR. Illustrative descriptors. Extended version 2016* (CoE, 2016). They were, however, eventually replaced with a different division of mediation (i.e., text mediation, concept mediation, communication mediation) in both the provisional and official CVs (CoE, 2018, 2020). The development of can-do statements for mediation also allowed the long-awaited move from theory to practice (Creanga, 2020). In total, twenty-four scales (including nineteen for mediation activities and five for mediating strategies) were developed within the CVs (CoE, 2018, 2020). Their formulation underlined the universality of mediation and, as argued by Martyniuk (2021), extended the use of mediation from the fields of language learning, teaching, and assessment to education in general.

In so far as the phenomenon of mediation had been examined in Polish glottodidactics prior to the publication of the CV (e.g., Andrzejewska, 2011; Janowska, 2017; Iluk, 2009; Rysak, 2010; Sujecka & Zając, 2016), the update of the CEFR quickly generated widespread interest among FLT specialists. For example, Martyniuk (2021) provided an account of the changes introduced to the 2001 framework pertaining to mediation. He outlined the theoretical background of the CV publication and examined the concept of mediation introduced in the updated framework. In 2020, a special issue of *Języki Obce w Szkole*, a Polish journal intended for FL teachers, was devoted to discussing theoretical and practical aspects of the concept in light of the CEFR and the CV. In their articles, Bartosik (2020), Dwużnik (2020), Gee-Milan and Gee (2020), Kucharczyk (2020), and Maciaszczyk

(2020) formulated the definitions of mediation, discussed the typologies of the concept, and put forward several examples of classroom mediation-oriented tasks. Significant contribution to introducing the concept of language mediation to Polish glottodidactics was made with the publication *Działania mediacyjne w uczeniu się i nauczaniu języków obcych. Od teorii do praktyki*[7] by Iwona Janowska and Marta Plak (2021). The Polish scholars provided a comprehensive account of the term both from a theoretical and practical perspective in the context of the action-oriented vision of language learning promoted by the CoE's educational initiatives.

1.3.2 Mediation-based practice in the action-oriented language classroom

1.3.2.1 Fundamentals of mediation-based tasks

The roots of the task concept can be traced to the communicative era in FLT. At the turn of the 1970s and 1980s, the use of a task as a unit of analysis and a learning tool was brought into sharp focus amid the growing appeal of a task-based syllabus (Gonzales-Lloret, 2007). The notion was subject to different interpretations. Long (1985) defined it as "the hundred and one things people do in everyday life, at work, at play, and in between" (p. 89), thus stressing its omnipresence in language users' lives. Crookes (1986) viewed a task as "a piece of work or an activity" which is performed in order to attain a given objective (p. 1). Prabhu (1987), similarly to Crookes (1986), treated a task as an activity; however, in his view, the achievement of a goal is possible only "through some process of thought" (p. 24). Skehan (1996b) compared a task to "activities which have meaning as their primary focus. Success in tasks is evaluated in terms of achievement of an outcome, and tasks generally bear some resemblance to real-life language use" (p. 20). In the CEFR (CoE, 2001), on the other hand, a task was described as "any purposeful action considered by an individual as necessary in order to achieve a given result in the context of a problem to be solved, an obligation to fulfil or an objective to be achieved" (p. 10). Despite a notable lack of consistency in defining the concept in FLT, it is possible to isolate several characteristics of tasks. The most distinguishing of them are listed in Table 1.4.

7 *Mediating activities in learning and teaching foreign languages: From theory to practice*

Tab. 1.4: *Key features of tasks (self-prepared)*

Long & Crookes (1991)	**Skehan (1996a)**	**Ellis (2003)**	**Littlewood (2004)**	**Willis (2004)**	**Janowska (2009)**
Input Cognitive processing Negotiation of meaning	Focus on meaning Relationship to real world Task outcome	Focus on meaning Real-world language use Use of any language skill Cognitive processing Communicative outcome	Communicative purpose Authenticity Learners' active involvement Focus on meaning	Outcome Focus on meaning Involvement of any language skill Real-world character	Workplan and action Meaning-oriented Real-life use of language Cognitive processing Communicative outcome

As clearly evident above, not every classroom activity can be classified as a task. Only those which draw learners' attention to meaning, create real-life contexts of language use, require (language- and non-language-related) decisions to be made by language users, necessitate interaction, involve cognitive processing, establish a clear communicative objective, and produce a non-language outcome can be referred to as tasks proper.

Mediation tasks are inherent to everyday communication, especially from the perspective of increasingly plurilingual and pluricultural societies (Dendrinos, 2013). They ensure the situated character of the learning process (North, 2021) and create authentic communicative situations that language learners encounter daily outside the language classroom (Janowska & Plak, 2021). Mediation tasks are individual and transactional tasks, in which focus is placed on information transformation (North, 2022). They not only increase language awareness and cultural knowledge, but also promote the use of communicative and learning strategies. Furthermore, the combination of three modes of communication (i.e., reception, production, interaction) within mediation (North, 2021) reflects the integrated view of language use promoted by the AOA (Piccardo et al., 2019).

The use of mediation tasks accentuates the action-oriented character of language learning. Learners, or mediators, assume the role of social agents who draw on their general and communicative competences to bridge the gap between source and target texts (Howell, 2017). They are expected to create target texts based on source texts in accordance with the principles of adequacy rather than equivalence (Howell, 2017). Mediation tasks require language users to linguistically and conceptually modify source texts in accordance with the needs of other interlocutors (CoE, 2018, 2020; Creanga, 2020). The type and scope of the changes introduced by mediators depends upon the communicative objective which shows what should be mediated and what should be omitted (Andrzejewska, 2011).

The specificity of mediation tasks is reflected in the process of their execution. Dendrinos (2013) described the process of mediation-based task performance by giving the example of KPG[8] cross-linguistic mediation tasks involving written and oral production. She isolated eight steps to successful task completion. The researcher argued that learners-mediators need to first identify the information gap and then determine what type of intervention is required based on interlocutors' needs. Next, they are expected to familiarise themselves with the context presented in the written/spoken source text and decide what to relay in terms of language and content. Later, they should rely on the gist or selected pieces of information from the source text to create the target text and organise the output. Finally, they are required to produce the target text and negotiate meanings with their (real or imagined) interlocutor(s).

Despite terminological differences, there has been a general agreement that mediation task performance requires mediators to have well-developed competences. For instance, Hallet (2009, p. 3-5, as cited in Janowska & Plak, 2021, p. 139-140) claimed that in order to mediate, learners need to demonstrate linguistic-communicative, intercultural, interactionist, and strategic-methodic competences[9]. Dendrinos (2013), similarly to Hallet (2009), argued that sociocultural awareness, competences (i.e., linguistic, sociolinguistic, discourse, strategic), and social skills underlie the ability to mediate. However, she also considered mediators' cognitive skills to be a prerequisite for successful mediation. According to the scholar, they enable learners to deal with the dynamicity of the mediation process since they allow students to "retain and recall information for use in a new context, combine prior knowledge and experience with new information, combine information from a variety of source texts" (Dendrinos, 2013, What KPG mediation involves).

---

8 *Kratiko Pistopiitiko Glossomathias* (KPG) is the National Foreign Language Exam System, which was introduced in Greece in 2003 (Anastasiadou & Tiliakou, 2015).

9 The English translations of the German terms *sprachlich-kommunikative Kompetenz*, *interkulturelle Kompetenz*, *interaktionale Kompetenz*, and *strategisch-metodische Kompetenz* were provided by the current Author.

The use of mediation tasks in the classroom brings definite advantages. Goodier (2020) claims that it facilitates a meaningful, collaborative, personalised, and authentic learning process. As reported by Gee-Milan and Gee (2020), it also helps students to develop the skills they need in the 21st century workplace. Some of the examples of must-have abilities that mediation tasks are found central to developing include collaborative working, critical thinking skills, autonomous learning, and empathy.

The neglect of mediation in the CEFR may heighten the false impression that this communicative language activity had been entirely overlooked in FL instructed settings until the CVs publication. However, in the education systems of Germany, Greece, and (later) Switzerland, the origins of mediation instruction go back to the 2000s, which was when cross-linguistic mediation was introduced to national core curricula and became a basic component in high-stakes exit FL examinations (Piccardo et al., 2019). Given an extremely brief description of mediation and the lack of descriptors in the 2001 framework, mediation tasks were conceptualised merely as "a communicative equivalent of the traditional translation" in the countries which were first to adopt mediation as an examination component (North, 2020, p. 553). Under the influence of the CEFR, mediation-based practice took the form of translation and interpretation exercises only. In the early 2000s, linguistic mediation appeared in the German national FL core curriculum. In line with the typology put forward within the CEFR, its understanding was limited to summarising and paraphrasing texts between L1 and L2.

One of the German researchers who attempted to categorise mediation tasks was Kolb (2009, as cited in Howell, 2017). She identified three types of tasks: paraphrasing visuals (e.g., signs), summarising in the L1 writing information presented orally in the FL, and summarising in the FL information written in the L1. In addition, her categorisation included pre- and post-mediation activities.

In her classification, Caspari (2013, as cited in Howell, 2017) divided mediation tasks into oral and written production of target texts. The former was further divided into relaying information in the L1 based on L2 spoken and written texts, spoken interaction based on a situational framework, and paraphrasing formal L1 written texts into colloquial L2. The latter included tasks requiring the preparation of L2 written text based on L1 text and picking out relevant information from L1 text and rewriting it in response to specific informational needs.

The research into mediation-based tasks also flourished in Greece. In their articles, Dendrinos (2013) and Stathapoulou (2014) overviewed the types of cross-linguistic mediation-oriented examination tasks developed within the

KPG. As reported by these scholars, mediation performance was measured at B1, B2, and C1 levels of proficiency, and the type of mediation task was correlated with the difficulty of the KPG written and spoken exam. As demonstrated in Table 1.5, mediation tasks were primarily limited to linguistic mediation, with summarising and relaying specific information presented in the L1 in a FL being the most common examples of tasks within the mediation component of the KPG.

Tab. 1.5: *Types of written and spoken mediation-based tasks in KPG (adapted from Dendrinos, 2013 and Stathopoulou, 2014)*

<table>
<tr><th></th><th>Written KPG</th><th>Spoken KPG</th></tr>
<tr><td>B1</td><td>- communicating the gist of an L1 text
- relaying information extracted from an L1 text</td><td rowspan="2">- relaying selected information from L1 texts
- expressing the gist of L1 texts
- talking about an issue discussed in an L1 text</td></tr>
<tr><td>B2</td><td>- conveying the main idea of a text in the L1
- making a summary of an L1 text
- relaying messages contained in an L1 text</td></tr>
<tr><td>C1</td><td>- conveying the main idea or supporting details of an L1 text
- summarising an L1 text
- interpreting in the TL the meaning(s) of one or more messages in the L1</td><td>- conversing for approximately ten minutes to provide an interlocutor with information from the source text and solve a problem which requires negotiation of meanings, ideas and factual information</td></tr>
</table>

With the CVs publication, the once impoverished understanding of mediation could be significantly enriched (CoE, 2018, 2020). The isolation of three broad types of mediation (i.e., text mediation, concept mediation, communication mediation) was a significant step towards acknowledging its (omni)presence in different areas, from personal, through public, to educational and occupational domains (Martyniuk, 2021). The development of twenty-four descriptors in the CV also facilitated an important move from theory to classroom practice (Creanga, 2020). The publication of fourteen subtypes of mediation-based tasks within text mediation (e.g., explaining data, note-taking), concept mediation (e.g., collaborating to construct meaning, managing interaction), and communication mediation (e.g., acting as an intermediary in informal situations), and five mediation strategies (e.g., to explain a new concept, to simplify a text) (CoE, 2018,

2020) could, as argued by Gee-Milan and Gee (2020) and Goodier (2020), inspire teachers (and other interested parties) to devise mediation-based tasks other than translation and interpretation.

1.3.2.2 Principles of mediation-oriented task design

The adoption of the action-oriented perspective on developing communicative competence carries certain pedagogical implications. A FL is taught first and foremost through task performance which imitates naturalistic language acquisition. Emphasis is therefore laid on collaborative, meaningful, and goal-oriented tasks. Their focus is on a non-language product, or outcome, such as "planning an outing, making a poster, creating a blog, designing a festival, choosing a candidate, etc." (CoE, 2018, p. 27).

The action orientation concept reflects a transition "from syllabuses based on a linear progression through language structures, or a pre-determined set of notions and functions, towards syllabuses based on needs analysis, oriented towards real-life tasks that are constructed around purposefully selected notions and functions" (CoE, 2018, p. 26). Educational procedures, such as designing syllabi, are established with reference to learners' communicative needs. This implies the introduction of tasks that are selected on the basis of their frequency and relevance to students' daily reality.

In the AOA, tasks should be designed after learners' needs have been identified in accordance with the backwards design principle (Howell, 2017). The procedure involving a systematic collection and analysis of subjective and objective information on the educational needs, goals, and wants of students is technically referred to as a task-based needs analysis (NA) (Brown, 2009). It constitutes the first step in the rationally and empirically motivated TBLT programme development and allows the planning of curriculum that meets the expectations of learners and teachers (Long, 2005, 2015; Norris, 2009). It is possible to isolate three steps in the process of task design (Long & Crookes, 1991). Once information on learners' educational needs has been collected and analysed, target tasks, or "real-world communicative activities" (Long, 2016, p. 6), are selected. If substantial discrepancies between the number of target tasks obtained from a NA and the amount of classroom time available for their teaching can be observed, target-type tasks, which create a foundation for pedagogic tasks, or "initially simple, progressively more complex approximations to the original target tasks" (Long, 2016, p. 7), need to be identified. If appropriately sequenced in accordance with their intrinsic complexity, they form a task syllabus (see Figure 1.8).

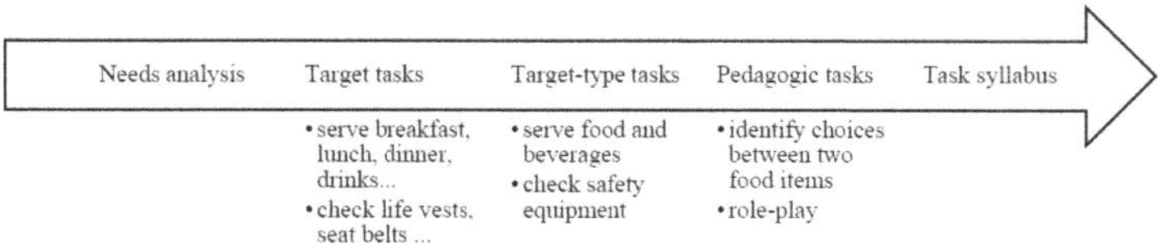

Fig. 1.8: *Process of task design on the example of airline flight attendants' NA (Long & Crookes, 1991, p. 21-22)*

In addition to the selection of target and pedagogic tasks, the task design process requires decisions to be made with regard to task features. Four general categories of characteristics which underlie task description were listed by Rod Ellis (2003b) in his seminal publication *Task-based language learning and teaching.* Input refers to information provided to students within the task, its medium (i.e., pictorial, oral, written) and organisation (i.e., tight, loose). Task conditions describe information configuration, interactant relationship, and interaction requirement. Task processes stand for the type of cognitive operation performed by learners during task performance (i.e., exchanging information, expressing opinions, explaining, reasoning) and the discourse mode (i.e., monologues, dialogues). Finally, task outcomes refer to the product, including its medium (i.e., pictorial, written, oral), the discourse domain/genre (i.e., description, recipe), and scope (i.e., close, open).

The choice of task features affects language learning, with some of the tasks being more effective in promoting language acquisition than others. Willis (2004) examined the influence of close and open tasks on the kind of discourse students produce during their performance. Since the former type of tasks have a very tight structure, they involve learners in more intense language production based on negotiation of meaning as opposed to the latter which involve only experience-sharing and anecdote-telling.

Task features were also found to determine the complexity of tasks, an important issue in the context of task grading, or the "rational sequencing of pedagogic tasks" (Long, 2015, p. 227). To give an example, a task with textual, familiar, and static input supported by visual information in which learners are expected to exchange information by writing an informal e-mail would be classified as easy. In contrast, tasks which require students not only to deal with oral, unfamiliar, and context-free input, but also require an exchange of opinions in a monologic discourse mode would be classified by Ellis (2003a, 2003b) as difficult.

FLT specialists' knowledge of task grading was also informed by research examining the effects of task complexity on the development of interlanguage. Conflicting approaches to the problem of task complexity emerged in the field.

One of the first proposals, the Capacity Hypothesis, was put forward by Peter Skehan (1996a, 1996b). The scholar claimed that cognitively challenging tasks "consume more attentional resources (...), with the result that less attention is available for focus on form" (Skehan, 1998, p. 97). Further, he argued that grading criteria ought to ensure a smooth progression from the least to most complex tasks. Equally importantly, tasks ought to be adjusted to students' proficiency level; too difficult tasks lead to fossilisation while too easy ones do not facilitate interlanguage development (Skehan, 1996b).

Another perspective on the problem of task complexity was provided by James Cummins (2000). He established a framework for designing tasks based on the range of contextual support (i.e., context-embedded versus context-reduced) and degree of cognitive involvement (i.e., cognitively undemanding and demanding).

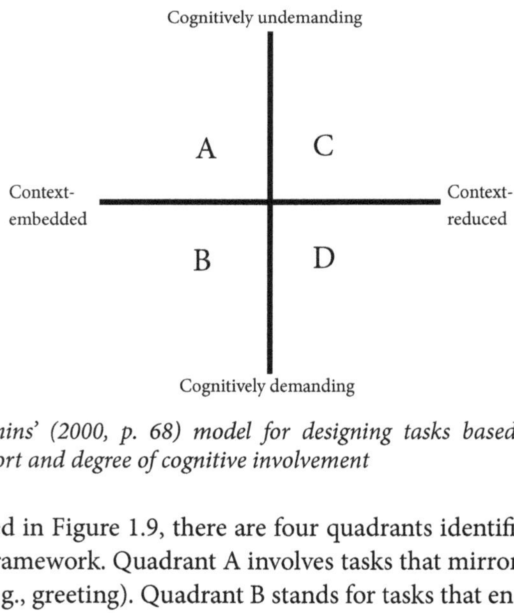

Fig. 1.9: *Cummins' (2000, p. 68) model for designing tasks based on the range of contextual support and degree of cognitive involvement*

As illustrated in Figure 1.9, there are four quadrants identified within Cummins' (2000) framework. Quadrant A involves tasks that mirror everyday social interactions (e.g., greeting). Quadrant B stands for tasks that encourage learners to process (e.g., compare and contrast) information on the basis of the context provided. Quadrant C tasks offer less contextual support; however, they do not require learners to process too much information (e.g., listening to a story). In addition to providing very limited contextual prompts, Quadrant D activities (e.g., interpreting evidence) are most cognitively demanding ones.

Cummins (2000) claimed that cognitively challenging tasks that offer a sufficient amount of contextual and linguistic support facilitate more successful language and content acquisition. This, however, conflicts with the findings of

Darmi's (2014) study, according to which "learners' use of the second language increases when they are not challenged cognitively, regardless of the contextual support provided" (p. 6). Robinson (2001) formulated the Cognition Hypothesis, in which he also highlighted the positive influence of task complexity on learning. The increase in the performative/procedural and cognitive/conceptual aspects of task complexity was said to promote the production of more complex FL structures by learners as the increased cognitive demands allow students to attend to new concepts and control their FL abilities more effectively (Robinson, 2007).

In addition, the nature of a mediation process itself should also be taken into account during task design. As already said, the need to mediate may occur anywhere, from personal to public, from occupational to educational domains (North & Piccardo, 2016; Stathopoulou 2015). The primary objective of a mediation task, regardless of the circumstances, is to make information available to an interlocutor who experiences linguistic, cultural, semantic, and/or technical difficulties in accessing it (CoE, 2018, 2020; Stathopoulou 2015). Mediation is used in this discussion to describe any language activity in which a learner takes on the role of an intermediary to improve other language users' understanding of the source text through the creation of the target text. In view of the above, the design and description of mediation-based tasks require information that accounts for the specificity of the process. Significant contribution in this respect was made by the Research Centre for Language Teaching, Testing, and Assessment at the University of Athens, Greece (Stathopoulou, 2014). A model for mediation task description was developed within the Task Analysis Project. A pre-defined set of six task features was put forward: topic of the text, discourse environment, text-type, communicative goal, generic process, and communicative roles of the mediator and their imagined interlocutor. The explanation of the mentioned task description parameters with examples can be found in Table 1.6.

Tab. 1.6: *Model for written mediation-based task description (adapted from Stathopoulou, 2011)*

Task description parameter	Example
Topic (What is the text about?)	environment, friendship, animals
Discourse environment (Where?)	magazine, newspaper, leaflet
Text-type (What type of text?)	article, email, report
Generic process (What text process?)	describe, argue, narrate, explain, instruct
Communicative process (For what purpose?)	urge, advise, disagree
Role relationships (Who is writing to whom?)	friend - friend, student - teacher

Another important contribution to promoting mediation-based classroom practice came with Brian North's (2021) *Plurilingual mediation in the classroom*. The set of ten examples of mediation tasks discussed therein was taken from the 2017 piloting of the new descriptors and was characterised by three common features. The first one relates to the combination of four language modes ensuring the complexity of a mediation task. The second one concerns learners' participation in a collaborative phase. The final one involves the construction of authentic scenarios.

The focus of mediation tasks is placed on information transformation (North, 2021). To achieve the intended effect, or to allow others to obtain the desired piece(s) of information, mediators need to comprehend the meanings articulated in verbal and/or visual source texts and create new meanings within target texts (Coste & Cavalli, 2015; Stathopoulou, 2015). This, however, calls for linguistic and conceptual modifications of source texts to be made by mediators in response to the needs of interlocutors, the situation, and the goal of the communication process (Andrzejewska, 2011). Therefore, from the perspective of mediation task design, what underlies successful mediation task performance (in addition to a well-developed repertoire of competences) is a well-developed set of instructions. Iluk (2009) argued that students are able to mediate successfully if they possess sufficient amount of information as to who the imagined interlocutors are and what is subject to mediation. The instruction ought to be formulated in such a way so that learners-mediators are able to decide what pieces of information to mediate and how to do it. The presentation of the details relating to the communicative situation and the mediator-interlocutor relationship helps the former create target texts (Iluk, 2009). A model of a mediating situation that considers task instruction development was designed by Janowska and Plak (2021) (see Figure 1.10). It took the form of a triangle, in which each of the angles stands for one of the components to be obligatorily included in instructions to a mediation task. 'A' stands for the mediator; 'B' refers to the visual and/or verbal source text, and 'C' describes an imagined interlocutor who awaits for target texts to be constructed and presented by mediators.

A number of practical guidelines on mediation task design have been recently provided in the (FL) literature. For example, it is possible to adapt existing speaking and writing tasks so that they involve learners in reformulating information from spoken/written source texts (Goodier, 2020). Inspiration for developing mediation tasks can be also drawn from the CV since the descriptors for aspects of mediation can be freely adapted to design course's objectives, materials, and tasks (Gee & Gee, 2020). Also, source texts for mediating tasks should be selected in accordance with the criterion of authenticity (Janowska & Plak, 2021). Moreover, balance between students' interests and the situations in which they may need to mediate outside the classroom should be maintained during source text selection (Chiappini & Mansur, 2020).

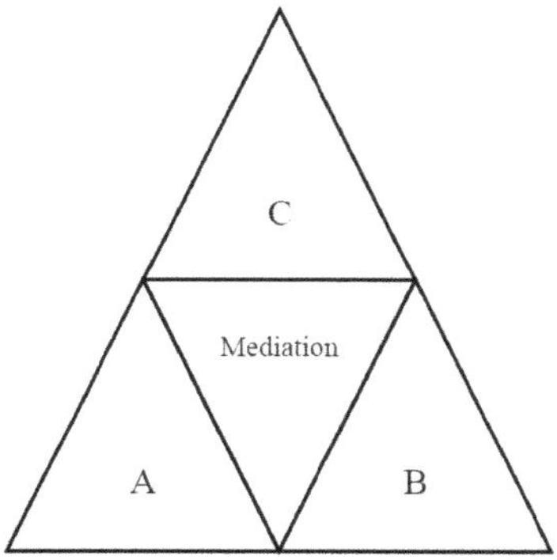

Fig. 1.10: *Model presenting the structure of instructions to mediation-based tasks (Janowska & Plak, 2021, p. 159)*

As pointed out by Howell (2020) and Janowska and Plak (2021), the assessment of mediation task performance had been explored prior to the CV publication. Pioneering research exploring the issue was conducted in Germany (e.g., Bohle, 2012). Since mediation is to ensure mutual understanding, it was generally agreed that the main point of reference in assessing mediation task performance should be adequacy. Bohle (2012) argued that "[t]he main criterion in the evaluation of crosslinguistic mediation must be whether or not the communicative aim is achieved in the (mediating) solution; that means, whether the information has been correctly selected and relayed completely and understandably" (p. 96, as cited in Howell, 2017, p. 150). A similar approach highlighting the communicative dimension of mediation assessment was adopted in the FL eighth-grader and New Matura exams in Poland in the wake of the 2017 education reform. As reported by Kucharczyk (2020), who investigated the mediation concept by confronting the Polish examination system with the CV, students' responses, even if they contain lexico-grammatical errors, are considered acceptable on the condition that they communicate meanings conveyed in verbal and or/visual source texts. Completion of mediation tasks may therefore be regarded as successful (or not) depending on whether learners/examinees have been able to communicate the key information from a source text in a comprehensible manner and in a way showing their consideration of the communicative situation (Iluk, 2009).

Chapter 2
EFL education in the Polish secondary school context

2.0 Outline

In Chapter Two, the literature related to English as a foreign language (EFL) learning, teaching, and assessment in post-war Poland is reviewed to provide background information on the state of Polish EFL secondary education. The present chapter has been divided into five main sections. The first subchapter provides a historical perspective on FLT in post-war Poland by presenting the major teaching trends that emerged in the field when the country was under the influence of the Union of Soviet Socialist Republics and when it underwent socio-political transformations due to the fall of communism. The following two subchapters offer a general overview of the selected education reforms implemented by the Polish government over the past thirty years by investigating their positive and negative impact on FLT and assessment in Polish instructed settings. The next subchapter presents basic information pertaining to the administration of EFL secondary school examinations in the selected European Union member states and Poland including the types of skills and knowledge tested therein. The final subchapter discusses Polish learners' challenges in developing their EFL communicative competence in the context of the recent 2017 education reform and the COVID-19 outbreak.

2.1 History of FLT in post-war Poland

2.1.1 FLT in Polish People's Republic: Under the influence of the Soviets

Decades of political, ideological, cultural, and economic oppression associated with three partitions of Poland and Poles' life-and-death struggle for freedom during national uprisings and military activities in the First and Second World Wars made an indelible imprint on Poland's autonomy. Such oppression continued to affect their hard-won independence in the post-war period despite Poles' fervent hopes and optimistic expectations for long-awaited freedom. Between 1947 and 1989, Poland, a communist and Eastern bloc country officially known as Polish People's Republic (*Polska Rzeczpospolita Ludowa*), yet again found itself in the clutches of an oppressor, the Soviet Union.

In line with the national policy of the Union of Soviet Socialist Republics, the communist party apparatus manipulated the Polish education system and curricula by adopting the socialist ideology (Pyter, 2015). This was manifested in a two-fold way in the area of FLT: through the promotion of the Russian language and introduction of propagandist texts to instructed settings.

A dark period in Poland's history spanning between 1944 and 1956, referred to as the Stalinist era, progressively undermined Polish inter-war period traditions pertaining to the teaching of Western languages. The initially lowly position of Russian as opposed to German and English (Opólska-Danecka, 1954, as cited in Zając, 2007) was gradually strengthened by the 1948 education reform. By virtue of the 1948 Ordinance of the Minister of Education, a new school system consisting of eleven-year comprehensive schools (including seven-year primary and four-year secondary schools) was adopted (Official Journal of the Ministry of Education from 1948, No. 5, item 86, as amended). Even though real-life application of the Russian language in the Polish society was severely limited, it became the "only foreign language in primary schools and the only required foreign language in secondary schools" (Reichelt, 2005a, p. 217) taught to learners aged eleven (i.e., grade five).

The influence of Stalinism on the Polish curricula was enormous. The need to discuss heavily politicised and socio-economic topics was the part and parcel of FL teachers' and learners' daily classroom routine. Illustrative examples of some of the common themes explored in FL instructed settings include *Exploitation and poverty of English workers in the first half of the 19th century*, *Social advancement of workers*, and *Marx's and Engels' views on labour movement in England* (Prejbisz, 1969). A generally sombre public mood did not favour the adoption of the Direct Method in FL instruction. Continual repressive measures taken by the government were reflected in the language classroom where learners and teachers reluctantly shared their personal opinions, the results of which was the restriction of FL instruction to text-based classroom work in accordance with the principles of the GTM (Komorowska, 2017).

The problems with teaching Western languages persisted in Polish instructed settings. An insufficient number of hours of instruction, the government's neglectful approach towards FL education, and limited contacts of teachers with Western teachers brought Polish adolescents' practical knowledge of FLs into disrepute, as reported by Sienicki (1957). Other unresolved issues which were responsible for limiting the field of FLT in Poland at that time included shortage of native speakers and authentic classroom materials (Kasztalska, 2014), "adversarial relationships" (Muchisky, 1985, p. 2) between teachers and learners, overcrowded classrooms, "dull, overloaded programs detached from reality, unfunctional syllabuses and drab, boring books" (Ehrenhalt, 1990, p. 8, as cited in Reichelt, 2005b, p. 217).

Greater liberalism caused by the 1956 Polish October Revolution, also known as Gomułka's Thaw, resulted in the introduction of English, German, French, and Latin as the second obligatory secondary school subject in the early 1960s. In accordance with the 1961 Act on the Education and Pedagogical System and the 1965 Ordinance of the Minister of Education, the length of compulsory primary school education was extended by one year in 1966 onwards (Journal of Laws from 1961, No. 32, Item 160, as amended; Official Journal of the Republic of Poland from 1965, No. 54, Item 281-282, as amended). New curricula adding some pragmatic elements to the language classroom proved salutary for FLT (Lipska, 1995; Prejbisz, 1966, 1969). The gradual shift from the GTM to Audiolingualism could be observed, with learners' development of the ability to communicate in every day contexts becoming the objective of FL education.

In spite of its low social utility, Russian grew in importance among Polish learners to the disadvantage of other languages (Komorowska, 2017; Komorowska & Krajka, 2020). The availability of instruction in three Western languages and Latin in secondary and technical schools did not prove effective in reversing this trend. What could explain the tendency to prioritise the Russian language was the elitist character of lycées combined with egalitarian non-full vocational schools (Prejbisz, 1961). Only around a quarter of learners attended secondary (approximately 14-20%) and technical schools (approximately 30%) which, as stated above, offered instruction in two FLs. For comparison, more than half of Polish teenagers (53%) attended vocational schools with Russian only (Komorowska, 2017, p. 64).

More friendly attitudes towards the West encouraged by Edward Gierek, the first secretary of the Polish United Workers' Party (*Polska Zjednoczona Partia Robotnicza*) elected in 1970, resulted in the promotion of relatively active collaboration with countries from outside the Socialist bloc (Komorowska, 2007). Given the liberalisation of a passport policy, a growing practical necessity to use English in contacts with native and non-native speakers in the context of business, trade, commerce, technology, science, and tourism increased Poles' awareness of the utility of FL education. British and American radio programmes and movies provided an additional source of exposure to the language for Polish learners. Close vicinity of the German Democratic Republic, the only Western country with which Poles could collaborate, popularised the learning of German on a par with English. Latin also gained greater significance as a symbol of ancient culture and Western democracies.

The 1980s government's preoccupation with political issues gave FLT specialists freedom to follow the latest developments in SLA and language education. This in turn allowed teachers to design state-of-the-art syllabi based on the Western standards, such as Wilkins' (1976) concept of notional-functional syllabi, van Ek's (1976) Threshold Level specifications, and increasingly powerful concept of CLT (Komorowska, 1986).

Even though the Soviet language policy of Russification combined with the anti-Western sentiment were meant to downplay the importance of languages other than Russian, English tended to occupy an increasingly influential position. According to the English teaching profile published by the British Council (1975, as cited in Reichelt, 2005a), 60% of Polish secondary school students chose to learn the language, whereas the remaining ones enrolled in German and French classes. The trend continued eleven years later, with 50% of secondary school students opting for English (British Council, 1986, as cited in Reichelt, 2005a).

The appeal of English could explain an increasing need for EFL instruction in communist Poland. The language became not only the symbol of the Western world for Poles, but also their way to display their loyalty to the United Kingdom and the United States. Moreover, many considered developing a high level of EFL competence their ticket to a more prosperous and prestigious life (Muchisky, 1985). To respond to the unmet educational needs of Polish people, the private sector of FL education flourished, with language schools, summer courses, exchange programmes, and English for Specific Purposes courses becoming increasingly popular.

Nonetheless, a steady demand for English language teaching failed to be addressed in the political decisions of the consecutive communist governments. The data provided by Komorowska and Krajka (2020) clearly illustrate the severity of the shortage of English teachers as a direct consequence of regulations promoting the education, training, and employment of teachers of Russian to the disadvantage of instructors of other FLs. To give an example, there were fifteen times more teachers of Russian than of English until 1989 (18,000 versus 1,200 respectively), with English instructors constituting the most numerous group of FL teachers as compared with those of German (800) and French (200). Ultimately, these pro-Russian tendencies did not weaken the position of English, which became a dominant FL not only amid the transformations of the late 1980s and early 1990s, but also in the new millennium.

2.1.2 FLT in post-communist Poland: Undergoing the 1989 transformations

The Polish education system remained the most frequently and fundamentally reformed aspect of the country's reality. Since the wartime, the socio-political and ideological mood of the country had been adding major impetus for educational policy changes. A few modifications to the field of FLT were yet again eagerly anticipated in the wake of the 1989 transformations.

The economic and political crisis of the system, as evident in the problem of hyperinflation, led to the 1989 Roundtable Talks between the Solidarity trade union and the communist party (Wiśniewski & Zahorska, 2020). After weeks of negotiations, an agreement was reached, which resulted in free elections and the formation of the first non-communist government headed by Tadeusz Mazowiecki (Śliwerski, 1999), which initiated a series of profound political and socio-economic changes in Poland from 1990 and onwards, including the reforms of banking, taxing, and health systems, and the privatisation of the public sector. The fall of communism proved to have a decisive impact on Poland's international relations by attracting foreigners and business investors. Greater freedom encouraged the foundation of social and (to a lesser extent) private schools (Leek, 2015). Given their larger degree of autonomy in designing syllabi and dealing with organisational issues (e.g., decreasing the number of students in each class), the schools opened public discussions on the widely anticipated (yet not priority) changes in state education (Grewiński, 2017; Krajewska, 1995; Levitas & Herczyński, 2012).

The critical period of transformations also affected the Polish education system. According to Levitas and Herczyński (2012), there were two contradictory activities undertaken by reformers within Solidarity. On the one hand, they aimed to decentralise education by delegating power over schools to local governments. On the other, they maintained the central control over the minimum Core Curriculum (*minimum programowe*), or a set of uniform guidelines on the required material to be covered by teachers within each subject. Also, attempts were made first to popularise secondary school education among Poles and second to provide them with an easier access to universities (Journal of Laws from 1991, No. 95, Item 425, as amended). The solution proposed by the reform was to limit the number of vocational schools (Krajewska, 1995), which referred to as the so-called "blind educational alleys" attracted justifiable criticism given their limited usefulness in the context of their graduates' university enrolment (Komorowska & Krajka, 2020, p. 226).

Despite the infamy of Russian in Poland, the language was not banned (to the surprise of the interested parties from abroad) from FL instructed settings (Komorowska, 2015b). With the abolition of obligatory instruction in Russian in 1989 (Zając, 2008), Polish learners – at least in theory due to lack of teachers in the rural areas – were provided with an opportunity to study a FL of their choice. Compulsory education for both the first FL (FL1) and second FL (FL2) started in grade five of primary schools and grade one of secondary schools respectively (Official Journal of the Ministry of Education from 1990, No. 2, Item 8). By the virtue of the aforementioned resolution, the teaching of languages other than Russian flourished. As evidenced by Figarski's (1995) survey conducted among eighth-grade primary school students, more than half of the respondents (51.2%) did not want to learn Russian in secondary and technical schools. Statistical data derived from the studies investigating Poles' participation in FL instruction do reflect their growing enthusiasm to study English and German to the decided disadvantage of Russian. To give an example, based on Wróblewska-Pawlak and Strachanowska's (2000) analysis of reports undertaken by Poland's Main Statistical Centre (*Główny Urząd Statystyczny*, GUS) in the three school years 1986/87, 1993/94, and 1997/98 presented in Table 2.1, the number of Polish students learning English steadily grew from more than 269,000 in the mid-1980s to over 2,000,000 in the late 1990s.

Tab. 2.1: *Number of primary and secondary school learners of English, German, and Russian in Poland: the 1980s versus the 1990s (Wróblewska-Pawlak & Strachanowska, 2000, p. 102)*

Foreign language	1986/87	1993/94	1997/98
English	269,400	1,669,900	2,333,400
German	338,100	1,363,900	1,718,200
Russian	3,646,000	2,024,900	1,417,300

Poles' high level of motivation to learn English could be attributed to reasons of both instrumental and integrative nature, as argued by Krajewska (1995), Muchisky (1985), and Reichelt (2005a). The special status of English as the most popular FL in Poland after September 1989 transformations can easily be explained given its very positive associations with EFL users' professional and financial success. Tempted by the mindset of pursuing more prestigious careers, cooperating with professionals from abroad, travelling, and satisfying their growing economic standards, Polish learners remained determined to study English. Learning the Western language, which as opposed to Russian did not carry any negative connotations and thus did not remind Poles of their past strained historical relations with an invader, opened up opportunities "to show their solidarity with the modern and free world" (Kasztalska, 2014, p. 246) and most importantly sever any ties with openly despised communism.

Increasing awareness on the lingua franca role of English in the context of Poland's economic, political, socio-cultural, and ideological opening towards the West also heavily reinforced a growing pro-English trend. As a natural consequence of Poland's cooperation with the Western countries in the 1990s, English began to further permeate various spheres of Poles' everyday personal and professional lives. Polish advertising, business, news, and Internet discourse received a large influx of Anglicisms and Americanisms (Borger, 2011; Chłopicki, 2005; Wieluniecka, 2010). Their influence on Polish vocabulary, syntax, and collocations was inevitable.

The spread of English borrowings reflected the emergence of novel phenomena, objects, technologies, etc., and the pressing need to describe them (Wieluniecka, 2010). Nevertheless, some extreme views representing English borrowings' corruptive and destructive effects on the Polish language were expressed. For example, Chłopicki (2005) provided a reference to a Polish opinion magazine *Polityka* (1996), in which one of the journalists considered English a threat to the Polish language, stating that "Poles are not even willing to look for Polish equivalents for English terms or even simply translate them… Our language is dying" (Chłopicki, 2005, p. 121). Poles' deep sensitivity over their national independence effected in the publication of the 1999 Polish Language Act (Journal of Laws from 1999, No. 90, Item 999, as amended). Even though the document did not outlaw the use of English in public discourse, it introduced restrictions on the application of loan words, which proved problematic especially for those who dealt with technical register on an everyday basis.

Moving forward in time, in view of the growing interest in FLs in the 1990s and 2000s, more secondary schools organised classes majoring in languages in order to respond to Poles' educational needs. The foundation of private language schools and the creation of bilingual and exchange programmes were attempts to meet a growing demand for FLT in Poland (CoE, n.d.). This raised questions relating to the organisational aspects of primary school graduates' recruitment and the relevance of FL education in Polish instructed settings (Kuliniak, 2010, 2013).

After Russian "became virtually obsolete" (Kasztalska, 2014, p. 250) because fewer students were willing to continue learning it, more and more language teachers reskilled to teach either English or German. Since a degree in philology was no longer required to teach at schools as a consequence of the 1989 transformations (Komorowska 2015a, 2015b), a practical solution to the problem of teacher shortage was provided by three-year FL teacher training colleges (*Nauczycielskie Kolegium Języków Obcych*), whose origin dates back to the 1991 Ordinance of the Minister of Education (Official Journal of the Ministry of Education from 1991, No. 3, Item 15, as amended), as reported by Aleksander and Szarota (1995). According to Komorowska (2015a, 2015b), the foundation of those colleges might be considered a milestone in the history of FL teacher education in Poland due to the innovative character of the institution with regard to the teaching content. Students were expected to pass courses in practical language use, linguistics, literary and cultural studies, didactics, psychology, and pedagogy. They were also required to undergo teacher training at primary and secondary school levels to gain first-hand teaching experience. The education system in question was soon adopted by Polish universities, which helped to modernise teacher education in Poland.

Notwithstanding this, persuant to the 2009 Act on Education (Journal of Laws from 2009, No. 202, Item 1553, as amended), the institutions were closed in September 2015. Przemysław Krzyżanowski (2013), the then undersecretary of state in the Ministry of National Education, explained in the letter to the Marshal of the Sejm of the Republic of Poland that the decision was driven by the demographic changes, understood here as the decreasing number of students enrolled in (FL) teacher-training colleges. This downward trend is reflected in the data presented in Table 2.2.

Tab. 2.2: *Number of students in teacher- and FL teacher-training colleges in Poland in the 2000s and the 2010s (adapted from Krzyżanowski, 2013)*

Number of students	2006/07	2008/09	2010/11	2012/13
Teacher-training colleges	7,198	6,508	5,485	3,660
FL teacher-training colleges	13,159	12,431	8,928	6,108
Total	20,357	18,939	14,413	9,768

Major setbacks concerning the dominance of the Russian language in FL education, initial teacher shortage, and insufficient provision of coursebooks and audio-visual materials were overcome in Poland in the 1990s. Nonetheless, new problems kept arising within the field of FLT in the country at that time. Wide availability of private language schools offering courses in different languages diversified learners' exposure towards their FL1 and FL2, emphasising striking differences between students in compulsory education (Komorowska & Krajka, 2020). Furthermore, unsatisfactory salaries of Polish FL teachers were most often the main cause underlying frequent turnovers in teaching staffs, which in effect translated into low efficiency of FLT (Kasztalska, 2014; Reichelt, 2005a).

2.2 ELT in Poland today: Towards European integration

2.2.1 The 1999 education reform: Building a modern school system

The implementation of the 1990 reform by the first non-communist government took place under the influence of Poland's contacts with Europe in 1989 (Komorowska, 2007; Komorowska & Krajka, 2020). At that time, fundamental changes in Polish FL education were effected by its cooperation with Western countries, preparation for admission to the North Atlantic Treaty Organisation and European Union (EU), and participation in international assessment programmes, such as Programme for International Student Assessment (PISA) (Wiśniewski & Zahorska, 2020).

Mirosław Handke's structural, curricular, and examination reform of the Polish education system (Szczepanek, 2018) was introduced in 1998 amid plans for decentralisation put forward by a new government under the leadership of Jerzy Buzek (Journal of Laws from 1998, No. 117, Item 759, as amended). Aware of the unsatisfactory results of educational practices and clear disparities in the access to education between urban and rural areas, Polish authorities introduced a three-tier school system based on six-year primary schools, three-year middle schools, and three-year secondary schools in September 1999. The reform was an important step forward in Polish FLT. The starting age for the FL1 and FL2 was lowered to grade four of primary schools (i.e., ten-year old learners) and grade one of middle schools (i.e., thirteen-year old learners) respectively.

The new national curriculum – its origin going back to the concept of the minimum Core Curriculum and the 1996 amendment to Act on the Education from 1991 (Journal of Laws from 1996, No 67, Item 329, as amended) – breathed some fresh air into the Polish school system. The document provided very general information on the education goals, tasks of the school, teaching content, and learners' expected achievements for each educational level. It was expected that learners would progress throughout the nine-year long FL education from a very basic communicative ability (i.e., primary schools) to the level which allows them to effectively communicate in different situations (i.e., secondary schools) (Journal of Laws from 1999, No. 14, Item 129, as amended).

With the adoption of the pluralist approach towards syllabi (Debaene, 2007), their design attracted the attention of wider audiences. They included among others publishing houses, whose number grew because of the de-monopolisation policy. In 2004, teachers were granted autonomy in the choice and development of their own syllabi (Jakubowski, 2015). The Ministry of National Education and

Sport, even though not directly involved in the organisation of a teaching programme, also controlled the overall educational content by granting authorisation for its use (Otwinowska-Kasztelanic, 2007).

The 1999 reform effected significant changes regarding teachers' perceptions of their everyday classroom work and professional development. The introduction of the so-called "interdisciplinary streaming" (*ścieżki międzyprzedmiotowe*) promoted the practice of group work among FL instructors and encouraged their closer cooperation with non-language teachers (Komorowska, 2017, p. 88). Also, the successive stages of career advancement laid down clear specifications for promotion, which acted as a positive financial incentive (Jakubowski, 2015).

Despite the then ruling party's ambitious plans to increase society's educational attainment by promoting equal access to secondary schools and universities and modifying the curricula with an intention of developing learners' life-long learning skills, the implementation of the 1999 reform caused serious public concern. An insufficient amount of time for critical reflection (the act was announced in February in 1999 and scheduled for September 1999; Journal of Laws from 1999, No. 12, Item 96; Journal of Laws from 1999, No. 14, Item 124, as amended) and the doubtful value of middle schools (their learners reaching the age of puberty were most likely to cause behavioural problems) called into question the advisability of the reform. Dissenting voices pointing out the insecurity of teachers' employment, their hasty and ill-informed decisions about syllabi and textbooks, and practical problems relating to delays in printing coursebooks were added to a heated discussion (Wiśniewski & Zahorska, 2020).

In the wake of the 1999 reform, the number of Poles who claimed to know English on a communicative level continued to rise. The upward trend was clearly visible in the findings of Eurobarometer 2001 and 2003.1 studies (European Commission, 2002, 2003). As compared with the survey carried out in 2001, according to which 28% of the Polish respondents claimed to be conversant in Russian and 21% in English, Eurobarometer 2003.1 revealed that 62% of the Polish respondents reported knowing English communicatively, with only 30% of these respondents knowing German and 16% knowing Russian.

A similar trend developed in regard to Poles' desire to learn a FL. Namely, 48% of the subjects opted for English (European Commission, 2002). In contrast, only 33% of the participants chose German and 27% French (European Commission, 2003). In 2006, the data published in Special Eurobarometer 243 (European Commission, 2006) indicated an overwhelming advantage for the English language over German and Russian, suggesting Poles' strong inclination to choose instruction in English as both most useful (English 72%, German 46%, Russian 9%) and desirable (English 90%, German 69%, Russian 10%).

It is worth adding at this point that the 1999 reform served as the foundation for establishing a modern education system without which its further reforms would not be practicable in Poland. The reform was therefore justly referred to as revolutionary changes by Jakubowski (2015).

2.2.2 The 2009 education reform: Adopting a plurilingual approach

Despite the fact that lively discussions on promoting FLT among EU countries had been taking place since the 1980s, Poland did not find itself under strong influence from the European language policy until the beginning of the 21st century (Kucharczyk, 2016). The modifications introduced to compulsory FL education based on the 2008 Regulation of the Minister of Education (Journal of Laws from 2008, No. 4, Item 17, as amended) fully accorded with the assumptions of the plurilingual approach promoted by the EU seminal documents, such as the CEFR (CoE, 2001), *A new framework strategy for multilingualism* (Commission of the European Communities, 2005), and *Key competences for lifelong learning – European reference framework* (Official Journal of the European Union, 2006). Regulations stipulating the plurilingual approach could also be identified in the decisions reached during the 2002 EU Barcelona summit, which gave priority to EU citizens' ability to communicate in L1 and two (and more) FLs. To comply with the Barcelona objective and apply the so-called mother tongue + 2 formula, the member states were required to introduce compulsory FLT at incrementally lower stages of education (European Commission, 2002).

Katarzyna Hall's 2009 education reform laid the foundations for the application of the European standards in Polish FL instructed settings. First, the starting age for the FL1 was significantly lowered, with learners starting their compulsory FL education in grade one of primary schools. The learning of the FL2 was still mandatory in grade one of middle schools. Second, in line with the principle of plurilingualism, Polish learners could learn up to three languages throughout the whole cycle of the FL programme.Having considered their individual preferences and the number of languages they want to learn over a twelve-year span of compulsory FL learning, Polish students selected one of the three options offered by the Core Curriculum (see Table 2.3). Their choices determined the length of FL instruction for each of the languages, that is either three, six, or twelve years.

Tab. 2.3: *Compulsory FL learning and teaching in Polish schools after the 2009 reform (MEN, n.d., p. 14)*

<table>
<tr><th></th><th>Primary schools</th><th>Middle schools</th><th>Secondary schools</th></tr>
<tr><td rowspan="2">Case 1</td><td colspan="3">FL1</td></tr>
<tr><td></td><td colspan="2">FL2</td></tr>
<tr><td rowspan="2">Case 2</td><td colspan="2">FL1</td><td>FL3</td></tr>
<tr><td></td><td colspan="2">FL2</td></tr>
<tr><td rowspan="2">Case 3</td><td colspan="3">FL1</td></tr>
<tr><td></td><td>FL2</td><td>FL3</td></tr>
</table>

The 2009 reform proved a real milestone in adopting a modern perspective on the process of FL teaching and learning in Poland as European trends could also be identified in the new Core Curriculum (Kucharczyk, 2013; Marczak et al., 2015; Szpotowicz et al., 2009). The CEFR, known in Poland as ESOKJ, performed a primary function in the Polish FL education system (Marczak et al., 2015). The document had a noticeable effect on the presentation of proficiency levels at different stages of education. As seen in Table 2.4, six common reference levels (A1-C2) were adopted to describe the expected learning outcomes for primary, middle, and secondary schools.

Tab. 2.4: *Expected levels of language proficiency for different stages of FL education in Poland after the 2009 reform (adapted from Szpotowicz, 2011)*

<table>
<tr><th></th><th>Stage of FL education</th><th>Variant of FL education</th><th>Level of FL proficiency</th></tr>
<tr><td>Lower primary schools (grades 1-3)</td><td>I.</td><td></td><td rowspan="2">≈ A1</td></tr>
<tr><td>Upper primary schools (grades 4-6)</td><td>II.</td><td></td></tr>
<tr><td rowspan="2">Middle schools</td><td rowspan="2">III.</td><td>III.0</td><td>≈ A2</td></tr>
<tr><td>III.1</td><td>≈ A2+</td></tr>
<tr><td rowspan="4">Secondary schools</td><td rowspan="4">IV.</td><td>IV.0</td><td>≈ A2/B1</td></tr>
<tr><td rowspan="2">IV.1</td><td>≈ B1/B1+ (basic level)</td></tr>
<tr><td>≈ B2/B2+ (advanced level)</td></tr>
<tr><td>IV.2</td><td>≈ C1/C2</td></tr>
</table>

Teaching objectives (*cele kształcenia*), also known as general requirements (*wymagania ogólne*), and teaching content (*treści kształcenia*), or detailed requirements (*wymagania szczegółowe*), drew from the CEFR's constructs of communicative language competences and activities, as reflected in the concept of language use involving reception, production, interaction, and mediation. Some references to the framework's general competences were also made in the context of learners' personality features and ability to learn. Main ideas underlying learning within AOA, such as the development of learners' strategies, ability to work in groups, autonomy, self-assessment skills, and language awareness, were also formalised in the Core Curriculum (Kucharczyk, 2016; Szpotowicz, 2011). The main assumptions of *Key competences for lifelong learning* also laid the foundations for the preparation of the detailed requirements (MEN, 2009).

Poland's implementation of the European directives helped to enforce FL educational standards. According to Gajewska-Dyszkiewicz et al. (2013), who compiled the Polish version of the report on the ESLC for the Educational Research Institute (*Instytut Badań Edukacyjnych*, IBE), there were several positive aspects to compulsory FLT in Poland in the wake of the 2009 reform. The majority of Polish middle schools offered extra-curricular classes in FLs, held FL contests, ran FL clubs, and celebrated the European Day of Languages. Half of schools participating in the ESLC were also said to arrange field trips connected with FLT, whereas one out of three schools organised a FL student exchange.

There was unfortunately a dark side to the 2009 reform. The results of BENJA[10] and BUNJO[11] revealed certain discrepancies between the objectives of the European language policy and the Polish school reality. Developing learners' ability to cooperate through pair- and group-work was largely neglected by primary school teachers (Muszyński et al., 2015). Despite EU's attempts to protect and promote the languages of its member states, very few Polish primary and middle schools (especially in the countryside) offered instruction in languages other than English and German (Paczuska et al., 2014). French and Russian were taught in one out of five middle schools, whereas Italian and Spanish were even less common. The

10 BENJA (*Badanie efektywności nauczania języka angielskiego w szkole podstawowej*) was the longitudinal study conducted at the first and second stage of education in 172 primary schools in the period between 2010 and 2015 (Muszyński et al., 2015).

11 BUNJO (*Badanie uczenia się i nauczania języków obcych w gimnazjum*) was the longitudinal study conducted among Polish 4700 lower secondary school students, 480 teachers, and 120 headteachers over a three-year period between 2012 and 2014 (Paczuska et al., 2014).

ESLC, which was conducted on the initiative of the European Commission in 2011, revealed that out of 14 countries participating in the study, Poland came in second to last with regard to the diversity of languages offered by schools. This did not only question the plurilingual approach, but also prevented learning European languages different than Polish, English, and German. As reported by Abramczyk (2015), students with different exposure to a FL were refused the right to continue their language education at the level that was adjusted to their language proficiency. Because in some school contexts no placements tests were organised at the beginning of instruction, learners were frequently assigned to "broad-banded classes" which encompassed individuals with different levels of language competence (Komorowska, 2017, p. 112). Headteachers' freedom in assigning the number of hours for two FLs in accordance with the framework teaching programmes (*ramowe plany nauczania*) contradicted the plurilingual approach. In the view of an obligatory exam in the FL1, learners were naturally provided with more intensive instruction in that language. This certainly happened to the disadvantage of the FL2, whose teaching and learning occupied a secondary role in the eyes of students and teachers.

Even though no official regulations on languages compulsorily taught in Poland had been issued by the Ministry of National Education, it was a commonly adopted practice to choose English either as the FL1 or FL2 (ORE, 2011). According to Centre for Education Development (*Ośrodek Rozwoju Edukacji*, ORE), the number of Polish students of English almost doubled (46.9% versus 86.2%) between 1999 and 2009. A stable tendency could be observed in regard to learners of German (30.7% versus 33.5%). On the other hand, French and Russian suffered a drastic decline in popularity; the number of learners of Russian (16% to 4.5%) and French (4.2% versus 2.7%) decreased by almost four and two times respectively (ORE, 2011).

Wysmułek and Oleksiyenko (2015) provided compelling evidence demonstrating a growing disproportion in the use of English, German, and Russian in Poland. The scholars contrasted the results of POLPAN[12] studies from 1993 and 2013. As demonstrated in Table 2.5, it is possible to observe a significant growth

---

12 POLPAN (*Polskie Badanie Panelowe*) is a kind of research based on a series of individual interviews conducted every five years since 1988 with a representative sample of Polish adults. The questions concern respondents' professional careers, education, qualifications, as well as their psychological and physical well-being in the context of Poland's socio-economic transformations (Słomczyński, 2014).

in the number of Polish EFL users in all age groups, with a simultaneous decrease in those who spoke German and Russian.

Tab. 2.5: *Percentage of Poles speaking English, German, and French: the results of POLPAN studies from 1993 and 2013 (Wysmułek & Oleksiyenko, 2015, p. 8)*

Age group	Year	English	German	Russian
26-35	1993	20%	25%	51%
	2013	76%	14%	4%
36-45	1993	16%	20%	59%
	2013	43%	15%	32%
46-55	1993	12%	18%	66%
	2013	24%	18%	55%

The growing superiority of English inspired journalists and public figures to engage themselves in the so-called "battle for English" amid plans for the 2009 education reform (Śliwa, 2010, p. 693, as cited in Kasztalska, 2014, p. 253). Attempts were made to establish English as an obligatory FL taught in schools. Despite a general support for this idea from the public and an official letter issued to the Polish Prime Minister, Donald Tusk, such an initiative was not met with the Ministry's approval. Following CoE's (n.d.) guidelines issued in *Language education policy profile. Poland: 2005-2007*, the authorities aimed to promote Polish citizens' multilingualism and the development of communicative competence in two languages (or more) instead of favouring English to the disadvantage of other FLs.

2.2.3 The 2014 education reform: Expanding the early start programme

The 2014 education reform was Poland's another attempt to further expand the early start programme. The starting age for the FL1 was lowered and a period of transition began with the 2014/15 school year initiating a series of reforms, which were gradually implemented on a yearly basis until 2017. They resulted in the introduction of compulsory FL education first among five-old year students in 2015/16 and second among all kindergarten learners in 2017/18 (Journal of Laws from 2014 r., Item 803, as amended). Table 2.6 demonstrates the direction of changes with reference to the early start programme outlined by the Polish educational authorities over a span of fifteen years from 1999 to 2014.

Tab. 2.6: *Evolution of the early start programme in Poland (1999-2014) (self-prepared)*

<table>
<tr><th></th><th>Kindergartens</th><th>Lower primary schools</th><th>Upper primary schools</th><th>Middle schools</th><th>Secondary schools</th></tr>
<tr><td rowspan="2">1999</td><td></td><td></td><td colspan="3">FL1</td></tr>
<tr><td></td><td></td><td></td><td></td><td>FL2</td></tr>
<tr><td rowspan="2">2009</td><td></td><td colspan="4">FL1</td></tr>
<tr><td></td><td></td><td></td><td colspan="2">FL2</td></tr>
<tr><td rowspan="2">2014</td><td colspan="5">FL1</td></tr>
<tr><td></td><td></td><td></td><td colspan="2">FL2</td></tr>
</table>

The government's decision to teach the FL1 to three through six year-old learners effected significant changes in regard to kindergarten teachers' acquisition of formal qualifications (Pamuła-Behrens, 2015). The new reform generated a growing demand for instructors who were to be prepared pedagogically and linguistically to teach pre-primary school children. By virtue of the resolution, those teachers who could present their documentation of language proficiency were not obliged to complete post-graduate studies or FL courses for pre-primary education. However, a deadline was established for those who did not meet the formal requirements imposed by the reform. They were expected to gain formal FL qualifications (without any interruptions to their teaching careers) before September 31, 2020.

The inclusion of a FLT component affected teachers' every day classroom work with their kindergarten students. In order to address the needs of a new target group of FL learners, one of twelve objectives of the Core Curriculum set out for pre-primary schooling specifically addressed a FLT context. In line with the official guidelines, pre-primary language teachers were expected to facilitate their learners' development of language awareness, intercultural sensitivity, and motivation (Journal of Laws from 2014, Item 803, as amended).

Practical solutions on how to apply the teaching objectives of the Core Curriculum to pre-primary learning environments were provided by Pamuła-Behrens (2015). She listed several examples of FL classroom activities, emphasising the fact that they should not only be adapted to children's cognitive and linguistic abilities, but they should also be designed in such a way so as to stimulate the development of a right and left hemisphere of the brain (e.g., memory exercises, spot-the-difference exercises, TPR activities).

Teaching a FL to very young Polish learners became a reality within a couple of years following the 2014 reform. As argued by Leix and Wiegerowa (2014), who examined FL instruction in Czech kindergartens, pre-primary FLT encountered a number of pedagogical and psychological problems. Students' young age and their partially developed speech apparatus posed a challenge to learning their mother tongue (let alone a FL), whereas most often repetitive character of teaching content and learning objectives in the consecutive stages of education constituted a source of frustration for learners and their parents.

Even though the topic had been extensively covered in professional educational settings, the public was fed with misinformation about the miraculous effects of pre-primary FL instruction on learners' future attainment of the language, especially FL pronunciation (Bogucka, 2009). Based on the Critical Period Hypothesis, which predicts that post-pubertal L2 learners are not able to eliminate the traces of their foreign accent in non-native speech (Birdsong, 2007), there is a deeply held, yet erroneous conviction that learners' early start guarantees their impeccable FL pronunciation. As indicated by Neufeld (1977) and Olson and Samuels (1973), the FL phonetic attainment is not necessarily an age-constrained process. Since the Critical Period Hypothesis concerns naturalistic settings, it cannot account for the process of pronunciation learning in FL instructed settings. Private language schools and kindergartens preyed on ambitious parents' lack of expertise in that subject matter, excelling at organising courses for increasingly younger learners, who were unfortunately most often far from expressing their school readiness.

According to the data published in *Key data on teaching languages at school in Europe* (Eurydice, 2017), Poland became one of three European countries, including the German-speaking region of Belgium and Malta, in which learners below six years of age began their FL instruction. As of the 2015/16 school year, the starting age for the remaining countries listed in the report ranged between six and seven (e.g., France, Italy, Spain, the UK) as well as eight and nine (e.g., the Czech Republic, Finland, Germany, Lithuania).

Nevertheless, the lowering of the starting age did not result in establishing more ambitious goals in FL education system in Poland. Even though Polish learners started learning the FL1 earlier than students from other member states, the former's early start did not lead to a heightened minimum level of FL attainment expected of them at the level of secondary school education. Such countries as France, Germany, Italy, and the Czech Republic introduced FL instruction to older learners than in Poland. They, however, established B2 as the minimum required level of proficiency for the FL in contrast to Poland, where the B1 level was a basic requirement.

2.2.4 The 2017 education reform: Increasing educational requirements

From the very beginning of its introduction, the 1999 education reform kept attracting widespread constructive and destructive criticism from a variety of backgrounds. Politicians, teaching professionals, academics, and parents kept contributing to a nationwide discussion on the purposefulness of a three-tier school system in the context of learners' social participation and their educational and professional development (Dąbek, 2016).

On the one hand, the results of PISA[13] did prove a positive influence of the 1999 reform on Polish fifteen-year old learners' abilities, as reflected in the gradual improvement of their performance in Reading, Mathematics, and Science (Sitek, 2019). As reported by Jakubowski et al. (2016), "in the first assessment, Poland ranked below the OECD country average in reading. In 2003, Poland reached the OECD average; and by 2006, Poland scored above average, ranking 9th among all countries in the world" (p. 4). According to the 2017 report prepared by the Evidence Institute and the Polish Teachers' Union (*Związek Nauczycielstwa Polskiego*, ZNP), Polish students comprised 7% of the most gifted students in Science in the EU, exceeding such countries as Spain (5.2%) and Italy (5.5%) (Jakubowski et al., 2017). As seen in the data in Table 2.7, the upward trend in Polish students' performance has been almost continuously reinforced since the first edition of PISA, with the exception of the 2015 and 2022 editions.

Tab. 2.7: *Average performance of fifteen-year old Polish learners in Reading, Mathematics, and Science (Kaźmierczak & Bulkowski, 2024, p. 47, 130, 163)*

Year	Reading	Mathematics	Science
2000	479	-	-
2003	497	490	-
2006	508	495	498
2009	500	495	508
2012	518	518	526
2015	506	504	501
2018	512	516	511
2022	489	489	499

13 PISA is a worldwide study conducted every three years by the Organisation for Economic Cooperation and Development (OECD) in its member and non-member states since 2000.

Recently, Polish students have been performing well in a European comparison. According to the latest 2022 PISA results, the Polish students' performance in Reading, Mathematics and Science was higher than the average score for the OECD member states (476, 472, and 485 respectively) (Kaźmierczak & Bulkowski, 2024).

On the other hand, notwithstanding spectacular improvements in Polish learners' performance since the implementation of the 2000 PISA, the inefficiency of Handke's school system took centre-stage when Anna Zalewska's plans for the latest education reform were made public in December 2016 (Journal of Laws from 2017, Item 59). Strong opponents of the three-tier system (e.g., Kołakowski, 2016; Sarnecki, 2008) underlined commonly encountered problems, such as the examination-driven organisation of teaching procedures, learners' tendency to learn for tests and grades, and the repetitiveness of teaching content. Nowak (2011) pointed out to students' lack of comprehension manifested in the phenomenon of rote-learning, which exerted a negative influence on their logical thinking and decision-making processes. According to Śliwerski (2015), stressful experiences of changing schools and accommodating to new learning environments were chiefly to blame for aggravating teenagers' notorious behavioural problems.

The reintroduction of the system based on eight-year primary schools and four-year secondary schools was meant to offer a remedy to the deficiencies caused by middle and secondary schools. To increase the quality of education, changes introduced to the Core Curriculum included emphasis on spiral teaching, cross-curricular integration, AOA, project-based learning, and the development of hard and soft skills (Journal of Laws from 2017, Item 356; Journal of Laws from 2018, Item 467, as amended).

Under the influence of the decisions taken by Beata Szydło's government, the reform took immediate effect in the 2017/18 school year (Journal of Laws from 2017, Item 356, as amended). The Polish education system found itself in a transitional period. No admission procedures to grade one of middle schools were followed, therefore primary school graduates continued their education in eight-grade primary schools since September 2017. Because the 2018/19 school year marked the expiration of middle schools, the graduates of both eight-year primary and middle schools were admitted to grade one of secondary and technical schools in 2019/20. This unprecedented phenomenon was referred to as the dual year (*podwójny rocznik*), the negative consequences of which were widely commented in the Polish media. According to the report prepared by the Polish Ombudsman Adam Bodnar (*Rzecznik Praw Obywatelskich*, RPO, 2019), hundreds of learners in several cities, such as Zielona Góra (552 learners) and Lublin (603 learners), were not accepted to schools later that year. In view of this, governmental plans to provide learners with equal access to education were open to reasonable doubt (RPO, 2018). In addition, the reform itself provoked great uproar over middle school teachers' mass decruitment, unresolved teenage behavioural problems, changing curricula (hence, examinations and coursebooks), and Poland's limited budget expenditure (Podczasik & Piotrowska, 2017). Concerns over the reform were also expressed in the *European social policy network* flash report. The document, enumerated a number of problems with the reform, such as government's undue haste in bringing in the new law, lack of rationale for its implementation, daunting teachers' employment prospects, extra costs, and ill-considered curricula (Chłoń-Domińczak, 2017). A generally tense situation in the country caused by public's ambivalent approaches towards the reform was further complicated by the teachers' strike in April 2019. Not only their extremely low salaries – one of the lowest among the OECD member states (Wiśniewski & Zahorska, 2020) – but also a general organisational and curricular chaos brought by the reform sparked widespread protests.

The reform, which as its predecessors was deeply grounded in the European language policies, did not revolutionise compulsory FL education in Poland (Kopeć, 2017). An exhaustive account of the changes introduced to the Core Curriculum within the 2017 reform was provided by Smolik and Poszytek (2017), who defined it as a final product of a continuous evolution taking place in FLT. In line with the new Core Curriculum, Polish learners invariably choose between two or three FLs that they want to learn throughout a twelve-year span of FL education. They start learning the FL1 in pre-primary schools and participate in the instruction until the end of secondary school education because the document ensures the continuation of FL1 learning from grade one of primary schools. This provides them with a total number of 990 hours in the whole cycle of the FL programme (excluding kindergartens where the number of hours of English per week is headteachers' individual decision). This allows students to reach the CEFR's B1+ or B2+ levels of language proficiency. Instruction in the FL2 begins in grade seven of primary schools. The introduction of optional bilingual education from grade seven of primary schools intensifies learners' exposure toward FLs and increases the total amount of instruction by 120 hours in the whole cycle.

Despite a general discussion on increasing primary and secondary school learners' level of expected linguistic attainment, the Core Curriculum underwent cosmetic changes in this respect. To give an example, as far as the FL1 is concerned, Polish EFL learners of eight-year primary schools are expected to reach the CEFR's A2+/B1 level of language proficiency as opposed to their middle school peers who, according to the 2008 curriculum, were required to reach A2+. Expectations were thus raised not in the context of their language production, which still approximates the A2+ level, but language reception which now requires an average FL

user to reach the B1 level. As illustrated in Table 2.8, analogous modifications in the treatment of proficiency levels were introduced in secondary school contexts.

Tab. 2.8: *Framework for teaching FLs in primary and secondary schools after the 2017 reform: the number of hours per week and expected level of language attainment (self-prepared)*

<table>
<tr><th colspan="2">Level of education</th><th colspan="3">Lower primary schools (I)</th><th colspan="5">Upper primary schools (II)</th><th colspan="4">Secondary schools (III)</th></tr>
<tr><td colspan="2">Grade</td><td>I</td><td>II</td><td>III</td><td>IV</td><td>V</td><td>VI</td><td>VII</td><td>VIII</td><td>I</td><td>II</td><td>III</td><td>IV</td></tr>
<tr><td rowspan="2">Number of hours per week</td><td>FL1</td><td>2h</td><td>2h</td><td>2h</td><td>3h</td><td>3h</td><td>3h</td><td>3h</td><td>3h</td><td>3h</td><td>3h</td><td>3h</td><td>3h</td></tr>
<tr><td>FL2</td><td colspan="3"></td><td colspan="3"></td><td>2h</td><td>2h</td><td>2h</td><td>2h</td><td>2h</td><td>2h</td></tr>
<tr><td rowspan="2">CEFR's level</td><td>FL1</td><td colspan="3">A1 (I.1) → 180h</td><td colspan="5">A2+/B1 (II.1) → 450h</td><td colspan="4">B1+/B2 (III.1.P) → 360h
B2+/C1 (III.1.R) → 360h</td></tr>
<tr><td>FL2</td><td colspan="3"></td><td colspan="5">A1 (II.2) → 120h</td><td colspan="4">A2 (III.2.0) → 240h
A2+ (III.2) → 240h</td></tr>
</table>

Since the crucial difference made by the reform may lie in the length of FL2 learning, it is worth considering two possible scenarios. If learners decide to learn three FLs, the one taught at a primary school level since grade seven is at a disadvantage to the remaining two given the shortest period of instruction (FL1=990h, FL2=120h versus FL3=240h). After the 2017 reform, primary school students learn the FL2 for only two years, which provides them with a possibility to achieve only the A1 level of language proficiency (in contrast, middle school graduates were expected to attain the A2 level) (Koper, 2017). If, however, they continue learning the same FL2 in secondary schools, the length of instruction and the expected level of language attainment correspond to the one from the pre-reform period (for the purpose of the comparison with the 2009 reform, see Table 2.4).

At this point, it must be added that English has continued to assume central importance in the Polish education system. The dominant position of the language as an obligatory course taught in Polish schools was clearly demonstrated by the 2018 GUS publication *Education in the 2017/18 school year.* Since the 2005/06 school year, English has been gaining in significance as opposed to three most popular FLs in Poland whose popularity has remained unchanged (German) and has gone into progressive decline (French and Russian) (see Table 2.9).

Tab. 2.9: *Percentage of students learning the most popular FLs as an obligatory course in Polish schools (GUS, 2018, p. 63)*

School year	English	German	French	Russian
2005/06	65.9%	33.6%	3.3%	6.1%
2010/11	89%	36.4%	2.9%	4.8%
2015/16	94.9%	33.7%	2.4%	3.9%
2017/18	95.5%	33.9%	2.3%	3.6%

Similarly, *Statistical yearbook of the republic of Poland* (GUS, 2019) demonstrated a decided advantage of English at all levels of compulsory FL education as opposed to German and Russian, two of the most popular languages in Poland, right behind English. The vast majority of Polish teenagers, on average 93% in 2010/11 and 98% in 2015/16 and 2018/19, chose English as their preferred FL in primary, middle, secondary, and technical schools.

2.3 EFL assessment in Poland today: Towards high-stake examinations

2.3.1 Problems with EFL secondary school exit exams in the 1990s

Even though history has come the full circle under the influence of the latest 2017 reform, a series of changes – the most significant of which have been examined above – have radically and irrevocably affected Polish EFL assessment.

According to the Ordinance No. 55 of the Minister of Education, neither written nor oral EFL secondary school exit examinations (i.e., the Matura exam) were obligatory in Poland in the 1990s (Official Journal of the Ministry of Education from 1989, No. 6, Item 56, as amended). There were five mandatory exams: two written (in Polish and a school subject selected by examinees) and three oral (in Polish, a FL, and an additional subject) ones.

The 1989 Ordinance clearly excluded or significantly limited EFL assessment. It might happen that by virtue of the resolution, learners did not take any examination in English. Since they were not required to choose a written exam of a FL, the evaluation of their EFL competence (if they chose English of course) could be based on the oral examination only. Even if selected individuals decided to sit for both written and oral exams in English, it could happen that their EFL examination was restricted to the written mode of communication. This was because those students who got grade five (or six) from the written part and received at least grade four from the subject in the last two school years were automatically exempted from the oral exam.

Since Local Education Authorities (*Kuratoria*) were responsible for preparing questions for written EFL exams, the range of topics differed among the voivodeships (Eckes et al., 2005; Sitek, 2014). This is clearly illustrated in Wojtaszek's (1998ab) compendia containing examples of examination papers from 1995, 1996, and 1998.

Tab. 2.10: *Examples of sets for the written part of the 1998 Matura exam in English (Wojtaszek, 1998a, p. 17-38)*

	Bydgoszcz	**Gdańsk, Elbląg, Słupsk, Toruń**
Part One – Listening comprehension	A: Multiple choice (10 p.) B: Multiple choice (10 p.)	A: Multiple choice (8 p.) B: Open-ended (7 p.)
Part Two – Reading comprehension	A: Ordering (10 p.) B: True or False (10 p.)	A: Multiple choice (8 p.) B: Matching headings to the paragraphs (6 p.) C: Matching missing sentences to the paragraphs (6 p.)
Part Three – A lexico-grammatical test	A: Open gap fill (20 p.) B: Transformation (5 p.) C: Multiple choice (10 p.) D: Putting the verb from the bracket (5 p.)	A: Transformation (12 p.) B: Translation (10 p.) C: Open gap fill (10 p.) D: Multiple choice (16 p.)
Part Four – Writing	Length: approx. 250 words Structure: not specified Topics: 1. School is a waste of time 2. Write an advertisement for a place – real or imaginary. Your ad should make tourists want to go there for a vacation. 3. Describe a time when you followed another person's advice and regretted doing so.	Length: 250-350 words Structure: freeform Topics: 1. Books are no longer a tempting source of knowledge and information. Discuss. 2. "When I saw the place in broad daylight, I was stunned." Write a story beginning with these words. 3. Write a letter in which you justify why you want to the telephone. 4. Commenting on the poem by Elma Mitchell, present your views on the significance of poetry in people's lives.

Even though each set could be divided into four parts (see Table 2.10), the number of examination questions and their length, type, and difficulty depended upon the Local Education Authorities (Eckes et al., 2005). They also selected the required length of a writing assignment and the number of topics to choose from in Part Four.

Theoretically, a framework for a speaking part of Matura was established. According to Wojtaszek (1998a), it could be divided into three parts. In Part One, students' reading comprehension was assessed. Part Two concerned learners' language use. Part Three checked learners' ability to roleplay a dialogue with an examiner and provide a brief response to two situations presented by the teacher. Practically, a great diversity of questions (and thus the incomparability of results) characterised oral assessment since secondary school teachers enjoyed freedom in preparing examination papers (Eckes et al., 2005).

It was commonplace to undertake the internal assessment of the Matura exam. Both written and spoken parts of students' exams were marked by teachers working in an educational institution (Journal of Laws from 1989, No. 6, Item 56, as amended). The school scale was used to evaluate examinees' performance. Given the lack of standardised criteria in the case of open-ended questions, it was graded according to the judgement of examiners. The conditions in which the exams were conducted left much to be desired, as argued by Konarzewski in an interview for *Dziennik Polski* (2005). Students' papers were not coded and the instances of dishonest behaviours were frequent, which questioned the reliability of results. The Matura exams were usually of little relevance before the 1999 reform. This, as presented below, was to gradually change in the new millennium.

2.3.2 Effects of education reforms on EFL exams

Under the influence of the consecutive curricular reforms, younger Polish learners were required to take FL examinations. The 1999 reform introduced elective written and oral exams taken by secondary school graduates in any modern FL (i.e., English, German, Russian, French, Spanish, Italian). The first national New Matura (*Egzamin maturalny*) took place in 2005. The written middle school examination (*Egzamin gimnazjalny*) was administered in 2009, whereas the sixth-grader exam (*Sprawdzian szóstoklasisty*) was first taken by primary school students in 2015. Given their cyclical nature, learners' attainment of educational objectives outlined in the Core Curriculum could be measured after each educational stage, that is every three years (Kucharczyk, 2016; Łochowska, 2009). In 2019, however, the first eighth-grader exam (*Egzamin ósmoklasisty*) took place, postponing students' first FL examination by two years and breaking the aforementioned continuity in FL assessment.

FL examinations received a massive makeover. They went through the process of standardisation (Kucharczyk, 2014; Smolik, 2012; Trzcińska, 2009). Selected general and detailed curriculum requirements, CEFR's descriptors of language proficiency, and can-do statements from European Language Portfolios (Smolik & Trzcińska, 2011) laid the foundations for establishing a uniform macrostructure of primary, middle, and secondary school exit exams. Communicative language activities based on reception, production, interaction, and mediation, and components of communicative language competence were introduced to evaluate Polish learners' FL achievement of objectives at each educational level. The New Matura syllabi (*Informatory maturalne*) published on the official website of the Central Examination Board provided a comprehensive description of the structure and assessment criteria for the exam.

In order to measure and compare examinees' progress and to evaluate the quality of the learning and teaching process at all stages of education in different regions of the country (Gajewska-Dyszkiewicz & Paczuska, 2015; Jakubowski, 2015; Wiśniewski & Zahorska, 2020), the concept of external and national examinations was introduced by the 1999 education reform. Central and Regional Examination Boards (*Centralna Komisja Egzaminacyjna*, CKE/*Okręgowa Komisja Egzaminaycjna*, OKE) were set up among others to prepare examination papers, establish assessment criteria, train examiners, and draw up reports to inform the public about exam results (Eckes et al., 2005; Śliwerski, 1999). By virtue of the resolution, external examiners assessed the written parts of exit examinations, whereas examination commissions (consisting of teachers working in a given educational institution and a representative from a different school) administered oral exams. The delegation of the responsibility for examining students from schools and teachers to CKE and OKE helped to draw a useful distinction between external assessment associated with national exams and an ongoing grade-based internal assessment regularly taking place in the language classroom.

In view of the above, FL exams have assumed more prominent roles, which allows conclusions to be drawn about the quality of FLT (Łochowska, 2009; Sitek, 2015; Wiśniewski & Zahorska, 2020; Zawadowska-Kittel, 2017). The statistical data prepared by the examination boards constitute an important source of feedback on Polish EFL students' linguistic achievements in the context of the general and detailed curriculum requirements. They also set a basis for discussions among teaching specialists who scrutinise examinees' results to evaluate how effective particular educational institutions are in preparing their students for examinations.

The investigation of the diagnostic and evaluative functions of FL exams and their usefulness in tracking educational deficiencies was provided by Cichmińska (2015), Komorowska (2017), Muszyński et al. (2016), and Paczuska et al. (2014). The Polish scholars attempted to explain the discrepancies in the mean scores achieved by students from Polish rural and urban areas. They attributed the former's lower EFL performance to a generally more limited educational offer of extra classes and tuition in English. A more frequent occurrence of the phenomenon of broad-banded classes seemed to translate into less favourable learning conditions prevailing in schools located in the countryside regions of Poland. Differences in the levels of EFL competence between students' parents from cities and villages also disadvantaged the latter.

The standardised, external, and national system of FL examinations has also performed a selective function. The New Matura formed the basis for secondary school graduates' university enrolment, replacing entrance examinations in 2005 (Zając, 2016). Also, the exit exam for primary schools started to be used as the basis for learners' admission to a higher level of education.

Over the years, Polish FL examinations have been modified a few times. Attempts were made to further increase the number and variety of spoken and written texts and to broaden the scope of abilities assessed in the exam (Trzcińska, 2015). The assessment criteria for examinees' written and oral language production placed more emphasis on the content of students' utterances and the qualitative aspects of language use, such as pronunciation and fluency (Smolik, 2012). A distinct category of cohesion and coherence was introduced to evaluate learners' written assignments. Some of the changes also concerned the levels of exams. Between 2012 and 2019, middle school students could choose between two versions of their FL exam, a basic and an advanced level. Moreover, in 2012, a new version of the speaking part of the New Matura, which combined activities from the two levels of the 2005 oral examination, was introduced (Krajewska, 2010). Some further changes made to the eighth-grader exam and New Matura with regard to the scope of examination questions and scoring procedures were also caused by the introduction of the 2018 Core Curriculum (see section 2.4.2). In conclusion, a series of reforms has radically changed the face of FL exams in Poland. A new examination system has in turn affected the Polish realities of FL teaching and learning.

2.3.3 Effects of exams on EFL education

Given their selective function, the eighth-grader exam and New Matura have taken on the role of high-stake exit examinations. Students' final results have therefore determined their future admission to schools and progression of their professional and educational career (Jakubowski, 2015; Niemierko, 2002; Sitek, 2015).

The influence of examinations, technically known as the washback or backwash effect, may be twofold in the area of language teaching and learning (Kołakowska, 2015; Taylor, 2005). If this effect is positive, it helps to maintain the link between language learning, teaching, and assessment; if not, classroom actors are likely to prioritise those skills and strategies that are bound to be tested by the exam and simultaneously background those less probable to be assessed. The washback effect can rarely be considered an explicitly positive or negative phenomenon (Kucharczyk, 2016). It is thus possible to consider several advantages and disadvantages to having introduced high-stake examinations to the Polish education system. Komorowska (2007, 2017) put forward some of the washback-related benefits. The positive washback effect is central to maintaining the connection between language teaching, learning, and assessment. To meet curriculum and examination requirements, teachers have to minimise the importance of lexico-grammatical exercises and complement their classes with communicative activities. This means that students' accuracy has ceased to be the only aspect of FL knowledge taught and tested in the language classroom in Poland (Komorowska, 2007). There is also an emotional aspect underlying the learning process. Learners feel more motivated to learn a language if they know that their competence is to be assessed (Komorowska, 2007). There are, however, several disturbing implications arising from the washback effect. According to Gajewska-Dyszkiewicz and Paczuska (2015), a FL exam has become an ultimate reference point for learners and teachers. The New Matura syllabi, which contain key information on the structures, scoring procedures, and linguistic means assessed in the examination are, as tentatively suggested by the scholars, followed closely by FL teachers more frequently than the guidelines issued in the Core Curriculum.

The importance of examinations in teachers' everyday classroom work was supported by the results of the survey reported by the Supreme Audit Office (*Najwyższa Izba Kontroli*, NIK, 2014). Out of 1,309 teachers from public and private schools, 82% and 67% respectively concentrated only on those aspects of the Core Curriculum that are likely to be assessed during their students' examination.

A similar tendency could be identified in BUNJO (Paczuska et al., 2014). Middle school teachers reported building their lessons around the content that is most likely to be tested during the exit exam. Students of grade one participating in the study agreed with this statement and confirmed their participation in the activities which prepare them solely for the examination.

Furthermore, the mandatory character of exit examinations in the FL1 reduces learners' motivation and willingness to learn the FL2 (Kucharczyk, 2016). This certainly translates into students' poorer performance which in the case of the most popular FL2 taught in Poland, German, does not meet the A2 level standards established by the Core Curriculum with regard to listening, reading and writing (European Commission, 2012).

2.4 Assessing EFL secondary school learners' communicative competence

2.4.1 The European perspective

2.4.1.1 General trends in FL national examinations

The concept of national language examinations is "a relatively new form of assessment" in Europe, as revealed by research findings published in the report *National testing of pupils in Europe: Objectives, organisation and use of results* (Eurydice, 2009, p. 14). Even though a few EU member states (i.e., France, Finland, Scotland) have 19th-century traditions in language assessment, the turn of the 20th and 21st century, as demonstrated in the report *Languages in secondary education: An overview of national tests in Europe – 2014/15* (Eurydice, 2015), proved revolutionary for the majority of European countries with regard to the popularisation of FL examinations.

As demonstrated in Figure 2.1, the vast number of EU member states (e.g., Cyprus, Hungary, Poland, Estonia, Slovakia, Bulgaria, Denmark, Croatia, the Czech Republic, Austria) administered their first FL examinations at the International Standard Classification of Education (ISCED) levels 2 and 3 only after the year 2001.

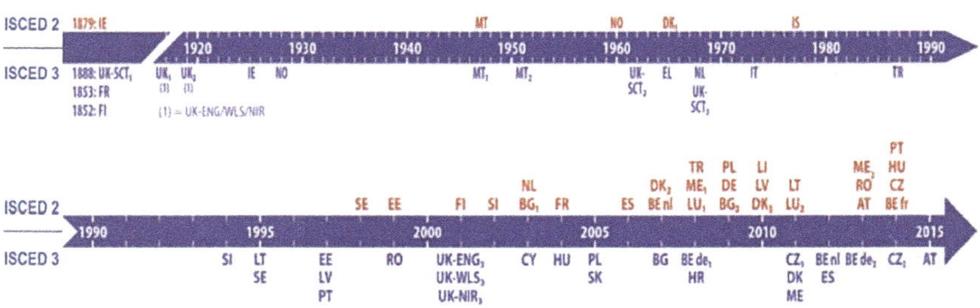

Fig. 2.1: *Introduction of the first national test in FLs at the ISCED levels 2 and 3 (Eurydice, 2015, p. 14)*

The wide spread of national language examinations coincided with the publication of the CEFR, whose six common reference levels have to a greater or lesser extent continued to influence the preparation of FL policy documents, coursebooks, and tests (European Parliament, 2013; Eurydice, 2015). Since then, more and more European educational institutions have implemented the horizontal and vertical descriptors to establish international standards in their language assessment procedures (Little, 2007).

Since the 1980s, the field of FL testing in Europe has undergone the process of professionalisation (Pizorn & Huhta, 2016). One of the indicators is the foundation of international organisations targeting language assessment. Some of the renowned ones include International Language Testing Association, Association of Language Testers in Europe, and European Association for Language Testing and Assessment. Individual countries have also set up bodies responsible among others for the preparation and administration of external examinations: Slovak National Institute for Certified Educational Measurements, Lithuanian National Examination Centre (NEC), and Czech Centre for Education Results (CERMAT), to mention just a few.

External language examinations most frequently "carry high-stakes for students" (Eurydice, 2015, p. 16). The admission to a higher level of education is granted to learners on the basis of their final score achieved in the school-leaving certificate, for example, the *Baccalauréat* in France, the *Abitur* in Germany, and the *Matura* in Slovenia (European Parliament, 2014). Apart from their key role in certification, examinations have also increased their practical usefulness. They have been developed as instruments to evaluate education systems, measure the achievement of curriculum objectives, and (in effect) improve FL learning and teaching practices (Eurydice, 2009, 2015).

The growing communicativeness of national language examinations could also be observed to take place (Pizorn & Huhta, 2016). Evolving conceptualisations of SLA and language proficiency, as reflected in the transition away from ALM to CLT in the late 1970s and early 1980s, effected changes in language examinations: "[w]hile decades ago test takers tested on a national level were supposed to translate sentences, recite grammatical rules and dialogues by heart, they are now expected to be able to skim, scan and infer information from an authentic newspaper article, talk about their views and attitudes to the topics of their interests and relevance and write a letter of application or complaint, as well as compose a narrative or a discursive essay" (Pizorn & Huhta, 2016, p. 247). The knowledge of lexico-grammatical structures took on a secondary role in view of the increasing importance of learners' ability to use language for communicative purposes.

It is also worth adding at this point that national language examinations measure students' mastery of FL reading, listening, speaking, and writing in varying degrees. Some countries (e.g., the Czech Republic, Poland, France) conduct examinations to test learners in all four language skills. Reading has proven to be the most commonly examined ability. There has been, however, a general tendency for exams to neglect the oral component. Even if speaking is assessed, it is not always the whole population of students that participates in the exam (e.g., Austria, Spain), and not all FLs are subject to oral assessment (e.g., Ireland) (Eurydice, 2015).

According to the 2017 *Key data on teaching languages at school in Europe* report, "English is unquestionably the main foreign language learnt in Europe" (Eurydice, 2017, p. 71). The universality of EFL instruction has led to the prevalence of EFL examinations in Europe. As of the 2014/2015 school year, learners' competence in the language was evaluated in almost all EU countries except German- and Flemish-speaking regions of Belgium, where French is a compulsory FL (Eurydice, 2015).

French, German, Spanish, Italian, and Russian are (right after English) top five FLs selected to be studied by students across Europe (Eurydice, 2012, 2017). The popularity of the languages, however, is conditioned by the country's location. It is more common for Eastern countries to administer FL examinations in Russian. The EU member states located in the southern regions of Europe, on the other hand, are more likely to choose Spanish and Italian.

Students are generally expected to reach the CEFR's independent user level at the end of the ISCED level 3 (Eurydice, 2017). An overview of the common reference levels covered by national tests in upper secondary schools demonstrates that the examinations are in line with the curriculum objectives since they oblige learners to attain either B1 or B2 levels of language proficiency (Eurydice, 2015). Varying requirements imposed on secondary school graduates arise from the differences in the implementation of the early start programme and the linguistic context of the country.

2.4.2.2 Examples of EFL examinations

In most EU countries, the national exit examinations administered at the ISCED level 3 are the most common (and sometimes the only) kind of students' FL assessment (Sitek, 2014). There are, however, differences between the obligatory and optional EFL exams with respect to their complexity and the range of skills assessed therein.

The FL *Maturitna Skuska* is a Slovak obligatory high-stake exit exam. There are three levels of the exam: students are free to choose either B1 or B2, whereas the C1 level is targeted at bilingual school graduates. The exam is composed of three centrally-designed parts, all of which differ with reference to assessment and scoring procedures. The first is an external written component, which consists of three sections: listening, language in use, and reading. The second is an internal written component in which students are expected to write an essay whose length may vary depending on the level of the examination. The third is an internal oral component assessed by schools. It examines learners' speaking which is elicited through picture-description, discussion-based, and role-play activities (*Maturita exam in Slovakia*, n.d.; NUCEM, n.d.).

There is one compulsory FL examination in the Czech Republic. It is an external part of the Czech *Maturitni Zkouška* prepared by CERMAT (Ruzkova et al., n.d.; *Petr Naske, Matura po czesku*, n.d.). There is only one level of the exam, which consists of three subtests based on close-ended questions (i.e., listening, reading, and gap filling), open-ended questions (i.e., writing), and speaking. The former is centrally assessed, whereas the two latter ones are marked by schools in accordance with externally established criteria. In contrast, the second school-level part of *Maturitni Zkouška* is composed of three mandatory centrally-designed examinations. The scope of the subjects tested within this part of the Czech Matura depends upon the profile of the school that conducts the examination. Some of the examples of the subjects to be selected by students include Math, Czech, a FL, Biology, Chemistry, and Social Sciences. The structure of a FL examination is similar to the one from the obligatory part discussed above (Ruzkova et al., n.d.).

The state secondary exit examination in Hungary is *Érettségi.* Students are required to take the exam in at least five subjects, one of which is a FL. It consists of written and oral parts, each of which contributing differently to the final grade: 66% and 33% respectively. To be awarded the Upper Secondary School Leaving Examination Certificate, students need to pass exams at the intermediate level of language proficiency. To enter the university, they need to sit their exams at the advanced level (UCAS, 2017).

In Romania, secondary school graduates are required to take the National Baccalaureate Exam, also known as the bac (*Examenul Național de Bacalaureat*). The examination consists of two (or three) oral and four (or five) written exams. The oral exam in a FL is compulsory. Examinees complete one reading comprehension task and one speaking task based on a randomly selected topic. Romanian students can also take a written exam in English provided that they choose a different FL in the speaking part (*Baccalaureate exam in Romania*, n.d.).

In order to be awarded a Maturity Certificate (*Brandos Atestatas*) and get into a higher level of education, Lithuanian graduates need to take national- and school-level maturity examinations. The secondary exit exam in a FL is not mandatory. However, an EFL national exam is the most popular optional state exam selected by students in Lithuania. It is conducted in a centralised manner by the NEC (Ministry of Education, Science, and Sport, n.d.; SKVC, n.d.). There is one level of the examination which consists of a written and oral part. The former includes listening, reading, and writing, whereas the latter requires learners to produce a monologue and dialogue. Language use is not tested in any of the parts.

The Finnish Matriculation Examination (*Ylioppilastutkinto*) is a high-stake national examination executed by the Matriculation Examination Board. It consists of four compulsory tests. One of them is taken in examinees' L1 (i.e., Finnish, Swedish, Sami). The remaining three tests are selected from four options possible, one of which is a FL test. There are two levels of the FL exam (i.e., advanced, basic), each of which consists of tests of listening comprehension, written comprehension, and language production. There is a difference in the length and number of written assignments between the advanced and basic version of the Finnish Matriculation Examination (*Description of tests*, 2021).

To enrol in the tertiary level of education, German students are expected to pass the *Abitur*. It consists of at least one oral and three written examinations selected by exiting students in such subject areas as Languages, Literature and Arts, Social Sciences, Mathematics, Natural Sciences, and Technology. The written exams need to cover at least two subjects at an advanced level. One of them can be a FL (UCAS, 2016). The tasks for examinations in German, Mathematics, and the FL1 are designed centrally by the Ministry of Education and Cultural Affairs. The EFL exam consists of skill-based tests, out of which the writing component is mandatory. Students select one out of three tasks based on the following instructions: "a) extract or sum up ideas from the source text, b) analyse content (explain, compare & contrast etc), and c) comment, or produce a new text creatively based on the source text(s)" (Petrescu, n.d.). Additionally, every year a different skill is examined. Both the exit examination results and students' class performance add up to the final grade of the *Abitur*.

By contrast, graduates of secondary schools in Sweden do not take exit examinations. Instead, each student receives a school-leaving certificate (*Slutbetyg*) based on their school grades. The final grade in English is awarded by the teacher on the basis of national tests (*Nationella prov*) prepared by the Swedish National Agency for Education (*Skolverket*). There are two types of English tests designed for basic and more advanced learners. Each of them consists of three subtests assessing oral interaction (i.e, speaking), reception (i.e., reading and listening), and written production (i.e., writing) (Skolverket, 2005).

Table 2.11 has been compiled to collect basic information on the types of national secondary school examinations administered in the selected EU member states.

Tab. 2.11: *Overview of FL examinations in the selected EU countries (self-prepared)*

Country	Secondary school examination	Character of FL examination	EFL examination	Parts of examination
Czech Republic	*Maturitni Zkouška*	obligatory	yes	oral and written
Finland	*Ylioppilastutkinto*	optional	yes	written
Germany	*Abitur*	optional	yes	written or written and oral
Hungary	*Érettségi*	obligatory	yes	oral and written
Lithuania	*Matura*	optional	yes	oral and written
Romania	*Examenul Național de Bacalaureat*	obligatory	yes	oral or written
Slovakia	*Maturitna Skuska*	obligatory	yes	oral and written

2.4.2 The Polish perspective

2.4.2.1 Eighth-grader exam

The primary school exit exam in a FL, known as the eighth-grader exam, is the first FL high-stake national examination taken compulsorily by learners in the last grade of eight-year primary schools (ISCED level 2). It was first administered in April 2019 as a direct effect of the implementation of the 2017 education reform, which as already mentioned re-instated a two-tier school system in Poland (PAP, 2019b).

The main objective of the exam is to evaluate FL students' compliance with the general and detailed requirements outlined in the Core Curriculum for the first and second stage of education, that is grades from one to eight of primary schools. The exam assesses students' communicative competence at the basic (A2+)/intermediate (B1) level of language proficiency based on their language reception, production, interaction, mediation, and language use (CKE, 2017a).

Learners take the exam in one of the FLs they have been compulsorily taught (GUS, 2020). In the vast majority of cases, they choose English (CKE, 2019a, 2020b). For example, in the Masovian voivodeship itself, almost 49,000 primary school learners took an EFL exam. In contrast, only 375 and 304 declared to write their examination in German and Russian respectively. Even fewer students sat for the exam in Spanish (29), French (21) and Italian (1) (OKE, 2020).

There are five parts of the EFL exam (CKE, 2017a). They test listening comprehension, language functions, reading comprehension, use of English, and written production. Each of the first four parts contains both close- and open-ended questions. Students' EFL writing skills are assessed in reference to four criteria: content, cohesion and coherence, accuracy, and range. The first of them, which is used to examine to what extent students manage to refer to and elaborate on the points from the instructions, accounts for 40% of the score. The overall score is 60 points: 36 points for close- and 24 points for open-ended questions. There is no minimum threshold level set for the exam.

Despite the primary goal of FLT in Poland, which is the development of the ability to effectively communicate in a FL both in speech and writing, students' productive skill of speaking is excluded from the examination. It is therefore impossible to specify to what degree the objectives established in the Core Curriculum for oral production, interaction, and mediation have been reached by eighth-graders at the end of the second stage of their FL education.

As opposed to other mandatory FL examinations administered in the past, the exam creates heightened expectations in reference to eighth-graders' performance (Pater, 2018; Zakolska, n.d.). As explained by the then Polish Education Minister, Dariusz Piontkowski in an interview for the Polish Press Agency (*Polska Agencja Prasowa*, PAP, 2019a), its difficulty has been increased first and foremost through the introduction of open-ended questions. The written assignment has become compulsory for all students, whereas the maximum word limit has been increased from 100 to 120. The introduction of mediation activities has placed greater challenge on examinees because they are expected to process selected pieces of information in both their L1 and a FL and respond to them accordingly. For the sake of comparison, Table 2.12 provides a summary of the crucial differences between the three FL examinations. For example, the range of activities in the sixth-grader exam and the basic level of the middle school exit exam was limited to close-ended questions while FL students' skill of writing was assessed in neither of the examinations.

Tab. 2.12: *Comparison of mandatory EFL exams in Poland (2011/2012-2018/2019) (adapted from CKE, 2010, 2013, 2017a)*

Type of FL examination	**Middle school exam after the 2009 reform**	**Sixth-grader exam before the 2017 reform**	**Eighth-grader exam after the 2017 reform**
School years	2011/12-2018/19	2014/15-2015/16	2018/19-
CEFR's level of proficiency	A2 (basic level) A2+ (advanced level)	A1	A2/A2+ (2019/20-2020/21) A2+/B1 (2022/23-)
Time	60 min	45 min	90 min
Parts	1. Listening comprehension 2. Reading comprehension 3. Use of English 4. Language functions/Writing	1. Listening comprehension 2. Language functions 3. Use of English 4. Reading comprehension	1. Listening comprehension 2. Language functions 3. Reading comprehension 4. Use of English 5. Writing
Types of questions	Close-ended questions/ Open-ended questions in Part Three	Close-ended questions	Close-ended questions/Open-ended questions in Part One-Five
Examples of activities	- Multiple choice questions - Matching - True/false questions - Gap filling - Answering to questions - Paraphrasing - Translation - Writing (an informal letter, e-mail)	- Multiple choice questions - Matching - True/false questions	- Multiple choice questions - Matching - Gap filling - Paraphrasing - Translation - Writing (an informal letter, e-mail, blog post, note)

The new structure of the eighth-grader exam seemed to place greater demands on Polish EFL learners. This can be noticed in their relatively lower average scores, 59% and 54%, obtained in 2019 and 2020 as compared with the 2016 sixth-grader exam and the basic level of the 2019 middle school exam, on which examinees scored 71% and 68% respectively (CKE, 2016, 2019b).

The reports published annually by the Central Examination Board highlight major weaknesses of Polish EFL primary school students (CKE, 2019a, 2020b). The analyses reveal two fundamental problems: their poorer overall performance in open-ended questions and a small degree of lexico-grammatical accuracy in Part Four (i.e., use of English) and Part Five (i.e., written production) of examination papers. Interestingly, the low level of Poles' accuracy seems to correlate with their lack of ability to transfer information in the writing part of the examination, as evident in the comparatively bad scores on content, that is one of the four assessment criteria (CKE, 2019a, 2020b).

Primary school students' results are rather disappointing in the light of the fact that the data presented above pertained to learners who took their exam at the A2/A2+ level after more than eight years of learning English. It must be underlined here that this level was only a temporary arrangement and higher requirements for students' language production (A2+) and reception (B1) were planned to be set.

2.4.2.2 Aptitude, achievement, and placement tests

As a general rule, results of the eighth-grader exam and selected final school grades serve as the basis for primary school graduates' admission to a higher level of education. Bilingual secondary schools and secondary schools with bilingual classes implement additional assessment procedures. Officially, the two instruments are used to measure students' special skills in FL learning (Journal of Laws from 2020, Item 910, as amended). Language aptitude tests are administered in Poland to recruit primary school graduates to a preliminary class, whose major objective is to prepare them for consecutive stages of bilingual education in grades one to four of secondary schools. They measure candidates' inherent ability to learn FLs, or "potentialities for achievement ideally independent of current knowledge" (Reber, 1985, as cited in Rysiewicz, 2008, p. 570). Language aptitude test results acted as a predictor of a FL learning success since, as demonstrated by Kuliniak in his 2010 and 2013 pilot studies, the secondary school students' top scores were found to strongly correlate with their high level of linguistic attainment. Achievement tests, on the other hand, serve a different purpose. They are designed to recruit secondary school candidates to grade one of bilingual schools based on their "current state of knowledge or skill (ability)" (Reber, 1985, as cited in Rysiewicz, 2008, p. 570) in a FL.

No governmental regulations on how to assess candidates' level of FL aptitude and expertise in the secondary school context with the help of language aptitude and achievement tests have been issued in Poland. Therefore, all the decisions concerning the choice of examination questions lie with a given educational institution (Kozińska, 2021). Key recruitment principles are posted on the official websites of schools. The analysis of selection criteria established for primary school graduates by twenty-seven bilingual secondary schools located in thirteen major Polish cities (see Appendix A) in the 2021/22 school year reveals that the structure of language aptitude tests designed for bilingual school candidates in Poland was generally uniform. They contained activities examining test-takers' L1 command, knowledge of idiomatic expressions, abstract thinking, analytical skills, and ability to deduce fictional language rules. They were conducted entirely in Polish. Since aptitude tests employed activities based both on fictional and untypical FLs, it was impossible to carry out the assessment of learners' oral language skill (Kuliniak, 2010, 2013). On the other hand, achievement tests administered at the level of secondary education showed greater inconsistency. They might assume a written and/or oral form. The differences could also lie in the types of tasks (e.g., paraphrasing, translations, open cloze exercises), the range of language skills (e.g., four language skills versus reading only), and the level of difficulty (e.g., A2/A2+ versus B1/B1+).

As the school year begins, it is also customary to organise placement tests for grade one learners. Their results help FL teachers to divide newcomers into groups of relatively comparable levels of language proficiency. To ensure efficient implementation and scoring, placement tests may take on a written form and implement multiple choice questions.

2.4.2.3 New Matura

The New Matura in English is an elective high-stake national examination taken by nineteen-year old secondary school graduates. It consists of a written and oral component, which assess learners' FL communicative competence based on their use of English and language reception, production, interaction, and mediation. The primary objective of this examination is to assess to what degree students have met the general and detailed requirements for the last stage of compulsory FL education in Poland (the ISCED level 3).

The EFL written New Matura is an external examination, which can be taken at two levels of language proficiency. The basic level is obligatory for those learners who have been studying English as the FL1 throughout their twelve-year cycle of language learning. Examinees are required to display their communicative competence at the intermediate (B1+)/upper-intermediate (B2) level of proficiency. The advanced level of New Matura, which is conducted at the upper-intermediate (B2+)/advanced (C1) level of language proficiency, is optional. Students' performance on communicative language activities (i.e., reception, production, interaction, and mediation) and their knowledge of lexico-grammatical structures are assessed via four main types of examination questions based on listening and reading comprehension, use of English, and writing. The passing threshold for the basic level is 30%.

As an aftermath of the latest 2017 education reform, an unprecedented situation took place in Poland. Two different Core Curricula were followed simultaneously for three consecutive school years, from 2019/20 to 2021/22 (PAP, 2019a). The last New Matura exam based on the 2012 curriculum was scheduled for 2022 while the first examination following the new 2017 curriculum was to be administered a year later. A set of heightened detailed requirements for the mastery of FL knowledge and skills has also been imposed on students (MEN, 2017). Increasing the ultimate level of expected linguistic attainment translates into greater complexity of examination questions at both basic and advanced levels: for instance, the duration of a listening comprehension assignment and the length of reading comprehension texts have been increased by five minutes and approximately 300 words respectively. Analogically to the changes made to the primary school final EFL exam, an open-ended type of questions has been introduced to Parts One, Two, and Three of the examination paper. The minimum word limit for the written assignment in Part Four of the basic level of Matura has been raised from 80 to 100 words (CKE, 2021; MEN, 2021). The comparison between the 2015 and 2023 versions of the EFL written New Matura has been presented in Table 2.13.

Tab. 2.13: *Comparison of the FL New Matura exam first administered in the 2014/2015 (adapted from CKE, 2013) and 2022/2023 school years (adapted from CKE, 2021)*

Type of FL examination	**EFL written Matura exam**			
Polish translation	*pisemny egzamin maturalny z języka angielskiego*			
School years	2014/15-2021/22		2022/23-..	
Level	basic	advanced	basic	advanced
Type	obligatory	elective	obligatory	elective
CEFR's level of proficiency	B1/B1+	B2/B2+	B1+/B2	B2+/C1
Time	120 min	150 min	120 min	150 min
Parts	1. Listening comprehension 2. Reading comprehension 3. Use of English 4. Writing		1. Listening comprehension 2. Reading comprehension 3. Use of English 4. Writing	

(Continued)

Tab. 2.13: Continued

<table>
<tr><th>Type of FL examination</th><th colspan="4">EFL written Matura exam</th></tr>
<tr><td>Types of questions</td><td>- Closed-item questions: Parts One-Three
- Open-ended question: Part Four</td><td>- Closed-item questions: One-Three
- Open-ended questions: Part Three-Four</td><td colspan="2">Closed-item and open-ended questions: Parts One-Four</td></tr>
<tr><td rowspan="2">Examples of activities</td><td colspan="2">- Multiple choice questions
- Matching
- True/false questions</td><td colspan="2">- Multiple choice questions
- Matching
- True/false questions
- Gap filling
- Transformation
- Word formation
- Translation
- Grammaticalisation</td></tr>
<tr><td>- Writing (a letter, e-mail, blog/forum post, etc.)</td><td>- Gap filling
- Transformation
- Word formation
- Translation
- Writing (a formal letter, article, argumentative essay etc.)</td><td>- Writing (an informal letter, e-mail, blog post, etc.)</td><td>- Writing (a formal letter, article, argumentative essay etc.)</td></tr>
</table>

According to the New Matura syllabus published by CKE, four criteria (i.e., content, cohesion and coherence, accuracy, range) are used to assess examinees' written performance on the FL exam (CKE, 2013, 2021). The practical aspects of language use and communicativeness are highly significant. Students are required to write a functional text based on four points included in the instructions in line with the 'refer to and elaborate on' principle. On average, 40% of the total score achieved by examinees in relation to writing pertains to the content of their assignment. If students fail to express the ideas formulated in the instructions, they achieve zero points not only in the category of content, but also in the remaining ones.

Since its first general administration, the EFL New Matura exam has strengthened its position in the Polish FL instructed settings. According to the 2005 report compiled by CKE, 76.1% of secondary school graduates chose English as their obligatory exam subject. More recent data reveals not only an almost 20% increase in the number of students selecting English, but also a decline of 12.7% and 5% decline in the examinations carried out in German and Russian respectively. Table 2.14 shows how the number of EFL learners has been changing over the span of fifteen years.

Tab. 2.14: *Popularity of modern FLs chosen by secondary school graduates as their obligatory examination subjects (CKE, 2005, 2009, 2015, 2017, 2020)*

Year	English	German	Russian
2005	76.1%	16.7%	5.4%
2009	82.2%	15.7%	5.7%
2015	90%	7%	2%
2017	91.9%	6.8%	1.9%
2020	94.2%	4%	1.4%

Interestingly, as reported by CKE, the EFL written exam has also been most frequently selected by secondary school graduates as an additional examination at the advanced level since 2015.

The speaking part of EFL New Matura, on the other hand, is an internal examination conducted by school examination committees since the 2011/2012 school year (Journal of Laws from 2020, Item 1327). It lasts approximately fifteen minutes and consists of four parts:

1. warm-up – students answer a few general questions;
2. role-play – students take on familiar roles (e.g., of a traveller, customer, learner) and hold a dialogue with an examiner to discuss four points included in the instructions;
3. description of a photograph – students comment on the content of the photograph and answer three questions connected with the illustration;
4. input-based utterance – students choose one photograph which in their opinion most satisfactorily meets the requirements laid down in the instructions, justify their choice, and answer two related questions

The maximum score adds up to 30 points: 18 points for examinees' communicative ability (Part One-Three) and 12 points for the quality of their utterances (Part One-Four), composed of range, accuracy, pronunciation, and fluency. The passing threshold is 30% (CKE, 2013, 2021). The scoring procedures implemented during the oral examination are in compliance with the objectives underlying the assessment of communicative competence in the CEFR (Kucharczyk, 2015). Given the pragmatic aspects to language learning promoted by the AOA, what is subject to examination is first and foremost students' ability to appropriately express their intentions in the FL and react to interlocutors' communiques. This fact can be observed in the criteria adopted by CKE for the purpose of assessing Polish students' performance in the speaking part of New Matura in a FL (confer Table 2.15).

Tab. 2.15: *Criteria for the assessment of FL pronunciation in the speaking part of New Matura (adapted from CKE, 2013, 2021)*

Points	Criterion of assessment: FL pronunciation
2	• No pronunciation errors OR pronunciation errors do not impede communication
1	• Pronunciation errors sometimes impede communication
0	• Pronunciation errors often impede communication OR pronunciation errors make students' utterances unintelligible • Silence OR utterances are unintelligible

According to the guidelines published in the New Matura syllabus (CKE, 2013, 2021), students' pronunciation is primarily evaluated in the context of how it affects the communicativeness of utterances. This principle also applies to the assessment of students' language use and fluency.

Based on the data presenting average New Matura scores for the 2015-2020 period (GUS, 2020), it is possible to observe a steady tendency. Out of three obligatory written exams, Polish students fared better in English (73%) than in Polish (57.7%) and Mathematics (55.8%). A satisfactory result in the EFL examination may therefore be indicative of students' positive achievement of the curricular goals regarding their development of communicative competence at the intermediate level of language proficiency (Muszyński et al., 2016).

Some scholars, however, questioned the relevance of EFL examinations taken by Polish adolescents. Walczak (2015) referred to *Gazeta Wyborcza*, a Polish daily newspaper, and cited a part of an interview with Jacek Członkowski, the chairman of the Polish Association for Standards in Language Education, who voiced justifiable criticism over the misleading character of the written FL New Matura. Członkowski criticised the surprisingly low minimum threshold and the structure based on close-ended questions, arguing that "the exam is designed in such a way so that the majority of students can pass it" (Walczak, 2015, p. 131).

Zawadowska-Kittel (2017) took a similar stance, advocating the introduction of a 50% minimum score for all communicative language and lexico-grammatical activities. In her opinion, a pragmatic approach towards language assessment reflected in the primacy of communicative language use over accuracy should also be subject to criticism. The scholar argued for the development of more detailed assessment criteria of productive skills and the adoption of a less liberal attitude towards examinees' lexico-grammatical inaccuracy.

2.5 Challenges to developing EFL communicative competence in Poland

2.5.1 EFL instruction in the wake of education reforms

Since the beginning of the new millennium, the education system in Poland has undergone a complete makeover with regard to its structure, content of the Core Curricula, and examination principles. Nevertheless, several problems underlying compulsory FLT in Poland have remained untackled.

One of the most fundamental issues which deservedly captured special attention among FLT specialists concerns the neglectful approach towards FL oracy (Gajewska-Dyszkiewicz & Paczuska, 2015; Marczak et al., 2015). Even though the development of the ability to communicate in speech and writing is, as we read in the Core Curriculum, the primary objective of FL education at all stages in Poland, no official examination of Polish students' oral communicative competence is administered until the facultative New Matura examination. The introduction of consecutive FL exams at lower stages of education did not solve the problem since, as presented in the previous sections, they all excluded the speaking component. The lack of an obligatory FL speaking exam did not only directly contradict the assumptions of the Polish Core Curriculum for FLs, but also adversely affected the realities of FL learning and teaching in Poland. Marczak et al. (2015) investigated the implementation of the curricula based on the BENJA and BUNJO and concluded that the observational data and the transcriptions of FL lessons revealed limited (or close to none) participation of Polish primary and lower secondary school students in activities developing their oral communicative competence. The researchers also stressed a general lack of awareness about the inferior position of speaking practice in FL education. Only 20% of headteachers acknowledged a specific need to emphasise students' oral language production in the FL classroom (Marczak et al., 2015).

Organisational aspects underlying EFL instruction in Poland also left much to be desired. Note-taking and grammar-teaching combined with coursebook-based work were commonly implemented in FL instructed settings, as demonstrated by Walczak (2015) who studied the comments of Polish parents and students posted on a forum of the Polish *Polityka* weekly. Muszyński et al. (2015) pointed out to other typical features of English language teaching at the primary school level: teacher dominance and students' scarce contribution (on average 20 words) in constructing classroom discourse. The data collected by Eurydice (2012) indicated that similar problems, such as overemphasis on theory and learners' limited FL speech production, occurred in Polish instructed settings.

Teachers' preoccupation with FL vocabulary and grammar practice, revealed by the results of the 2011 ESLC, does not guarantee students' accurate language production (European Commission, 2012). This was evidenced by the analyses of the 2011 mock middle school exam (Szpryngier, 2012), the 2015 sixth-grader exam (Cichmińska, 2015), and the 2015 New Matura exam (Muszyński et al., 2016; Trzcińska, 2015). As unanimously observed by the Polish scholars, EFL learners' performance on examination questions which assess the latter's use of English was generally poorer as opposed to those which measure their skills of listening, reading, and writing. The main reason underlying the tendency may be students' inadequate amount of the contextualised use of lexico-grammatical structures in combination with language skills (Paczuska et al., 2014).

Furthermore, even though some students in Poland obtained very good results on FL tests and their level of proficiency approximated C1 and C2, the learners' success might not necessarily depend upon their participation in FL instruction provided by Polish schools. According to the Polish ESLC report (Gajewska-Dyszkiewicz et al., 2013), half of the respondents that achieved the highest scores received private tuition. Following that line of reasoning, some of the Polish students' high levels of language competence might be attributed to out-of-class language instruction rather than the compulsory FL courses taught at schools.

As already mentioned, the speaking part of New Matura is the only examination of Polish students' oral communicative competence. In most cases, however, its results are not taken into consideration in the process of admission to a tertiary level of education. This, unfortunately, affects students' attitudes not only towards the perceived usefulness of this examination, but also towards the importance of the speaking skill during everyday language practice. In a study conducted with secondary school students, Zawadowska-Kittel (2017) demonstrated subjects' ambivalence towards the speaking part of the EFL New Matura. She explained that learners' patronising attitudes towards the exam provoked by the dubious validity and authenticity of the three exam questions and the insignificance of the score during the recruitment process lower their motivation towards EFL speaking-based classroom practice.

2.5.2 Effects of the COVID-19 outbreak on compulsory FLT

It is difficult to disagree that the COVID-19 pandemic has had an overwhelming effect on the education system. Both negative and positive aspects of the recent global health crisis have been identified so far.

The relevance of developing communicative competence was called into question in the light of the pandemic. Nationwide school closures and sudden transitions towards online teaching and learning in March 2020 brought about by the Polish governments' preventative measures to minimise the negative effects of the coronavirus outbreak took its toll on the Polish educational reality (Deczewska, 2020; Miśkowiec, 2020; Uchwat-Zaród, 2020). Since not all teachers were able (or willing) to readily adapt to new conditions, the quality of online FL classes in some cases significantly deteriorated in the early period of distance learning. Karolczuk (2020) cited one of the comments made by a student in which he negatively judged his online classes: "But for Netflix, I would forget how to speak English" (p. 41). The report prepared by Plebańska et al. (2020) clearly demonstrated how limited and passive students' in-class participation in online classes was. Having been asked about their typical online lessons, three quarters of Polish learners stated that their teachers sent them self-study e-materials (42%) and assigned them to complete coursebook activities (35%). Extensive use of multimedia presentations and films during online classes, as reported by 46% of learners, did not encourage their active learning, promoting instead a deeply-rooted transmission model of teaching (Plebańska et al., 2020). Buchner and Wierzbicka's (2020) study yielded similar results: the vast majority of teachers provided students with links to online materials (90%) and guidelines on the types of coursebook activities to complete (95%). YouTube and e-versions of students' books proved two top sources of materials used by instructors.

With time, however, more and more practical suggestions on how to encourage learners' active participation in remote classes and increase the authenticity of the learning process began to circulate in the specialist literature. Krajka and Białek (2021) drew attention to problem- and project-based technology-mediated language learning involving the use of the Internet, social networking sites, *Kahoot*, and *Moodle*. They also presented the series of online WebQuest-based projects carried out within *The teaching English in Poland* programme in the context of Puentedura's (2006) SAMR (standing for Substitution, Augmentation, Modification, and Redefinition) model. In addition, the use of multimedia applications was a common example provided by FLT specialists in response to the SARS-CoV-2 outbreak. Some of the programmes referred in the literature included *Padlet* used to create virtual boards (Uchwat-Zaród, 2020), *Mentimeter* introduced to make presentations and carry out polls (Kordus 2020), and *AnswerGarden* utilised to build word clouds (Pałczyńska, 2021).

Despite teachers' attempts to modernise language instruction during the pandemic, the period of distance education in Poland generally received fierce criticism in view of the negative effects it had on students' emotional well-being. As argued by Grabowski (2021) in his report prepared for the Ombudsman for Children Mikołaj Pawlak, online education severely limited students' interaction with their peers, negatively affected learners' psycho-physical state, and destroyed the child-parent relationship, with average and poor students being particularly vulnerable to experiencing these problems. The findings of the report published by the Supreme Audit Office highlighted similar issues. NIK (2021) argued that the main cause underlying the poor quality of remote classes, wider educational gaps between students, and run-down mental state of teachers and learners was primarily the lack of clear guidelines issued by the Polish Ministry of Education and Science at the beginning of the pandemic.

What is more, the results of the 2021 Test for International Comparisons of Knowledge and Skills[14] conducted by Jakubowski et al. (2022) suggest that the period of online education in Poland in 2019/20 and 2020/21 school years combined with implementation of the 2017 education reform might have had a negative impact on the Polish education system. The findings of this research study administered by the Evidence Institute among Polish learners from Warsaw schools demonstrated that students' scores were lower when compared with the previous 2003-2018 PISA editions; the differences were significant and ranged from 14 to 60 points (Jakubowski et al., 2022).

It must be stressed at this point that Poland was not the only country whose education system was destabilised under the influence of the pandemic. The COVID-19 outbreak also represented a serious organisational and technological challenge in different parts of Europe. Germany, Denmark, Estonia, Greece, and Italy were some of the countries listed by DW which had to solve problems similar to those encountered in Poland, including teachers' reluctance to take online classes, insufficient computer equipment, and Internet outages (*Pandemia a problemy ze zdalnym nauczaniem,* 2021).

---

14 The Test for International Comparisons of Knowledge and Skills is based on the methodology adopted in PISA. It tests Reading, Math, and Science, each supplemented with questions relating to the Core Curriculum. The results can be compared with those of PISA (Jakubowski et al., 2022).

In addition to the doubtful character of distance and hybrid learning, EFL instruction might have been further complicated by Polish government's controversial proposals. Given the introduction of the epidemic state on March 20, 2020, Minister of National Education Przemysław Czarnek announced his decision to cancel the speaking-based examinations in the 2019/2020-2022/2023 school years (PAP, 2021). Moreover, by the virtue of the ministry's resolution announced in December 2020 (MEN, 2020), the scope of requirements for the 2021 eighth-grader exam and written New Matura was reduced (Journal of Laws from 2020, Item 2314, as amended). The most significant changes concerned the ultimate level of linguistic attainment; it was lowered from A2+/B1 to A2/A2+ for the eighth-grader exam and from B1/B1+ to A2+/B1 for the basic level of the New Matura exam.

Despite several negative aspects of the COVID-19 pandemic (just a handful of which have been enumerated above), the introduction of remote classes as a preventative measure taken to reduce the spread of the coronavirus has greatly facilitated the digitalisation of schools (Szostek, 2020). According to the *OECD digital education outlook 2021* (OECD, 2021), "the experience has catapulted education systems, traditional laggards when it comes to innovation, years ahead in what would have been a slow slouch towards smart schooling" (p. 3). An illustrative example demonstrating the trend in Poland was provided by Igielska (2021) and Sewastanowicz (2021). They reported that ICTs utilised by academics and university students within the period of distance education are highly likely to be used in the post-pandemic reality of tertiary education.

The concept of digital transformation has recently taken on the status of a buzzword in the European context, as evident in the EU pro-technology policies. A good example illustrating the significance of digitalisation in Europe is the continuation of the 2018-2020 edition of the *Digital Education Action Plan* in the years 2021-2027. The European Commission determined two objectives to be given priority within the period of the plan's implementation, namely establishing efficient digital education systems and facilitating the development of digital competences (European Commission, 2020).

The consequences of the recent global health crisis combined with the latest pro-technology trends in the EU policy initiatives have suggested a growing need to reconsider the shape of the education system in Poland. In the light of the growing relevance of digital technologies in instructed settings, changes to compulsory FL education reflecting the pro-technology trends have been more than justified. Since the Fifth Generation students used their personal devices on a daily basis (Pyżalski et al., 2019) and they all gained the experience of learning with their computers and mobile devices within the period of distance education in 2019/20 and 2020/21 school years, it is worthwhile considering introducing technology-mediated language learning activities, which, as illustrated in Chapter Three, offer a reasonable alternative to traditional methods of language teaching (Nussbaum-Beach & Hall, 2012).

Chapter 3
Voice assistants in ESL/EFL learning

3.0 Outline

Chapter Three focuses on exploring the phenomenon of voice assistance in ESL/EFL learning contexts. It consists of five subchapters. The first one introduces the idea of Computer-Assisted Language Learning (CALL) and traces the evolution of the concept against the backdrop of developments within linguistics, psychology, SLA, and ICTs. The second one underlines the growing mobility of computer technologies and discusses implications involved in their implementation in language instruction. Next, the technological advancements facilitating the emergence of Intelligent Mobile-Assisted Language Learning (IMALL) and the basic tenets underlying this young subfield of CALL and Mobile-Assisted Language Learning (MALL) are discussed. The following subchapter is devoted to the presentation of task-oriented IMALL; it provides an overview of the technological ancestors of VAs and offers basic information about the technology under discussion. The final subchapter presents the research trends and locates the sources of limitations of the selected empirical studies investigating the use of VAs in (out-of-class) ESL/EFL learning.

3.1 Computer usage in language education: Development of CALL

3.1.1 Concepts and definitions

The repertoire of pedagogical tools used in instructed settings has expanded substantially over the last century. Once equipped with a blackboard, chalk, and course book only, learners and teachers witnessed the arrival of technological innovations, such as television, film, and radio into classroom environments (Braga et al., 2017; Cuban, 1986). Out of these, the advent of computers has been considered particularly noteworthy for giving language education a new lease of life (Butler-Pascoe, 2011; Salaberry, 2001; Yaman & Ekmekci, 2016).

In *Dictionary of computing*, Collin (2009) defines the concept of a computer as "an electronic machine that receives, stores and processes data very quickly using a program kept in its memory." As far as its history is concerned, the computer has undergone a gradual evolution amid a plethora of technologically and socially motivated developments. As a matter of fact, its earliest version has its origin in the counting devices constructed by Wilhelm Shickard and Blaise Pascal in the 17th century (Randell, 1982). The major breakthrough in the creation of a program-controlled computer came in the 19th century with Charles Babbage's Difference and Analytical Engines and the sequence-controlled mechanisms popularised by Joseph Jacquard under the name of the automatic draw loom (Craig, 2021; Randell, 1982). Combined with ongoing technological progress and changes in public and governmental attitudes towards the role of computers, which were fuelled by World War II, Babbage's inventions proved to be the cornerstone in the development of the earliest mechanical computers and their 20th and 21st century successors, from electro-mechanical and electronic computers, through transistor and personal computers, to laptops, mobile devices, and netbooks (Copeland, 2000; Craig, 2021; Pericherla, 2016).

In the modern era, the idea of applying computer technology to language education dates back to the Programmed Logic for Automatic Teaching Operations (PLATO) developed at the University of Illinois in 1960 (Dębski, 1993). Based on the GTM principles, this drill-and-practice tutoring system for teaching reading in Russian involved vocabulary and grammar drills, translations, and grammar explanations (Ahmad et al., 1985). The program was later designed to include multiple languages (including English) and was soon implemented at several universities (Butler-Pascoe, 2011).

Growing interest in the use of computers in language learning and teaching opened up a new interdisciplinary subfield of applied linguistics in the early 1980s (Chapelle, 1997, 2006; Martins & Moreira, 2012). It was referred to as Computer-Aided Language Instruction (CALI) and CALL by American and British scholars respectively (Higgins, 1983). The former was incorporated into the name CALICO standing for Computer-Assisted Language Instruction Consortium, which is a professional association established in the United States of America in 1982. The origins of the latter are not entirely known, with the earliest reference found by Davies et al. (2013) in the 1981 conference paper by Davies and Steel.

In view of the increasing prominence of the learner-centredness concept, CALI, although once preferable, lost favour due to close associations with top-down programmed instruction (Davies, 2006; Davies et al., 2012; Jarvis & Achilleos, 2013). When the first attempts to introduce computer-based projects into instructed settings were made in the 1960s and 1970s through PLATO and its likes (e.g., Computer-Assisted Learning Exercises for French, Time-Shared Interactive Computer-Controlled Information Television), it was believed that technology could contribute to language learning through conscious drill- and dialogue-based language practice (Dębski, 1993). However, the advancements in the field of SLA gave prominence to such notions as subconscious language acquisition and comprehensible input (Krashen, 1981, 1985), thus calling into question the effectiveness of a traditional chalk-and-talk method. As a consequence, computers have ceased to be utilised for language learning and teaching purposes only, taking on new roles: they began to be used as a source of authentic content to stimulate language acquisition by providing numerous affordances through multimodal input and offering a means of communication (Jarvis & Krashen, 2014).

Ultimately, CALL has remained a widely accepted generic term (Hubbard, 2021; Levy & Hubbard, 2005). A number of professional associations (e.g., AsiaCALL, EUROCALL, PacCALL,), journals (e.g., *On-CALL*, *ReCALL*, *CALL Journal*), and events (e.g., GLoCALL WorldCALL), which have been established worldwide to popularise computer application in language education, demonstrate marked preference for the term.

When the definition of CALL was formulated by Mike Levy (1997) in his seminal work *Computer-assisted language learning: Context and conceptualization*, CALL was referred to as "the search for and study of applications of the computer in language teaching and learning" (p. 1). Over the course of its sixty-year-long history (to be briefly overviewed in the following section), the concept of a computer has branched out in several directions (Kern, 2006), with the field remarkably widening in scope. Once limited to behaviourist computer systems, CALL spans now a wide range of ICTs. Some of the examples include online blogs, social networking sites, podcasts, e-learning platforms, virtual worlds, corpora and concordances, computer-mediated communication, interactive whiteboards, natural language processing (NLP), and mobile apps (Jarvis & Achilleos, 2013; Walker et al., 2012). It is therefore common to observe the changing status of CALL in its recent conceptualisations (e.g., Egbert, 2005; Hubbard, 2021). In contrast to Levy (1997), who in the late 1990s equated CALL with the use of computers in language education, Hubbard (2021) broadened the scope of the field by comparing it to "any endeavor involving the use of computers and associated technologies of all types – desktops, laptops, tablets, smart phones, mp3 players, interactive whiteboards, etc. – in some significant way in language learning and teaching" (p. 1). Since Levy's (1997) first suggestions about the implementation of computers to language learning and teaching were put forward, the understanding of CALL has significantly broadened, with the field not only covering an increasingly wider range of language learning contexts, but also involving a broader array of computer technologies.

Despite a number of problem areas connected with CALL implementation, some of which concern money investments, availability of the courseware, teachers' and learners' technological expertise, and Internet access (Palacios-Hidalgo, 2020), existing literature on the subject is profuse in linguistic and affective benefits accruing from computer technology use in language learning. One asset of CALL is seen in the fact that new types of technology-mediated activities, especially those involving Web quests, e-mailing, social networking etc., help learners practise the language in an interactive way without constant teacher's intervention (Lee, 2016; Rahimi & Bigdeli, 2014). The other merit recurring in literature is related to increased authenticity of language use by guaranteeing easy access to a range of multimedia resources and authentic content (Chan & Chan, 2011; Davies & Hewer, 2012; Reinders & Hubbard, 2013). Another point worth making is that computer technologies generate learner-centred activities which allow students to learn at their own pace in stress-free environments (Lewoc, 1994). By giving learners the opportunity to access materials independently of the teacher and outside of instructed settings, ICTs support self-directed learning and personal knowledge management, both of which are central to promoting learner autonomy (Gitsaki & Taylor, 1999; Warschauer et al., 1996). Further, students can immediately receive multimodal and personalised feedback on their language use (Reinders & Hubbard, 2013). This facilitates language learning by turning it into an efficient, effective, individualised, convenient, and motivating process (Hubbard, 2021).

The contemporary meaning of a computer (and CALL) is far too broad now to include just personal computers (PCs) and laptops (Kern, 2006). In view of the continuous technological progress leading to the rise of the World Wide Web and the development of Artificial Intelligence (AI) systems, computer technologies have evolved into portable and wireless forms (Arvanitis & Krystallis, 2020; Bączkowska, 2021). The field has undergone numerous transformations and has seen various branches, some of which include Technology-Enhanced Language Learning (TELL, Bush & Terry, 1997), Network-Based Language Teaching (Kern & Warschauer, 2000), Web-Enhanced Language Learning (WELL, Taylor & Gitsaki, 2004), MALL (Chinnery, 2006), ICALL (Intelligent Computer-Assisted Language Learning; Schulze & Heift, 2012), and IMALL (Taher & Hussein, 2019). Despite a variety of terms that describe the process of language learning with the help of computer technologies and the Internet, we treat CALL as an umbrella term that successfully spans a number of its forms (Hubbard & Levy, 2016; Stockwell, 2012, 2022). It is therefore used in this overarching sense in this discussion.

3.1.2 Methodological, pedagogical, and technological evolution of CALL

History has shown that CALL is not merely a "shorthand for 'the use of technology' ", but rather, as argued by Garret (2009), "a dynamic complex in which technology, theory, and pedagogy are inseparably interwoven" (p. 719-720). The interdependent relationship between technology capabilities, learning theories, language teaching paradigms, the extent and scope of CALL practices, as well as the roles of computers, learners and teachers were well demonstrated against the background of the methodological, pedagogical, and technological development of CALL (Bax, 2003; Blin, 2016; Chun, 2016, 2019; Davies, 1997; Davies et al., 2012; Gruba, 2004; Warschauer, 1996, 2000, 2004; Warschauer & Healey, 1998). Since its early beginnings in the 1960s, CALL has been profoundly shaped not only by the trends in SLA and language pedagogy, but also by the state of computer technology (Bączkowska, 2021; Davies et al., 2013; Dębski, 1993).

Overlapping in time with the audio-lingual methodology of the 1960s and 1970s, the first phase Behaviourist CALL[15] (Warschauer, 1996) fell under the strong influence of the then dominant structural linguistic theories and Skinner's (1957) Operant-Conditioning Model (Alemi & Tavakoli, 2016; Liu & Shi, 2007). In this period, the drill-and-practice courseware was based on the model of computer as tutor (Taylor, 1980; Davies, 1997). The CALL tutoring systems served "as a vehicle for delivering instructional materials" (Warschauer, 1996, Behavioristic CALL). They provided accuracy-oriented language practice in selected areas (e.g., morphology, lexis, syntax) through repetitive drills, multiple-choice and cloze exercises, feedback, positive reinforcement, and self-pacing in line with the programmed instruction (Moras, 2001).

In Behaviourist CALL, students were entirely dependent on the computer program (Ahmad et al., 1985). It gave a visual stimulus (e.g., a monochrome text displayed on the screen) to which they were expected to respond appropriately (e.g., either by typing their own answer or selecting one of the options already provided in a close-ended question) (Davies, 2006). As a result, learners interacted solely and exclusively with the machine (Bączkowska, 2021). Teachers were to serve as mediators (Gruba, 2004) between the computer and students throughout the learning process to make sure that the latter "understand instructions and can supply the kind of responses required to make the program advance" (Abraham

15 The name Behaviourist is changed into Structural in a later publication (Warschauer & Healey, 1998).

& Liou, 1991, p. 104, as cited in Gruba, 2004, p. 637). Since such applications of computer technologies, described as instructional by Dębski and Gruba (1991), did not facilitate social interaction (or even stifled it), Bax (2003) referred to this behaviourist phase of CALL as Restricted CALL.

The extent of the early computer-based projects, such as PLATO, was severely reduced by the technological limitations of computers. Since they were usually stored on mainframes located on campuses, they could be accessed by university students at connecting terminals only (Butler-Pascoe, 2011; Chapelle, 2001). Given the fact that mainframes could not play sound and video, the first phase can be also tellingly referred to as Dumb CALL (Davies et al., 2012).

Grounded in Skinner's (1957) Stimulus-and-Response Theory, drill-and-kill programs of Behaviourist CALL fell out of favour, attracting a barrage of criticism as they did not favour authentic communication (Stevens, 1989; Underwood, 1984). Problems with developing learners' communicative competence within the ALM combined with the growth of cognitive and humanistic psychology effected transition away from the programmed learning to the communicative and functional language use associated with the CLT paradigm (Butler-Pascoe, 2011). The communicative phase of CALL fell on the late 1970s and early 1980s. Greater attention was paid to ensuring that the programs of this period encouraged not only student-computer, but also student-student interaction (Stevens, 1989). Implicit grammar instruction, creation of natural learning environments through the TL use both on- and off-screen, and students' freedom with regard to the choice of language produced were some of the principles formulated by Underwood (1984) with an intention of increasing learner accuracy and fluency within Communicative CALL.

The development of PCs in the late 1970s brought about the idea of educational computing within the reach of a wider audience, encouraging the development of courseware by teachers through authoring programs (Gruba, 2004; Hubbard & Levy, 2016). The first graphics, even though very primitive, could be displayed in the 1980s, and they increased the attractiveness of the computer software (Davies, 2006).

In view of the methodological, pedagogical, and technological advancements, computers took on new roles in the classroom. The behaviourist computer as tutor model was extended in non-drill skill practice of Communicative CALL through simulation, text reconstruction, gap-filling, speed-reading, and vocabulary games to provide students with a greater degree of choice, control, and interaction (Levy, 1997). With the arrival of word processors, spelling and grammar checkers, and concordances, the computer became a tool (Taylor, 1980). It also acted as a stimulus for discussion, writing, and critical thinking, thus encouraging student interaction in the spirit of CLT (Piper, 1986). The use of computers for playing games (including simulations), carrying out collaborative projects (using *Storyboard* and *HyperCard*), and establishing computer-mediated communication in enriched chat environments called multi-user domains permitted learners and teachers more freedom with regard to their roles in the classroom. To imply the change in the interaction dynamics effected by the advent of Communicative CALL, an alternative term Open CALL was used (Bax, 2003).

Critique of "teaching compartmentalized skills or structures" (Warschauer, 1996, Communicative CALL) combined with the growing influence of psychological theories of development, such as constructivism (Piaget & Inhelder, 1967), social-constructivism (Vygotsky, 1978), and constructionism (Papert, 1980), caused increasing dissatisfaction with CLT, encouraging scholars to teach in a more integrative way by using task-, project- and content-based approaches. The primary aim of the last phase Integrative CALL (Warschauer, 1996, 2000; Warschauer & Healey, 1998) was to integrate language skills and technology into language learning (Yang, 2010) in line with "a socio-cognitive view that emphasizes real language use in a meaningful, authentic context" (Lee, 2000, p. 2). This could be fulfilled due to two major developments of the early 1990s (Davies, 2006; Moras, 2001), the arrival of multimedia personal computers (MPCs) and the rise of the World Wide Web, which laid the basis for Multimedia and Web CALL respectively (Davies et al., 2012).

With the increasing affordability of MPCs, their number started to grow. So did the sophistication of CALL programs increase. More powerful graphics cards and soundcards were some of the innovations which made it possible for colourful fonts, animations, and high-quality photographs to be displayed and sound to be played and recorded (Davies, 2006). The arrival of MPCs extended the types of stimuli offered to learners, from plain texts and line drawings, to the combination of texts, still images, sounds, and videos (Davies, 2006). This automatically changed the ways in which learners could interact with computers; instead of just typing at the keyboard, they could point-and-click and drag-and-drop with a mouse and speak into a microphone.

Even though the launch of the Internet was considered a breakthrough for CALL (Chapelle, 2001), the field "took a step backwards for a while" (Davies et al., 2012, para. 6). Behaviourist CALL made a comeback with one-way traffic, slow broadband Internet access, and point-and-click exercises of Web 1.0. Once traffic became two-way, and sound and video quality improved thanks to the arrival of Web 2.0, the Internet provided numerous opportunities for collaborative language practice inside and outside instructed settings (Walker et al., 2012).

With the concepts of learner agency, authenticity, and social interaction coming to the foreground with the rise of Integrative CALL, the role of computers in language learning changed again. Emphasis was placed on the use of technology as a social space (Toyoda & Harrison, 2002), a medium of global communication, and a source of authentic materials (Davies, 2006; Warschauer, 1996). While in the earlier phases of CALL learners interacted primarily with computers, in the integrative phase interaction began to involve learners via networking (Bączkowska, 2021). Thanks to the technology capabilities to for example record and playback voice and analyse speech via Automatic Speech Recognition (ASR) software, students were also enabled to learn autonomously without the presence of language instructors. Accordingly, teachers were advised to step back to give their pupils a chance to define learning objectives, design syllabi, and self-assess progress, to mention just a few examples.

The transfer of computer functions to mobile devices and improvements in mobile devices processing power, storage space, and wireless connectivity have encouraged the use of easily portable devices as pedagogical tools for ESL/EFL learning and teaching (Kukulska-Hulme & Shield, 2008; Park & Slater, 2014; Stockwell & Hubbard, 2013). The subsequent proliferation and widespread ownership of increasingly sophisticated mobile and wearable devices in the first decade of the 21st century made it possible for language acquisition to take place not only in formal classroom settings, but also outside, in the physical confines of one's home and on the go (Miangah & Nezarat, 2012).

In response to the changing FL learning landscapes and growing appeal of the ecological perspective on SLA (e.g., Kramsch & Whiteside, 2008; van Lier, 2008), the fourth phase referred to as Ecological CALL has recently been added to the aforementioned historical typology of CALL by Blin (2016), Chun (2016, 2019), and Lafford (2009). Once borrowed from natural sciences and applied in language education, the ecology metaphor and the notion of an ecosystem have offered a more comprehensive view of language acquisition at a time when technology usage is moving towards normalisation, or "the stage when the technology becomes invisible, embedded in everyday practice" (Bax, 2003, p. 23). According to Blin (2016), CALL ecosystems comprise interactive elements, or living and non-living components, such as language learners, teachers, TL users, technological devices, applications and platforms, and multimodal resources. As digital technologies enable their users to create texts, which in addition to writing incorporate audio, images, music and video, voices have been expressed wanting to go beyond traditional definitions of literacy and move towards digital literacies and multiliteracies (Chun, 2016).

For convenience, the key theoretical aspects covering among others the language teaching paradigms, types of technology, and learning objectives associated with each of the phases of CALL development discussed above are summarised in Table 3.1.

Tab. 3.1: *Theoretical perspectives in different phases of CALL (adapted from Chun, 2016, 2019)*

Phase of CALL	Behaviourist	Communicative	Integrative	Ecological
Time frames	1970s-1980s	1980s-1990s	2000s	2010s
Type of technology	Mainframes	PCs	Multimedia and Internet	Mobile and wearable devices
Primary use of computer technologies	Drills	Communicative activities	Authentic discourse	Global communication
Language teaching paradigm	Grammar-Translation Method, Audiolingual Method	Communicative Language Teaching	Content-based, Specific purposes	Digital literacies, multiliteracies
View of language	Structural	Cognitive	Socio-cognitive	Symbolic and intercultural competence
Learner status	Dependent	Independent	Collaborative	Collaborative
Learning objective	Accuracy	Accuracy and fluency	Accuracy, fluency, agency	Identity as global citizens

According to the *Research agenda 2014* (TESOL International Association, 2014), investigating the use of technology in language learning became one of the major research priorities for the TESOL members. More importantly, however, examining learners' uses of learning opportunities afforded by mobile devices, also referred to as portable, wireless, handheld, and nomadic (Chinnery, 2006), was formulated as one of the first research problems addressed in the document. In light of the increasing significance of the mentioned devices in both personal and educational domains, we continue the discussion by exploring the phenomenon of MALL.

3.2 Greater mobility of computer technologies: Growth of mobile learning

3.2.1 From CALL to MALL

Amid the changing technological landscape, "the object of interaction of the human [with technology] has changed accordingly, from stationary computers, through portable ones (laptops, palmtops, tablets), to mobile phones (smartphones)" (Bączkowska, 2021, p. 11). Increased use of mobile devices in the language classroom opened up a new field called MALL (Kukulska-Hulme, 2019; Polakova & Klimova, 2019). The term was first used by George Chinnery (2006) in his influential article *Going to the MALL: Mobile assisted language learning*. The term stands for the use of "mobile technologies in language learning, especially in situations where device portability offers specific advantages" (Kukulska-Hulme, 2013, p. 3701). MALL is not a genuinely independent field (Czerska-Andrzejewska, 2016; Park & Slater, 2014; Viberg & Gronlund, 2012). In addition to clear connections to SLA, the two bodies of knowledge, CALL and mobile learning, also known as m-learning, have been found instrumental in informing theory, research, and practice within MALL (Cakmak, 2019; Kim & Kwon, 2012; Stockwell & Hubbard, 2013).

As pointed out in Section 3.1.1, the status of CALL has changed in response to the rapid technological development. This is reflected in its definitions which illustrate the transition away from computers to computer technologies in language learning. Since the latter cover now "the full range of digital devices and the networks that connect them, as well as the software, including mobile apps" (Hubbard, 2021, p. 3), it is justified to treat MALL as a subfield of CALL (Park & Slater, 2014). Once we have adopted this broad meaning of the computer technology and accepted the fact that mobile devices are nothing else than handheld computers (Yang, 2013; Singh & Samah, 2018), a number of insights from CALL research can be found relevant for MALL. Some of the examples include the principles for task design (Doughty & Long, 2003) and evaluation in e-learning (Chapelle, 2001). Further, acknowledging the effects of individual and cultural differences on the success or failure of collaborative learning (Belz, 2001), limitations of self-reporting (Fischer, 2007), and novelty effect of technology (Murray & Barnes, 1998) can provide a point of departure for MALL research.

A traditional sense of the computer notion can, however, be retained in the understanding of CALL. It is then justified to argue that MALL differs markedly from its sister field in the "use of personal, portable devices that enable new ways of learning emphasising continuity or spontaneity of access and interaction across different contexts of use" (Kukulska-Hulme & Shield, 2008, p. 273). Following that line of reasoning, CALL and MALL support language learning via different yet complementary ways, through language learning computer software and mobile applications respectively (Stockwell, 2022; Yaman & Ekmekci, 2016). Whilst the former "is better (…) for handling various types of information such as visual, sound, and textual information", the latter "is superior (…) in portability" (Yamaguchi, 2005, p. 57, as cited in Chinnery, 2006, p. 13). Given this portability dimension, mobile devices free students from the spatio-temporal limitations of traditional (i.e., classroom) language learning (Koole, 2009; Wang, 2017). In view of this, MALL can also be unanimously classified as a subarea of m-learning (Cakmak, 2019; Lindaman & Nolan, 2015; Viberg & Gronlund, 2012).

There is a lack of consensus among FL teaching specialists as to the definition of m-learning (Taylor, 2006). For instance, Traxler (2005) applied it in reference to the use of mobile devices in learning. Having adopted a learner-centred perspective, O'Malley et al. (2005) defined it as "any sort of learning that happens when the learner is not at a fixed, predetermined location" (p. 7). Conde Gonzales et al. (2008) placed m-learning on the continuum between e-learning and u-learning, describing it both as "an evolution of eLearning" and "the first step towards the creation of ubiquitous learning" (p. 61). El-Hussein and Cronje (2010) provided the most comprehensive account of the concept of all, explaining that it "takes place in learning environments and spaces that take account of the mobility of technology, mobility of learners, and mobility of learning" (p. 20). In view of the above, it is justified to argue that m-learning can take place anytime and anywhere regardless of learners' age, place, and time. As a consequence, it creates opportunities for language learning to be a personalised, authentic, situated, collaborative, and, probably most importantly, life-long process (Kukulska-Hulme, 2009; Kukulska-Hulme et al., 2017; Reinders & Benson, 2017; Traxler, 2009). As pointed out by Roschelle (2003) in his influential paper *Unlocking the learning value of wireless mobile devices*, handheld computers show enormous potential for revolutionising education. They facilitate the movement away from the episodic and supplementary technology use associated with computer labs to its regular and complete implementation inside and outside language classrooms through portables, which is to be discussed below.

3.2.2 Proliferation of mobile devices: From dumbphones to smartphones

Since the first use of MALL in the late 1980s, when Twarog and Pereszlenyi-Pinter (1988) provided assistance and feedback to distant language learners through telephones, the repertoire of mobile technologies discussed in the literature has broadened significantly. It now includes smartphones, tablet computers, digital audio players, electronic dictionaries, e-book readers, and handheld game consoles, to give some of the most common examples (Davie & Hilber, 2015). Generally speaking, any portable and wearable devices which deliver content and instruction through the Internet and satellites and enable users to perform a variety of tasks involving communication (i.e., calling, texting, e-mailing), organisation of content (i.e., address, calendar), access to information (i.e., websites), and relaxation (i.e., camera, music, games), fit into the category of a mobile device (El-Hussein & Cronje, 2010; Kukulska-Hulme & Shield, 2008; Stockwell & Hubbard, 2013; Trinder, 2005). The key educational properties of these devices include their portability, social interactivity, context sensitivity, connectivity, and individuality (Klopfer et al., 2002).

In this discussion, a mobile technology stands for "...any device that is small, autonomous, and unobtrusive enough to accompany us in every moment" (Trifonova et al., 2004, p. 3). Also, it is "owned and controlled by an individual rather than an institution" and allows its user to access the Internet and perform many tasks, especially those communication-based (UNESCO, 2013). Laptop computers, although portable to some extent, are beyond the scope of MALL as they are still more like PCs in that they are too sizeable to be freely carried in their users' pockets and handbags while walking around (Viberg & Gronlund, 2012).

Over the last forty years, MALL has been impacted by technological advancements (Stockwell, 2022). As suggested by Squire (2009), MALL apps of the 2000s were a mere replication of CALL software, as evident in "stripped down versions of their more complex desktop predecessors" (p. 71). In addition, the first wave of MALL programs and projects bore close resemblance to the concept of Web 1.0 in that "the interaction was not virtually user-centred or -created." (Yang, 2013, p. 20). The situation changed when Mobile 2.0, which was based on the premises of Web 2.0, made its way into learning environments, contributing to the upsurge of collaborative activities (Wang & Heffernan, 2009).

With the advent of mobile devices, interest towards MALL started to grow (Godwin-Jones, 2011), with great diversification of contexts, ranges of use, and language areas and skills investigated within the field (Stockwell, 2022). MALL may thus be used with reference to different learning situations, both formal and informal. For example, depending on the functionality of the mobile device involved, it may be applied with reference to the use of QR codes (Rivers, 2009), video-recording (Toland et al., 2016), *Instagram* (Azlan et al., 2019), and self-study with the help of mobile apps (Thuy & Yukawa, 2021). Researchers have been examining how to use mobile technology to support language learning given the technology's flexibility, low cost, small size, and user-friendliness (Huang et al., 2012). As illustrated by Burston (2013) in his extensive annotated bibliography of implementation studies from 1994 to 2012, electronic dictionaries, personal digital assistants (PDAs), mobile phones, MP3 players, and tablet PCs were the core subject of research within MALL. Moreover, the powerful appeal of MALL has recently lain in an increasing ownership of smartphones (Stockwell & Hubbard, 2013; Yang, 2013). According to Taylor (2023) (see Figure 3.1), the number of smartphone users worldwide rose from 3,668 billion in 2016 up to 6,648 billion in 2022 (the latter is equivalent to 84% of the world's population) and is expected to be on the rise in the upcoming years.

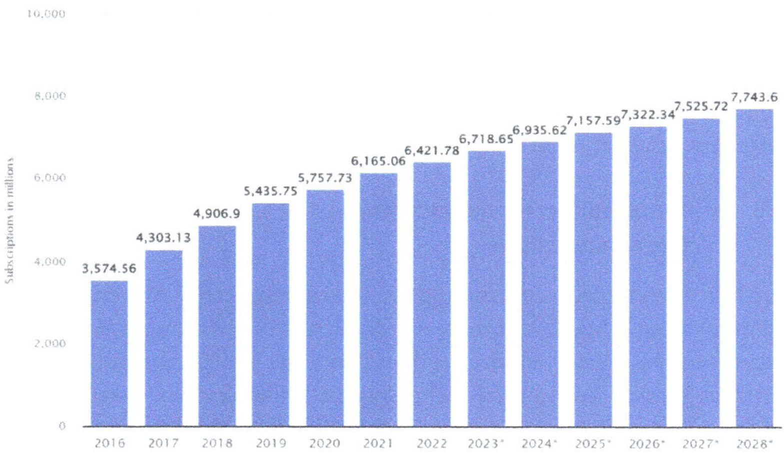

Fig. 3.1: *Number of smartphone mobile network subscriptions worldwide (2016-2028) (Taylor, 2023)*

Smartphones have been increasing in prominence both in personal and educational domains due to their growing sophistication. Since the first call made in 1973 on the prototype handheld mobile phone Motorola DynaTAC by Martin Cooper, a co-founder of ArrayComm and Dyna LLC (Wang, 2012), the device has undergone a complete transformation, from the so-called bricks to lightweight smartphones (Dudley, 2018). Despite their early technological constraints, such as small screen size, limited storage capacity, low processor speed, short battery life, low bandwidth, and limited input and output capabilities reported in the MALL literature (e.g., Kim & Albers, 2001; Koole, 2009; Nah et al., 2008; Thornton & Houser, 2003), it has recently acquired the nickname of a pocket computer (Jackson, 2018) thanks to its shape and the increase in speed, memory, and functionalities (Arvanittis & Krystalli, 2021; Stockwell, 2022).

In 2007, a smartphone revolution began with the launch of the first iPhone by Steve Jobs, a co-founder of Apple Inc. (Jackson, 2018). As compared to a traditional mobile phone[16], which is also pejoratively referred to as a dumbphone by Davie and Hilber (2015, p. 71), its successor, a smartphone, or "a mobile phone that can be used as a small computer and that connects to the internet" (Cambridge dictionary, n.d.), has considerably increased its capabilities. It can function as a camera, video and audio recording device, Internet browser, calendar, alarm clock, music and radio player, note pad, social media outlet, etc. (Yang, 2013). Access to free and commercial apps available through various stores (e.g., *Apple Store*, *Google Play*) even further increases the capabilities of already technologically sophisticated smartphones (Miller, 2012; Stockwell, 2022), strengthening their influential position in different areas of life (Miangah & Nezarat, 2012). In light of the above, we attempt to consider some of the implications involved in the smartphone application in language education.

3.2.3 Implementation of smartphones in MALL: a learner's and teacher's perspective

There is little consensus surrounding the smartphone use in education, with the issue remaining a highly controversial topic not only among researchers and FL teaching specialists, but also students, parents, and administrators. Insofar a few problems related to their technological limitations have been overcome, smartphones have earned poor reputation in view of their increasing misuses and excessive uses.

According to some researchers, smartphone use tends to have a disruptive effect on the process of learning (Froese et al., 2012; Neiterman & Zaza, 2019). As Glass and Kang (2018) state, dividing attention between the content of classroom lectures and smartphone use impairs long-term retention of the material, as demonstrated by the subjects' poorer exit exam performance. Smartphones

16 According to Stockwell (2022), a cell phone is another term used in some geographical regions to refer to a traditional mobile phone.

are also held responsible for increasing the number of cheating incidents during exams (BBC, 2019). They are considered cheating tools because they enable students to get notifications during tests, text friends for answers, and share photos of exam questions (Walker, 2017). Experimental interventions to ban mobile devices from schools proved to have a beneficial influence on students' learning outcomes. Researchers found out that the students from schools in which phone bans had been imposed scored higher on tests (Beland & Murphy, 2015) and performed better with regard to such aspects as the quality of note-taking and information recall (Kuznekoff & Titsworth, 2013).

Another disturbing trend is the changing character of smartphone use, from a habit to an addiction (Roberts et al., 2014), effected by the increasing frequency and amount of time spent by the youth in front of smartphone screens (Lee et al., 2014). Behavioural and mental problems known as no mobile phone phobia (nomophobia for short), or the fear of being separated from one's phone (Bhattacharya et al., 2019), have a negative impact on the psychological well-being and result in elevated levels of anxiety (Hwang et al., 2012). Smartphone addiction kills not only the moods of their users, but also their manners, as stressed by Popescu (2018, Inattentional blindness is a problem), who argued that " 'always-on' behaviour that smartphones contribute to causes us to remove ourselves from our reality (...). And aside from the health consequences, if we're head down, our communication skills and manners are slumped, too." The use of the device was also found to have a destructive influence on social interaction. According to Sherry Turkle (2015), the author of *Reclaiming conversation: The power of talk in a digital age*, it decreases the quality of conversation and empathy between speakers.

Furthermore, it was claimed that smartphones may be a serious cause for concern in relation to health. On the one hand, the World Health Organisation (*Electromagnetic fields and public health: Mobile phones*, 2014) warned against the potential carcinogenic effect of radiation from phones, to which children are particularly vulnerable. On the other, Cancer Research UK explained that "the radiation that mobile phones or phone masts transmit and receive is very weak", and therefore it "does not have enough energy to damage DNA" (*Do mobile phones cause cancer?*, 2022, para 2). Notwithstanding the conflicting information, it is hardly disputable that excessive smartphone use causes several health issues including users' fatigue, headache, eyesight problems, and wrist pain (Lange et al., 2018).

In view of the potential hazards that smartphone use poses in educational settings, some countries, such as France and Greece, decided to ban the devices from schools (Rubin & Peltier, 2018; Vourdoumpa, 2018). Similar preventative measures have already been taken by some states in Australia (Cambell & Third, 2020), whereas in the United Kingdom, there are plans for imposing similar restrictions on pupils (Shadwell, 2021). In Poland, on the other hand, no official rules on whether students are allowed to use smartphones at schools (or not) have been formulated by the government. The responsibility for addressing this controversial issue has been therefore delegated to school authorities who are obliged to set out conditions for smartphone use on their school property (Journal of Laws from 2016, Item 59, Article 99, as amended). According to the Daily Legal Newspaper (*Dziennik Gazeta Prawna*), there is a marked tendency to disallow smartphone use in Polish instructed settings. To be precise, 66% of schools in Poland reported having introduced bans on the technology use while almost one-third declared to impose similar prohibition in the future (Klinger & Otto-Duszczyk, 2019, as cited in Grodecka, 2020).

All the above-mentioned problems, ranging from poorer academic performance, through worse emotional and physical health, to superficial face-to-face interactions, might have been exacerbated by the outbreak of the COVID-19 pandemic. According to the App Annie report (i.e., a report that details an average monthly number of hours spend by users in mobile apps in 2019 and 2020) discussed by Kristianto (2020), it further increased the time people spent on their mobiles.

Avoiding the effects of the technologisation of the 21st century society is, however, near to impossible (Bhattacharya et al., 2019), as best demonstrated by the angry reactions of American students and parents to the cell phone ban imposed on schools in New York (*School cell phone ban causes uproar*, 2006). Since in Poland 82% of the students aged 9-17 use smartphones with an Internet access every day (Pyżalski et al., 2018), banning mobile devices at school seems counterproductive. It leads to the secretive use of the technology in the classroom, widens the gap between students' school and private lives, and deprives them of the ability to exploit the potential of smartphones as learning tools (Polakova & Klimova, 2019). Smartphone-based MALL is fully justified in view of its consonance with Generation Z (Gen Z for short) students' expectations. What distinguishes the members of Gen Z born between 1996 and 2012 from their predecessors[17] (i.e., Traditionals, Baby Boomers, Generation X, Generation Y) is the fact that the

17 There is little agreement among sociologists on the nomenclature and time spans used with reference to different generational groups, as demonstrated in different publications (e.g., Lancaster & Stillman, 2002; Martin & Tulgan, 2002; Oblinger & Oblinger, 2005). In this discussion, we adopt the labels and dates provided by Gonzales-Lloret (2017), Levonius (2015), Polakova and Klimova (2019), and Schroer (2008).

former's "existence is more connected to electronics and digital world" (Singh & Dangmei, 2016, p. 2). Having grown up with unprecedently easy access to cutting-edge technologies and multimedia tools from a very young age (Cilliers, 2017; Rothman, 2016), these digital natives, to use the term introduced by Prensky (2001), constitute the most technologically sophisticated generational group according to the *2012: Investing in generation Z* report published by the Institute for Emerging Issues (Singh & Dangmei, 2016). Other nicknames formulated to define this generational group, such as Screensters, Net Generation, Digital Generation, Viral Generation, and Google Generation (Cruz, 2016; Rothman, 2016) have one common denominator: the regular use of ICTs. As opposed to digital immigrants, or "those [...] who were not born into the digital world but have, at some later point in [...] lives, become fascinated by and adopted many or most aspects of the new technology" (Prensky, 2001, p. 1-2), digital natives come to classrooms with different experiences and expectations and are "more Internet savvy and expert than their Gen Y forerunners" (Schroer, 2008, Generation Z section). Students of this generation value speed, convenience, and ease of use. They perceive technology as an integral part of everyday life as they prefer to google their problems rather than to consult books and instructors (Gaston, 2006). "It is the first generation that has never known a world without the Internet" and, unsurprisingly, they show a low level of tolerance for being without high-tech equipment (Polakova & Klimova, 2019, p. 4).

It has been posited in the literature that regular use of ICTs has effected changes in the way Gen Z learns. One of the controversial examples relates to the brain structure (Prensky, 2001). Rothman (2016, para. 6) claimed that in case of Gen Z members, "the part of the brain responsible for visual ability is far more developed, making visual forms of learning more effective." She further added that digital natives are excellent task-switchers, although side effects of this include a short attention span and lack of ability to analyse complex information. Screensters are experimental learners who thanks to technology, learn through exploration and interaction both inside and outside classrooms (Gaston, 2006; Rothman, 2016). They have "a very high level of near-instantaneous interactivity" and "a very high expectation of response time", which means that they do have little patience for engaging in asynchronous communication (Gaston, 2006, p. 12). They are therefore characterised as socially open, fast, and interactive learners (Cruz, 2016). Repeated calls for introducing changes to educational systems have been therefore issued in the field due to the presence of Gen Z in today's classroom (Cilliers, 2017; Gaston, 2006; Prensky, 2001; Oblinger & Oblinger, 2005).

Despite this, there has been a strong criticism voiced at the claims made in the digital native literature. In so far as Prensky's (2001) concept of digital natives has held considerable appeal, neither empirical evidence nor undeniable facts examined in everyday practice have been provided to support his conjecture (Benett et al., 2008). As a matter of fact, studies proved that digital natives' inclination to use technology in every sphere of their life does not necessarily translate into their willingness to use in the classroom. Margaryan and Littlejohn (2008) reported that learners were not necessarily enthusiastic about mixing their private sphere, in which they used social networking sites and services, with their classroom sphere. An interesting adjunct to this are the findings of the study conducted by Lohnes and Kinzer (2007), which revealed that students' views of the education system were primarily traditional in that they expected the classroom to be a separate space where they were guided by the subject expert.

Similarly, scepticism was expressed over the implementation of technology into the pre-pandemic education system in Poland. Plebańska's (2017) study revealed that half of the respondents stated that there are no ICTs used in their schools. To be more specific, according to the report published by IBE (2020), it was a combination of technology-related and non-technology-related factors that dampened Polish teachers' enthusiasm to integrate smartphones into the learning process, some of which included the specificity of the device itself, teachers' classroom management problems, increased responsibilities, heightened public expectations, and waning authority. As a result, students mistakenly perceived smartphone use merely as a form of entertainment (Pyżalski et al., 2019). According to the Centre for Public Opinion Research (*Centrum Badania Opinii Społecznej*, CBOS, 2018), the majority of the respondents (87%) found it inappropriate to use smartphones in school and academic settings in Poland.

Nevertheless, with the growing demand for acquiring FLs and the decreasing amount of time for traditional language courses, the use of mobile devices appears to be a very attractive alternative for today's students (Miangah & Nezarat, 2012). Smartphones provide a range of contexts for language learning in which learners may undertake activities tailored to their personal needs (Kukulska-Hulme et al., 2007; Pachler et al., 2010; Yang, 2013). These mobile devices provide students with easy and instantaneous access to authentic resources through apps and online sites both on- and off-site (Wang, 2017; Zaranis et al., 2013). According to the United Nations Educational, Scientific and Cultural Organisation (UNESCO, 2013), smartphones show the potential for enabling underprivileged students to receive language education and undergo language learning experiences by gaining access to language materials. Yedla (2013) even went as far as to call MALL a paradise for English language learners. Since they allow for flexible use of time and space, mobile devices maximise chances for out-of-school learning (Wang,

2017; Zaranis et al., 2013) and facilitate the shift from teacher- to student-led learning (Polakova & Klimova, 2019). They enable learners to study the language in the so-called digital wilds, or "digital spaces, communities, and networks that are independent of formal instructional contexts" (Sauro & Zourou, 2017, p. 186), without traditional sine-qua-nons, such as classrooms, teachers, and coursebooks (Yaman & Ekmekci, 2016). They thus create opportunities for sustained language practice outside instructed settings during everyday activities, such as walking and commuting (Kukulska-Hulme, 2018). In addition, the technology facilitates the development of digital literacy (Kukulska-Hulme et al., 2015; Wang, 2017; Zaranis et al., 2013) and students' participation in both individualised and collaborative language learning activities, synchronously and/or asynchronously (Kukulska-Hulme, 2018).

From psychological and pedagogical perspectives, the use of mobile devices has been found to support current theories of learning. Smartphones aid the development of learner agency and autonomy (Godwin-Jones, 2011; Kukulska-Hulme et al., 2015), which is in line with Piagetian constructivism (Piaget & Inhelder, 1967) assuming that individuals construct their world knowledge through the cognitive effort based on the internalisation of experiences involving assimilation and accommodation. Also, the devices encourage interactive, collaborative, and situated learning practices. This is in harmony with the externalisation of experiences underlying Vygotsian social-constructivism (Vygotsky, 1978). According to the socio-cultural theory, the interaction between individuals and their social milieu stimulates the former's development by mediating between their existing knowledge and new information. Furthermore, smartphones create environments in which technology facilitates learning through doing (Kukulska-Hulme et al., 2015; Kukulska-Hulme & Viberg, 2018). It thus applies the principles of constructionism. Papert's (1980) theory shares some similarities with Piaget's, in that for both theorists knowledge is built by an individual as structures, and Vygotsky's, in that the learning process relies on the externalisation of personal experiences (Bączkowska, 2021). It, however, puts into the foreground the active construction of a product, which is the driving force for individuals' development.

MALL implementation can thus be found congruent with the CEFR's (CoE, 2001, 2018, 2020) AOA to developing communicative competence (see section 1.2.2). As Carol Chapelle (2001), the author of a publication *Computer applications in second language acquisition*, had it: [a]nyone concerned with second language teaching and learning in the 21st century needs to grasp the nature of the unique technology-mediated tasks learners can engage in for language acquisition and how such tasks can be used for assessment" (p. 2). Introduction of technology-mediated tasks, described by Gonzales-Lloret (2017) as "meaning- and goal-oriented, communicative, authentic, and oriented to learning by doing" (p. 235), enables keeping the field of FLT in the vanguard by increasing the relevance of learning. To give an example, Kiernan and Aizawa's (2004) study examining the use of mobile phones in TBLL revealed that technology-mediated task performance can promote L2 acquisition and enable students to focus on meaning.

There is no doubt that technology use calls for urgent teacher-student role redefinition (Lam & Lawrence, 2002; Makrakis, 2005). As language learners find more opportunities for active participation in learning by adapting its path and pace to their personal needs, teaching becomes more learner-centred, with teachers stepping aside from their traditional roles of decision-makers and assuming new ones, those of guides, facilitators, and supporters (Bancheri, 2006; Polakova & Klimova, 2019). Since neither students' high levels of digital literacy nor their regular use of technology in personal domains increases their willingness to use it for educational purposes and guarantees their skillfulness at doing so (Abdous et al., 2009), the role of the teacher takes on yet greater significance. According to Tafazoli and Golshan (2014), language instructors should engage students in such projects that motivate them to use technology as a part of their out-of-class learning routines.

FL teachers are generally amenable to technological innovations; however, many of them resist the idea of using ICTs extensively (Liaw et al., 2007) and limit their technological experiences to "low-range applications such as email services or getting information from the Internet" (Abdelhalim, 2016, p. 163). Teachers' decisions whether or not to integrate technology into their language teaching is, as argued below, the result of a plethora of factors. CALL teacher education whose primary objective is "to equip current and future language teachers with the knowledge and skills, both technical and pedagogical" is believed to help teachers incorporate technology into language teaching (Hubbard, 2008, p. 180). To date, a number of frameworks for digital capability development in teacher training have been established. An important contribution to the ongoing debate of what CALL teachers should know and do about CALL was made by the International Society for Technology in Education (ISTE, 2017). The ISTE Standards for Educators Framework listed teacher skills in seven areas underlying teacher digital literacy: commitment to continued personal learning, digital leadership, digital citizenship, digital collaboration, digital learning environment designer, effective digital learning facilitator, and digital data analyst. Furthermore, the updated version of UNESCO's (2018) ICT Competency Framework for Teachers identified three

levels, each standing for a different stage of the ICTs use in education: knowledge acquisition, knowledge deepening, and knowledge creation. Once crossed with six different aspects of teachers' work, including understanding ICT in education policy, curriculum and assessment, pedagogy, application of digital skills, organisation and administration, and teacher professional learning, they added up to eighteen competences for teachers. There was, however, a caveat made in connection to CALL teacher education by Pokrivcakova (2019), who cast doubt on the usefulness of "long lists or complicated charts of 'key skills' " (p. 146), which in her opinion lay down unreasonable requirements for language teachers. According to the researcher, they are first and foremost language professionals and instructors, who in order to use a modern technology willingly need be convinced that it "can help them achieve educational objectives more effectively (in shorter time and with less effort)" (p. 146). In addition to their ICT competence, teachers' attitudes and preferences toward CALL determine success or failure of its implementation (Beatty, 2003; Liu et al., 2004; Peters, 2006). A combination of context- (e.g., technical equipment, curriculum, classroom time) and teacher- (e.g., ICT skills, attitudes, perceived usefulness of technology, experience with using technology as a learner) related factors may therefore be considered in an attempt to explain teachers' decision whether or not to implement MALL (Cichowska et al., 2020; Davis, 1989; Milbrath & Kinzie, 2000; Sabzian & Gilakjani, 2013; Son et al., 2011).

Technological advancements have continuously changed the face of mobile learning, provoking greater divisions between its proponents and opponents. The MALL landscape, already abundant in controversies and nuances related to the debatable use of smartphones and their influence on teaching and learning, learners, and teachers, is being further complicated by the wave of recent developments. Given their increasing ingenuity, personal technologies show considerable potential for rendering assistance to their users. Kukulska-Hulme (2016) suggested that a wide range of possibilities for mobile assistance, defined by the researcher as "a generic term that can include direct help, collaboration on a task, supportive words and actions, and provision of helpful scaffolds or resources", for language learning and communication exist (para. 4). She identified thirteen forms of mobile assistance, ranging from motivation (e.g., rewards for achievement) and well-being support (e.g., mood monitor, confidence coach), through progress monitoring (e.g., feedback on performance) and direct help (e.g., instruction), to social support (e.g., conversational partner) and mediation (e.g., translation aid), to mention just a few. Depending on the needs of learners, mobile assistance may be rendered on a regular basis and in response to a situation-specific problem (Kukulska-Hulme, 2019). One of the examples illustrating the practical application of mobile assistance was the MASELTOV project designed to provide effective linguistic support to migrant populations arriving in Europe (Kukulska-Hulme et al., 2015). Several context-aware services were offered in the prototype MASELTOV app, including translation, navigation guide, information resource, and language learning (Kukulska-Hulme, 2017).

With the launch of VAs in the 2010s, the era of mobile assistance powered by communicative AI systems began. Considered a major human achievement in the history of AI (Hawking, 2014), the rise of smart technologies and services available via mainstream smartphones has afforded interesting possibilities for humans to establish communication with machines.

3.3 Arrival of artificially intelligent technologies: Rise of Intelligent MALL

3.3.1 AI and human-machine communication: Towards Intelligent CALL

The dreams of human-machine communication (HMC) – once an inspiration for science-fiction scenarios – have been gradually realised against the backdrop of advancements within information and computer sciences, mathematics, linguistics, psychology, and most importantly AI (Chowdhury, 2003; Edwards, 2020). The artificial intelligence phrase was first used by John McCarthy during summer research project known as the Dartmouth Conference in 1956 (Benko & Lanyi, 2009). Generally, scholars emphasised the polysemy of the term (Guzman & Lewis, 2020), which can be used to refer to computer systems (Russell & Norvig, 2010), specific skills of computers (Copeland, 2022), and science and engineering of making intelligent machines (McCarthy, 2007). In this discussion, we have adopted a definition formulated by Lucking et al. (2016), in which AI stands for "computer systems that have been designed to interact with the world through capabilities (for example, visual perception and speech recognition) and intelligent behaviours (for example, assessing the available information and then taking the most sensible action to achieve a stated goal) that we would think of as essentially human" (p. 14).

Even though AI has become omnipresent, from systems underlying smart and financial technologies, through e-commerce and marketing, to manufacturing and car industries (Pokrivcakova, 2019), intelligent machines, or those thinking and acting like human beings (Chamberlain, 2017), have come into greater public attention fairly recently motivated by the launch of the first VAs on mainstream smartphones in the 2010s (Arif, 2018; Kukulska-Hulme, 2019). It is worth stressing here that the research into AI in fact began over 70 years ago. The development of the Imitation Game, or the test for AI which examines a machine's ability to display intelligent human-like behaviours (Zemcik, 2019) created by Alan Turing in 1950, generated a wave of interest in programs reproducing human intelligence (*Personal digital assistant*, 2019).

The application of AI concepts, algorithms, and technologies to language teaching and learning opened up a subfield of CALL referred to as Intelligent Computer-Assisted Language Learning, or ICALL for short (Gamper & Knapp, 2002). ICALL is a young field of research that draws from a number of disciplines: CALL and SLA on one side and computational linguistics on the other (Levy, 1997). AI systems used in education can be divided into three broad categories: learner-, teacher-, and system-facing ones. Each of them supports students, teachers, and administrators in their everyday education-related work respectively (Baker et al., 2019). For the purpose of the current dissertation, we focus on the first type only.

It is possible to isolate several reasons behind the initial failure to apply AI into educational devices. According to Anderson et al. (1985), the costly and time-consuming character of the procedure made it impossible for ICALL to develop between the 1950s and 1980s. Since the first publication on ICALL from the late 1970s, which documents the intelligent computer software designed by Weischedel et al. (1978) for teaching German as the L2, attempts to ensure the increased and more regular use of ICALL applications have not proven entirely successful either (Amaral & Meurers, 2011). Intricacies involved in the process of language learning and computational processing of a human language, combined with the complexity of the language itself, have been the major culprits held responsible for impeding the development of the field (Schulze & Heift, 2012).

Given the steady progress in areas of AI research, such as user modelling, expert systems, and NLP (Schulze, 2008), needs and aspirations for the technologies having the capacity to "talk with users in a way that feels natural and personalized" could be gradually fulfilled (Reaburn, 2019, para. 1). User modelling enables computational systems to say "the 'right' thing at the 'right' time in the 'right' way" (Fischer, 2001, p. 70) by collecting information about their users and using it to offer services adapted to their needs (McTear, 1993). Within research conducted on user modelling, student modelling is of particular importance to ICALL (Schulze & Heift, 2012) since it allows a program to gain insights into learners' knowledge and abilities by analysing their actions (Self, 1994). Expert systems "use human knowledge captured in a computer to solve problems that ordinarily require human expertise" (Khanna et al., 2010, p. 109). In education, expert systems contain relevant information from a particular learning domain. In ICALL applications, it is the grammatical system of the TL (Schulze & Heift, 2012). NLP is used to refer to "the analysis of linguistic data, most commonly in the form of textual data such as documents or publications, using computational methods" (Verspoor & Cohen, 2013, p. 1495). As illustrated in Figure 3.2, it involves two processes (Chopra et al., 2013; Rus, 2013): natural language understanding (NLU), which "helps software understand user interactions' intent and context" (Ahmad, 2021, para. 6), and natural language generation (NLG), which describes the "process of deliberately constructing a natural language text in order to meet a specified communicative goal" (McDonald, 1986, p. 2).

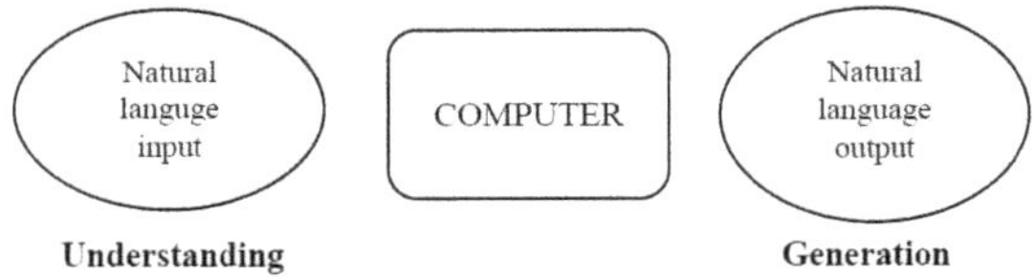

Fig. 3.2: *Process of natural language processing (Chopra et al., 2013, p. 131)*

Due to the implementation of the aforementioned AI technologies, ICALL software differs from that of CALL and MALL in the former's ability to establish HMC (Schulze & Heift, 2012). Using Levy's (2009) tutor-tool distinction, cases of HMC within the field of ICALL were divided into two types, tutorial and non-tutorial interactions. They take place through the medium of intelligent language tutoring systems (ILTSs) and dialogue systems (DSs) respectively (Schulze & Heift, 2012).

ILTSs assume the role of a human tutor (Moundridou & Virvou, 2003) thanks to the integration of four components into their architecture (Kang & Maciejewski, 2000): the Expert Knowledge Module, which stands for the content to be taught; the Student Model Module, which represents student's competence; the Tutoring Module, which controls instructional interactions with the learner, and the User Interface Module, which regulates interactions between the system and its user. Some of the best known examples of ILTSs include *Robo-Sensei* (Nagata, 2009) and *The E-Tutor* (Heift, 2010). As Schulze and Heift (2012) explained, ILTSs are more effective than traditional CALL programs. Instead of string-matching algorithms, which compare students' answers with the answer key letter by letter, ILTSs apply NLP systems to offer highly individualised feedback. In her commonly cited article *Computer vs. workbook instruction in second language acquisition*, Noriko Nagata (1996) argued that intelligent (i.e., immediate and appropriate) feedback offered by NLP produces higher learning results.

It was suggested that such AI-powered systems have a decided advantage over human tutors. Pokrivcakova (2019) claimed that "AI-powered tools are ahead of human teachers who simply do not have capacity to continually analyse each and every learner's outputs, diagnose their individual learning needs, adapt the learning content accordingly and give learners well-grounded feedback in the span of several seconds – and that all in the class of twelve or more students" (p. 138). It does seem to be a very promising feature of the technology, albeit is worth stressing here that the feedback provided to FL learners should consider a range of information both on the learner and the learning context. However, the fact is that most tutoring ICALL programs focus on the language aspect (or the grammatical competence) only hence "the activity and context in which the error was made and individual learner differences are not taken into consideration (Amaral & Meurers, 2011, p. 11).

Having said that, we would like to make it clear that the focus of interest in this discussion is on the presentation of HMC through DSs, also known as conversational agents (CAs)[18] (Jurafsky & Martin, 2021). As opposed to ILTSs, these computer programs take on the role of an interlocutor and thus have the capacity to establish non-tutorial communication with human users (Stewart & File, 2007). According to Hudson and Self (1982), the beginnings of instructional DSs date back to 1970, which was when Jaime Carbonell (1970) published a report *AI in CAI: An artificial intelligence approach to computer aided instruction* based on the SCHOLAR system. The SCHOLAR program is regarded as the first attempt to conduct mixed-initiative dialogues in which both the user and the computer can ask each other questions. In SCHOLAR, the scope of human-computer interactions (HCIs) was limited to the topics related to the South American geography. With time, the successors of SCHOLAR, such as WEST and SOPHIE, were programmed to establish more purposeful HCIs through the creation of game-playing and problem-solving environments respectively (Hudson & Self, 1982).

A well-known example of a DS used in ICALL are FLUENT projects. They aimed to provide "conversation in the target language, uninterrupted by discussions of grammar, use of first language, and difficulties of other students" (Hamburger, 2014, p. 183). In FLUENT 1 and FLUENT 2, there are actions to be performed by both a computer and a human user with the moveable objects found in bathroom and kitchen settings (Hamburger, 2014). As argued by Stewart and File (2007), the designers of a prototype DS for L2 practice called *Let's Chat*,

18 In this discussion, DSs and CAs are used interchangeably with reference to any AI-powered program that can hold conversations with human users.

learners are better-prepared to handle natural human-human communication (HHC) thanks to the well-constructed and native-like TL input that they receive from the conversational ICALL program.

So far different classifications of CAs have been made. Based on the type of input they are able to process, there are three types of DSs (Arora et al., 2013): text-based DSs involve chatting, spoken DSs use oral language, whereas their multimodal counterparts are able to combine different user input modes, ranging from speech, through touch and gaze, to body movement. Depending on the purpose of HMC, DSs can be divided into two types: chatbots and task-oriented DSs (TODSs) (Fellows et al., 2021; Jurafsky & Martin, 2021). Each of them will be briefly discussed below.

Even though the idea of the chatbot technology is almost sixty years old now (more information on its historical development can be found in section 3.4.1) – it dates back to Weizenbaum's *ELIZA* program – the term chatterbot, to be later clipped to chatbot (Arif, 2018), was first used only in the 1990s with reference to a non-human TINYMUD player whose main function was to chat with other human players (Mauldin, 1994)[19]. Regardless of differences in their communication channel and level of advancement, chatbots are defined as conversational interfaces (Joshi, 2018) which emulate human oral and written conversations (Campo, 2022; Frankenfield, 2022; Higgins, 2021) through the medium of an app, a messaging platform, and a social network (*Chatbot*, n.d.). Generally, the more conversational AI-driven technologies underlie their architecture, the richer the experience of HMC (Carter, 2019). The majority of basic chatbots, referred to as 'set guidelines chatbots' (Frankenfield, 2022), combine the rule-based programming with NLU to answer user questions according to the patterns of conversations which have already been pre-established in their database (Carter, 2019). Even though NLU engines help chatbots better understand user language and respond to questions more effectively, only such AI functionalities as machine learning allow them to learn from their interactions with humans to improve future responses (Carter, 2019). Therefore, 'self-learning chatbots', which can identify similar key words,

19 In addition to chatterbot and chatbot, other names that have also been in circulation nowadays are bot, chat robot, talkbot, interactive agent, and artificial conversational entity (*Chatterbot*, 2019; Frankenfield, 2022; Shewan, 2022). Even though it is commonplace to use the above-mentioned concepts interchangeably, some differences do exist among them. For example, bots (short for robots – Cambridge Dictionary, n.d.) are programs designed to perform software-based tasks either automatically or on command. Chatbots are the same technological tools; they, however, are created to automate interactions with human users (Joshi, 2018; Lin, 2021; Ramos, 2018).

know that "How much does this cost?" and "What's the price?" are the same questions and require the same response (Reaburn, 2019). 'Contextual chatbots', on the other hand, are programmed to provide the most accurate responses by using a battery of AI technologies (Carter, 2019). The human input, speech or text, is first recorded and then interpreted within NLP. NLU allows computers to make inferences from the user input (Ahmad, 2021). The meaning obtained by chatbots determines their reaction which, be it a question or a response, is turned into human speech in the process of NLG (Reaburn, 2019).

Due to a number of benefits associated with their application, chatbots have been playing an increasingly important role in (language) learning. Colace et al. (2018) suggested that chatbots can tackle learners' problems resulting from brief and prolonged absence at school and unfavourable learning conditions resulting from overcrowded classrooms. In view of language students' increased levels of self-confidence and self-perceived convenience of use, chatbot infrastructure seems to be both a successful language tutor and a language learning tool. This was evidenced by Haristiani's (2019) study with Japanese learners using *Gengobot*, "a chatbot-based dictionary application about multi-language grammar" (p. 4). The participants listed six advantages to using chatbots, including among others reduction of FL anxiety levels, presentation of multimodal input, provision of quick feedback, and attractiveness of the technology.

TODSs, just as chatbots, are able to converse with their users, but they do it purposefully to support humans in their digital task performance. They underlie the architecture of VAs, which are built into the operating systems of mainstream smartphones and available through downloadable mobile voice apps (to be discussed in a greater detail in section 3.4). HMC via VAs is facilitated by the combination of several AI technologies (Goksel-Canbek & Mutlu, 2016). A wakeword detector continuously listens for the key word or phrase. The command which activates the assistant differs in each VA: it is for example "Hey Siri" for Apple's *Siri*, "Alexa" for Amazon's *Alexa*, and "OK Google" for *Google Assistant*. An alternative way to turn an VA on is through a push-to-talk button. An ASR system transforms the user utterance into text transcription which is then used to identify their intentions through NLU. Depending on the type of command, the dialogue manager chooses the best course of action to follow. In this case it is a response that should be provided to the user which via the text-to-speech solution is communicated by the assistant's synthesised voice (Mutchler, 2019). This allows users to hold real-life conversations with VAs during digital task performance given the latter's ability to understand and carry out voice commands and to produce automatic responses to user queries (Hoy, 2018). Figure 3.4 demonstrates the combination of different types of AI technologies involved in the functioning of any TODSs underlying VAs.

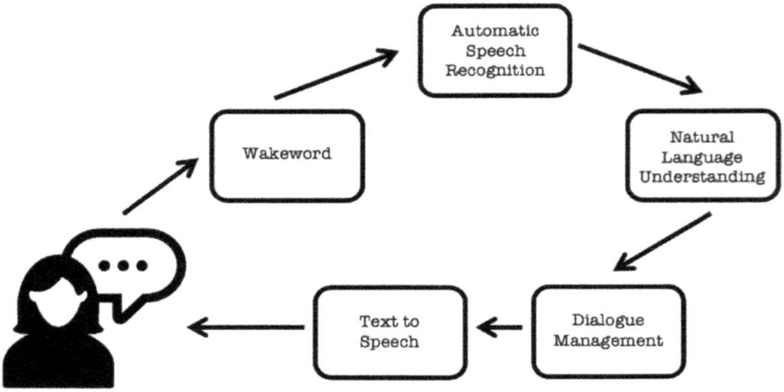

Fig. 3.3: *Model presenting the functioning of VAs during task performance (Mutchler, 2019)*

A noteworthy initiative to promote the use of conversational AI in EFL learning through TODSs was implemented by the French government in the summer of 2019 when the call for proposals for "the conception, creation, and supply of a voice assistant to teach English to elementary school kids" was released by the French Ministry of Education (Hue, 2019, para. 1). The main reason to introduce VAs to EFL French instructed settings was the poor English pronunciation of elementary French teachers. The Ministry of Education issued a list of requirements to be fulfilled by the program, some of which included its compliance with different types of hardware (from smart speakers and smartphones, through tablets, to computers), the ability to work online and offline, and the possibility to use it both on- and off-site (Hue, 2019).

3.3.2 Emergence of IMALL

With AI-driven technologies having acquired the status interlocutors (Guzman & Lewis, 2020), language learners' limited HHC in the TL inside and outside instructed settings may be compensated for by ICALL programs. Once constrained by spatio-temporal limitations, ICALL – similarly to CALL – has been liberated from the confines of traditional classrooms and language labs by smaller and less expensive, but more powerful mobile technologies (Motivalla, 2007). In MALL, the shift from language learning based on Short Message Service to the use of more technologically sophisticated multimedia and intelligent learning systems could be observed around the 2010s (Viberg & Gronlund, 2013).

In their 2010 article *The application of artificial intelligence in mobile learning*, Liu et al. isolated five uses of AI in m-learning programs. The Mobile Intelligent Teaching Expert System simulates the behaviours of specialist instructors by providing the interactivity component and adapting methods to learners' aptitudes. The Mobile Intelligent Decision Support System supports students in decision-making by providing necessary materials to facilitate this process. The Mobile Intelligent Information Retrieval Engine gives users access to relevant data based on their actual needs and past searching behaviours. The Mobile Intelligent Induct-Learning System uses a fact-finding function to analyse mistakes in learning and introduce changes required to make the process more successful in the future. Finally, the Intelligent Hardware Network provides efficient networking facilities with high levels of processing capabilities to support the above-mentioned AI features for mobile devices.

The beginnings of IMALL date back to the ILTSs application in MALL (Taher & Hussein, 2019), with one of the representative examples being found in Stockwell (2007), who conducted a small-scale study among a group of Japanese EFL university students using *VocabTutor*, an intelligent mobile phone-based vocabulary tutor. Due to the technological limitations of the mobile phones, such as small screens and high cost of Internet connection, the subjects preferred performing the vocabulary tasks on the computer rather than with their mobile phones. Notwithstanding this, Stockwell (2007) noted down the affordances offered by his IMALL system, stating that it "had the potential to provide learners with sophisticated vocabulary learning activities through mobile devices that they already possess, as well as to store information about the learners that may be used to assist them with their vocabulary learning" (p. 380).

Another case illustrating the AI application in MALL is *English practice*, the system developed for EFL learners by Pham et al. (2018). It is a chatbot that can be installed on mobile devices to interact with users through a window chat. The program takes on the role of an intelligent personal assistant; it is designed to send learners reminders and assist them with learning vocabulary and performing exercises. As Pham et al. (2018) reported, the majority of the chatbot features was utilised by its users, which according to the authors, augured well in favour of the use of the system in the future.

In addition to tutorial HMC established via FL learning systems, the number of opportunities for non-tutorial interactions with portable devices has been growing (see section 3.5). With the proliferation of VAs in the 2010s, which are built into the mobile operating systems and can be downloaded to learners' personal mobile devices in the form of mobile voice apps, smartphone users have gained unrestricted access to intelligent mobile assistance (Dizon, 2021).

Despite the growing interest in the use of AI-enhanced mobile devices in language education, the IMALL term has been neglected (Taher & Hussein, 2019). Google and Google Scholar searches conducted on August 21, 2023 using the exact phrase "intelligent mobile assisted language learning" to assess the popularity of the concept yielded nine and five hits on Google and Google Scholar search engines respectively, not only proving the novelty of the field, but also suggesting a need to further define it. IMALL investigates the use of AI-powered mobile and wearable devices in language education. To the best of the present author's knowledge, the term was first introduced as late as in 2019 in the article *A review of intelligent mobile assisted language learning (IMALL) system* by Taher and Hussain (2019). In this discussion, it is described as an emerging interdisciplinary subfield of ICALL and MALL. By applying the techniques underlying ICALL software to IMALL programs, it enables learners to engage in tutorial and non-tutorial interactions with their portables. Thanks to the mobility dimension inherent in m-learning, it may expand language learning opportunities to out-of-class contexts. The mobility of the technology, learner, and HMC therefore facilitates anytime-and-anywhere learning. Given the combination of ICALL and MALL principles, IMALL provides learners with a 24/7 access to ILTSs and CAs offering opportunities for unlimited reception and production of language input and output respectively through the medium of students' personal mobile and wearable devices. This mentioned affinity of IMALL with ICALL and MALL is illustrated in Figure 3.5.

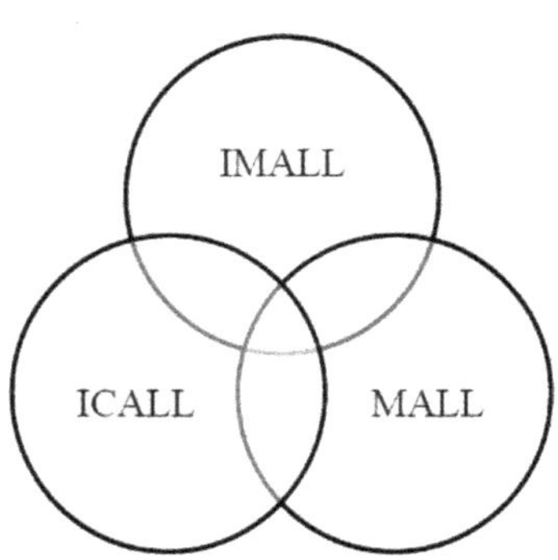

Fig. 3.4: *Relationship between ICALL, MALL, and IMALL (self-prepared)*

For our purposes, we limit the field of IMALL to the use of TODSs underlying the architecture of VAs. Thus, in this discussion, we introduce the term task-oriented IMALL to describe the implementation of mobile technologies that thanks to AI algorithms are capable of rendering voice assistance understood here as the performance of digital tasks requiring human intelligence. Language learning theories fully support the use of VAs in FL learning. According to the Interactionist Theory, interaction with another speaker stimulates language development through the negotiation of meaning, production of modified input, and attention to linguistic form (Long, 1996). As argued by Dizon (2017), VAs are not able yet to adapt their output in such a way so as to improve their interlocutors' comprehension; they can, however, promote negotiation of meaning. HCIs themselves can improve FL abilities: Bibauw et al. (2019) argued that "meaningful practice of a target language, as it occurs in conversation, leads to improve the learner's proficiency in that language, and that, even if a native speaker remains the ideal interlocutor, a computer can provide opportunities for such practice" (p. 829). It can thus be speculated that learners may draw benefits for their L2/FL learning from their dialogic interactions with VAs.

Despite promising perspectives for HMC, IMALL raises several burning questions. The influence of HCI via TODSs on students' development of FL language skills and subsystems, successfulness of a HMC process per se, adaptation of pedagogical principles, teachers' changing roles, and students' attitudes towards AI-driven technologies are just a handful of issues that need to be better understood. Even though several attempts to investigate the use of VAs in language learning have already been made (see section 3.5.1), these and other problems relating to their in IMALL have remained under-researched areas in the field of FL learning in view of the study limitations which will be addressed in section 3.5.2. The presentation of the current state of research into the use of VAs in formal and informal language learning will, however, be preceded by the description of the historical background of the concept of VAs and the introduction of basic information relating to this technology.

3.4 Introduction to task-oriented IMALL

3.4.1 Origins of chatbots and personal digital assistants

The phenomenon of voice assistance earned a wider recognition only a few years ago (Arif, 2018). It may thus come as a surprise that it has its origins in the architecture of traditional and AI-powered chatbots of the 1960s and the concept of personal assistance offered by hand-held PDAs in the 1980s (Goksel-Canbek & Mutlu, 2016; Ismail, 2019; Kukulska-Hulme, 2016).

With its innovative ability to ask questions in a therapeutic manner based on a very simple script (Debecker, 2017), *ELIZA*, the classic example of traditional chatbot architecture, was hailed "the technological predecessor to today's conversational agents" (Guzman & Lewis, 2020, p. 77) and "the mother of all chatbots" (Ismail, 2019, para. 3). *ELIZA* is a keyboard-operational, conversational program, which as the simulation of a psychotherapist developed in 1966 by Joseph Weizenbaum (Kluwer, 2011), was the earliest technology to pass the Turing Test by mimicking human-like behaviours (Lin, 2020). Given the use of key-words and pattern-matching, it could respond to users' typed statements with open-ended questions and simple replies based on decision trees (Debecker, 2017; Higgins, 2021). Practically, this conversational program and similar ones (e.g., *Parry*, or a schizophrenic patient, designed in the 1970s) were unable to respond to more complex questions and handle intelligent interactions with human users (Ahmad, 2021; Campo, 2022).

Developments in AI were viewed as an important driving force behind approximating the principles of HHC to HMC by enhancing the architecture of traditional decision-tree-based chatbots. NLP, information retrieval, and ML systems have opened up a new field of research known as conversational (or communicative) AI (Fernandes, 2017; Guzman & Lewis, 2020). Even though still in its infancy (IBM Cloud Education, 2020), conversational AI enables chatbots to enhance their ability to simulate written and spoken interactions with humans by adding AI functionalities to visual and audio interfaces.

A number of attempts to establish HMC have already been made within conversational AI. The pursuit of AI technologies simulating human conversations began in the late 1980s. The first artificially intelligent chatbot *Jabberwacky* was introduced in 1988 (Lin, 2020). It could engage in meaningful verbal exchanges using a simulated human voice. As opposed to its predecessors, it relied on feedback rather than key-wording to elicit responses. This means that "the more it chatted, the more it learned" (Lin, 2020, para. 5). *Sound blaster artificial intelligent text to speech operator*, also known as *Dr. SBAITS*, which was a simulation of a psychologist created in 1991, employed the Sound Blaster sound card to synthesise speech and simulate verbal communication with its users (Arif, 2018; Zemcik, 2019). It was the first bot to make use of the text-to-speech technology (Lin, 2021). This, according to Zemcik (2019), made the chatbot more human. *Artificial linguistic internet computer entity* known as *ALICE* was the first online chatbot[20]. Created in 1995, *ALICE* displayed NLP and had a heuristic function (Arif, 2018; Kavliwashere, 2018) thanks to which, as argued by Lin (2021), it was

20 It is worth mentioning here as a curiosity that *Alice* provided a source of inspiration for the creation of *Siri*, the first voice-enabled IVA introduced by Apple Inc. in 2011 (Arif, 2018).

able to retain an impressively natural flow of conversation. The program won a Loebner prize, or the annual Turing Test award (Okonkwo & Ade-Ibijola, 2021).

In addition to a purely conversational function, the technologies were soon to acquire a new set of abilities allowing them to assist human users in task and service performance. The beginning of the 21st century represented an important breakthrough in the application of chatbot technologies. The 2001 *SmarterChild* was "the instantaneous fact-finding technology" available on America Online's Instant Messenger (Olsen, 2003, para. 3). Given its ability to support humans in everyday task performance by allowing them access to information systems and tools through chat, it was described as "the forerunner of Siri, Alexa and other virtual assistants" (Kavliwashere, 2018). *SmarterChild* could assist its users in retrieving relevant pieces of information related to weather, prices and sport, and performing tasks, such as translating, to mention just a few of its capacities (Molnar & Zoltan, 2018).

Another development in the chatbot architecture came with the 2006 *Watson* created by International Business Machines Corporation. The technological superiority of the program was established by its ability to satisfactorily answer user questions by retrieving only specific information from a mass of unstructured online and offline data through NLP algorithms (Giacaglia, 2019; Kavliwashere, 2018). Considered a supercomputer, "Watson showed off its encyclopaedic knowledge of topics ranging from ancient languages to fashion design", beating its human champion rivals in the popular United States trivia quiz show *Jeopardy* in 2011 (Gabbatt, 2011, para. 6).

The refinements of the traditional rule-based chatbot architecture have made it possible for computer programs to assist humans in everyday digital task performance at the beginning of the new millennium. Despite this, the first occurrences of digital assistance, whose scope was comparatively narrow due to technological limitations, predate the use of AI-driven technologies. Its origins date back to the 1970s, when the first PDA called *Dynabook* was designed by Alan Kay. Wiggins (2004) described Kay's PDA as "an interactive computer similar to a book with wireless communications abilities and a flat panel display" (p. 6). Even though the device had never been released to the market, it laid the foundations for laptop computers and the future generations of PDAs (Wiggins, 2004). In 1984, Psion Organiser, which combined the functions of a calculator and clock, was the first PDA in the history that was put on market (Viken, 2009) and the "world's first practical pocket computer" (*Psion organiser 1*, n.d., para. 2).

Despite this, the first known use of the term PDA dates back to 1992, when the then chief executive officer and chairman of Apple Inc., John Sculley, coined the phrase to describe the Apple Newton during his presentation at Consumer

Electronics Show in Las Vegas (McCracken, 2012). Other names, such as a handheld PC and personal data assistant, were used to refer to PDAs, too. Palmtops were also used for that purpose. The difference between the two, however, lies in the input device: an integrated keyboard versus a pen-like stylus respectively (Lenox & Woratschek, n.d.). Broadly speaking, a PDA "is a portable device that functions as a personal information manager" (*Personal digital assistant*, 2016). As a matter of fact, the understanding and scope of personal digital assistance have broadened significantly in the wake of the technological revolution in the mobile industry (Beal, 1996). In the traditional sense of the term, a PDA can be defined as "a small handheld device equipped with a microprocessor that is used especially for storing and organizing personal information (such as addresses and schedules)" (Merriam-Webster dictionary, n.d.). The device was used primarily by "businesspeople to track appointments and contact information" in the 1990s and early 2000s (Smith & Wempen, 2011, p. 140).

The earliest PDAs that could be used as address books and to-do lists were considered obsolete (Smith & Wempen, 2011) once their successors had acquired many of smartphone features including among others wireless access to the Internet, Bluetooth connectivity, memory card slots, software apps, and multimedia support (*Personal digital assistant*, 2016). Even though PDAs differ in regard to the input device, RAM memory capacity, battery life, size, price etc., they are now nearly indistinguishable from smartphones in that both can be used for calling, Web browsing, watching videos, viewing photos, and much more. AI-driven developments of the chatbot architecture have considerably increased the humanness of HMC, at the same time extending the technology capabilities from those of conversationalists to those of assistants. At the same time, the concept of personal digital assistance has broadened in scope, with new generations of PDAs far surpassing their ancestry devices in the ways digital information is obtained, stored, organised, accessed, and retrieved by their users. Recently, the term has been further redefined by the technology industry. PDAs are now more commonly used with reference to the software that is able to recognise human voice and respond appropriately by performing different kinds of digital tasks (e.g., Dara, 2019; Enge, 2019; Hoy, 2018).

3.4.2 Fundamentals of VAs

The 2010s marked a milestone in the development of PDAs with the arrival of voice-based AI-powered technologies easily accessible via mainstream smartphones and dedicated appliances. The first VA was Apple's *Siri* (2011) followed by its likes, such as *Google Assistant* (2012), Amazon's *Alexa* (2014), Microsoft's

Cortana (2016), and Huawei's *Celia* (2020). These "software agents using NLP in an integrated system" (Bozkurt & Goksel, 2018, p. 4291) are "cloud-based virtual assistants" (Dizon & Tang, 2020, p. 108, Dizon, 2021, p. 1), or "pieces of digital software that specifically help individuals perform daily tasks" (Carter, 2019, So, What's a Chatbot?).

VAs assist humans in everyday task and service performance in many areas of life (Chamberlain, 2017). They can be requested to control home devices and media, and manage digital tasks based on e-mail, to-do lists, and calendars via voice (Adamopoulou & Moussiades, 2020; Hoy, 2018). Users can also ask their assistants to schedule appointments, make calls, and set alarms (Carter, 2019). The number of tasks that assistants are able to perform is constantly increasing (Petrock, 2019). For instance, Amazon publishes regular updates called "Alexa's Monthly Roundup" on the new features acquired by its VA. The abilities of these technologies may further be developed once users have installed skills, which are the equivalents of mobile apps for smartphones. These skills, according to Gerencer (2019) are "key to making the best use of these assistants." Most popular examples include *Dominos* and *Pizza Hut* for ordering food, *Uber* and *Lyft* for requesting a ride, *Jeopardy* for offering entertainment, and *Kayak* for estimating travel distance (Gerencer, 2019).

There are four frontrunners in the voice assistance industry, Apple's *Siri, Google Assistant*, Amazon's *Alexa*, and Microsoft's *Cortana* (Bushnell, 2021). A number of attempts have been made so far to compare them. Different criteria have been considered in the evaluation of particular assistants, some of which include usefulness (Pyae & Joelsson, 2018), skills and users' experiences (Yang et al., 2019), task performance and privacy problems (Hoy, 2018), accuracy and naturalness of responses (Lopez et al., 2017). Although VAs are being constantly updated and upgraded, it must be stressed here that they are recent technologies which still require further improvements (Bushnell, 2021). Since each of each them has its strengths and weaknesses, the choice of an IVA remains a matter of personal preference.

A plethora of terms have been applied to describe technologies which assist humans in everyday task performance. Such terminological heterogeneity was indicated by Bozkurt and Goksel (2018). Having conducted the analysis of almost 300 research papers published between 1984 and 2017, they proved that "intelligent assistants exist in diverse forms" (p. 4295). As evident in scientific research papers, news articles, business website posts, and blog entries analysed for the purpose of this discussion, the most common names used to refer to the technology in question include:

a. voice assistants (e.g., Aron, 2011; Burbach et al., 2019; Ramos, 2018; Terzopoulos & Satratzemi, 2019);
b. intelligent virtual assistant (e.g., Alexandru, 2020; Beamon, 2021; Gray, 2016; Joshi, 2018; Nobles at al., 2020; Srikanth, 2020; Vainu, 2021);
c. intelligent personal assistants (e.g., Berdasco et al., 2019; Bozkurt & Goksel, 2018; Chamberlain, 2017; Dizon, 2017, 2020; Dizon & Tang, 2020);
d. intelligent assistants (e.g., Kukulska-Hulme, 2019; Kukulska-Hulme & Lee, 2020);
e. digital voice assistants (e.g., Box, 2022; Suarez, 2021);
f. smart personal voice assistants (e.g., Adamopoulou & Moussiades, 2020);
g. virtual assistants (e.g., Srikanth, 2020);
h. voice interaction assistants (e.g., Underwood, 2021);
i. task-oriented dialogue agents (e.g., Jurafsky & Martin, 2021).

A Google search on September 21, 2024 was conducted to assess the popularity of the selected VA-related terms listed above. The results were as follows: intelligent virtual assistant, intelligent personal assistant, and voice assistant yielded 90,600, 272,000, and 12,900,000 hits respectively. It is why for the purpose of this discussion, the VA term will be used interchangeably with IVA and IPA.

There are other popular terms used with reference to technologies that have been developed to offer assistance to humans. Despite apparent similarities, they should not be confounded with IVAs. Some of the examples have been provided below. Smart assistants, such as smart speakers (e.g., Amazon's *Echo*, Google's *Nest*, Apple's *HomePod*), are IVA-powered voice-activated speakers. These "external AI home-assistant devices" are programmed to help individuals with everyday tasks at home by controlling household appliances (Pyne, 2020, para. 16). Their use is limited to one's abodes, which means that they do not give access to virtual assistance on the go. The most popular home areas in which they are kept include the living room, bedroom, and kitchen (Adobe Inc., 2019). Some Internet sources use the term chatbot with reference to *Alexa*, *Siri*, and their likes (Strauss, 2016). As previously stated, chatbots are applied inter alia in business areas to relay product-related information and book meetings. Nevertheless, they are not intelligent enough to provide virtual assistance and, as argued by Joshi (2018), if requested, "they get confused, and ultimately keep asking the same questions for clarification" (para. 4). Given this, chatbots and IVAs should not be treated synonymously (*Wirtualni asystenci AI a chatboty*, 2019). Also, one should be particularly wary of the two-fold nature of the virtual assistant concept. The term can obviously be used to define a non-human figure of an online personal assistant (Srikanth, 2020). However, it is also correct to use it with reference to a human being, that is an "independent contractor who provides administrative services to clients while operating outside of the client's office" (Kenton, 2022, para. 1).

IVAs can now be accessed through a variety of intelligent devices. The vehicles of the assistants include smartphones, tablets, laptops, desktops, smart speakers, smartwatches, cars, and smart home appliances, such as smart TVs, lights, thermostats, alarm systems, and outlets/switches (Accenture, 2017; PWC, 2018; Social Lens Research, 2018). The most popular device used to access the assistant is unquestionably a smartphone (PWC, 2018; Social Lens Research, 2018).

The way in which people prefer to use their smartphones to conduct searches has been subject to change. As demonstrated by the results of the 2019 Voice Usage Survey conducted by Perficient (Enge, 2019), voice search is slowly taking on greater significance. Figure 3.6 shows that mobile browser still remains the most common first choice. However, a major increase in the use of voice control in 2018 could be observed, with voice search remaining the runner up.

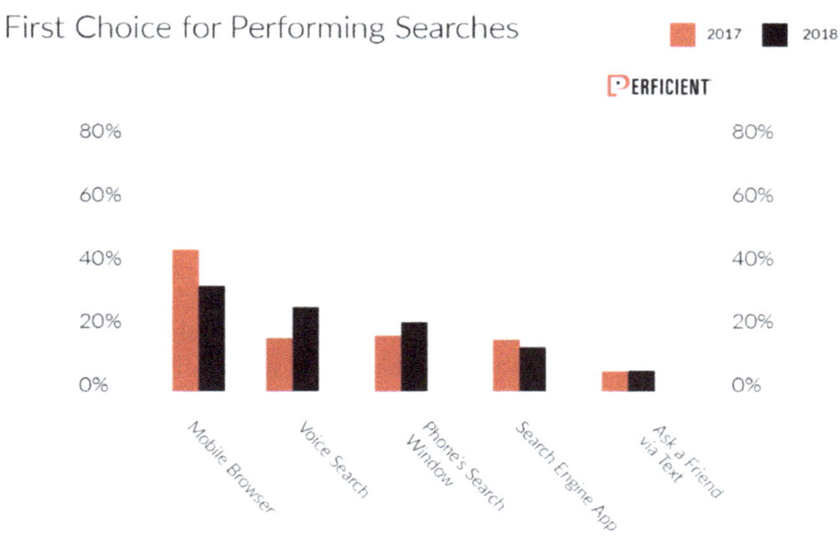

Fig. 3.5: *Participants' first choices for performing searches on smartphones according to the 2019 Perficient Voice Usage Survey (Enge, 2019)*

Even though HMC can take place through different communication channels – text, voice, images, haptics, or gestures (Kluwer, 2011) – voice assistance deserves particular attention, with speech-to-text and text-to-speech conversion systems, in contrast to computers with keyboards and mouses or smartphones with touch-screens, increasing the naturalness of the process (Adobe Digital Insights, 2019; Mutchler, 2019). Since IVAs are programmed to understand voice commands (Adamopoulu & Moussiades, 2020) and "vocally respond to human questions and requests" (Guzman & Lewis, 2020, p. 72), they justly deserve to be hailed "the realization of the science fiction dream of interacting with our computers by talking to them" (Hoy, 2018, p. 82).

Interestingly, the beginnings of voice-controlled technologies date back to the 1950s, which was when Bell Labs developed *Audrey*, the first speech recognition system able to discern between spoken digits, from zero to nine (Martynenko, 2019; Moskvitch, 2017). In 1962, the International Business Machines Corporation presented *Shoebox*, a mathematical tool which could recognise sixteen spoken words in addition to doing mathematical calculations (*Science: Shoebox is listening*, 1961). Carnegie Mellon's *Harpy*, created a decade later in cooperation with the United States' Defense Advanced Research Projects Agency, was able to identify 1,000 words and, unlike its predecessors, even entire sentences (Moskvitch, 2017). With time, voice-control technologies became more efficient, coming into practical use in toys (e.g., Worlds of Wonder's *Julie Interactive Talking Doll*), computers (e.g., Apple's *PlainTalk*), and healthcare industries (e.g., Dragon's *NaturallySpeaking*) in the 1980s and 1990s (Ramos, 2018). They underwent a revival of interest in the 2010s when, as already mentioned, VAs entered into the mainstream mobile industry.

Several survey studies have been conducted to date to examine the scale of voice assistance. According to Capgemini Research Institute (2019), HMC via TODSs is a very recent phenomenon as 83% of those using VAs started doing so between 2016 and 2018. The findings of the report published by PricewaterhouseCoopers (PWC, 2018) indicated that 90% of the population was aware of the existence of IPAs. The findings from the 2019 Digital Consumer Survey (Accenture, 2019) revealed that voice interface became a global trend, with 50% of online customers globally using IVAs.

Selected research studies also tried to understand the usage of VAs. The prime motives behind the technology uptake listed by Adobe Digital Insights (2019) included convenience, accessibility, enjoyment, possibility to automate time-consuming activities through voice, and inclusiveness for people with visual impairments. The most common applications of VAs ranged from communication, through home and media control, to transactions (Gillett, 2020). The top ten uses of IPAs enumerated by Gerencer (2019) included playing music, keeping a shopping list, creating a smart home and office, running a TV set, managing timers, entertaining kids, using assistants' skills to simplify everyday task performance, driving hands-free, getting news, weather, and traffic reports, and having fun. Even though communication with VAs is usually limited to transactional interactions only, the findings of the survey focusing on user behaviours with smart speakers (Nielsen, 2018) indicated that 68% of the respondents conversed with their assistants for fun. Such data displayed a clear tendency on the part of IVA users towards establishing social interactions with their virtual assistants in addition to handling transactions.

VAs have been used in a variety of settings. The top five places listed in the descending order of popularity include the home, car, outdoors, work, and the store (Social Lens Research, 2018). Even though the device can be accessed anywhere, almost three out of every four consumers (74%) used their assistants at home (PWC, 2018). The respondents explained that they preferred keeping their conversation with an IVA private and, in their opinion, speaking to the assistant in public "just looks weird" (p. 3). The results of the 2019 Digital Consumer Survey (Accenture, 2019), however, displayed a contradictory tendency. IVAs moved beyond home surroundings to cars where, in addition to strictly home-related tasks, such as searching for information, setting timers/alarms, browsing news, and checking e-mail, they were used for voice calling, text messaging, getting directions, checking the traffic, and playing music.

Conversations with IPAs are far from unproblematic. As argued by Kukulska-Hulme (2019), they could be compared to those held with a very bad human personal assistant. One of the major obstacles to successful HMC via an IVA is posed by communication breakdowns. VAs have comprehension difficulties when they hear background noises and non-standard language input resulting from speakers' use of dialect, accent, slang, and language that is considered unscripted for the technology. Another problem is the human factor. IPAs lack true human conversational skills because they are not able to use facial expressions to improve communication (Adobe Digital Insights, 2019). Emotions, sarcasm, and other conversational undertones referred to by Fernandes (2017) as empathy understanding, make it impossible for the device to interpret intended user meanings and to respond appropriately.

As the interest towards exploiting the potential of AI increases, some concerns around security and privacy breaches saw the daylight too (Terzopoulos & Satratzemi, 2020). IVAs record users' conversations and other pieces of personal information (e.g., location) via smartphones to improve services and future responses. As with any other computer program, they are vulnerable to technical failures and hacking which puts users' privacy at stake. Several controversial incidents involving the unauthorised use of IVAs were reported in the media. For example, 1,700 *Alexa* audio files which contained sensitive information (e.g., names, habits, jobs) belonging to a VA user were accidentally sent to a German man (Dara, 2019) while approximately 1,000 Dutch *Google Assistant* users were secretly recorded by their VA (Strzałkowski, 2019).

Another caveat surrounds the alleged (physical) threats that HMC via VAs might pose to their users, especially those under-aged. In a *New York Post* article, David Cost (2021) wrote about "a potentially deadly TikTok challenge" recommended to a ten-year old by Amazon's smart speaker in December 2021 (para. 2). In her viral tweet, the child's mother explained how *Alexa Echo* issued the penny challenge, or "a viral stunt from several years back with the potential to create sparks, damage electrical outlets and even start fires" (Cost, 2021, para. 5). In response to the girl's query of "Tell me a challenge to do," the device responded, "Here's something I found on the web. According to ourcommunitynow.com: The challenge is simple: plug in a phone charger about halfway into a wall outlet, then touch a penny to the exposed prongs" (Segal, 2021, para. 5). Fortunately, the parent intervened on time to save her child from disaster.

Since *Alexa* retrieves information from the Web to respond to users' questions, it seems understandable why it may make such a mistake. Nevertheless, what is alarming is "human oversight in these systems – especially when they are aimed towards children" (Wise, 2021, para. 10). In a statement for the British Broadcasting Corporation, the Amazon spokesman confirmed that changes preventing *Alexa* from suggesting similar activities had been made to ensure the assistant provides "accurate, relevant, and helpful information to customers" (BBC, 2021).

In addition, several other factors might be held responsible for slowing down the voice technology adoption (Accenture, 2019; Childnet, 2018; PWC, 2018; Social Lens Research, 2018). They result from technological limitations of IVAs including, as argued by their users, low reliability of information and slow processing time. Also, the public's limited knowledge of IVAs capabilities, lack of trust to voice control, and hesitation due to its complexity and/or price may stifle the idea of intelligent virtual assistance.

In view of rapidly evolving voice technology capabilities and new voice-controlled product lines being launched regularly, the account of the scale and scope of voice assistance we have attempted to provide above may not be entirely accurate. In addition to the fact that some of the data on the IVA usage might already be outdated, the majority of the survey reports cited in this discussion were limited to consumers from the United States. Even though Internet users from some geographical regions and age groups are more inclined to adopt voice technologies than others, there is no doubt that at the moment of preparing the current publication intelligent virtual assistance is still in its infancy.

What is, however, hardly disputable is that voice-assisted technologies are steadily gaining popularity. Software developers more and more often decide to feature voice-assisted technologies in a variety of devices: cars, wearables, TV sets, and other connected gadgets (Petrock, 2019). Tom Dorf, the Vice President of MocoSpace, speculates that "voice commands are on the cusp of being a primary way to interact with all electronics/appliances, search the internet and conduct e/m-commerce" (Social Lens Research, 2018, p. 16). A good example reflecting the pro-AI trend is Estonia, the number one digital country in the 2018 Digital Life Abroad report (InterNations, 2018). According to Grzegorczyk (2021), the Estonian government is planning to launch "the world's first public service AI-based virtual assistant" called *Bürokratt* in 2022 (para. 3). Since the technology applies the systems underlying communicative AI to perform tasks and render services, it removes the necessity for citizens to call government agencies and visit the facilities in-person. Thanks to *Bürokratt*, Estonians will be able to arrange payments, make application submissions, and introduce personal data updates through the voice assistant (Schwartz, 2021).

With an increasing number of tasks that voice assistants are capable of performing, the idea of intelligent virtual assistance per se is most likely to be taken for granted in the foreseeable future (Arif, 2018). It is expected that over time the number of IVA users is likely to grow (Reaburn, 2019) and so is the number of VAs, which, according to Laricchia (2022), is going to double from 4.2 to 8.4 billion between 2019 and 2024.

3.5 Pedagogical use of VAs in ESL/EFL learning

3.5.1 Overview of research studies

Alongside the exponential growth of VAs, an apparent increase in the research interest in the use of the technology in in-class and out-of-class L2/FL learning environments has been observed over the last few years. Several studies have already examined the voice assistance phenomenon among different age groups, from children, through adolescents, to young adults in formal and informal ESL/EFL learning contexts. The following four research trends could be identified in the research investigating the use of mainstream VAs:

a. assessing the feasibility of VAs in formal and informal language learning, as reported by the study participants;
b. evaluating the reliability of HMC with regard to the VA's ability to comprehend ESL/EFL accented speech of the study participants;
c. investigating HCIs in terms of the strategies adopted by the study participants in the face of HMC breakdowns, or the situations when a user's command is not understood by the VA;
d. examining the effects of experimental interventions involving VAs on different aspects related to language learning, namely speaking, listening, motivation, willingness to communicate (WTC), and FL anxiety.

Much of the research on the VA use in L2/FL education has been conducted to explore the subjects' opinions on the application of the technology in language learning. In their study conducted in Canada, Moussalli and Cardoso (2016) investigated four ESL students' views on *Alexa*, reporting that according to the learners, using *Alexa* was not only easy and fun, but also beneficial for their L2 development. However, one important challenge mentioned by the four subjects was the appearance of communication breakdowns, which had been caused by *Alexa*'s failure to understand their commands. The findings of Dizon's (2017) study conducted among four Japanese students were similar to those of Moussali and Cardoso (2016). The EFL learners positively evaluated *Alexa*, stating that the IPA offered opportunities for speaking practice and provided implicit feedback on pronunciation. In his follow-up ten-week, quasi-experimental study focusing on the in-class use of *Alexa* for speaking and listening practice, Dizon (2020) reported that twenty-eight subjects considered the VA a valuable language learning tool. The use of these voice-assisted technologies was also warmly welcomed by eleven primary-age EFL learners in a nine-month study conducted in Spain by Underwood (2017). By adopting the 'in the wild' design approach, the teacher attempted "to stimulate children and teachers to think about current and future opportunities for using AI in natural classroom settings" (p. 318). According to Underwood (2017), the participants of his study were excited by any case of the AI implementation. They also remained highly motivated to engage in interactive TL speaking by asking *Alexa*, *Siri*, and *Google Assistant* questions (e.g., *How do you spell (…)?, What does (…) mean?, How do you say (…) in English?*) and giving commands (e.g., *Play some music!*). Even though neither did the IVAs work properly when students spoke simultaneously nor were the technologies able to answer all learners' questions, the children found the experiences of talking to the voice recognition systems very enjoyable on the whole. The findings of the study conducted by Chen et al. (2020) with twenty-nine Taiwanese university students indicated that the major problem addressed by the subjects was the appearance of communication breakdowns caused by their pronunciation errors. Tai and Chen's (2020) study conducted with 112 Taiwanese junior high school students demonstrated that the subjects took a very positive attitude towards *Google Assistant*. The learners stressed the fact that the mentioned VA made their language learning more pleasurable and increased the authenticity of their communication in the TL. Lastly, Dizon and Tang (2019, 2020) explored the use of *Alexa* for autonomous EFL learning among Japanese university students. In so far as learners in their studies reported that the IPA was enjoyable to use, issues with its speech comprehensibility were again raised by some of the participants. In sum, the results of the selected IVA research demonstrated that on the one hand the students very positively evaluated the technology; yet, on the other, they reported a problem resulting from the fact that IPAs had often struggled to understand their speech.

The data obtained from the quantitative studies investigating the reliability of VAs in understanding L2/FL accented speech seemed to support the claim that the technology is not able to consistently comprehend the subjects' utterances. For instance, the study undertaken by Daniels and Iwago (2017), which was designed to compare the accuracy of *Google Assistant* and *Siri* in transcribing the utterances of 41 Japanese ESL learners, revealed different findings: it was reported that *Google Assistant* was able to successfully transcribe on average only 82% of the input, whereas the mean accuracy rate of *Siri* was considerably lower, 66%. In a similar vein, in his study conducted with Japanese EFL learners, Dizon (2017) revealed that *Alexa* could fully understand as little as 50% of the learners' oral requests. Nevertheless, the findings from Moussalli and Cardoso's (2019) study conflicted with the above-mentioned results since according to the scholars, *Alexa* could understand the ESL learners 83% of the time. Despite a comparatively high accuracy score, the results indicated that the VA did seriously fall behind the human raters who, in contrast to the assistant, were able to comprehend 95% of the ESL learners' utterances. Interestingly, Chen et al. (2020) observed a correlation between the Taiwanese EFL participants' proficiency level and the VA's comprehensibility score. The scholars reported that the advanced L2 subjects in their study were understood far more frequently than those at low and intermediate levels of language competence. An important addition to the current discussion are the findings obtained by Moussalli and Cardoso (2017), who listed most common causes underlying HMC breakdowns. The reasons behind frequent misunderstandings between a human user and an IVA included the former's highly varied speech rate (from fast to slow), segmental errors in pronunciation (e.g., *How many cups in a liter* ([lajtər])?), hesitations (e.g., *um... could you... help me with pronouncing b.i.t...s?*), incorrect sentence structures (e.g., *From Montreal and Quebec, what is the distance between?*), atypical demands (e.g., *Can you shout for me?!*), phrases not requiring a response (e.g., *Wow, that's great!*), and complex questions (e.g., *I'm thinking what to have for lunch; suggest something which is Mexican cuisine*) (Moussalli & Cardoso, 2017, p. 220). Little consistency in the study findings with reference to the reliability of the selected VAs in understanding accented commands of ESL/EFL learners could be observed.

Several empirical studies have been also designed to investigate the process of HMC via mainstream VAs in the context of the strategies that the subjects implemented to handle HMC breakdowns. Based on the speech samples of 11 ESL participants, Moussalli and Cardoso (2019) found that the repetition (43%), paraphrase (32%), and abandonment (23%) were three most frequent reactions to breakdowns produced by the learners. Chen et al. (2020) reported similar results; namely, in a group of 29 Taiwanese students who communicated with *Google Assistant*, repetition and rephrasing were the most common responses to communication breakdowns. Dizon and Tang's (2020) study also focused on exploring the subjects' linguistic behaviours when faced with HMC breakdowns. It, however, demonstrated conflicting findings: the group of 14 Japanese university students most frequently abandoned their attempts to communicate with *Alexa* (63%), whereas the use of the strategies involving paraphrase (20%) and repetition (17%) was comparatively rare. The striking difference in the results of the mentioned studies might arise from the disparate data collection procedures. In Moussalli and Cardoso (2019) and Chen et al. (2020) the data were gathered during a single session while in Dizon and Tang (2020) the procedure covered a span of two-months. Further, in Moussalli and Cardoso (2019) and Chen et al. (2020) the subjects were video-recorded, whereas in Dizon and Tang (2020) they communicated with the VA in their own homes.

Relatively little research has been undertaken to examine the effects of VA-based experimental interventions on the participants' development of language skills and attitudes towards language learning. One of very few exceptions is Dizon's (2020) study investigating the influence of the *Alexa* use on Japanese EFL students' listening and speaking development. In this study, 13 learners in the experimental group underwent a ten-week intervention involving weekly VA-student interactions. The results of the pre- and post-tests demonstrated that even though *Alexa* did not promote L2 listening development, it significantly improved learners' speaking skills. The findings presented by Tai and Chen (2022) contradict those published by Dizon (2020). In their ten-week, quasi-experimental study, the Taiwanese researchers investigated the effect of two VAs, *Google Nest Hub* using multimodal responses and *Google Nest Mini* using only audio responses, on adolescent EFL learners' listening comprehension. The results demonstrate that *Google Assistant*, especially *Google Nest Hub*, facilitated the participants' listening comprehension development thanks to the presentation of multimodal responses and interactive listening. In another study, Tai and Chen (2020) evaluated the influence of the VA-student communication on the participants' WTC. In their two-week study conducted with a group of 112 Taiwanese junior high school students, the participants from the experimental group performed activities through interactions with *Google Assistant*. The findings based on the results of the pre- and post-study questionnaires revealed that the communication with the VA did have a positive effect on learners' WTC. Namely, the students from the experimental group reported lower levels of anxiety and higher levels of confidence in the TL as opposed to the controls involved in the conventional EFL speaking classroom practice. Similarly, the findings of the study undertaken by Chen et al. (2020) among 29 Taiwanese university students who communicated with *Google Assistant* indicated the learners' increased level of motivation and reduced level of FL anxiety. The preliminary studies referred to above showed that the VAs had considerable potential to improve students' TL speaking and listening and to enhance their WTC by lowering FL anxiety and increasing motivation.

For convenience, Table 3.2 has been compiled to supply essential details on the mentioned studies investigating the use of VAs for ESL/EFL learning. The information relating to the country in which the study was conducted, the VA used by the learners, the objectives formulated in the research, the number of the subjects participating in the study, the duration of the study, and the instruments of data collection has been provided below.

Tab. 3.2: *Overview of the selected research into the VA use in in-class and out-of-class ESL/EFL learning (self-prepared)*

Study	**Country**	**VA**	**Research objectives**	**Subjects**	**Duration**	**Data collection instruments**
Moussalli & Cardoso (2016)	Canada	*Echo*	1. to investigate the learners' perceptions of the use of the IVA	n=4	a thirty-minute session	- background questionnaires - surveys - participants' interviews
Daniels & Iwago (2017)	Japan	*Siri* *Google Assistant*	1. to find out which voice recognition system is more successful at transcribing the subjects' EFL speech 2. to examine which tool can be used more effectively in EFL speaking practice	n=41	no information	- transcriptions taken from the speech recognition systems
Dizon (2017)	Japan	*Alexa*	1. to assess the IVA's ability to understand EFL utterances 2. to examine the students' opinions on the IVA	n=4	a twenty-minute session	- learner-generated command performance - interactive storytelling performance - interviews
Moussalli & Cardoso (2017)	Canada	*Echo*	1. to find out how much accented speech of the ESL learners the IVA can understand 2. to compare the IVA's and the human raters' ability to understand ESL speech 3. to examine the strategies the ESL learners use when their communication with the IVA fails	n=11	a thirty-minute session	- background questionnaires - surveys - judges' ratings and transcriptions of the participants' speech

Underwood (2017)	Spain	*Alexa* *Siri* *Google Assistant*	1. to find out if the IVA can provide the children with satisfactory answers to their questions 2. to suggest the ways in which the IVA can be used to encourage the children to speak in the TL	n=11	nine months	- co-design activities, such as developing playdoh models, designing posters, preparing short presentations
Dizon & Tang (2019)	Japan	*Alexa*	1. to assess the extent to which the EFL learners use the VA in autonomous language learning 2. to find out how the learners use the VA 3. to examine the learners' views on the use of the IVA in autonomous language learning	n=2	four weeks	- surveys - learner usage data available on the *Alexa* website
Chen et al. (2020)	Taiwan	*Google Assistant*	1. to investigate how the EFL learners at different proficiency levels perceive the use of the IVA	n=29	a sixty-minute session	- surveys - interviews
Dizon (2020)	Japan	*Alexa*	1. to examine the impact of the VA-student interaction on the subjects' listening comprehension and speaking proficiency 2. to investigate the EFL students' views on the use of the VA in in-class language learning activities	n=28	ten weeks	- pre and post-listening assessment tests - speaking proficiency tests - surveys

(Continued)

Tab. 3.2: Continued

Study	Country	VA	Research objectives	Subjects	Duration	Data collection instruments
Dizon & Tang (2020)	Japan	*Alexa*	1. to assess the students' views on the use of the IVA in autonomous language learning 2. to investigate the students' usage habits concerning the VA in autonomous language learning 3. to find out what strategies the students use to resolve breakdowns in communication with the VA	n=14	two months	- surveys - learner usage data available on the *Alexa* website
Moussalli & Cardoso (2019)	Canada	*Alexa*	1. to find out if the IVA can understand accented speech of the EFL learners 2. to find out if the EFL learners can understand the speech of the IVA 3. to compare the IVA and the native-speaker raters in their ability to understand accented speech 4. to find out what strategies the learners use to solve the communication breakdowns with *Alexa*	n=11	a single session spanning from thirty to forty-five minutes	- background questionnaires - surveys - participants' ratings and transcriptions of the IPA's speech - interviews - judges' ratings and transcriptions of the participants' speech

Tai & Chen (2020)	Taiwan	*Google Assistant*	1. to investigate the potential of the VA in developing the adolescent EFL learners' WTC 2. to investigate their perceptions of the VA for EFL learning	n=112	two weeks	- pre and post-study questionnaires - interviews
Tai & Chen (2022)	Taiwan	*Google Assistant (Google Nest Hub, Google Nest Mini)*	1. to assess the effect of the VA on the participants' listening comprehension 2. to evaluate the subjects' views on the use of the IVA in in-class language learning activities	n=92	ten weeks	- English listening tests - questionnaire - interviews

The preliminary VA research generally yielded promising results. The participants evaluated the technologies as enjoyable, motivating, effective, helpful, and easy to use in different contexts of language learning, ranging from single-session use (Dizon, 2017; Moussalli & Cardoso, 2016, 2017, 2019), through in-class learning (Chen et al., 2020; Dizon, 2020; Tai & Chen, 2020, 2022; Underwood, 2017), to autonomous off-site learning (Dizon & Tang, 2019, 2020). In addition to the fact that *Alexa, Google Assistant*, and their likes were well-received by the students, the mentioned VAs have had a positive impact on language- (Dizon, 2020; Tai & Chen, 2022) and psychology-related (Chen et al., 2020; Tai & Chen, 2020) aspects to language learning.

Several benefits accruing from the use of the very technology in formal and informal language learning were of special importance to language learners and teachers. HMC was first and foremost considered a valuable addition to traditional L2/FL learning and teaching as it increases the quantity and quality (i.e., multimodality) of the language input that learners receive (Moussalli & Cardoso, 2019) and promotes learner autonomy by providing extra opportunities for non-stop communication support outside language classrooms and in personalised, stress-free, meaningful, and fun environments (Kukulska-Hulme, 2019; Kukulska-Hulme & Lee, 2020; Underwood, 2021). Further, since the VAs enable students to practice language on their own, the introduction of the technology saves classroom time for practicing those forms of language input that the machine is not able to understand and generate (Kukulska-Hulme & Lee, 2020). Lastly, communication with IVAs was said to be less stressful, whereas HMC breakdowns encouraged learners to pay greater attention to accuracy and self-correction (Underwood, 2021)

Despite this, some problems underlying HCIs via VAs were foregrounded. For example, Kukulska-Hulme (2019) expressed ethical concerns over the introduction of IVAs, stressing the fact that humans may use the technology to deceive other human users. Kukulska-Hulme and Lee (2020) argued that the problems of task design and types of guidance required from teachers represent other challenges with the introduction of IPAs to language learning. Underwood (2021) addressed issues relating to data protection of VA's users and untrustworthiness of information provided by the technology. Most importantly, however, some of the findings raised doubts about the reliability of VAs in understanding L2/FL accented speech (Daniels & Iwago, 2017; Dizon, 2017; Moussalli & Cardoso, 2016, 2017; Underwood, 2017), with their to comprehend L2/FL accented utterances precluding the use of the technology by heavily accented learners. More investigation, however, is required in this respect as other studies (Moussalli & Cardoso, 2019) demonstrated that VAs are able to comprehend over 80% of learner output.

The findings of the twelve studies into the use of IVAs in formal and informal L2/FL learning environments referred to above suggested that the technology did have a positive linguistic and affective impact on language learners. Although the empirical studies demonstrated the effectiveness of VA-mediated activities, more research focusing on exploring the potential of voice assistance in language education is vital to clarify some of the unresolved issues.

3.5.2 Study limitations

Having overviewed the empirical studies into voice assistance, we have been able to identify at least four sources of methodological limitations pertaining to the sample size, (treatment/research) duration, data collection instruments, and data collection procedures. The above-mentioned research findings can therefore be called into question.

One of the problems concerns the sample. As evident above, small-scale studies dominated, with most of them involving low numbers of participants, for instance, eleven (Moussali & Cardoso, 2017, 2020; Underwood, 2017), four (Dizon, 2017; Mousalli & Cardoso, 2016), and two (Dizon & Tang, 2019).

Another problem is related to the short study duration. As far as the studies investigating the reliability of HMC are concerned (Moussalli & Cardoso, 2016, 2017, 2019), the data were collected from single sessions only. Studies examining the effects of VA-based experimental interventions, however, were not better designed in this regard, with Dizon and Tang (2019) and Tai and Chen (2020) undertaking research that lasted only four and two weeks respectively.

The next problem is connected with the data collection instruments. In some of the studies, the principle of triangulation of sources and methods was not applied. To give an example, Dizon based his findings on the participants' self-report, with the interview (Dizon, 2017) and survey (Dizon, 2020) being the only source of the data on the students' opinions on *Alexa*. Similarly, Tai and Chen (2020, 2022) took into consideration the analyses of the learners' interviews only. A valuable addition to these studies would be:

a. the triangulation of sources based on the examination of the learners' usage logs containing information on the frequency of VA-student interactions and details relating to the communication process accessible through the dedicated websites;
b. the triangulation of methods involving the administration of both quantitative and qualitative methods of data collection through survey questionnaires and interviews either to corroborate or repudiate the findings.

The last problem to be addressed here is connected to data collection procedures. As already said, the study by Moussalli and Cardoso (2019) looked at the communication strategies that ESL learners used when faced with HMC breakdowns. The data were, however, collected in a non-naturalistic environment where the subjects were observed and video-recorded. The phenomenon known as the Hawthorne effect, or "the behaviour-modifying effects of being the subject of social investigation, regardless of the context of the investigation" (Wickstrom & Bendix, 2000, p. 363), might have influenced the participants' behaviours and their choices of communication strategies. More naturalistic research is therefore required to obtain a better insight into how not only ESL, but also EFL IVA users resolve communication breakdowns in real-life settings.

Even though several studies have already been conducted to examine the use of IPAs in L2/FL learning, some areas are still under-studied in the literature on the topic. Controversial issues which do require further investigation in view of the inconsistent study results include the reliability and accuracy of VAs in understanding the accented speech of ESL/EFL learners and the impact of VA-mediated activities on the ESL/EFL students' listening comprehension ability. The effects of VA-based experimental interventions on the development of the remaining language skills and subsystems are not clear either, this certainly deserving urgent attention from the researchers as well. Also, more research needs to be conducted in naturalistic settings to investigate informal out-of-class uses of VAs so as to examine the potential of the very technology to increase learner autonomy. To date, only one small-scale pilot study (Dizon & Tang, 2019) and the follow-up study (Dizon & Tang, 2020) have been conducted in this context in Japan.

In view of the variable quality of the methodology underlying the reported studies, conflicting research findings, and gaps in the VA-oriented research, there appears a need for designing and undertaking more longitudinal empirical studies that would not only involve more numerous groups, but would also triangulate the sources and methods of data collection to further explore voice assistance and evaluate its long-term effects on L2/FL learning-related aspects.

Chapter 4
VAs in action-oriented mediation practice in a Polish EFL secondary school context: Research methodology

4.0 Outline

Chapter Four provides crucial information on the methodology underlying the current research study conducted with the aim of investigating the use of VAs in Polish EFL teenage learners' action-oriented mediation-based self-instruction. The chapter has been divided into six sections. The first one offers an explanation of the research problem. Research questions and research design are then defined, followed by the presentation of the population and sample of the present study. Next, the six-stage procedure involving the needs analysis, target task selection, instructional treatment design, pilot testing, study proper, and programme evaluation is presented. The data collection plans and analysis methods are also discussed in the context of the selected stages of the research procedure. The chapter ends with a section on ethical considerations outlining the fundamentals of learners' protection within research involving human participation.

4.1 Research problem

The introduction of increased requirements within the 2018 FL Core Curriculum to four-year secondary schools in September 2019 coincided later that school year with the outbreak of the COVID-19 pandemic and the implementation of remote learning techniques in March 2020. As a direct consequence of the public health preventive measures, the several-month long period of distance education led to an unprecedented situation in Polish instructed settings in which education was moved away from the physical confines of traditional schooling to the digital realm of online learning. This presented learners and teachers with constantly new challenges in their virtual classroom environments. The dubious educational value of e-learning in Polish primary and secondary schools was vividly commented upon amid the coronavirus outbreak, with limited student-student and teacher-student interaction and inadequate exposure to instruction in an EFL context being just some of problems demonstrated by the results of research studies (see section 2.5.2).

In response to the expectations of Polish FL learners whose preparation for classes and exams was seriously hampered by the pandemic, the requirements for the eighth-grader exam and New Matura (further referred to in this discussion as Matura) were lowered from school years 2019/20 to 2021/22 from A2+/B1 to A2/A2+ and B1/B1+ to A2+/B1 respectively. The decision was also reached to cancel the oral FL examination taken by secondary school graduates in 2019/20, 2020/21, 2021/22, and 2022/23 school years (see section 2.5.2).

Even though some attempts were made by the Polish government to mitigate the negative effects of the COVID-19 pandemic on students' performance during their FL exit examinations, no attention was paid to four-year secondary school students almost throughout the duration of the current research study carried out in the 2021/22 school year[21]. Despite being equally as affected by the coronavirus crisis and national school closures as their eighth-year primary and three-year secondary school peers, they would be faced with a more difficult version of the written Matura exam. Not only the expected level of the linguistic attainment (A2+/B1 versus B1+/B2), but also the types of examination questions, as suggested by the official document prepared by the Central Examination Board, or the Matura syllabus, would be subject to change from the 2022/23 school year onwards (see Table 2.13).

It transpired that mediation, defined here as any situation in which "the user/learner acts as a social agent who creates bridges and helps to construct or convey meaning, sometimes within the same language, sometimes across modalities (e.g., from spoken to signed or vice versa, in cross-modal communication) and sometimes from one language to another (cross-linguistic mediation)" (CoE, 2020, p. 90), assumes greater importance in the written 2023 Matura. As compared with its 2015 version, text mediation would be included in each of its four sections: Listening, Reading, Use of English, and Writing. It was more than certain then that this communicative language activity should require special attention from both learners and teachers not only in view of the increasingly plurilingual and

---

21 In the first half of February 2022 when the participants entered Phase Two of the current quasi-experiment with the factor rotation technique (Week 12 out of 18; for the schedule, see section 4.5.5), the Polish Ministry of Education published a list of 2023 and 2024 Matura examination requirements (gov.pl). As far as the basic level of the FL exam is concerned, the decision was reached that firstly, the level of language proficiency to be tested therein would be lowered from B1+/B2 to B1/B1+, and secondly, that the exam would be based on the guidelines contained in the Matura syllabus rather than the national Core Curriculum for FLs.

pluricultural communities in Europe, but also the high-stake character of Matura in Poland.

The 2017 structural, curricular, and examination reform together with the COVID-19 pandemic took their toll on grade two and three students of four-year secondary schools. What added to greater uncertainty to Polish EFL instructed settings, putting the learners at an obvious educational disadvantage, was the publication of the examination guidelines only in March 2021, slightly more than two years prior to the administration of the 2023 Matura. Further, given an unpredictable character of the coronavirus crisis, it was impossible to foresee to what extent and for how long traditional schooling would be practicable in the forthcoming months.

There was no doubt that additional practice that could take place irrespectively of the circumstances, whether on-site or at a distance, was not only justified in light of the new curricular and examination requirements, but also more than welcome by learners who, in spite of everything, had to pass their obligatory written language exit exam to enter into tertiary education. Considering the unfavourable situation in which Polish FL teenage learners were placed (specifically grade two and three secondary school students), we planned the intervention which consisted of action-oriented text mediation practice. Task-oriented IMALL (i.e., voice assistance), self-instruction, and AOA underlay the experimental intervention to apply the principle of learner-centredness. Norris' (2009) six-step framework for developing a TBLT programme was adapted by the present author to develop, introduce, and evaluate the technology-mediated EFL text mediation practice.

In the age of conversational AI when the assistance offered by software agents widely available on mobile and portable devices had facilitated everyday task performance, it was more than justified to investigate the effects of VAs on the process of language learning to fill in the gap in CALL research (see section 3.5). To the present author's best knowledge, no empirical study had been conducted with an intention of investigating the effects of VAs, understood here as the product innovation, and the voice assistance in out-of-class task performance, that is the process innovation, on FL learners' text mediation. No such intervention was provided in Polish instructed settings with a view to preparing secondary school students for the performance of text-mediating activities within the new version of the written Matura exam, and no commercial mediation activities were prepared at that time in line with the March 2021 examination guidelines. Both of these factors further added to the novelty value of the study.

4.2 Research questions

The uncertain future of on-site learning, complicated by the volatile coronavirus pandemic, called for urgent measures to create opportunities for out-of-class EFL learning. Cognizant of the pressing need for supporting Polish secondary school students in their preparation for the Matura exam in the wake of the COVID-19 health crisis (see section 2.5.2) and filling in the research gap by investigating the use of VAs for EFL learning (see section 3.5), we aimed to explore the potential of Amazon's *Alexa* in the Polish students' mediation-oriented self-instruction. VAs, referred to as automatic speech recognition systems by Dizon and Tang (2020) (for other definitions, see section 3.4.2), were said to provide learners who have limited opportunities to interact with FL speakers with a chance of meaningful HMC. A set of *Alexa*-based homework assignments was therefore designed by the present author within technology-facilitated oral homework (TFOH) (Shanks, 2021) to provide additional opportunities for extra EFL practice in low-stake self-regulated out-of-class learning.

In view of the above, we attempted to find out if supporting regular classroom instruction with VA-based and action-oriented self-instruction (i.e., the independent variable) had an effect on Polish teenage learners of EFL with regard to their performance in intralinguistic text mediation (i.e., the dependent variable). We also set out to determine the strengths and weaknesses of the treatment in providing text mediation practice based on the analysis of HMC and the learners' perceptions of the use of *Alexa* during self-instruction. Based on these research aims, the study sought the answers to three central research questions (CRQ):

CRQ1: How does the VA-based and action-oriented self-instruction affect intralinguistic text mediation of the Polish EFL learners?

a. Does it affect their intralinguistic text mediation at within-group levels?
b. Does it affect their intralinguistic text mediation at between-group levels?

CRQ2: How do the Polish EFL learners evaluate the VA?

a. How useable do they find it?
b. How effective do they find it?
c. How satisfactory do they find it?
d. What are the benefits of the interaction with the VA?
e. What are the challenges of communicating with the VA?

Considering the quantitative character of the CRQ1, we formulated the following null hypotheses:

H_{01}: VA-based and action-oriented self-instruction has no influence on the experimental group students' intralinguistic text mediation skills at within-group levels. The participants do not perform better with regard to intralinguistic text-mediating activities having participated in the VA-based and action-oriented self-instruction.

H_{02}: There is no difference in the participants' intralinguistic text mediation skills at between-group levels. The students involved in the VA-based and action-oriented self-instruction do not perform better with regard to intralinguistic text-mediating activities than the students assigned to do traditional paper-and-pencil homework.

In response to the null hypotheses statements, we also put forward alternative hypotheses:

H_{A1}: VA-based and action-oriented self-instruction has a positive influence on the experimental group students' intralinguistic text mediation skills at within-group levels. The participants perform better with regard to intralinguistic text-mediating activities having participated in the VA-based and action-oriented self-instruction.

H_{A2}: There is a difference in the participants' intralinguistic text mediation skills at between-group levels. The students involved in the VA-based and action-oriented self-instruction perform better with regard to intralinguistic text-mediating activities than the students assigned to do traditional paper-and-pencil homework.

The specific procedures followed by the present author to answer the research questions and test the hypotheses enumerated above are presented in the sections below.

4.3 Research design

A research design can be defined as "the overall plan for collecting data in order to answer the research question" (Fraenkel et al., 2011, Glossary). It is central not only to gathering and analysing data, but also to finding answers to research questions in accordance with the research objectives (Wilczyńska & Michońska-Stadnik, 2010). For the purpose of the current investigation, a mixed-methods design (MM) was used. It is a relatively new methodology which, also referred to as an integrating, synthesis, and multimethod approach to research, originated in education, management, sociology, and health sciences in the 1980s and 1990s (Creswell, 2014). MM, defined as "the collection or analysis of both quantitative and qualitative data in a single study" (Dörnyei, 2007, p. 163), was adopted because it combines the strengths of the two approaches (Terrell, 2012). According to Mugenda and Mugenda (2003), the quantitative approach yields the data needed to meet particular research objectives and test hypotheses, whereas the qualitative approach offers comprehensive explanations of the issues under examination. As suggested by Greene et al. (1989), MM may be used to inform the process of instrument design and broaden the scope of treatment evaluation through product and process assessment. The investigation of research questions via different methods of data collection and types of data, also known as methodological triangulation, or "validation-through-convergence" (Dörnyei, 2007, p. 165), improves the validity of the study (Fraenkel et al., 2011). This triangular approach, as explained by Miles and Huberman (1984), allows to gain a broader perspective on the problem "by seeing or hearing multiple instances of it from different sources by using different methods and by squaring the finding with others it needs be squared with" (p. 267).

The experimental research was undertaken to answer the CRQ1 related to investigating the effects of the VA use during task performance on the Polish EFL students' intralinguistic text mediation. This quantitative research method allows the examination of the cause-and-effect relationships between independent (IV) and dependent (DV) variables (Konarzewski, 2000) (see Figure 4.1). By manipulating the variables, that is by holding the IV constant throughout the experimental intervention, performing the operationalisation of the DV, and developing its precise measurement techniques, the researcher is able to deduce whether the changes in the DV result from the treatment (Łobocki, 2003).

Fig. 4.1: *Logic model presenting associations between the VA use during action-oriented self-instruction and the EFL learners' ability to mediate (self-prepared)*

A typical experimental study comprises an experimental intervention, also known as treatment. There are usually two groups involved, the treatment (or experimental) group (henceforth ExG), which is exposed to the experimental factor, and the control group (henceforth CtrlG), which continues with traditional instruction and most importantly serves as a point of comparison. To make CtrlG and ExG as similar as possible, the principle of randomisation should be applied (Creswell, 2014). To estimate the effect of the intervention, pre-and post-tests are administered in each group before and after the treatment takes place (Wilczyńska & Michońska-Stadnik, 2010).

The realisation of classic experiments based on probability sampling procedures represents a considerable challenge for educational researchers (Dörnyei, 2007). In situations where random assignment of students to the ExG and CtrlG is not feasible, quasi-experiments, which differ from true experiments in that they make use of intact grouping, can be conducted (Campbell & Stanley, 1963). Such a research methodology, however, is accepted only if group differences are accounted for and dealt with in the research design (Dörnyei, 2007).

The quasi-experimental research design underlay both the pilot project and the study proper. A small-scale preliminary study was carried out to pilot-test and evaluate the data collection instruments and samples of the tasks to be distributed among the ExG and CtrlG in the main study (Grzeszkiewicz-Radulska, 2012). The objective of the pilot-testing stage was to identify the potential weaknesses of the research design, instructional treatment, and data collection tools in order to introduce the required changes to the main study conducted in the subsequent stage of the research (Larsen-Freeman & Long, 1991).

The quasi-experiments were divided into two phases in the pilot project and the main study. In view of the researcher's inability to ensure the CtrlG and ExG equality, the factor rotation technique was employed to account for the group differences caused by intact grouping and the impact of extraneous variables on the realisation of the experimental treatment (Sirotova et al., 2021). In the first phase, the effects of the experimental intervention were investigated in Group A, or the ExG, whereas Group B served as the CtrlG. In the second phase, the groups switched their position, that is the CtrlG acquired the status of the ExG and vice versa (Łobocki, 2003; Wilczyńska-Michońska & Stadnik, 2010) (see Figure 4.2).

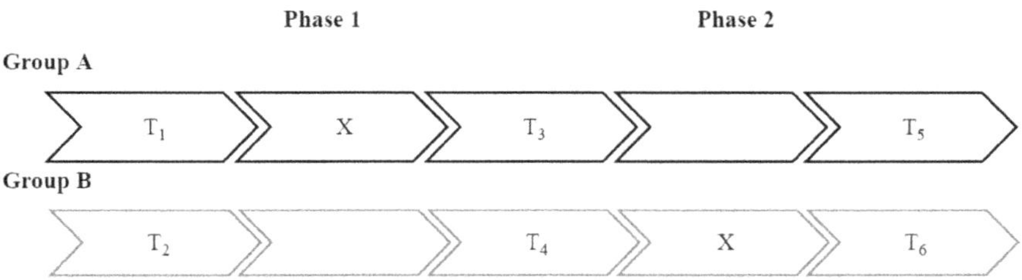

Fig. 4.2: *The quasi-experimental design with the factor rotation technique adopted in the pilot project and the main study (T=data collection on the participants' intralinguistic text mediation) (self-prepared)*

The descriptive research was conducted to gather quantitative and qualitative data in response to the CRQ2 investigating the participants' attitudes towards voice assistance during task performance to help interpret the results of the quasi-experiment with the factor rotation technique. The explanatory sequential MM approach (Creswell, 2014) was taken to explore the learners' views on the introduction of *Alexa* during self-instructed text mediation practice. The quantitative results from the questionnaire were used to select a group of the participants to be interviewed during the qualitative phase. The strategy referred to as the QUAN→qual technique[22] (Dörnyei, 2007) was found to overcome the limitations of quantitative research, with interview questions adequately explicating and adding to the survey results (see Figure 4.4).

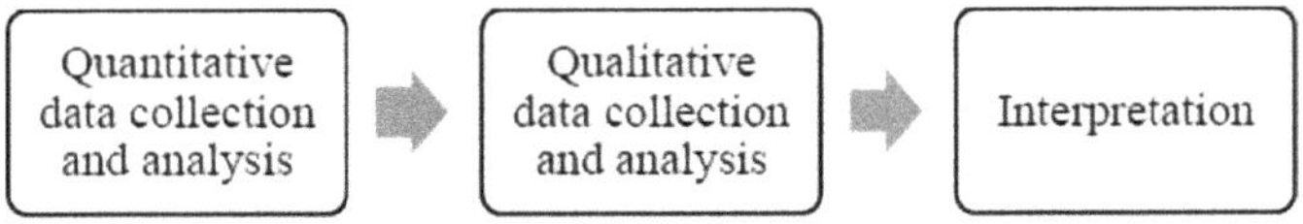

Fig. 4.3: *The explanatory sequential MM design used to answer the CRQ2 (adapted from Creswell, 2014)*

The identification of the participants' needs during the technology-mediated task-based NA – even though not formulated as a specific research objective and research question – also followed a specific research plan. The NA involved the convergent parallel MM procedure described above (see Figure 4.3). Also, the small-scale qualitative study based on semi-structured interviews (SSIs) (Step One; see section 4.5.1) was conducted in line with the qual→QUAN technique (Dörnyei, 2007) to facilitate the process of questionnaire development (Step Two) (see Figure 4.5). To be precise, the exploratory sequential MM approach was adopted to improve the content representation of the survey and to increase the internal validity of the research into the learners' needs.

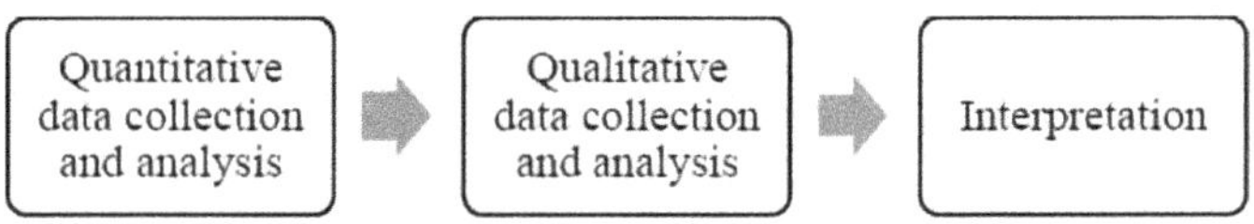

Fig. 4.4: *The exploratory sequential MM design used during the NA (adapted from Creswell, 2014)*

Despite obvious advantages to the MM procedures implemented in the research design, the collection, analysis, and interpretation of both quantitative and qualitative data represent some challenges. The most frequently encountered problems include the complexity of the research design, vast collection of

22 In the MM research designs developed by Creswell (2014), capitalisation (QUAN, QUAL) suggests that given data are more important in the analysis and interpretation than those in lowercase (quan, qual).

research data, time-consuming analysis, and researcher's inadequate expertise in both quantitative and qualitative forms of research (Terell, 2012).

4.4 Population and sample

In its broadest sense, the current study aimed to address the population of Polish FL secondary school learners (the ISCED level 3), namely the graduates of eight-year primary schools[23]. Given the vast diversity of the population in terms of learners' proficiency, amount of in- and out-class exposure to the language, levels of autonomous learning, FL-related plans for the future, and a whole host of other related variables, delimiting the setting from which a sample for the study would be drawn was an obligatory step.

Since the implementation of sampling strategies involving randomisation is highly impracticable in educational settings (Dörnyei, 2007), convenience sampling, also referred to as haphazard and accidental sampling (Etikan et al., 2015), was used. As a non-probability sampling strategy, it allows to select members of the target population according to a set of specific criteria, that is the participants' accessibility, geographical location, availability within fixed periods, and their readiness to participate in the study (Dörnyei, 2007). The learners who participated in the current quasi-experiment were selected because of their easy accessibility. It was convenient for the author to choose the sample because she had been working in the school for three years at the time when the study was being conducted.

Due to the subjectivity involved in choosing the sample, non-random sampling has a lot of limitations. First and foremost, it involves the risk of displaying sampling and selection bias as opposed to probability sampling strategies because some groups can be deliberately included in (or excluded from) the sample (Cohen et al., 2000, as cited in Dörnyei, 2007). Also, there is a problem with under- and over-representation of the population. Furthermore, convenience sampling represents a threat to external validity. It excludes the possibility of making generalisations because the sample is not representative of the total population (Hatch & Farhady, 1982). In view of these limitations, the current study did not aim to produce results that could be used to create generalisations about

23 For clarification, the middle school graduates were excluded from consideration by the present author in view of significant differences between them and four-year secondary school students (i.e., the participants of the quasi-experiment) in the number of English lessons per week, Core Curricula, and the 2015 versus 2023 Matura examination requirements.

the entire population of Polish FL secondary school students (Etikan et al., 2015). In other words, we avoided taking such a broad view during the interpretation of the findings (see section 5.5) given the fact that the sample represented only a specific group of Polish EFL students at the ISCED level 3 (Dörnyei, 2007).

In so far as the external validity of the study was low because of the convenience sampling strategy, due care was taken to improve its internal validity to ascertain that the change observed in the ExG with regard to the DV was effected by the experimental influence. The selection of the CtrlG similar to the ExG in terms of a recruitment process and pre-test scores enables the rejection of the rival hypotheses related to test, history, instrumentation, and maturation of the study participants. As explained by Campbell and Stanley (1963), the main effects of these variables "should be manifested equally in experimental and control groups" (p. 14). Additionally, the factor rotation technique was followed to control for the group inequality. As explained by Sirotova et al. (2021), "the cornerstone of this technique is the exchange of position between the experimental and control groups during the experiment. The exchange is caused by working with the independent variable" (p. 192).

The sample drawn from the population consisted of Polish EFL learners from a private secondary school in Lublin, a city located in the eastern part of Poland. The participants were 74 teenage students (46 girls and 28 boys), all of whom at the time of the research being conducted were enrolled in the second and third year of a four-year EFL programme offered by the school. They began their secondary school education either in September 2019 (the grade three students) or September 2020 (the grade two students) as the graduates of eight-year primary schools. The students were members of six intact groups. In line with the policy of the school, the groups were formed at the beginning of their language education (i.e., in grade one) based on the results of the written and oral placement tests administered by EFL teachers in the first two weeks of September. It is to be noted that these six groups had been formed without any influence of the researcher.

Due to the absence of over a dozen participants from English classes at the time of the administration of the study and their refusal for their data to be analysed within the current research, 61 students (39 girls and 22 boys) managed to fully participate in two phases of the eighteen-week quasi-experiment and the programme evaluation. They voluntarily completed sixteen homework assignments as both the CtrlG and ExG members, performed three written text mediation tests, and responded to the post-study questionnaire (for learners' protection within research involving human participation, see section 4.6). Twelve of them also took part in SSIs in which they were asked about their interaction with *Alexa* (see section 4.5 for the details concerning the research procedure, data collection instruments, and analysis methods).

The overall proficiency level of the learners was rather low. According to the results of the placement tests conducted in September 2019 and 2020, their knowledge of English did not exceed the A2 level. They were therefore assigned by their EFL instructors to work with a series of coursebooks adjusted to their then current level of language competence, *New Enterprise A1* (the grade three students) and *New Enterprise A2* (the grade two students) by Express Publishing. In the 2021/22 school year, six groups of Polish teenage learners started learning the English language at the B1 level of proficiency. Prior to the intervention, each of them was randomly assigned by the researcher to either Group A or Group B.

The two groups were comparable in regard to the variables which could have an effect on the study findings, namely the level of language proficiency and the type of language instruction. The participants met three times a week to attend four forty-five-minute lessons of English. They were taught English by two Polish EFL instructors with a similar level of work experience. A series of coursebooks entitled *New Enterprise B1* by Express Publishing, consisting of a student's book, workbook, grammar book, and exam skills practice component, laid the basis for the majority of classroom activities and homework assignments performed by the students in in- and out-of-class settings respectively. They were also exposed to a similar form of instruction and assessment based on the same coursebook. The lessons were organised by their EFL teachers in accordance with the functional-notional syllabus adopted in the coursebook. This involved the teaching of four language skills (i.e., listening, reading, writing, speaking) and language subsystems (i.e., grammar, vocabulary) in an integrated way. Nevertheless, as commented by the teachers in informal conversations with the present author, deductive teaching of English grammar and vocabulary took a considerable amount of classroom time.

In addition, Group A (n=39) and Group B (n=35) were similar in other important aspects. This was evident in the analysis of the students' responses to the background questionnaire (see Appendix B) that they had been asked to fill in anonymously in the first week of November 2021, that is before the first pre-tests (T_1 and T_2) were administered[24]. The questionnaire consisted of six close-ended and five open-ended questions, in which the participants were asked about their

24 The same procedure involving the implementation of the background questionnaire to identify similarities and differences between the ExG and CtrlG was applied by Kruk (e.g., 2011, 2012, 2014, 2015) in a number of his quasi-experimental research studies.

personal history of EFL learning, attitudes, motivations, and out-of-school exposure to English. The survey was written and filled out in the learners' L1 to avoid comprehension problems. It had been pilot-tested in Stage Four of the current research procedure a month before the study proper began. Mean scores and percentages of agreement values for responses to close-ended questions were calculated, whereas the students' answers to open-ended questions were categorised in themes with the assistance of *Taguette*, a free open source tool for coding textual qualitative data, and reported in a narrative form below. Content Analysis, "a research technique for making replicable and valid inferences from texts (or other meaningful matter) to the contexts of their use" (Krippendorf, 2019, p. 24), underlay the analysis of the data.

The examination of the responses to the background questionnaire revealed that on average, the students in Group A had been learning English for 10.85 years while those in Group B had been learning it for an average of 10.94 years. To be more specific, the majority of the students (22 participants from Group A, 56%, and 18 from Group B, 51%), had been learning English for 10 years. As for other participants, they reported having studied English for 11 to 14 years.

The participants' attitudes toward EFL instruction were also quite uniform, that is mainly positive. The claim can be supported by the fact that 35 participants from Group A (90%) and 30 from Group B (86%) declared that they enjoyed learning English (a lot). By contrast, only 4 in Group A (10%) and 3 in Group B (9%) expressed the opposite opinion. When asked to explain their choices, the students most frequently pointed to the role of English as a lingua franca (n=68), its importance in tertiary education and future professional career (n=59), and its usefulness in gaining access to popular culture (n=54).

As far as the participants' out-of-class EFL instruction is concerned, no significant discrepancies between the two groups were found. The majority of the students from Group A (51%) and Group B (54%) had had no English instruction outside of school before the study. Similarly, more than half of the students in Group A (56%) and Group B (54%) had no extracurricular classes at the beginning of the study. None of the students revealed possession of any language certificate in English. Students' limited participation in extracurricular EFL learning-related activities was welcomed by the author as this helped her to reduce the probability of the out-of-class instruction affecting the results of the study.

Almost 90% of the students in Group A (n=35) and Group B (n=31) reported using English outside school rather often. Nevertheless, this was reserved for a limited number of purposes. The top three out-of-school uses in the two groups of the participants included entertainment (i.e., listening to songs, watching movies and series with Polish subtitles, playing computer games), translation and interpretation (i.e., helping relatives who do not know the language), and communication with their English-speaking friends and family members as well as workers in shops, hotels, and restaurants during holidays abroad.

When asked about the most frequently implemented techniques for learning English on their own, the students pointed out revising lexico-grammatical structures. Approximately 64% and 57% of the students in Group A and 77% and 69% in Group B focused on vocabulary and grammar respectively in their out-of-class EFL learning.

Worryingly, only 27 out of 74 of the students (15 in Group A, 38%, and 12 in Group B, 34%) stated that they performed EFL activities other than completing compulsory homework assignments set by their instructors and studying for upcoming English language tests and quizzes. They listed filling in past Matura exam papers (n=17, 23%), learning the rules for using English tenses (n=10, 14%), reading graded readers (n=3, 4%), and doing activities available on the *LearnEnglish Teens* website operated by the British Council (n=1, 1%).

The majority of the students (28 from Group A, 72%, and 24 from Group B, 69%) usually devoted from five to fifteen minutes to their daily EFL learning routines. They used that time to complete their homework assignments. The students, however, complained that they could not focus on English more because of the necessity to prepare for their majors, or the school subjects in which they specialise within their class profile. Four students from Group A (10%) and 3 from Group B (9%) claimed that they did not study English at home at all. In relation to the amount of time they spent in their EFL learning routines, none of the students learned English for more than thirty minutes.

The above-mentioned information from the background questionnaire gave a rather disconcerting view of the EFL learning habits of the participants. Nevertheless, from the perspective of the current research study, such a situation could be regarded as favourable as it could considerably minimise the likelihood of the learners practising the targeted communicative language activities on their own during the experimental intervention prepared by the present author.

The key information relating to the characteristics of Group A and Group B together with the selected aspects examined within the background questionnaire are presented in Table 4.1. Judging by the data demonstrated below, it can be argued that the two groups were closely comparable with regard to a number of criteria.

Tab. 4.1: *Participants of the quasi-experimental study with the factor rotation technique (self-prepared)*

	Group A	**Group B**
Number of the students	39	35
Number of English lessons per week	4	4
Years of studying English	10.85	10.94
Level of language proficiency	A2+/B1	A2+/B1
(Very) positive attitude to EFL learning	35	30
(Very) frequent out-of-class use of English	35	31
Number of students with English language certificates	0	0
Participation in extracurricular EFL classes	22	19

4.5 Research procedure, data collection, and data analysis

4.5.1 Needs analysis

For the purpose of this quasi-experiment, Norris' (2009) framework was adapted by the present author. She divided the research study into six stages, that is 1) the technology-mediated task-based NA, 2) target task selection, 3) instructional treatment design, 4) pilot testing, 5) main study, and 6) programme evaluation. The research procedure underlying each of the stages is discussed below.

The objectives of Stage One were to explore task, language, and technology-related needs of the teenage Polish EFL students in the personal, public, and educational domains, on the basis of which the target tasks typical of an English for general purposes context would be identified (Stage Two). The procedures of data collection discussed below were implemented in the last week of August 2021 and the first two weeks of September 2021.

The implementation of a NA seems truly fundamental in such countries as Poland, where the government decides upon learning objectives and standards. The top-down approach to national FL Core Curricula development entails the risk of mismatch between learners' needs and administrators' decisions on what should be given priority in the language classroom. As opposed to a priori educational goals established by the Polish authorities, listening to teachers' and students' voices is found critical to promoting a democratic process of curriculum design and highlighting the issue of learner-centredness, the key tenet underlying good educational practices (Watanabe, 2006) and systematic curriculum building (Brown, 1995).

The approach to course design worked out within TBLT was adopted for the purpose of the current investigation. "The non-technical, everyday, real-world" (Long, 2015, p. 108) definition of a task, "the hundred and one things people do in everyday life, at work, at play, and in between", formulated by Long (1985, p. 89) provided a unit of analysis in the programme development for the quasi-experiment. The choice of a task as a unit of analysis in the language programme design gained momentum in view of SLA theories and research as well as principles of the philosophy of education. Defined as "the kinds of activities that learners want to or have to be able to do with the new language", tasks were said to broaden the understanding of language learning by shifting the perspective from a strictly linguistic to social goal-oriented activities (van Avermaeat & Gysen, 2009, p. 144). Focus on form brought to life by tasks offered an attractive alternative to structural syllabi, which, as already suggested in Chapter One, were discredited by the lack of an empirically-sound rationale for their introduction to instructed settings (Long, 2015; Long & Crookes, 1991).

Following Gonzales-Lloret's (2014) new model for technology-mediated TBLT, we extended the objectives of a traditional NA to match the requirements of technology-supported language learning. Apart from identifying learners' real-life communicative needs, or the instances of target tasks (Long, 2005), the NA involved the collection of data on the participants' smartphone and/or tablet use habits and their experiences with VAs. This was necessitated by the implementation of technological tools, such as mobile devices and VAs, within the treatment.

Four philosophies informed the procedure (Stufflebeam, 1977, as cited in Stufflebeam et al., 1985). To gather the information necessary to identify target tasks, the democratic philosophy was embraced by investigating perceptions of all the parties involved, from learners, through teachers, to administrators. The diagnostic philosophy helped to isolate the necessities, or "what the learner has to know to function effectively in the target situation" (Hutchinson & Waters, 1987, p. 55), understood here as such tasks which, if missing, would negatively affect their future performance, as perceived by all the stakeholders. The results of the diagnostic test triangulated with learners' and teachers' evaluations of the former's lacks helped to isolate the gap between the students' present-day competence and their desired future performance in accordance with the discrepancy philosophy. Following the analytic philosophy, the test results were also used to exclude such tasks from the syllabus for the performance of which the learners had already been well prepared.

Amid the plethora of terms creating slight confusion in NA-oriented EFL contexts (Dudley-Evans & St John, 1998), the current technology-mediated task-based assessment of the participants' needs aimed to examine the necessities, lacks, and wants, as defined by Hutchinson and Waters (1987), of the Polish EFL secondary school students. Sources of data (i.e., learners, teachers, administrators) were triangulated in the current NA to gather information on the learners' real communicative needs, the target tasks. For that purpose, Hutchinson and Water's (1987) definition of the concept, as demonstrated in Table 4.2, guided the process of data collection.

Tab. 4.2: *Sources of information on the participants' needs and the data collection methods: the NA (self-prepared)*

	NECESSITIES		LACKS		WANTS	
	Source of data	Method of data collection	Source of data	Method of data collection	Source of data	Method of data collection
Perceived needs	-Administrators -Teachers	-Analysis of official documentation -Needs questionnaire	-Teachers -Learners	-Needs questionnaire -Diagnostic tests	-Teachers	-Needs questionnaire
Self-perceived needs	-Learners	-Written retrospection -Needs questionnaire	-Learners	-Written retrospection -Needs questionnaire	-Learners	-Written retrospection -Needs questionnaire

A consensus of opinions among scholars was reached in favour of conducting multi-methodological research in learners' needs identification (Brown, 2009; Hutchinson & Waters, 1987; West, 1994). The methodology for the current NA was carefully selected and sequenced so that the learners' perceptions of their needs could be compromised with those of the administrators and teachers. As suggested by Long (2015), the NA was begun with open-ended techniques of data collection and followed by implementing closed techniques and follow-up procedures. Following that line of reasoning, we started with SSIs (Step One) which provided the basis for isolating the elements of interest to be further investigated through the needs questionnaire (Step Two). The latter combined with students' written retrospection (Step Three), analysis of official documentation (Step Four), and the diagnostic tests based on the requirements of the 2023 Matura (Step Five) set the basis for the multimethodological NA (see Figure 4.6).

Fig. 4.5: *Logic model for the methodology implemented during the NA (self-prepared)*

To inform the process of the questionnaire design, the first step in the NA was qualitative. Online SSIs were conducted in Polish with a group of volunteers in the last week of August 2021. Since SSIs involve both close- and open-ended questions frequently followed by additional "Why" and "How" questions, they are "superbly suited for a number of valuable tasks, particularly when more than a few of the open-ended questions require follow-up queries" (Adams, 2015, p. 493). The interviews were conducted in Polish by means of the *Zoom Cloud Meetings* video conferencing software program. Five major categories of the data were elicited: 1) bio-data, such as the participants' age and length of learning English, 2) reasons to study and use English in Poland and abroad, 3) the target tasks they found difficult, would like to perform, and have to perform in English, 4) mobile devices use habits, and 5) experiences with IVAs together with perceptions of their potential for EFL self-instruction.

The present researcher transcribed the interviews to find out the learners' self-perceived necessities, lacks, and wants. An open-coding analysis focused on revealing the respondents' motivations behind their study and use of English, target tasks, their smartphone and/or tablet use habits, familiarity with IPAs, and the tool's potential in language learning. Open-coding, the first stage in the Grounded Theory, involves asking questions and making comparisons "to break through subjectivity and bias" (Corbin & Strauss, 1990, p. 13). It is used to extract distinctive parts from the qualitative data by identifying similarities and differences between events, actions, and interactions, labelling them and making further examination through generative and comparative questions (Corbin & Strauss, 1990). The qualitative data were categorised in themes in line with the research objectives with the assistance of *Taguette*. To achieve intercoder reliability, 10% of the interviews were analysed by the author's colleague, an EFL secondary school teacher.

Based on the information from SSIs, the online needs questionnaire for the participants and the two EFL teachers was designed in Step Two of the NA. Its aim was to provide more specific information on the self-perceived and perceived needs of the participants by gathering quantitative data. Thirty-five closed-item responses were organised into four sections. They all utilised a six-point Likert scale moving from negative (1) to positive (6) (i.e., from *extremely unimportant, absolutely not, strongly disagree* to *extremely important, a lot, strongly agree*). The forced-choice question format was used on purpose to avoid neutral responses which "can give survey takers an easy out, creating a temptation to breeze through the question without much thought" (Thompson, 2018: para. 6). Even though odd numbers of response categories were generally preferable over even numbers in that the former allows a respondent not to take sides (Colman & Norris, 1997), no recommendations regarding the length of the Likert scale were made since as reported by Taherdoost (2019), the choice of a particular scale, be that five- or six-point, has no effect on the measurement quality.

In Section One, called necessities, the respondents were asked to assess the significance of the selected aims of learning English. In Sections Two and Three, that is EFL task-related lacks and wants, they were to point out the most problematic and desirable tasks given the communicative language activities (i.e., reception, production, interaction, mediation) involved in their performance. Section Four sought to find out how the respondents evaluated the learning potential of mobile devices. The questionnaire was written in Polish to circumvent learners' comprehension problems.

Before the final version was released for use through *Google Forms*, the informal testing was conducted with a group of 12 grade one students and a Spanish teacher in the first week of September 2021. The questionnaire was piloted to ensure validity by identifying the items that cause troubles for the respondents (Presser et al., 2004). As explained by Nanda et al. (2013), informal tests based on unstructured reviews "can provide very useful information on shortcomings of the instrument, which includes: questions that might be misunderstood, confusing layout, misleading instructions, typographical problems and so on" (p. 70). The participants of the pilot study were asked to fill in the online needs questionnaire, evaluate the wording and content, list the items that, in their opinion, should be added and/or removed and, if necessary, provide additional comments.

The reliability of the aforementioned instrument was evaluated on the sample of 12 participants. The correlation matrix was analysed to check whether the questions should be reversed or not. The Cronbach's alpha coefficient (α) was calculated for each of the four sections of the needs questionnaire to examine the internal consistency of the scale by describing the extent to which all the items measure the same latent variable (i.e., the students' self-perceived necessities of using English, their English-related lacks, their EFL learning wants, the potential of mobile devices in the respondents' EFL learning) (Bonett & Wright, 2014). It was established that $\alpha \geq 0.70$ is good, $\alpha \geq$ is 0.80 is better, and $\alpha \geq 0.90$[25] is best. The analysis of the correlation matrix revealed no necessity to reverse the questions in Sections One through Three. The Cronbach's alpha coefficient value for Section One was reported to be 0.74, Section Two 0.93, and Section Three 0.92, which shows that each of them had a high level of reliability. In Section Four, however, Statement One had an inverse (negative) correlation. The Cronbach's alpha coefficient value for this section was low (0.49), but if the statement was removed, it rose to 0.66. Once the statement had been reversed following the correlation matrix, the Cronbach's alpha coefficient was reported to be 0.72, which is satisfactory.

After the pilot stage had been completed, the necessary revisions, that is the editorial corrections and simplification of lengthy closed-response items, were made in the needs questionnaire. The final draft laid the basis for the online needs questionnaires (for the paper version, see Appendix C), which was distributed to the sample (n=74) and their EFL teachers (n=2) in the second week of September 2021. Once the online survey had been closed, the quantitative data were downloaded, coded, and entered into the computer for the computation of the percentages of the respondents' (n=60) self-perceived necessities, lacks, and wants, and their attitudes towards the use of mobile devices.

The objective of the third step of the NA, written retrospection, was to triangulate the needs questionnaire by collecting qualitative data relating to participants' out-of-class opportunities for the use of English and the functions of smartphones and/or tablets that were perceived by the teenagers as useful in their everyday life. The students were asked to elaborate on the two mentioned issues within their homework set in the first week of September 2021. They were given a weekend to complete the assignment and asked to hand it in during the following English class.

Corbin and Strauss' (1990) open-coding analysis was performed to uncover those circumstances which favoured the respondents' (n=74) out-of-school use of English and encouraged their reliance on mobile devices. The qualitative data generated from the open-ended questions in the written retrospection were

25 The coefficient value that is too high, or close to 1, may, however, mean the questionnaire contains similar questions.

categorised in themes with the help of *Taguette* and presented in the form of a narrative in the next section. Again, 10% of the students' retrospections were examined by an EFL secondary school teacher to achieve intercoder reliability in the data analysis process.

The next step in the NA was the investigation of the secondary school EFL course-related official documentation. The primary objective of Step Four was twofold: firstly, to identify the general and detailed requirements of the national Core Curriculum for FLs taught at the basic level (B1+/B2) and secondly, to isolate the types of examination questions from the 2023 Matura syllabus published by CKE in March 2021. The information collected from the documents helped the author to triangulate the needs questionnaire and written retrospection with regard to the task-related necessities.

Based on the general and detailed requirements of the Core Curriculum and the guidelines issued in the 2023 Matura syllabus, the diagnostic tests were prepared by the researcher and administered by the EFL teachers in the second and third week of September 2021. It took the EFL teachers four forty-five minute periods of instruction to follow the assessment procedure. The main aim of the written and oral parts of the test was to assess participants' EFL reception, production, interaction, and mediation, and also to supplement the information gathered in the needs questionnaire by providing an objective perspective on participants' lacks. It was assumed that by isolating the instances of students' most and least satisfactory performance, the language activities which proved least and most problematic could be excluded from and included in the instructional treatment.

Three out of six groups of the students participating in the study (n=38) were randomly selected by the researcher to take the diagnostic tests. Her decision to conduct the written and oral diagnostic tests only with a limited number of participants was motivated by the two teachers' concerns over the lengthy procedures involved in the administration of the tests and their negative impact on the regular language instruction.

The written diagnostic test was divided into four sections: Listening, Reading, Use of English, and Writing. Eight close- and six open-ended tasks at the B1+ (production) and B2 (reception) levels were adapted from *Learning Club* and *My Perspectives*, the Polish EFL learner and teacher websites operated by two printing houses, Express Publishing and Nowa Era.

To identify learners' problems with oral language production, interaction, and mediation, an oral diagnostic test based on the guidelines from the 2023 Matura syllabus was administered during a forty-five minute lesson. The students were provided with one of three topics – *Studying for an exam*, *Throwing a birthday party*, and *Going to the cinema* – each of which required them to refer to and elaborate on four points included in the instructions. To increase the authenticity and practicality of the test, the students worked in dyads formed at random to reach an agreement on one of the familiar issues that they had been presented with in the role-play. All the dialogues were recorded with the oral consent from the participants. The author and her colleague marked the dialogues with regard to five criteria: content, range, accuracy, pronunciation, and fluency. As already pointed out in section 2.4.2.3, students' oral accuracy, pronunciation, and fluency were evaluated in the context of how each of them affected the communicativeness of learners' utterances. The quantitative data obtained from the diagnostic tests were coded and entered into the computer for the computation of statistics. The *Statistica* software package was used to run descriptive statistics, such as means, medians, modes, standard deviation (SD), and minimum and maximum values so as to present the quantitative data in form of the tables.

4.5.2 Target task selection

The NA, although not formulated as a specific research problem and research objective, was a fundamental step in the treatment design. Its basic aim was to provide a sound and empirically motivated rationale for the selection of target tasks in line with the widely recommended principle of the backwards design.

A series of SSIs was conducted within Step One of the NA in the last week of August 2021 with a group of 14 volunteers from the sample (12 female and 2 male students). The interviews lasted for 20 to 35 minutes and were recorded with the computer recording tool *Apowersoft* with the oral consent of the interviewees.

The main findings pertaining to respondents' use of English that emerged from the interviews included the following. The 16- and 17-year old respondents had learned the language approximately for 11 years. In the majority of cases, their EFL self-instruction was limited to coursebook-based study of grammar and vocabulary. Six students searched for extra opportunities for language practice, such as listening to music, watching films, and reading books in English. All the learners, however, voiced disappointment over their autonomous EFL learning, suggesting some anticipated changes.

An analysis of the transcribed interviews indicated that participants' motivation to study English was entirely instrumental. The respondents (n=14) highlighted the importance of having well-developed EFL communicative competence in the view of their more or less regular temporary stays abroad during holiday time. Two of them (14%) underlined the need to communicate in English in future tertiary education and work settings. The learners unanimously reported having few occasions to use English in Poland. The instances, in the descending order of frequency, were entertaining oneself with English films and music, translating written and spoken texts to help others understand their meaning, instructing foreigners on how to reach their destination, and searching the Web. As for the examples of English use abroad, learners' answers remained consistent: all the interviewees (n=14) needed the language to deal with holiday-related activities, such as checking in and out at the hotel reception, ordering food, renting towels, and asking for directions, price, and information. They all stressed the importance of oracy in their out-of-class use of English. Tasks involving learners' spoken interaction with other native and non-native users of the language both in Poland and abroad proved, in their opinion, most desirable and problematic at the same time. Also, they were convinced that developing good speaking skills was required of them after secondary school graduation. The teenage students (n=14) who had participated in the SSIs reported the use of their mobile devices mainly for spoken and written communication. They stressed the fact that smartphones and tablets assisted them during everyday task performance. The functions of the mentioned technologies most frequently used by the learners were the notes, calendar, search engine, dictionary, and music/video player. All the participants (n=14) were familiar with the idea of voice assistance available on their mobile devices, and they had tried using it at least once in the Polish and English language. However, their opinions relating to the potential of technology for EFL self-instruction were divided. Six respondents (43%) were positive about IVAs, suggesting that they could increase their exposure to English by boosting their language production and reception. On the other hand, the remaining eight learners (57%) rejected VAs and deemed them pretty useless. The main reason underlying their decision was the unsatisfactory nature of their past HMC, which had frequent communication breakdowns and unsuccessful search results obstructing the process.

The analysis of students' responses (n=60)[26] to the first section in the needs questionnaire administered in Step Two of the NA in the second week of September 2021 revealed some interesting tendencies (see Table 4.3). When asked about their self-perceived needs relating to their uses of English, the vast majority of the participants regarded as important and very important the following contexts of language use: travelling and sightseeing (93%), access to popular culture (87%), using English in the future job and achieving a high score in the written part of Matura (83%), reading news and articles and staying abroad (70%), and

26 Despite their EFL teachers' repeated reminders, 14 participants out of 74 did not fill out the online needs questionnaire.

communicating with English-speaking friends and achieving a high score in the oral part of Matura (67%). The context found the least relevant for the biggest number of learners (20%) was communication with English-speaking family members, which probably pointed out mainly monolingual and monocultural social backgrounds of one-fifth of them.

Tab. 4.3: *Significance of the selected necessities of the English use as reported by the students (n=60) (self-prepared)*

	Not important at all %	**Not important** %	**Important** %	**Very important** %
1. Communication with English-speaking family members	13	7	20	30
2. Communication with English-speaking friends	3	0	27	40
3. Access to popular culture in English	0	3	20	67
4. Access to news and articles in English	0	0	27	43
5. Travelling and sightseeing	0	0	20	73
6. Achieving a high score in the written part of Matura	3	0	20	63
7. Achieving a high score in the oral part of Matura	7	3	13	53
8. Attending university classes in English in Poland	0	0	27	27
9. Studying abroad	3	0	23	30
10. Using English in the future job	0	0	30	53
11. Staying abroad	3	3	23	47

In the second section, the respondents were asked to identify the areas which, in their opinion, were most problematic. Eight communicative language activities based on the classification adopted in the CEFR (see Table 4.4) were selected for that purpose and included in the needs questionnaire. The investigation of learners' self-perceived problems with using English showed that communicative language activities involving aural and written language reception were found least problematic by the biggest number of the respondents, 33% and 47% respectively. On the other hand, the data presented in Table 4.4 clearly demonstrate that the respondents claimed to have (a lot of) problems not only with oral language interaction (33%), but also oral (33%) and written (23%) language production. Nonetheless, no clear tendency could be observed with regard to students' self-perceived problems with written language production (23%) and written interaction (16%) since a similar number of the students (20% and 17% respectively) also found them simple to deal with in the English language. What is, however, even more interesting in the context of the current discussion is the students' attitude towards the performance of language mediating activities. 30% and 27% of the students reported not having problems with written and oral language mediation respectively. On the other hand, 3% and 17% claimed the opposite. As demonstrated later, students' conviction about their good performance during mediation-based tasks clashed with the results of the written and oral diagnostic tests conducted by the present author with the intention of identifying students' lacks.

Tab. 4.4: *Students' perception of their difficulties with the performance of communicative language activities (n=60) (self-prepared)*

I (rather) have no problems with…	I have (a lot of) problems with …	
47%	0%	1. Written language reception
33%	17%	2. Aural language reception
20%	23%	3. Written language production
23%	33%	4. Oral language production
17%	17%	5. Written interaction
17%	33%	6. Oral interaction
30%	3%	7. Written language mediation
27%	17%	8. Oral language mediation

Judging by the participants' answers to the third section, no clear trend indicating students' marked preference for developing the ability to perform one particular type of communicative language activity over the other could be observed. All eight reception-, production-, interaction-, and mediation-based language activities were almost equally relevant for the respondents because they expressed a strong wish to develop all of them. The top two activities selected by the students were aural language reception and oral interaction (83%), each followed by oral language production and written language mediation (77%), written language production (73%), written language reception (70%), oral language mediation (63%), and written interaction (57%). Only 5 respondents out of 60 did not wish to improve their ability to perform any type of the activities.

In the last section, the students were asked to evaluate their uses of mobile technologies. A vast majority of the respondents (90%) used mobile devices (i.e., smartphones and tablets) daily, found them useful in learning (87%), and regarded their ability to use the devices as very good (83%). Over 60% had an unlimited Wi-Fi access at home, which probably further strengthened their reliance on the above-mentioned technologies. As far as their experiences with VAs are concerned, only 20% and 23% claimed to have frequently used the technology in Polish and English respectively. Equally importantly, approximately over one-third of them agreed with the statement that VAs could support their EFL learning (40%) and improve their language skills (37%).

Tab. 4.5: *Mobile device use habits as perceived by the participants (n=60) (self-prepared)*

	Strongly disagree %	**Disagree** %	**Agree** %	**Strongly agree** %
1. I use my smartphone and/or tablet every day.	0	0	7	83
2. I judge my ability to use mobile devices to be very good.	0	0	17	50
3. I have an unlimited Wi-Fi access at home.	7	0	10	53
4. I find smartphones and tablets useful in learning.	0	0	13	73
5. I often use IVAs in Polish.	40	27	3	17
6. I often use IVAs in English.	40	23	67	17
7. I believe that IVAs may support my EFL learning.	0	27	33	7
8. I believe that I will improve my language skills by interacting with IVAs.	10	20	27	10

An important fact to be considered was that only one-third of the students regularly used VAs either in Polish or English. This fact had to be accounted for in the preparation phase before the treatment was introduced. An *Alexa* user guide on how to install and interact with the IVA was written in the L1 to ensure that all the students, regardless of their past experiences with voice assistance, had equal chances to successfully complete a set of tasks within the treatment.

Students' answers to the needs questionnaire were triangulated with those of their EFL teachers' within Step Two. The two English instructors were invited to complete exactly the same questionnaire as the students. As far as the necessities are concerned, teachers' responses overlapped with those of the students, with the former pointing out the importance of students' EFL communicative competence in gaining access to popular culture, travelling, and sightseeing. According to the two teachers, the performance of communicative language activities based on reception was slightly less problematic for their learners than those involving interaction, production, and mediation. The instructors were convinced about students' willingness to develop the ability to perform all eight language activities enumerated in the questionnaire.

In so far as teachers' answers to the first three sections of the questionnaire remained pretty consistent and matched those provided by the participants, their responses to the last section expressed divergent opinions on their students' mobile technology use habits. One of the teachers clearly underestimated the role of the technologies in learners' lives, claiming that her pupils neither used mobile devices on a daily basis nor interacted with VAs. In addition, she believed that the VAs had no positive influence on her students' EFL learning. The second teacher adopted a more pro-technology attitude; namely, she agreed with the statements that not only her students made use of smartphones and tablets every day and talked to VAs, but also that the assistants may aid pupils' EFL learning. Despite divided opinions, the teachers were convinced that their learners were adept at using mobile devices and could do this freely because of unlimited Wi-Fi access at home.

As for the instances of the real-life use of English identified within learners' written retrospection (Step Three), students' answers (n=61)[27] were grouped under two categories: English use in Poland and English use abroad. The English

27 A few students (n=9) did not return the written retrospection despite their teachers' repeated reminders. In addition, 4 learners either provided too little information or

use in Poland category was further divided into such themes as "mediating texts" (i.e., interpreting spoken utterances and translating manuals, clothes and cosmetics labels, T-shirt letterings, recipes, and lyrics), "maintaining social relationships" (i.e., talking to English-speaking friends and family members), "helping foreigners" (i.e., giving directions), and "entertaining" (i.e., playing computer, smartphone, and tablet games, watching films and series, listening to music, reading books). The English use abroad category, on the other hand, comprised "surviving" (i.e., doing simple errands, namely ordering food, shopping, renting beach chairs and towels, asking for information at the tourist information centre), and "socialising with local communities" (i.e., chatting with all-round entertainers at hotels, talking about weather and recent national events with other tourists, comparing the Polish and regional cuisine while conversing with locals).

Three themes were established for the situations in which the students used their smartphones and/or tablets. They included "entertaining" (i.e., watching films/series, searching the net, playing games, listening to music), "surviving" (i.e., reaching intended destinations, translating, note-taking, writing down important dates in the calendar, preparing shopping lists, looking at bus timetables), and "learning" (i.e., attending online classes during pandemic, note-taking, translating, recording notes and listening to them).

In Step Four of the NA, the present author explored the needs of the participants, as perceived by the Polish authorities based on the selected EFL course-related documentation. Specifically, two documents, the 2018 national Core Curriculum for FLs and the 2023 Matura syllabus, were analysed to unravel those necessities that were deemed significant by the Polish Ministry of Science and Higher Education. Five general curricular requirements for FLs could be identified: Use of English, Language reception, Language production, Interaction, and Language mediation. They could be further divided into detailed requirements[28]. The examples found most significant in the context of the Matura examination are presented in Table 4.6.

wrote their answers unintelligibly. Their papers were therefore excluded from the analysis.

28 The English translations of the general and detailed core curriculum requirements for FLs were provided by the present author.

Tab. 4.6: *General and detailed curricular requirements for FLs evaluated within the written Matura examination in Poland (adapted from CKE, 2021)*

Activity	General FL core curriculum requirement	Examples of detailed FL core curriculum requirements
1	II. Oral language reception	II.7. Examinees draw conclusions from the utterance based on the information provided therein. II.3. Examinees identify the intentions of the author of the utterance. II.2. Examinees get the gist of the utterance.
2		II.7. Examinees draw conclusions from the utterance based on the information provided therein. II.5. Examinees find selected pieces of information in the text. II.6. Examinees put information in the right order.
3	II. Oral language reception V. Oral language mediation I. Use of English	II.5. Examinees find selected pieces of information in the text. VIII.2. Examinees present in a FL information formulated in a FL.
4	II. Written language reception	III.1. Examinees identify the main ideas of the text.
5	II. Written language reception V. Written language mediation I. Use of English	III.2. Examinees identify the intentions of the author of the text. III.3. Examinees identify the context of a situation. III.4. Examinees find selected pieces of information in the text. VIII.2. Examinees present in the L1 information formulated in a FL. VIII. 1. Examinees present information based on the content of the visuals.
6	II. Written language reception	III.4. Examinees find selected pieces of information in the text. III.6. Examinees put information in the right order. III.7. Examinees draw conclusions from the utterance based on the information provided therein. III.1. Examinees identify the main ideas of the text.
7		III.5. Examinees identify connections between text fragments.

(Continued)

Tab. 4.6: Continued

Activity	General FL core curriculum requirement	Examples of detailed FL core curriculum requirements
8	I. Use of English IV. Written interaction V. Written language mediation	I. Examinees use varied lexico-grammatical structures VII.4. Examinees express their opinions. VII.13. Examinees express emotions. VII.3. Examinees communicate information and explanations. VIII.3. Examinees formulate in a FL information presented in the L1. XIV. Examinees have language awareness.
9		
10		
11	I. Use of English	I. Examinees use varied lexico-grammatical structures.
12		
13		
14	I. Use of English III. Written language production IV. Written interaction V. Written language mediation	I. Examinees use varied lexico-grammatical structures. VIII.3. Examinees formulate in a FL information presented in the L1.

As already pointed out in sections 2.4 and 4.1, greater requirements were placed on Polish secondary school graduates in the wake of the 2017 education reform. As compared with the 2015 version of Matura, the 2023 examination would consist of both close- and open-ended questions in each of its four sections: Listening, Reading, Use of English, and Writing (see Table 2.13). In addition, either oral or written text mediation activities would be included in each of the exam components. Also, the expected level of language proficiency would be raised from B1/B1+ to B1+/B2, and the spoken and written texts in the Listening and Reading sections would be lengthened. The minimum word limit and scoring would also be subject to change in the Writing section as opposed to the 2015 Matura exam. Namely, the former would be increased from 80 to 100 words, whereas the latter from 10 to 12 points, with greater importance given to content (5 points versus 4 points) and range (3 points versus 2 points). The 2023 Matura would display a greater variety of examination activities. In addition to close-ended questions (i.e., multiple-choice, matching, true/false) in Listening, Reading, and Use of English and an open-ended question (i.e., writing an informal letter, e-mail, blog post, etc.) in Writing, different types of the latter (e.g., gap filling, transformation, word formation, translation) would be introduced to the first three sections of the exam.

The curricular requirements and examples of examination activities provided the basis for the development of the written diagnostic test in Step Five of the NA. It must be noted that at the time of conducting the NA, there were no examples of the 2023 version of Matura available commercially apart from the one presented and discussed in the examination syllabus. The results of the written diagnostic test administered among three intact groups of students (n=36)[29] randomly selected from Groups A and B in Step Five of the NA are summarised below. Table 4.7 presents descriptive statistics (i.e., mean, median, mode, SD, minimum and maximum values) for 14 activities completed by 36 participants in the written diagnostic test.

Tab. 4.7: *Descriptive statistics for the written part of the diagnostic test (Activities 1-14) based on the general and detailed curricular requirements and the Matura syllabus (n=36) (self-prepared)*

		n	Mean	Median	Mode	SD	Min	Max
Listening	1	36	2.69	2	2	1.618	0	5
	2		2.36	2	2	1.437	0	5
	3		0.69	0	0	1.009	0	3
Reading	4		1.00	1	Multiple	0.986	0	4
	5		2.17	2	1	1.483	0	5
	6		2.78	3	3	1.551	0	5
	7		2.89	3	Multiple	1.545	0	5
Use of English	8		1.72	2	2	0.615	0	2
	9		1.36	2	2	0.867	0	2
	10		0.75	1	0	0.874	0	3
	11		0.44	0	0	0.695	0	2
	12		0.17	0	0	0.378	0	1
	13		0.78	2	1	0.485	0	2
Writing	14		6.13	6	Multiple	2.198	2.0	10.0

29 It was expected that 38 students would take the diagnostic test. Two learners, however, were absent from school when the test was administered by their EFL instructors.

The data presented above illustrate that the mean scores for the 14 examination activities were very low. As far as the detailed curricular requirements are concerned, the students (n=36) had most problems identifying the selected pieces of information from the aural source text and presenting them in a FL in the written target text (Activity 3, or oral language mediation). It was the least satisfactory performance in the Listening section, with the mean of 0.69 points and the majority of the students scoring zero points (mode) in the activity. In the Reading section, the activity requiring the learners to identify the main ideas in the written text (Activity 4) proved equally challenging, as evidenced in the low mean score (1.00). A similar problem could also be observed in Activity 5 (2.17), which examined learners' ability to mediate written source texts. The modal value there was 1 point. Further, very low mean scores for Activities 12 (0.17) and 11 (0.44) were indicative of the fact that the students had difficulties with the correct and appropriate use of lexico-grammatical structures. In addition, none of the learners correctly performed Activity 12 (max. 2 points), as demonstrated by the maximum value of 1 point.

The mean scores for each of the four sections, Listening (max. 15 points), Reading (max. 20 points), Use of English (max. 13 points), and Writing (max. 12 points), were very low. It must be pointed out that some students were not able to successfully complete any of the activities in the first three sections, as demonstrated by the minimum values presented in Table 4.8. Further, none of the students achieved the maximum number of points in any of the sections.

Tab. 4.8: *Descriptive statistics for four sections of the written diagnostic test (n=36) (self-prepared)*

	n	Mean	Median	Mode	SD	Min	Max
Listening	36	5.75	6	4	3.228	0	13
Reading		8.83	9	8	3.418	0	16
Use of English		5.22	6	6	2.392	0	11
Writing		6.13	6	Multiple	2.198	2	10

SD, which stands for the measure of how dispersed the data is in relation to the mean, varied from 2.198 to 3.418 points out of 15, 20, 13, and 12 points. Since high SD indicates that data are spread out around the mean value, there were significant individual differences between the participants because they had not performed the diagnostic test around the same level. All in all, there is no doubt that participants' performance in the written diagnostic test was somewhat disappointing.

Students' answers (n=36) to the last open-ended question (Activity 14) were marked by the author and her colleague. To examine interrater reliability, Pearson Correlation Coefficient (r), which assesses the degree to which ratings covary, was calculated (Surface & Dierdoff, 2003). It assigns the value between – 1 and 1 where '0' is no correlation, '1' is total positive correlation, and '–1' is total negative correlation (Hatch & Farhady, 1985). A correlation value of 0.69 points between the two judges' ratings indicated that a moderately positive relationship existed between the two in the assessment of participants' answers to Activity 14 (confer Figure 4.7).

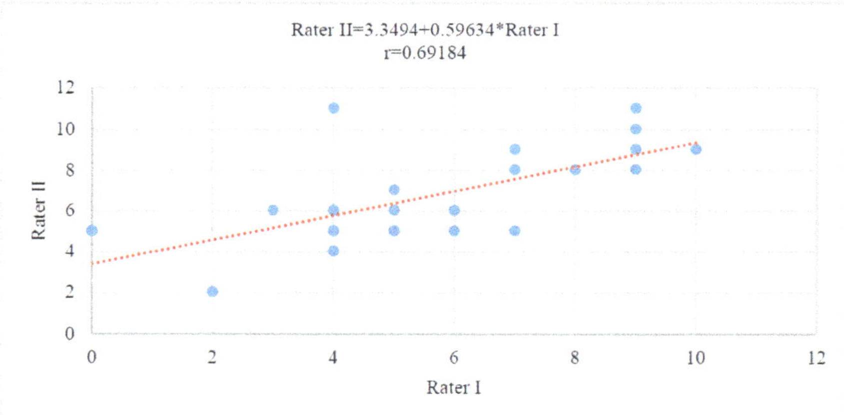

Fig. 4.6: *Scatter diagram with the Pearson correlation coefficient: Activity 14 in the written diagnostic test (self-prepared)*

Closer investigation of learners' performance in writing with regard to the four categories of content (max. 5 points), cohesion and coherence (max. 2 points), range (max. 3 points), and accuracy (max. 2 points) revealed that the students had serious problems formulating in a FL information presented in the L1 (i.e., written language mediation). That was demonstrated by the low mean score (2.39) and the modal value (2 points) appearing most frequently in the set of the data statistically analysed in the content category (see Table 4.9).

Tab. 4.9: *Descriptive statistics for Activity 14 in the written part of the diagnostic test (n=36) (self-prepared)*

	n	Mean	Median	Mode	SD	Min	Max
Content	36	2.39	2.0	2	1.030	0.5	5.0
Cohesion and coherence		1.29	1.5	1	0.496	0.0	2.0
Range		1.26	1.0	1	0.546	0.0	2.5
Accuracy		1.19	1.0	1	0.495	0.0	2.0

Based on the speaking EFL Matura exam, one activity was designed for the oral diagnostic test by the author. Sixteen dialogues were recorded with the oral consent from the participants (n=31)[30] in Step Five of the NA. Given the odd number of the students, one of the learners had to role-play a dialogue twice; her performance, however, was evaluated only once. Pearson correlation (r) was used again to assess the interrater reliability. A value of 0.85 between two judges' ratings indicated that a significant and positive relationship existed between the two (confer Figure 4.8).

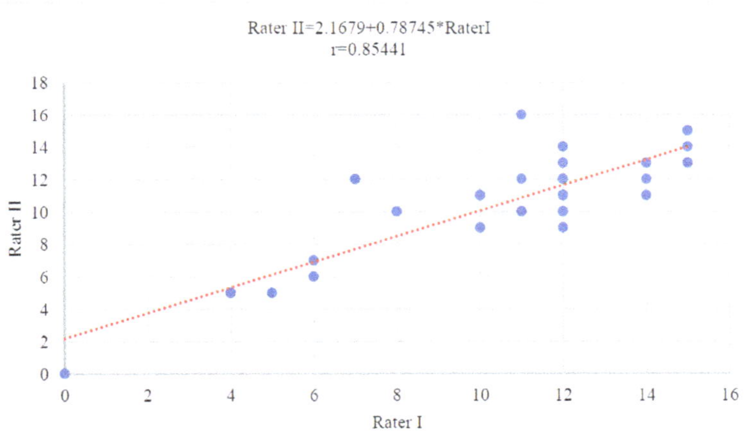

Fig. 4.7: *Scatter diagram with the Pearson correlation coefficient: the oral diagnostic test (self-prepared)*

30 Out of 38 participants, only 31 were present during the class when the dialogues were role-played in pairs.

The analysis of the students' (n=31) oral performance in the diagnostic test with regard to five criteria – content (6 points), range (4 points), accuracy (4 points), pronunciation (2 points), and fluency (2 points) – revealed that the mean values achieved by the learners for content were really low (2.73), with the majority of the participants scoring only 2 points out of 6. This suggested that the students found it challenging to communicate and elaborate on the information (i.e., written language mediation) presented in the instruction to the speaking-based activity within the test. In addition, as presented in Table 4.10, the variance was rather high in the aforementioned category (1.322 points out of 6). That again indicated the considerable diversity with regard to the teenagers' performance during the assessment of oracy. The statistical analysis of the range and accuracy suggested that the learners had performed better in these categories than in that of content, achieving the moderate mean scores of 2.61 and 2.23 points respectively. What has to be stressed here is the fact that students' oral performance was evaluated positively by the two raters in the pronunciation and fluency categories, with the mean scores of 1.68 and 1.50 points respectively and the modal value of 2 points.

Tab. 4.10: *Descriptive statistics for the oral part of the diagnostic test based on the general and detailed curricular requirements and the Matura syllabus (n=31) (self-prepared)*

	n	Mean	Median	Mode	SD	Min	Max
Content		2.73	2.5	2	1.322	0.0	6.0
Range		2.61	3.0	3	0.803	0.0	4.0
Accuracy	31	2.23	2.5	2.5	0.717	0.0	3.0
Pronunciation		1.68	2.0	2	0.556	0.0	2.0
Fluency		1.50	1.5	2	0.707	0.0	2.0

It transpired from the analysis of the relevant FL course-related documentation (Step Four), students' and teachers' responses to the needs questionnaires (Step Two), written retrospection (Step Three), and results of the written and oral diagnostic tests (Step Five) that the practice of oral and written language mediation within the instructional treatment was more than desired (see Table 4.11). The development of EFL students' ability to mediate proved necessary from the perspective of the Polish authorities, as evidenced in the guidelines issued in the latest Core Curriculum for FLs and the examination syllabus (i.e., perceived necessities and wants). Mediating language activities were also one of those which the students had difficulty completing, as demonstrated by the statistical analysis of the written and oral tests (i.e., perceived lacks). As reported by the students in the written retrospection, mediating a text was one of the activities which required their use of English in Poland (i.e., self-perceived necessities). Additionally, when asked about their self-perceived wants of using English, students themselves pointed out performing language mediation activities as one of the abilities they were willing to develop. Nevertheless, as presented in Table 4.11, the students had a false impression that they had no serious problems with oral and written language mediation (i.e., self-perceived lacks). This, as tentatively suggested above, clashed with their low score on text mediation activities that they had obtained in the written and oral diagnostic tests (i.e., perceived lacks).

Tab. 4.11: *Perceived and self-perceived needs of the participants (self-prepared)*

	NECESSITIES	LACKS	WANTS
Perceived needs	▪ aural/written language reception ▪ oral/written language production ▪ oral/written interaction ▪ **mediation of written/spoken texts**	▪ **oral/written language mediation** ▪ written language reception ▪ written interaction ▪ use of English	▪ oral/written language reception ▪ oral/written language production ▪ oral/written interaction ▪ **mediation of written/spoken texts**
Self-perceived needs	▪ travelling abroad and sightseeing ▪ gaining access to popular culture ▪ passing the written EFL New Matura ▪ **mediating texts**	▪ oral interaction ▪ oral language production	▪ aural language reception ▪ oral language production ▪ **mediation of written/spoken texts**

Based on the results of the NA, the decision was reached to design real-life text mediation tasks that could potentially be performed by the students in their personal and public domains. The contexts of the English language use both in Poland (i.e., talking to English-speaking friends and family members, assisting Polish relatives who do not know English well, helping foreigners solve a problem in English, entertaining) and abroad (i.e., chatting with all-round entertainers at hotels, sightseeing, doing simple errands in the place of the holiday destination) that were identified in the written retrospection provided the basis for the target task selection and the development of the treatment.

Equally importantly, what the NA findings revealed was that the use of mobile devices by the students was very commonplace (at least from the participants' perspective). Mobile technologies became, what Bax (2003) called it, normalised for the Polish learners for the purposes of entertainment, learning, and survival in the EFL context. In addition, students' (n=60) answers to the needs questionnaire indicated participants' inclination to use mobile devices and VAs. 90% of the students reported utilising smartphones and/or tablets on a daily basis. On the other hand, one-fifth of them reported using IVAs often, whereas approximately 40% of them were convinced that their interaction with the AI-driven technology could support their EFL learning.

In view of the above, real-life tasks identified in the course of the NA as relevant to the students' needs were combined with VAs. Task-oriented IMALL was therefore implemented within the treatment in the ExG, which took the form of TFOH defined for the purpose of this discussion as VA-based and action-oriented homework assignments focusing on intralinguistic text mediation practice. For the purpose of comparison, the CtrlG also received homework targeting language mediation, yet it comprised a set of conventional tasks which were to be performed by the students without the VA.

4.5.3 Treatment design

In view of the information amassed in the theoretical chapters of the current dissertation and the results of the NA, the treatment was implemented in the quasi-experiment with the intention of enhancing Polish EFL learners' ability to mediate a text. The instruction provided by the author was designed in such a way so as to fulfill this aim.

Given the unpredictable character of the COVID-19 pandemic and its destabilising influence on the state of education in Poland at the time of the preparation of the research study by the author, the decision was made to develop such instruction which could be implemented regardless of the circumstances, both during on- and off-site EFL learning. TFOH, the approach proposed and discussed by Shanks (2021), was adopted to overcome EFL learning challenges associated with distance education by providing the Polish students with extra opportunities for practising English in their low-stake home surroundings. In this discussion, TFOH stood for the ExG students' VA-based self-instructed TBLL for text mediation.

Self-instruction, defined by Dickinson (1987) as "a neutral term referring generally to situations in which learners are working without the direct control of the teacher" (p. 11), was an attractive option in light of the global health crisis. Given its practicality and significance in the promotion of increased educational objectives, such as learner autonomy and life-long education (Dickinson, 1979, 1987), it was implemented both in the experimental and conventional intervention underlying the current treatment. Moreover, the application of the self-instruction concept in FLT is in line with the psychology of learning, or the works of Jean Piaget and Jerome Bruner, both of whom underlined the importance of active problem-solving in the process of child development (Little, 1991).

The treatment was implemented to investigate the effects of task-oriented IMALL on the learners' ability to mediate EFL texts. As already said in section 3.5, the use of VAs in CALL is fully justified in view of language learning theories. IMALL enables FL learners to engage in non-tutorial interactions with their mobile devices in the TL (here smartphones and tablets). According to Moussalli and Cardoso (2019), the use of IPAs is fully justified since the technology is said to meet the criteria established for CALL tools by Chapelle (2001). Specifically, VAs satisfy learners' needs (i.e., learner fit). Their use enhances learning through increased input and output (language learning potential) and facilitates meaningful HCIs (interactiveness and focus on meaning). Additionally, they display a potential to positively affect the development of learner autonomy (positive impact) and to be easily used outside the language classroom (practicality).

For the purpose of the current quasi-experiment, Amazon's *Alexa* was chosen (for the application of this assistant in other empirical studies, see Dizon, 2017, 2020; Dizon & Tang, 2019, 2020; Moussalli & Cardoso, 2019). It is by far the most financially successful assistant, with over 30,000 skills, or apps (whose number is constantly on the rise) that allow it to complete voice tasks (Sabharwal, 2020). *Alexa*, just like any other VA, is a voice-based AI-powered technology. When asked "What is Alexa?", the programme responds "Alexa is me! I'm a virtual assistant who can help you with lots of things – like timers and alarms, the weather forecast, the latest news and sports updates, as well as shopping lists and recipes. I can even tell you a joke – just ask." It is easily accessible via mainstream smartphones and dedicated appliances; it can be downloaded on learners' personal mobile devices with Android and iOS operating systems in the form of a mobile voice app through *Google Play/Gallery App* and *App Store* respectively.

In accordance with the AOA to language use adopted within the treatment, the learners were expected to act as individuals and social agents (Piccardo et al., 2011). In other words, they took on the familiar roles of friends, relatives, tourists, and students who function in the communicative situations in their personal (i.e., family relations, individual social practices) and public (i.e., leisure activities of public nature) domains. Action-oriented learning enabled the author to contextualise the learning process by transporting it outside the language classroom and to reduce the probability of the language being practised for its own sake (CoE, 2001).

The participants engaged in an action under the guise of tasks, which hold a dominant position in action orientation (see section 1.2.2). As highlighted by some researchers (e.g., Ellis, 2003b; Long, 1985), it is more probable that learners will acquire the TL when a FL learning process mirrors real-life and out-of-class contexts. In the NA, the data on students' current and future needs had been derived from different sources and through multiple methods (see section 4.5.1). This allowed the author to select such tasks which preserved their real-life character, ensured relevance to students' needs, and displayed a motivational quality (Long, 2015). The features of tasks already discussed in Chapter One (see Table 1.4) were taken into consideration by the present author while developing the tasks for the ExG and CtrlG. The tasks were designed to ensure learners' focus on meaning, clear outcomes, and the relation to the real world. Also, they were based on cognitive and interactionist theories of SLA because they promoted learning by doing and involved rich and elaborate input (Doughty & Long, 2003), in this discussion represented by the source texts and *Alexa*'s feedback.

Based on the results of the NA (see Table 4.11), communicative language activities involving language mediation were found to be students' necessity, lack, and want. In the CV (CoE, 2020), mediation was defined as any situation in which a language user "acts as a social agent who creates bridges and helps to construct or convey meaning, sometimes within the same language, sometimes from one language to another" (p. 90) (for other definitions of mediation, see section 1.3.1.1). Text mediation tasks based on the requirements of the 2023 Matura exam became the focus of this treatment. The tasks were limited to intralinguistic mediation, which meant that students needed to mediate a text within one language, that is English. They were based on the CV's (CoE, 2020) "Relaying specific information" descriptor, which "refers to the way some particular piece of information of immediate relevance is extracted from the target text and relayed to someone else" (p. 93). The emphasis was therefore placed on the specific content of the source texts that was found relevant by the mediator rather than the main ideas and lines of argument presented in the texts. Three concepts were operationalised within this type of text mediation activities:

1. relaying information on times, places, and names of events from announcements,

2. relaying sets of instructions,
3. relaying specific information from informational texts, such as guides and brochures, from correspondence, and from longer texts, such as blog posts (CoE, 2018).

The results of the NA provided the basis for the development of intralinguistic text mediation tasks within the instructional treatment. The contexts of English language use both in Poland and abroad enumerated by the students in the written retrospection, that is "establishing informal communication to help relatives, friends, and foreigners gain access to the text they cannot read and/or understand because of technical and/or linguistic barriers", underlay the design of the tasks. A set of mediation tasks for both the ExG and CtrlG (consisting of eight tasks each) to be performed by the students on a weekly basis was developed by the author in the context of the necessities found particularly important by the respondents in the needs questionnaire (i.e., travelling and sightseeing, gaining access to popular culture).

Authentic and semi-authentic materials provided the basis for the source texts within the tasks. They comprised the pieces of information searched by *Alexa* online in the ExG and *YouTube* videos, blog posts, travel and tourism websites, and food websites in the CtrlG. Based on the data provided by the assistant and those available on the Internet, the present author developed the target texts to be filled out by the participants.

The parameters for task description identified by Stathopoulou (2011) (see section 1.3.2.2) were used to characterise the tasks implemented within the treatment. As presented in Table 4.12, the topics of tasks developed for the ExG and CtrlG covered travelling and popular culture. In the ExG, the discourse environment was limited to *Alexa*. In the CtrlG, there were two types of tasks. Task 1, 3, 5, and 7 targeted listening, which meant that the comprehension of the source texts involved mediators' aural language reception. Tasks 2, 4, 6, and 8, on the other hand, required learners' written language reception and were focused on reading. The students were to fill in the gaps in the target texts, which for the purpose of the current study took the form of informal messages and e-mails. Based on their responses to the needs questionnaire, the participants took on familiar social roles of friends, relatives, and tourists. The performance of each task was motivated by the attainment of a specific communicative objective (e.g., to instruct a cousin who does not have access to the recipe on how to prepare the Yorkshire pudding in Task 4 in the ExG). A set of sixteen tasks developed for the ExG and CtrlG by the current author is listed in the table below (for samples, see Appendix E).

Tab. 4.12: *Description of IVA-based text mediation tasks designed for the ExG and CtrlG (self-prepared)*

		Topic and title of the task	Discourse environment	Text-type	Communicative objective	Mediator-interlocutor relationship
ExG	1	Popular culture and travelling – *Greece*	*Alexa*	informal email	to provide a friend with basic facts about Greece	friend-friend
	2	Popular culture and travelling – *Palace of Culture and Science*		*WhatsApp* notification	to help a friend do her homework by sending her key information on the landmark	friend-friend
	3	Popular culture and travelling – *Madrid and Paris*		*Facebook* group post	to find basic facts about Madrid and Paris to help friends choose their holiday destination	friend-friend
	4	Popular culture – *Yorkshire pudding*		text message	to instruct a cousin on how to prepare Yorkshire pudding	relative-relative
	5	Popular culture and travelling – *London Eye*		note	to provide other tourists with fun facts about London Eye	tourist-tourist
	6	Popular culture – *Star Wars*		written online conversation	to provide other classmates with information about your and your friend's favourite movie	student-student
	7	Popular culture – *McDonald's*		*Messenger* notification	to provide a hotel worker with information about McDonald's to help him find employment	tourist-worker
	8	Popular culture – *BTS*		*Facebook* group post	to find basic information about BTS to choose the birthday present for a friend	friend-friend

CtrlG	1	Popular culture and travelling – *Madame Tussaud's Museum*	interview	note	to provide other tourists with basic information about Madame Tussaud's Museum	tourist-tourist
	2	Popular culture and travelling – *Malta*	leaflet, map, forum, infographic	informal email	to provide a friend with basic facts about Malta	relative-relative
	3	Popular culture – *Boxing Day*	informative talk	informal email	to help a cousin do his English homework	relative-relative
	4	Popular culture and travelling – *Wieliczka Salt Mine*	map, leaflet, forum, ticket office information	*Messenger* notification	to help a student finish her English school project	student-student
	5	Popular culture – *Daniel Craig*	actor's biography	*WhatsApp* notification	to help a friend collect biographical information about the actor who featured in *James Bond* movie series	friend-friend
	6	Popular culture and travelling – *Disneyland*	map, forum, infographic, leaflet	informal email	to convince a friend to visit Disneyland	relative-relative
	7	Popular culture and travelling – *Eiffel Tower*	informative talk	informal email	to provide a younger brother with key facts about the landmark	relative-relative
	8	Popular culture – *Borek*	infographic, leaflet, forum, blog post	note	to help grandma learn basic information about borek	relative-relative

A set of exhaustive instructions was developed by the author to introduce each of the tasks. In accordance with Janowska and Plak's (2021) model (see Figure 1.10), information on the mediator (A), the source text (B), and the imagined interlocutor (C) was accounted for in the preparation process. The instructions to the tasks and the tasks themselves were pilot-tested within Stage Four (see section 4.5.4). To give an example, the English translation of the instructions developed for Task 4 to be completed by the ExG can be found below: "During the Christmas break, your cousin Linda [C] is planning a surprise for her family. She wants to prepare a popular side dish, Yorkshire pudding. However, despite all her efforts, she is not able to achieve her culinary goal because the paper version of her special BBC recipe [B] has gotten destroyed. To finish the dish on time, she begs you for help. Read the text message from Linda below. Ask *Alexa* for assistance and help your cousin fill in her incomplete recipe [A]."

The imagined interlocutors could not familiarise themselves with the source texts because of technical and linguistic problems. The students' intervention as mediators was necessary due to their friends', relatives', and classmates' inadequate EFL competence (e.g., Task 7 in ExG, Task 3 in CtrlG), physical inability to access the source texts (e.g., Task 1 in CtrlG), lack of time (e.g., Task 3 in ExG), and Internet blackout (e.g., Task 2 in ExG, Task 5 in CtrlG). Given the structure of mediation activities within the 2023 Matura, the students-mediators needed to fill in the gaps in the target texts to help their interlocutors access the source texts. In each of the sixteen tasks, there were either six or seven gaps in each of the target texts.

There was, however, a fundamental difference between the ways in which the ExG and CtrlG students accessed the texts. As illustrated in the logic model presented in Figure 4.9, the ExG students were expected to read the target text and identify the kind of information missing (e.g., number, date, temperature, height, activity, attraction, name and surname, place, title, etc.), ask *Alexa* an appropriate question, and fill in the gap in the target text with the missing information. In other words, to gain access to the source text, they needed to ask the IVA a question. *Alexa* provided the students with multimodal input: written (i.e., a text), visual (i.e., a photograph), and aural (i.e., sound) (for sample screenshots, see Appendix F). In the CtrlG, on the other hand, the students did not need to negotiate meanings. Instead, they were expected to read the target text to identify what kind of information is missing in order to find the desired pieces of data in the source texts, be that written (i.e., forums, blog posts), visual (i.e., infographics, maps, diagrams, photos) or aural (i.e., interviews, biographies, informative talks). Next, they needed to use the ideas from the source texts to fill in the gaps in the target text. As a consequence, as demonstrated below, the aural/written language reception and written language production underlay traditional text mediation tasks. The performance of *Alexa*-based mediation tasks, on the other hand, required multimodal HCIs between the student and the VA in addition to written language reception and production.

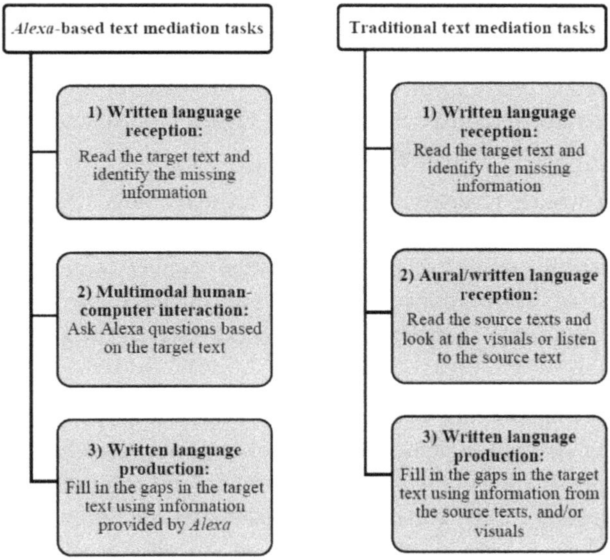

Fig. 4.8: *Logic model underlying the performance of tasks by the ExG and CtrlG (self-prepared)*

The process of designing technology-mediated tasks for language teaching should account not only for the main task alone, but also for warm-up and consolidating activities (Lopez & Ruiz-Cecilia, 2017). Based on the most commonly applied and frequently cited model of lesson design within TBLT proposed by Willis (1996, p. 50) and Willis and Willis (2007, p. 254), which offered a classical division into the pre-task, task, and post-task phase, we isolated three phases in the performance of the task within the instructional treatment in the current quasi-experiment (see Figure 4.10).

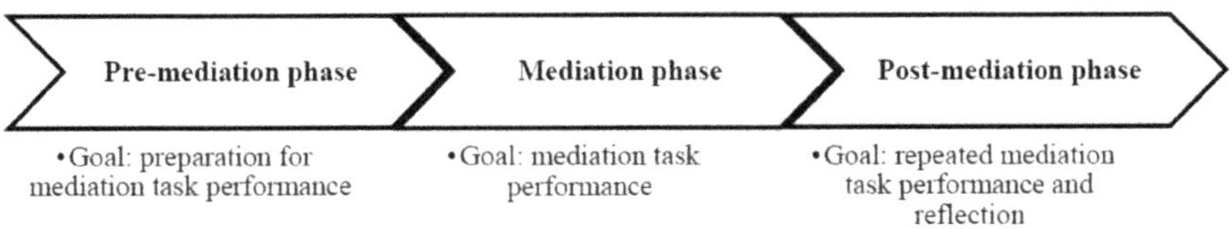

Fig. 4.9: *Logic model underlying text mediation tasks in the treatment (self-prepared)*

The goal of the pre-mediation phase was to prepare the students for their future task completion. Skehan's (1996a) concept of restructuring was adopted therein to reduce the processing load. This was achieved through foregrounding, or introducing the topic of the task through the presentation of instructions, and planning by the students what kind of information they might need to successfully complete the mediation process.

The mediation phase involved learners' performance of the task. It could be further subdivided into three stages (confer Figure 4.9), each of which involved a different communication mode:

1. written language reception – the learners read the target text to decide what kind of information was missing
2. oral interaction in the ExG/aural and written language reception in the CtrlG – the learners searched for the required information in the source texts
3. written language production – the learners filled in the gaps in the target text

The activities implemented in the last stage of the mediation task implementation, the post-mediation phase, involved learners' repeated task performance and reflection. The former was found helpful in "inducing effective use of attentional resources during tasks, and of balancing the various goals that are desirable" (Skehan, 1996, p. 20). The latter, on the other hand, encouraged the students to evaluate the outcome of the task and their mediation performance (Willis, 1996).

In total, there were sixteen tasks targeting intralinguistic text mediation. They were to be performed by the ExG and CtrlG students individually within their weekly homework assignments throughout the period of sixteen weeks. Each task was preceded and followed by the pre- and post-mediation phase, which were to support the learners in the mediation of the source texts within the main phase and encourage their critical reflection on their performance respectively (for samples, see Appendix E). The selected tasks were pilot-tested and evaluated by the students within Stage Four of the current research procedure.

4.5.4 Pilot project and the main study

As already mentioned, the aim of the pilot-testing stage was to identify problems with the research design, treatment design, and data collection and analysis methods to improve the research procedure underlying the main study. Based on students' written responses and informal comments provided by the EFL instructor who was in charge of running the pilot project, a number of modifications to the main study were carried out. Each of the changes introduced to the main stage is presented and accounted for below.

It was highlighted by the students that they had been provided with too little time to prepare for the performance of the technology-mediated tasks. As reported informally by the EFL instructor, the learners complained during the in-class discussion that the *Alexa* user guide had been handed out too late. Those students who had never used *Alexa* (and any other VA) also expressed their strong wish to have a warm-up activity assigned in order to practise HCIs. The author decided to include such a preparation activity in the instructions and gave students more time (i.e., two weeks) to familiarise themselves with the basics of HMC to be better prepared for the experimental intervention.

As pointed out by the majority of the students, the instructions to the ExG and CtrlG tasks required editing. The learners from Group A and Group B agreed that the instructions were excessively long and highly complicated. The participants stressed the fact that they provided too many intricate details on the imagined interlocutors and the causes underlying mediator's intervention. Having perused the instructions again, the author decided to abbreviate the texts from nine-eleven to six-eight sentences to include only the pieces of information that were absolutely necessary for the students to perform the mediation tasks. Some tiny details were therefore omitted to provide the learners with possibly short yet informative introduction to each task.

Another modification concerned the key to the ExG and CtrlG tasks. Once the participants of the pilot project had performed their homework assignments and checked them with their EFL instructor, it turned out that based on the source texts and the information provided by *Alexa*, more than one answer was correct. More elaborate answer key was thus developed for the sixteen tasks by the author in collaboration with her colleague who agreed to perform the tasks on her own, compare her answers with the key, and if necessary, supply it with alternative acceptable answers.

The EFL teacher also drew author's attention to several spelling mistakes that she had identified in the instructions as well as the source and target texts. This encouraged her to adequately address this problem to avoid similar issues in the study proper. She reread the tasks distributed among the participants of the pilot project to locate and correct the mistakes. In addition, another EFL instructor was requested to take the printed copies of the remaining twelve tasks home and mark any typographical and grammatical errors that she had managed to spot.

The next change to the data collection plans to be discussed here occurred in the area of the programme evaluation. In the pilot project, both the ExG and CtrlG were asked to complete the post-study questionnaire and participate in the SSIs simultaneously. In so far as it was not a problem in the case of the one-month pilot project, it would be a problem in the main study. Group A students, who took on the ExG status in Phase 1 of the quasi-experiment, would be asked to evaluate the *Alexa*-based instruction eight weeks after they had completed it. The decision was therefore made that the participants would immediately enter into Stage Six of the present research procedure (i.e., programme evaluation) as soon as the experimental intervention had been completed.

Finally, two questions were added to the interview guide. Their aim was to invite the students to express their personal opinions on the experimental intervention. The first question in Section 3 asked the participants to decide whether they would continue to use the technology with the aim of improving their EFL learning (to mediate) and explain their decision. The second one encouraged the students to critically evaluate the treatment by suggesting expected improvements.

As previously stated, the experimental research design with the factor rotation underlay the research study conducted in Stage Five of the current research procedure. Six intact groups consisting of 61 Polish EFL secondary school students, 39 girls and 22 boys, divided into Groups A (n=31) and B (n=30) successfully participated in two phases of the eighteen-week quasi-experiment. They completed the background questionnaire (see section 4.4 and Appendix B), performed sixteen homework assignments both as CtrlG and ExG members (for sample tasks, see Appendix E), and took three written intralinguistic text mediation tests (see section 4.5.4 and Appendix G).

Throughout the duration of the treatment, Groups A and B were expected to perform eight intralinguistic text mediation tasks with the help of *Alexa*. When they took on the role of CtrlG students, they were expected to complete a set of eight traditional paper-and-pencil text mediation-oriented homework assignments. Detailed schedule for the homework assignments and the implementation of the data collection instruments can be found in Table 4.28. For convenience, italics are used to denote the ExG.

In mid-October 2021, three weeks before the beginning of the quasi-experiment, the author consulted two EFL teachers to finalise the details on how the research should be conducted. The instructors were provided with the research plan outlining the dates of the meetings during which particular data collection instruments and the ExG and CtrlG homework assignments should be implemented. All the required documents (i.e., the background and post-study questionnaires, mediation tests, homework assignments) were sent to the EFL

Tab. 4.13: Schedule for the homework assignments and the implementation of the data collection tools: the quasi-experimental study with the factor rotation technique (self-prepared)

			Homework assignment	**Group A (n=31)**	**Group B (n=30)**
Phase 1	**Week 1**	Nov 8-12		Background questionnaire	
				T_1	T_2
	Week 1-8	Nov 8-12	Homework assignment 1-8	*Intralinguistic text mediation-oriented IVA-based tasks*	Traditional intralinguistic text-mediating tasks
		Nov 15-19			
		Nov 22-26			
		Nov 29-Dec 3			
		Dec 6-10			
		Dec 13-18			
		Dec 20-22			
		Jan 10-14			
	Week 9	Jan 17-21		T_3	T_4
Phase 2	**Week 10-17**	Jan 24-29	Homework assignment 1-8	Traditional intralinguistic text-mediating tasks	*Intralinguistic text mediation-oriented IVA-based tasks*
		Jan 31-Feb 4			
		Feb 7-11			
		Feb 28-Mar 4			
		Mar 7-11			
		Mar 14-18			
		Mar 21-25			
		Mar 28-Apr 1			
	Week 18	Apr 4-8		T_5	T_6

teachers in an electronic version via e-mail. The instructors maintained regular contact with the researcher throughout the duration of the eighteen-week quasi-experiment, informing her about the progress and delays in the study. They also committed neither to performing any mediation activities in-class nor assigning homework involving mediation practice throughout the experimental intervention.

The author randomly selected Group A students as those that would receive the treatment in the first place. The EFL instructors were therefore asked to inform the participants two weeks before the study proper began (Oct 25-29) that the latter would be assigned to do one technology-mediated homework assignment a week. To prepare the students for the performance of the tasks, each of the three groups was provided with the *Alexa* user guide two weeks prior to the introduction of the treatment. The file was uploaded by the EFL instructors on the *Google Classroom* platform so that each student could read the document whenever and wherever they wanted. At the same time, Group B students became the CtrlG. They did not receive any extra materials to work with on their own within their English homework prior to the experimental intervention.

One week before the launch of the treatment in the ExG and the introduction of conventional mediation tasks to the CtrlG (Nov 3-5), the EFL instructors asked the students whether they had managed to successfully install the app on their smartphones or tablets and perform the preparation activity assigned within the instructions. They also informed their learners that from the following week on they would be provided with one VA-based mediation task to perform on a weekly basis through the period of eight weeks. Similarly, the CtrlG students were notified that in addition to conventional homework assignments based on the *New Enterprise B1* coursebook, they would be expected to perform one text mediation task, which would be regularly uploaded on *Google Classroom*. The teachers also explained the reason behind the introduction of the tasks and briefly presented the key information on the 2023 Matura examination. The students met three times a week, which meant that one out of three assignments would include the performance of a mediation task.

The study proper began in the second week of November 2021 (Nov 8-12) with the administration of the background questionnaire by two EFL instructors among Group A and Group B students, the first round of text mediation tests (T_1 and T_2), and the implementation of the first mediation task. Throughout the following eight weeks (Nov 8-Jan 14), ExG and CtrlG students were required to perform one mediation-based homework assignment in addition to conventional homework they were assigned to do by their EFL instructors. Each task was uploaded by the teachers on *Google Classroom*. Students' answers provided to the tasks were checked and discussed during the English class following each ExG and CtrlG homework assignment.

In Week 9 of the quasi-experiment (Jan 17-21), the second round of mediation tests (T_3 and T_4) was administered in the ExG and CtrlG. This marked the end of Phase 1 and the beginning of Phase 2, when Group A and B switched their roles as the ExG and CtrlG. As soon as the students completed all the technology-mediated tasks, which marked the end of the experimental intervention, they took part in the programme evaluation (for details, see section 4.5.6).

Similarly to Phase 1, throughout the following eight weeks of Phase 2 (Jan 24-Apr 1), the ExG and CtrlG students were expected to complete one mediation task in addition to conventional homework that they were assigned to do by their EFL instructors. As already said, Group A students were expected to complete traditional tasks, whereas Group B interacted with the VA to perform their homework. Students' answers were checked with the teachers during the following English class.

In Week 18 of the quasi-experiment (Apr 4-8), the third (and final) round of mediation tests (T_5 and T_6) was administered in the ExG and CtrlG. This marked the end of the quasi-experiment with the factor rotation technique. As soon as the experimental intervention had drawn to an end, Group B students took part in the programme evaluation.

To evaluate the change in participants' EFL intralinguistic text mediation brought about by *Alexa*-based and action-oriented self-instruction in the current study, Group A and Group B took three written text-mediating tests prior to the experimental intervention and after they had changed their position from the ExG and CtrlG and vice versa. During the first measurement (T_1 and T_2), one third of the learners completed version A (i.e., G_A1 and G_B2), one third version B (i.e., G_A2 and G_B3), and one third version C (i.e., G_A3 and G_B1). As presented in Table 4.29, the versions were subsequently swapped around; the students who had been given version A during T_1 received version B during T_3, those pretested with version B were provided with version C, and those who had been asked to complete version C were asked to work with version A. At the end of Phase 2, the tests were swapped again to ensure that each of the participants received the same version of the test only once.

Tab. 4.14: *Distribution of the testing instrument in the quasi-experiment with the factor rotation technique: the main study (G_A: Group A students who served as the ExG in Phase 1; G_B: Group B students who served as the CtrlG in Phase 1) (self-prepared)*

	The beginning of Phase 1		**The end pf Phase 1/ The beginning of Phase 2**		**The end of Phase 2**	
	T_1	T_2	T_3	T_4	T_5	T_6
	Written measure					
Intralinguistic text mediation	G_A1: A	G_B1: C	G_A1: B	G_B1: A	G_A1: C	G_B1: B
	G_A2: B	G_B2: A	G_A2: C	G_B2: B	G_A2: A	G_B2: C
	G_A3: C	G_B3: B	G_A3: A	G_B3: C	G_A3: B	G_B3: A

The data collected in the text mediation tests (T_1-T_6) were subjected to quantitative analysis. The mean, median, mode, SD, minimum and maximum scores were calculated for the ExG and CtrlG. Depending on the result of the *Shapiro-Wilk Normality Test*, which examines the distribution of a statistical dataset, either parametric or non-parametric tests (or the two) were performed. To contrast scores obtained by the ExG, the *Paired Samples T-Test* or the *Wilcoxon Signed Rank Test* were run. For the comparison of the two groups (i.e., ExG versus CtrlG), the *Two Sample T-Test* or the *Mann-Whitney U Test* was chosen. If the parametric *Independent Samples T-Test* was chosen, the *Levene's F Test* needed to be performed in the first place to assess the homogeneity of variances. The 0.05 level of statistical significance was chosen for the purpose of the current research study.

4.5.5 Programme evaluation

In the final stage of the research procedure, the evaluation of the treatment by the ExG students began. It was carried out to amass the data necessary to answer the

Tab. 4.15: Schedule for the programme evaluation: the quasi-experimental study with the factor rotation technique (self-prepared)

<table>
<tr><th></th><th></th><th></th><th>Homework assignment</th><th>Group A (n=31)</th><th>Group B (n=30)</th></tr>
<tr><td rowspan="4">Phase 1</td><td rowspan="2">Week 1</td><td rowspan="2">Nov 8-12</td><td rowspan="2"></td><td colspan="2">Background questionnaire</td></tr>
<tr><td>T_1</td><td>T_2</td></tr>
<tr><td>Week 1-8</td><td>Nov 8-Jan 14</td><td>Homework assignment 1-8</td><td>Intralinguistic text mediation-oriented IVA-based tasks</td><td>Traditional intralinguistic text-mediating tasks</td></tr>
<tr><td rowspan="2">Week 9</td><td rowspan="2">Jan 17-21</td><td rowspan="2"></td><td>T_3</td><td rowspan="2">T_4</td></tr>
<tr><td rowspan="4">Phase 2</td><td>Post-study questionnaire
Post-study SSI</td></tr>
<tr><td>Week 10-17</td><td>Jan 24- Apr 1</td><td>Homework assignment 1-8</td><td>Traditional intralinguistic text-mediating tasks</td><td>Intralinguistic text mediation-oriented IVA-based tasks</td></tr>
<tr><td rowspan="2">Week 18</td><td rowspan="2">Apr 4-8</td><td rowspan="2"></td><td rowspan="2">T_5</td><td>T_6</td></tr>
<tr><td>Post-study questionnaire
Post-study SSI</td></tr>
</table>

CRQ2. Quantitative and qualitative methods of data collection and analysis were adopted in the descriptive research design underlying Stage Six of the current research procedure. Two data collection instruments (i.e., the post-study questionnaire and post-study SSI) were introduced by the present author to examine participants' views on the use of *Alexa* during the experimental intervention. The schedule for the implementation of these research tools within the programme evaluation can be found in Table 4.30. For convenience, bolding is used to mark the moment when Stage Six began in the ExG.

To explore the participants' views on their HMC, the post-study questionnaire on technology was used. It was developed to assess students' perceptions of using *Alexa* for their out-of-class EFL learning. Each of twelve items asked the students to assess the degree to which they agreed with the statements by using a six-point Likert scale ranging from *strongly disagree* (1) to *strongly agree* (6). The items to the questionnaire were written in English by Dizon and Tang (2019, 2020) and then translated by the present author into participants' L1 (Polish) to prevent comprehension problems. Students' acceptance of *Alexa* was measured therein based on Davis' (1989) technology acceptance model (TAM), which consists of the following components:

1. the usability of the VA in EFL learning to mediate (Statement 1-4)
2. the effectiveness of the VA in EFL learning to mediate (Statement 5-8)
3. satisfaction with the implementation of the technology in TFOH (Statement 9-12)

The data were subjected to statistical analysis. Mean, median, mode, SD, minimum and maximum values, and percentages of agreement values of the Likert-type items were calculated.

In addition to the application of the post-study questionnaire to all the study participants, post-study SSIs were conducted. They were completed individually at a time convenient for the selected interviewees via the *Zoom Cloud Meetings* video conferencing software programme. The interviews were conducted in Polish to explore learners' perceptions of the use of *Alexa* in their EFL learning (to mediate). They lasted for 20 to 30 minutes.

The participants were selected through purposive MVS, which is viewed as contributing to the validity of research by making the findings more generalisable (Dörnyei, 2007). Twelve learners (i.e., six proponents and six opponents) were chosen from the sample to participate in the interview based on their answers to the survey.

An interview guide which consisted of a set of seven questions prepared by the researcher was used. The interview questions were divided into three blocks: students' acceptance of *Alexa* based on the TAM (Davis, 1989), students' self-perceived advantages and disadvantages to using the IVA for the purpose of EFL learning (to mediate), and students' attitudes to implementing *Alexa* in their regular EFL learning (to mediate). Part One included three questions. They asked the interviewees to express their opinions on their self-perceived usefulness and effectiveness of *Alexa* (Question 1-2) and their satisfaction with the use of the IVA (Question 3). The students were requested to share their comments on why (or why not) they thought the voice assistant had been useful, effective, and satisfactory in their EFL self-instruction. In Part Two, there were two questions related to the advantages and disadvantages to using the VA in participants' EFL learning. To be specific, Question 4 asked the learners to think of the benefits that, in their opinion, could be derived from the introduction of *Alexa* to their EFL education. Question 5, on the other hand, encouraged the participants to consider any challenges that they had identified and/or experienced during the performance of their homework assignments. Part Three comprised two questions. They aimed to reveal students' final thoughts related to the technology use in learning English. Question 6 asked whether the participants would continue to use technology with the aim of improving their English and in particular their ability to mediate a text. Question 7, on the other hand, invited the learners to share their suggestions to improve the task-oriented IMALL treatment and add their comments related to the use of technology in their EFL self-instructed learning.

The transcriptions of the interviews were categorised in the context of five topics of the CRQ2 (i.e., usefulness, effectiveness, satisfaction, benefits, and challenges) with the help of *Taquette* to reduce tedious work (Kondracki et al., 2002). To find out how the learners evaluated their interaction with the IVA, Qualitative Content Analysis was performed. An inductive approach to data analysis was adopted, which means that the themes were directly taken from the data (Kondracki et al., 2002) and developed in accordance with the aims of the study (Charmaz, 1996). Finally, to support the reliability of the data analysis process, 10% of the qualitative data were analysed by another EFL teacher.

4.6 Ethical considerations

Research ethics is crucial in any study involving human participation. "Standards for behaviour that suit their particular aims and goals" (Resnik, 2015, para. 7) should be maintained by researchers throughout the research process, including the planning stage and data collection, analysis, and interpretation (Dooly et al., 2017).

Before the data collection process and the treatment began, the present author had obtained an oral approval of the school administration to conduct the study.

Also, she was given the oral informed consent from the two English teachers to participate in the research, that is to gather the required data from the students, implement the experimental procedures, and adapt their EFL in-class and out-of-class instruction to the requirements of the eighteen-week study.

One of the key ethical considerations, the principle of informed consent, requires the study participants to agree to participate in the study on a voluntary basis and to be fully acquainted with the purposes and procedures involved in a particular research procedure (Terrell, 2012). Nevertheless, in the current study neither of the six groups had been informed about the experiment until it was performed. It was our intentional action to avoid the potential collection of unreliable data inherent to the Hawthorne effect.

Once the participants had been notified of their participation in the experimental procedure and the research aims, they could withhold the approval for their data to be processed during the analysis and interpretation stages of the research. It must be emphasised here that only the pieces of data obtained from the students who had provided their oral consent to participate in the study were stored and then subjected to analysis and interpretation.

A step-by-step user guide on how to create an account, log into the Amazon's website, download the *Alexa* app, and interact with the VA was distributed among all the students two weeks prior to the experimental intervention. The participants had time to familiarise themselves with the software and perform a few simple tasks with the help of *Alexa* to identify potential difficulties which could be successfully overcome with the help of their instructors before the treatment arrived. The English instructors had been trained beforehand by the researcher in how to use *Alexa* to help students solve potential technology-related problems.

Clear instructions written in participants' L1 were provided before any data gathering procedure was implemented, be it a test, a questionnaire, or an interview. Efforts were made to guarantee that no threatening questions were asked to the participants and that they could answer the questions within the planning times and other times at their convenience (Bradburn et al., 1979).

The factor rotation technique was employed not only to control for the group inequality and increase the internal validity of the study, but also to deal with the ethical concerns pertaining to the provision of the best instruction to all the students (Pawlak & Kruk, 2012). As the ExG and CtrlG swapped their roles in two phases of the quasi-experiment, the intervention was equally distributed among all the study participants.

The treatment did not inflict any physical, emotional, and psychological harm to the study participants. Honesty was maintained when conducting online video interviews during needs assessment and programme evaluation because oral permission for voice recording was obtained from the interviewees.

Appropriate measures were taken to protect participants' identity. Confidentiality of their written and recorded responses to the survey and interview questions was ensured. The names of the individual learners, teachers, school administrators, and institutions were anonymised during the presentation of the methodology adopted in the study, data analysis, and the discussion of findings. The students were assured that any information provided by them in the study would be used for the purpose of the research only.

Ethical standards oblige researchers to retain integrity in the interpretation of the data. As any conclusions should be drawn from the data themselves, due care was taken "to not over-interpret or misinterpret the data and represent the possible conclusions as closely as possible" (Dooly et al., 2017, p. 352). Experimental and descriptive approaches to research design were adopted to triangulate and corroborate the findings, with the former helping to test hypotheses and the latter providing explanations of the issues under examination. A MM research design was also followed to combine the advantages of quantitative and qualitative methods in light of the requirements of the three CRQs.

The researcher did her best to take into account all these ethical considerations in the current research. First and foremost, she made sure that all the parties involved gave their informed consent to participate in the study, preserved the privacy of the students, and maintained integrity throughout the research process.

Chapter 5
VAs in action-oriented mediation practice in a Polish EFL secondary school context: Study results and discussion

5.0 Outline

The chief aim of Chapter Five is to report upon the research study examining the use of *Alexa* in out-of-class TBLL for text mediation. For this purpose, the analysis was conducted on the quantitative and qualitative data which were collected in Stage Five (Main study) and Stage Six (Programme evaluation) of the current research procedure. The chapter is divided into five subchapters for this purpose. The first subchapter reports the findings from the examination of the pre- and post-tests, the post-study questionnaires and SSIs. In the second subchapter, the findings related to the CRQs and their subquestions are discussed by making references to the relevant literature. The pedagogical implications related to the findings of the study are reviewed in the third subchapter. Finally, following the presentation of the conclusions from the study in the fourth subchapter, the limitations to the current quasi-experiment and recommendations for future research based on the results of the present study as well as the past VA research are shared.

5.1 Data analysis and presentation

5.1.1 Main study findings

5.1.1.1 Pre- and post-tests

In total, 183 mediation tests (93 copies from Group A and 90 copies from Group B) were collected from November 2021 to April 2022. They were scored by the present author and her EFL colleague and subjected to quantitative analysis to answer the CRQ1 and test the null hypotheses related to the influence of the treatment on participants' text mediation skills at within- and between-group levels. The mean, median, SD, minimum and maximum scores, and percentages of correct answers were calculated for oral and written text mediation in the tests administered in Group A (T_1, T_3, T_5) and Group B (T_2, T_4, T_6) in two phases of the quasi-experiment (see Table 5.1).

Tab. 5.1: *Descriptive statistics for Activities 1 and 2 in the pre- and post-tests administered in Group A (n=31) and Group B (n=30) in Phase 1 and Phase 2: the main study (self-prepared)*

				Mean	Median	SD	Min	Max	Percentage of correct answers
Group A	n=31	T_1	1	1.71	2	0.902	0	3	34%
			2	2.77	3	0.884	1	4	55%
		T_3	1	3.39	3	0.495	3	4	68%
			2	3.61	4	0.667	3	5	72%
		T_5	1	4.19	4	0.601	3	5	84%
			2	4.23	4	0.762	3	5	85%
Group B	n=30	T_2	1	1.80	2	0.887	0	3	36%
			2	2.40	2	0.814	1	4	48%
		T_4	1	2.80	3	0.761	2	4	56%
			2	3.00	3	0.910	2	5	60%
		T_6	1	4.00	4	0.643	3	5	80%
			2	4.20	4	0.761	3	5	84%

The mean scores and median values for Activities 1 and 2 in T_1 and T_2, which were administered at the beginning of the study, were low, ranging from 1.71 to 2.77 out of a maximum 5 points. As demonstrated by the data in Table 5.1, Group A and Group B students were very similar in their ability to mediate oral texts. This can be confirmed by the mean scores (1.71 versus 1.80) and median values (2 versus 2 points) achieved by the two groups. A subtle difference, however, could be observed in the students' performance in written text mediation, with Group A slightly outperforming Group B in this respect, as evidenced in its slightly higher mean score (2.77 versus 2.40) and median value (3 versus 2 points). It is interesting to note that none of the students scored a maximum of 5 points in both oral and written text mediation activities in T_1 and T_2.

The results of T_3 and T_4 (or the post-tests taken by the ExG and CtrlG at the end of Phase 1) indicate that both Group A, which received the treatment, and Group B, which was exposed to conventional self-instruction, performed better on oral and written text mediation. To be precise, the mean scores increased in the ExG from 1.71 to 3.39 and from 2.77 to 3.61 for oral and written text mediation respectively. The increase in the mean scores from 1.80 to 2.80 (Activity 1) and from 2.40 to 3.00 (Activity 2) could also be observed in the CtrlG after the students completed traditional homework. At the same time, the comparison of T_3 and T_4

suggest that the ExG performed better than the CtrlG, as evidenced in the mean scores for oral (3.39 versus 2.80) and written (3.61 versus 3.00) text mediation.

T_5 and T_6 were administered at the end of Phase 2, that is when Group A and Group B changed their status from the ExG to CtrlG and from the CtrlG to ExG respectively. The mean scores for Activities 1 and 2 suggest that having participated in Phase 2 of the quasi-experiment, Group A and Group B students further improved their ability to mediate oral and written texts, as illustrated by an increase from 3.39 to 4.19 (Activity 1) and from 3.61 to 4.23 (Activity 2) in the CtrlG as well as from 2.80 to 4.00 (Activity 1) and from 3.00 to 4.20 (Activity 2) in the ExG. It can be observed that in Phase 2, Group B (the ExG) caught up with Group A, as evidenced in the similar mean scores for oral (4.19 versus 4.00) and written (4.23 versus 4.20) text mediation. It must be added here that the minimum and maximum values for oral and written text mediation in T_5 and T_6 changed considerably compared to those in T_1-T_4, rising from 0 to 3 and from 3 to 5 points respectively.

To determine whether the differences between the data were statistically significant, an appropriate method of statistical analysis had to be selected. For that purpose, the *Shapiro-Wilk Test* was run on each of the dataset (T_1-T_6) to check whether the variables followed a normal distribution. The normality test statistic (W) was used to detect any departures from normality. The H_0 for this test states that the sample was taken from a normal distribution, and the H_A predicts the opposite. When the p-value is less than or equal to 0.05, the hypothesis of normality has to be rejected, with a smaller p-value showing stronger evidence against the null hypothesis. As presented by the data in Table 5.2, the results of the normality test indicated that the distribution of ExG (i.e., T_1, T_3, T_5) and CtrlG (i.e., T_2, T_4, T_6) variables deviated significantly from normality. The p-values for all the variables were < 0.05. The normality assumption was therefore rejected.

Tab. 5.2: *Results of the* Shapiro-Wilk Test *for variables T_1-T_6: the main study (self-prepared)*

			Pre-test	W	p	Post-test	W	p
Group A (n=31)	Phase 1	1	T_1	0.88	0.002*	T_3	0.62	0.000*
		2		0.86	0.0009*		0.76	0.00001*
	Phase 2	1	T_3	0.62	0.000*	T_5	0.76	0.0001*
		2		0.76	0.00001*		0.79	0.00003*
Group B (n=30)	Phase 1	1	T_2	0.85	0.00074*	T_4	0.80	0.00005*
		2		0.86	0.00083*		0.81	0.00010*
	Phase 2	1	T_4	0.80	0.00005*	T_6	0.79	0.00004*
		2		0.81	0.00010*		0.80	0.00005*

In view of the above, the *Wilcoxon Signed Rank Test* (or a non-parametric alternative to the *Paired Samples T-Test*) was performed to assess whether the treatment had an effect on the learners' ability to mediate oral and written texts at within-group levels. To be precise, it was run to compare two sets of scores for Activity 1 and 2 obtained from the same group (i.e., T_1 versus T_3, T_4 versus T_6) and to determine whether the two variables are different from each other in a statistically significant manner based on ranks. The median values standing for the middle numbers in a sorted list of numbers rather than the means (or average scores) were examined. The statistical significance of the tests (p) was judged at the 0.05 significance level.

As already said, the mean scores and median values for oral text mediation (Activity 1) were higher in the post-tests, T_3 (3.39; 3) and T_6 (4.00; 4), than in the pre-tests, T_1 (1.71; 2) and T_4 (2.80; 3). This indicates that Group A and Group B students performed better in the examined area in question after the experimental factor had been included in their EFL self-instruction. The eight-week treatment introduced in Phase 1 for Group A ($Z= 4.54$; $p=0.000006$) and in Phase 2 for Group B ($Z=3.96$; $p=0.000074$) led to statistically significant changes in the ExG students' ability to mediate oral texts. The results of the *Wilcoxon Signed Rank Test*, which was run to compare the sample medians from the pre- and post-test scores, allowed us to refute the H_0 for this test stating that the median of differences of ExG students' answers to Activity 1 in the post- and pre-tests equals 0 ($p<0.05$). H_A, according to which the median of differences of ExG students' answers to Activity 1 in the post- and pre-tests is higher than 0, could be accepted.

Similarly, the mean scores and median values for written text mediation (Activity 2) in the post-tests, T_3 (3.61; 4) and T_6 (4.20; 4), and the pre-tests, T_1 (2.77; 3) and T_4 (3.00; 3), demonstrate that Group A and Group B students performed better on written text mediation having been exposed to the treatment. As demonstrated by the data in Table 5.3, eight technology-mediated tasks introduced in Phase 1 for Group A ($Z=3.49$; $p=0.000477$) and in Phase 2 for Group B ($Z=3.68$; $p=0.000231$) led to statistically significant changes in the ExG students' ability to mediate written texts. The results of the *Wilcoxon Signed Rank Test* challenged the H_0 for this test that the median of differences of ExG students' answers to Activity 2 in the post- and pre-tests equals 0 ($p<0.05$). The H_A, according to which the median of differences of ExG students' answers to Activity 2 in the post- and pre-tests is higher than 0, was accepted.

Tab. 5.3: *Mean scores, median values, and* Wilcoxon Signed Rank Test *results for the pre- (T_1, T_4) and post-tests (T_3, T_6) in Group A (the ExG in Phase 1) and Group B (the ExG in Phase 2): the main study (self-prepared)*

			Pre-test	**Mean**	**Median**	**Post-test**	**Mean**	**Median**	**Z**	**p**
Group A (n=31)	Phase 1	1	T_1	1.71	2	T_3	3.39	3	4.54	0.000006*
		2		2.77	3		3.61	4	3.49	0.000477*
Group B (n=30)	Phase 2	1	T_4	2.80	3	T_6	4.00	4	3.96	0.000074*
		2		3.00	3		4.20	4	3.68	0.000231*

In addition, the same non-parametric test was used to examine the effects of the traditional self-instruction on the CtrlG students' ability to mediate oral and written texts. Its findings indicated that conventional mediation tasks also had a statistically significant effect on CtrlG students' intralinguistic oral text mediation in Phase 1 ($Z=3.86$; $p=0.000112$) and Phase 2 ($Z=4.01$; $p=0.000060$). Again, the H_0 stating that the median of differences of CtrlG students' answers to Activity 1 in the post- and pre-tests equals 0, was refuted as there was a statistically significant difference in students' answers before and after traditional homework was introduced, as evidenced in $p<0.05$. The mean scores and median values for the post-tests, T_4 (2.80; 3) and T_5 (4.19; 4), were higher as compared with the pre-tests, T_2 (1.80; 2) and T_3 (3.39; 3), suggesting that Group A and Group B students accomplished oral text mediation activities more successfully having participated in traditional self-instruction. The H_A, according to which the median of differences of CtrlG students' answers to Activity 1 in the post- and pre-tests is higher than 0, was accepted.

The findings of the *Wilcoxon Signed Rank Test* also revealed that conventional mediation tasks had a statistically significant effect on CtrlG students' intralinguistic written text mediation. Again, the H_0 stating that the median of differences of CtrlG students' answers to Activity 2 in the post- and pre-tests equals 0 was refuted as there was a statistically significant difference in CtrlG students' answers before and after traditional homework was introduced in Phase 1 ($Z=2.83$; $p=0.004676$) and Phase 2 ($Z=2.41$; $p=0.016043$), as evidenced in $p<0.05$. The mean scores for the post-tests, T_4 (3.00) and T_5 (4.23), were higher than for the pre-tests, T_2 (2.40) and T_3 (3.61). This shows that Group A and Group B students performed better on written text mediation having performed traditional mediation homework assignment. The H_A predicting that CtrlG students improved their written text mediation could therefore be accepted as the median of differences of participants' answers to Activity 2 in the post- and pre-tests was > 0. Even though the median values were the same in Phase 2 (4 points), the mean scores (3.61 versus 4.23) indicate that Group A performed better on Activity 2 after rather than prior to traditional self-instruction.

Tab. 5.4: *Mean scores, median values, and* Wilcoxon Signed Rank Test *results for the pre- (T_2, T_3) and post-tests (T_4, T_5) in Group B (the CtrlG in Phase 1) and Group A (the CtrlG in Phase 2): the main study (self-prepared)*

			Pre-test	Mean	Median	Post-test	Mean	Median	Z	p
Group B (n=30)	Phase 1	1	T_2	1.80	2	T_4	2.80	3	3.86	0.000112*
		2		2.40	2		3.00	3	2.41	0.016043*
Group A (n=31)	Phase 2	1	T_3	3.39	3	T_5	4.19	4	4.01	0.000060*
		2		3.61	4		4.23	4	2.83	0.004676*

To find out whether the eight-week treatment had any effect on the DV at between-group levels, either the parametric or non-parametric test, which compares the scores achieved by the two groups, should be run. To find out if the variables followed a normal distribution, the *Shapiro-Wilk Normality Test* was run before any statistical test was selected. For that purpose, the mean gain scores for the ExG (T_3-T_1 and T_6-T_4) and CtrlG (T_4-T_2 and T_5-T_3) for Activities 1 and 2, that is the differences of students' scores for EFL oral and written text mediation on the post- and pre-tests, were calculated. For example, in Group A, which became the ExG in Phase 1 of the quasi-experiment, the scores achieved by the students in Activities 1 and 2 in T_1 (the pre-test) were subtracted from those from T_3 (the post-test). At the same time, in Group B, which served as the CtrlG in Phase 1, the scores obtained by the students in Activities 1 and 2 in T_2 (the pre-test) were subtracted from those from T_4 (the post-test). The same procedure was applied to calculate the differences of students' scores for oral and written text mediation on the post- and pre-tests in Phase 2. The differences of mean scores for T_3 and T_1,T_4 and T_2, T_5 and T_3, and T_6 and T_4 were > 0. This allows us to argue that both experimental treatment and traditional mediation homework had a positive effect on ExG and CtrlG the students' oral and written text mediation skills. The results of the *Shapiro-Wilk Test* are presented in Table 5.5

The data suggest that the normality hypothesis had to be challenged for all the variables ($p<0.05$).

Tab. 5.5: *Results of the* Shapiro-Wilk's Test *for variables* T_3-T_1, T_4-T_2, T_5-T_3, *and* T_6-T_4: *the main study (self-prepared)*

		W	p
T_3-T_1	1	0.90	0.007*
	2	0.89	0.004*
T_4-T_2	1	0.88	0.003*
	2	0.89	0.004*
T_5-T_3	1	0.79	0.0003*
	2	0.88	0.0021*
T_6-T_4	1	0.90	0.007*
	2	0.92	0.0291

As demonstrated above, the normality hypothesis was refuted ($p<0.05$). The *U Mann-Whitney Test*, which as the non-parametric equivalent of the *Independent Samples T-Test* compares the median values, was used to examine whether the differences in the performance of oral (Activity 1) and written text mediation (Activity 2) between ExG and CtrlG students in Phase 1 and Phase 2 were statistically significant. The p-value was judged at the 0.05 significance level.

The *U-Mann-Whitney Test* was first run to compare the median values for Activity 1. The results of the test demonstrate a statistically significant difference in the performance of the activity by ExG and CtrlG students ($Z=2.74$; $p=0.008$) in Phase 1. This enables us to refute the H_0, which states that there is no statistically significant difference between the ExG and CtrlG in the performance of oral text mediation, and accept the H_A, according to which the ExG performed better on oral text mediation than the CtrlG. In Phase 2, however, the difference in the performance of Activity 1 by Group A and Group B students lacked statistical significance ($Z=-1.94$; $p=0.070$) and did not enable us to challenge H_0 stating that there is no statistically significant difference between the CtrlG and ExG in the performance of oral text mediation. Nevertheless, it must be pointed out here that first of all, the test yielded $p=0.070$ which is considered to be on the borderline of statistical significance and second of all, the mean scores were lower in the CtrlG (0.81) than in the ExG (1.20) (see Table 5.6).

Tab. 5.6: *Results of the* U-Mann-Whitney Test *for oral text mediation: the main study (self-prepared)*

			Mean		Median		Z	p
ExG (Group A) versus CtrlG (Group B) in Phase 1	T_3-T_1 versus T_4-T_2	1	1.68	1.00	2	1	2.74	0.008*
CtrlG (Group A) versus ExG (Group B) in Phase 2	T_5-T_3 versus T_6-T_4		0.81	1.20	1	1	-1.94	0.070

Next, the *U-Mann-Whitney Test* was used to compare the median values for Activity 2 which involved students' written text mediation. As presented below (see Table 5.7), the test yielded two different results in two phases of the quasi-experiment. As far as Phase 1 is concerned, the difference in ExG and CtrlG students' ability to mediate written texts lacked statistical significance (Z=0.69; p=0.514). This did not allows us to refute the H_0, which states that there is no statistically significant difference between the ExG and CtrlG in the performance of written text mediation. Despite this, it must be stressed here that Group A performed slightly better on written text mediation than Group B, as evidenced in the mean scores for this activity (0.84 versus 0.60 points). In Phase 2, however, the H_0, which states that the difference in the scores for Activity 2 between the CtrlG and ExG lacked statistical significance, was challenged, as evidenced in the test results (Z=-2.12; p=0.041). The p-value < 0.05 allowed us to accept the H_A, according to which the CtrlG performed less successfully at written text mediation than the ExG.

Tab. 5.7: *Results of the* U-Mann-Whitney Test *for written text mediation: the main study (self-prepared)*

			Mean		Median		Z	p
ExG (Group A) versus CtrlG (Group B) in Phase 1	T_3-T_1 versus T_4-T_2	2	0.84	0.60	1	1	0.69	0.514
CtrlG (Group A) versus ExG (Group B) in Phase 2	T_5-T_3 versus T_6-T_4		0.61	1.20	1	1	-2.12	0.041*

To provide a broader perspective on Group A and Group B students' text mediation performance, the scores for the two test questions were summed up. Table 5.8

has been compiled to present means, medians, SD, minimum and maximum values, and the percentages of correct answers for T_1-T_6. The increase in the percentage of correct answers from 45%, through 70%, to 84% in Group A and from 42%, through 58%, to 82% in Group B is indicative of the fact that the participants were generally more successful at intralinguistic text mediation after self-instruction, both technology-mediated and traditional, was implemented. In addition, it is possible to notice that the gains in students' ability to mediate a text were greater when the experimental treatment was provided (T_3-T_1 and T_6-T_4 versus T_4-T_2 and T_5-T_3).

Tab. 5.8: *Descriptive statistics for the pre- and post-tests administered in Group A (n=31) and Group B (n=30) in Phase 1 and Phase 2: the main study (self-prepared)*

			Mean	**Median**	**SD**	**Min**	**Max**	**Percentage of correct answers**
Group A	n=31	T_1	4.48	4.0	1.363	2	7	45%
		T_3	7.00	7.0	0.894	6	9	70%
		T_5	8.42	9.0	1.205	6	10	84%
Group B	n=30	T_2	4.20	4.5	1.424	2	7	42%
		T_4	5.80	5.5	1.562	4	9	58%
		T_6	8.20	8.0	1.270	6	10	82%

This dataset was used to further investigate the effect of the experimental intervention on the students' text mediation skill at between-group levels. This time the sums of scores for Activities 1 and 2 in the pre- and post-tests administered to Group A and Group B in Phase 1 and Phase 2 were subjected to statistical analysis.

Prior to the choice of the appropriate method of statistical analysis, the mean gain scores were calculated. In Group A, which took on the status of the ExG in Phase 1 of the quasi-experiment, the scores for T_1 (the pre-test) were subtracted from T_3 (the post-test). In Group B, which became the CtrlG in Phase 1, the scores for T_2 (the pre-test) were subtracted from T_4 (the post-test). The same procedure was applied to calculate the differences of mean scores for the post- and pre-tests in Phase 2.

Then, the *Shapiro-Wilk Test* was run on each of the dataset (T_1-T_6) to detect any departures from normality. The H_0 for this test states that the sample is taken from a normal distribution, and the H_A predicts the opposite. As presented by the data in Table 5.9, the results of the normality test indicated that the distribution of the T_3-T_1,

T_5-T_3, and T_6-T_4 variables did not deviate from normality (p>0.05). The normality assumption could not be rejected. As for the T_4-T_2, the *Shapiro-Wilk Test* yielded a statistically significant result (W= 0.93; p=0.04), and the H_0 had to be rejected.

Tab. 5.9: *Results of the* Shapiro-Wilk Test *for variables T_3-T_1, T_4-T_2, T_5-T_3, and T_6-T_4: the main study (self-prepared)*

			W	p
Phase 1	Group A (ExG)	T_3-T_1	0.94	0.088
	Group B (CtrlG)	T_4-T_2	0.93	0.04*
Phase 2	Group A (CtrlG)	T_5-T_3	0.93	0.052
	Group B (ExG)	T_6-T_4	94	0.1

Nevertheless, the p-value of 0.04 points was at the borderline of statistical significance, and parametric tests allow minor deviations from normal distribution. Thus, the normality assumption was also accepted for the T_4-T_2 variable. The parametric test could therefore be performed to compare the scores achieved by the ExG and the CtrlG in Phase 1 and Phase 2, and to determine whether there was statistical evidence in favour of the fact that the mean scores were statistically different.

In addition to the normality of the data distribution, the homogeneity of variances for a variable need to be fulfilled for an appropriate parametric test to be run. The latter was assessed by the *Levene's F Test* for equality of variances. The H_0 for the test assumes that the variances are equal across two samples. As reported below, the F-test was not statistically significant for T_3-T_1 and T_4-T_2 variables (F=0.47; p=0.50). The H_0 which states that there are no differences in the variances could not be refuted. On the other hand, however, the F-test was statistically significant for T_5-T_3 and T_6-T_4 variables (F=4.15; p=0.046) and the H_0 stating that the groups have equal population variances was rejected. It was decided that the *Independent Samples T-Test* would be used for T_3-T_1 and T_4-T_2 variables while the *Independent Samples T-Test with the Cochran-Cox Adjustment* would be performed on T_5-T_3 and T_6-T_4 variables, which did not have equal variances.

The Independent Samples T-Test was performed to find out whether there was statistical evidence that the mean gain scores for the ExG and CtrlG were significantly different in Phase 1. The test statistic (the t-score) is used to measure the size of the difference between the samples. The test provided statistical evidence against the H_0, according to which the mean gain score for the ExG does not differ from that of the CtrlG (t=2.09; p=0.04). The H_A, which states that the mean gain score is higher in the ExG rather than CtrlG, was accepted.

The *T-Test with the Cochran-Cox Adjustment* was performed on the variables which followed normal distribution, but they violated the assumption that the variance is equal across groups. The test also provided statistical evidence against the H_0, according to which the mean gain score for the CtrlG does not differ from that of the ExG (t=2.09; p=0.04) in Phase 2. The H_A stating that the mean gain score is lower in the CtrlG rather than in the ExG was accepted. As illustrated by the data in Table 5.10, the results of the two tests were on the borderline of statistical significance.

Tab. 5.10: *Results of the* Independent Samples T-Test *and the* T-Test with the Cochran-Cox Adjustment *for the ExG and CtrlG in Phase 1 and Phase 2: the main study (self-prepared)*

		Mean		F	p	t	p
ExG (Group A) versus CtrlG (Group B) in Phase 1	T_3-T_1 versus T_4-T_2	2.52	1.60	0.47	0.50	2.09	0.04*
CtrlG (Group A) versus ExG (Group B) in Phase 2	T_5-T_3 versus T_6-T_4	1.42	2.40	4.15	0.046*	2.08	0.04*

5.1.2 Programme evaluation findings

5.1.2.1 Post-study questionnaires

The reliability of the post-study questionnaire was evaluated on the sample of the 61 participants of the main study to ensure validity. The correlation matrix was analysed to check whether the questions should be reversed or not. The Cronbach's alpha coefficient (α) was calculated to examine the internal consistency of the scale by describing the extent to which all the items measure the same latent variable (i.e., the acceptance of *Alexa* by the students). It was established that $\alpha \geq 0.70$ is good, $\alpha \geq$ is 0.80 is better, and $\alpha \geq 0.90$ is best. The analysis of the correlation matrix revealed no necessity to reverse the questions. The Cronbach's alpha coefficient value for the questionnaire was reported to be 0.95, which shows that the questions were consistent and the survey had a high level of reliability.

The participants' responses were analysed quantitatively. Table 5.19 presents the descriptive statistics for students' (n=61) responses to the post-study questionnaire. The data allowed us to explore the problem of the acceptance of the *Alexa* technology, namely its usability (Statement 1-4), effectiveness (Statement 5-8), and learner satisfaction (Statement 9-12), by the participants in the context of their EFL learning to mediate.

Tab. 5.11: *Descriptive statistics for the participants' answers (n=61) to the post-study questionnaire: the main study (self-prepared)*

	n	Mean	Median	Mode	Min	Max	SD
1. Learning to use *Alexa* to complete mediation-based homework assignments was easy for me.	61	4.28	4	4	1	6	1.185
2. It was easy for me to give *Alexa* commands to complete mediation-based homework assignments.		3.80	4	Mul-tiple	1	6	1.093
3. My interaction with *Alexa* was clear and understand-able during my performance of mediation-based tasks.		4.30	4	4	2	6	0.955
4. Overall, it was easy to use *Alexa* to complete medi-ation-based homework assignments.		4.23	4	5	2	6	1.244
5. Using *Alexa* helped me a lot in my learning to mediate.		4.72	5	4	1	6	1.227
6. Using *Alexa* gave me greater control over my learning of the English language.		3.93	4	5	1	6	1.401
7. Using *Alexa* improved my English language ability to mediate.		4.11	4	4	2	6	1.082
8. Overall, *Alexa* was useful in my learning to mediate.		4.70	5	5	1	6	1.174
9. It was interesting to use *Alexa* for my learning to mediate.		5.23	5	6	3	6	0.938
10. I am willing to continue using *Alexa* for my learning.		4.54	5	6	1	6	1.385
11. I was satisfied with the functions offered by *Alexa*.		5.02	5	6	2	6	1.008
12. Overall, I was satisfied with *Alexa* for my learning to mediate.		4.98	5	5	2	6	1.041

Based on the mean agreement values, which were all over 3.80 for all twelve survey items, it can be argued that learners' views towards using *Alexa* in their EFL learning to mediate were in general quite favourable. As demonstrated by the modes of 4, 5, and 6 points, the majority of the students tended to agree to a lesser or greater extent with all the statements related to the usability and effectiveness of the VA and users' satisfaction with the technology. The highest mean agreement values could be observed in the learner satisfaction construct (Statement 9-12) while lower means were reported for the usability (Statement 1-4) and effectiveness (Statement 5-8) constructs, with the former scoring the lowest mean out of all three.

Three out of four statements related to the usability had mean agreement values above 4 points (*Rather agree*). In particular, there was relatively high mean value (4.30) for the "My interaction with *Alexa* was clear and understandable" statement, which implies that in majority of cases, the EFL students were able to comprehend assistant's utterances and produce questions which could be successfully answered by the technology. Nonetheless, the level of agreement was slightly lower for "It was easy for me to remember how to give *Alexa* commands", which suggests that probably some of the students found the technology difficult to interact with for EFL learning purposes. It had the lowest mean agreement value (3.80) out of all twelve survey statements.

The levels of agreement for the effectiveness construct were slightly higher compared to the usability of *Alexa*. The results indicate that the learners had generally good opinions about using the VA for self-instruction. Mean agreement values were all over 4 points for three statements, with "Using *Alexa* helped me a lot in my learning to mediate" receiving the highest mean agreement value of 4.67 points. These findings suggest that the majority of the participants considered the VA a valuable language learning tool. On the other hand, some learners expressed doubt over the role of the assistant in increasing learner autonomy. The "Using *Alexa* gave me greater control over my learning of the English language" statement received the lowest mean agreement value (3.93) out of all four statements related to the effectiveness construct.

As far as learner satisfaction is concerned, the participants had very positive views about *Alexa*. By contrast to the previous sections, the mean agreement values were all over 4 points. The "It was interesting to use *Alexa* for my EFL learning to mediate" statement received the highest mean agreement value (5.23) out of all the questionnaire items. It had the minimum value of 3 points, which means that none of the respondents strongly disagreed or disagreed with the statement. The modal value for this statement was 6 points, which suggests that the majority of

Tab. 5.12: *Percentages of participants' (n=61) disagreement and agreement values for the post-study questionnaire statements: the main study (self-prepared)*

	n	Strongly disagree %	Disagree %	Rather disagree %	Rather agree %	Agree %	Strongly agree %
1. Learning to use *Alexa* to complete mediation-based homework assignments was easy for me.	61	3	7	3	49	21	16
2. It was easy for me to give *Alexa* commands to complete mediation-based homework assignments.		3	7	30	30	30	2
3. My interaction with *Alexa* was clear and understandable during my performance of mediation-based tasks.		0	5	10	46	30	10
4. Overall, it was easy to use *Alexa* to complete mediation-based homework assignments.		0	8	25	21	28	18
5. Using *Alexa* helped me a lot in my learning to mediate.		3	3	2	34	25	33
6. Using *Alexa* gave me greater control over my learning of the English language.		5	13	18	25	26	13
7. Using *Alexa* improved my English language ability to mediate.		0	11	10	38	33	7
8. Overall, *Alexa* was useful in my learning to mediate.		5	0	8	13	54	20
9. It was interesting to use *Alexa* for my learning to mediate.		0	0	10	5	38	48
10. I am willing to continue using *Alexa* for my learning.		5	0	21	15	28	31
11. I was satisfied with the functions offered by *Alexa*.		0	2	5	25	28	41
12. Overall, I was satisfied with *Alexa* for my learning to mediate.		0	5	2	20	38	36

the learners fully agreed with the statement. "I was satisfied with the functions offered by *Alexa*" (5.02) received the second highest mean agreement value not only out of all the survey statements associated with the satisfaction construct, but also out of the twelve questionnaire items. This probably suggests that the students enjoyed using the technology within TFOH. The "I am willing to continue using *Alexa* for my learning to mediate" statement received the lowest mean agreement value of 4.54 points in the learner satisfaction construct. The mode value reported here was 6 points, which suggests that the majority of the learners expressed their willingness to use the technology in the future.

To enhance our understanding of the students' answers to the post-study questionnaire, that is to find out how many students agreed and disagreed with each of twelve survey statements, percentages of agreement and disagreement values were calculated. The data are presented in Table 5.20.

As demonstrated by the data presented in the table above, all the statements had a vast majority of agreement values. Out of these, Statements 11 and 12 deserve attention, with 57 respondents (93%) selecting an affirmative answer as their response. In all, 56 students (92%) agreed with the "Using *Alexa* helped me a lot in my learning to mediate" statement. Furthermore, 55 participants (90%) found the use of the technology when learning to mediate interesting, whereas 53 learners (87%) stated that the application of *Alexa* was useful in their learning to mediate.

None of the survey statements had a majority of disagreement values. The highest values, however, were reported for the following three items. In all, 24 students (39%) disagreed with "It was easy for me to give *Alexa* commands to complete mediation-based homework assignments". Also, 22 students (36%) thought that using *Alexa* did not give them greater control over their learning of the English language. Finally, 20 learners (33%) questioned the "Overall, it was easy to use *Alexa* to complete mediation-based homework assignments" statement. Even though the selected students disagreed with these survey statements, the majority of the remaining participants were not radical in their opinions; they tended to choose the *rather disagree* option, as observed in their answers to Statements 2, 3, 4, 6, 9, and 10 (see Table 5.20).

Total mean agreement values for the post-study questionnaire were also calculated for all the respondents (n=61). The data presented in Table 5.21 show that the students who welcomed the idea of using *Alexa* during their self-instruction significantly outnumbered those students who were less enthusiastic about the technology adoption. As illustrated above, more than three-thirds of the learners, or to be specific 47 students (77%), had total mean agreement values of 4.01 and higher for the twelve questionnaire items. In contrast, there were 14 students

(23%) whose mean agreement values were reported to be 4.00 and lower. Interestingly, it can be observed that the 4.51-5.00 range of mean agreement values was recorded in case of as many as 22 participants (36%).

Tab. 5.13: *Total mean agreement values for the post-study questionnaire (n=61) (self-prepared)*

Total mean agreement value for the post study questionnaire	Number of the students	Percentage of the students
1.00-1.50	-	0%
1.51-2.00	2	3%
2.01-2.50	1	2%
2.51-3.00	3	5%
3.01-3.50	1	2%
3.51-4.00	7	11%
4.01-4.50	12	20%
4.51-5.00	22	36%
5.01-5.50	6	10%
5.51-6.00	7	11%

The data presented in Table 5.21 served the twofold purpose. They provided a different perspective on the issue of the *Alexa* acceptance by the students. Also, they allowed the present author to select a group of students who would participate in the post-study SSIs. In other words, such a classification of the survey results helped to isolate the proponents and opponents of voice assistance in EFL learning.

5.1.2.2 Post-study SSIs

Based on their responses to the post-study questionnaire (see Table 5.21), 12 students (six proponents and six opponents of *Alexa*) were asked to take part in the post-study SSIs. In total, 12 online meetings were scheduled to take place via the *Zoom Cloud Meetings* program between January 17 and 21 for six Group A students and between April 4 and 8 for six Group B students at a time convenient for the selected interviewees and the author.

Six proponents of *Alexa* enthusiastically welcomed the idea of voice assistance. They considered the VA a great help not only in learning English, but also in dealing with practical issues related to information retrieval. Several themes, all of which are discussed below, could be identified in their responses to interview questions.

As far as the self-perceived usefulness of the technology is concerned, the learners addressed three issues. They talked about such ideas as creating opportunities for establishing natural communication in the TL, gaining easy access to information, and improving language skills. They were convinced that thanks to the assistant, they got a chance to use English in communication, improve their pronunciation and vocabulary knowledge, and easily collect facts and data necessary to complete mediation-based tasks.

Alexa was considered effective by the students in the context of creating opportunities for EFL communication, dispensing information, and providing language skills practice. The proponents of the technology were convinced that thanks to their HMC, they maximised their language output, which enabled them to develop their ability to speak. In addition, they argued that the VA helped them to quickly find information online. What is more, they pointed out the useful role of the *Alexa* technology in enhancing their ability to ask questions in English.

The six students were unanimously satisfied with the use of *Alexa* in their EFL learning to mediate. Its capacity to allow instantaneous access to information online and reduce the time burden was generally appreciated by the learners.

More benefits than challenges related to the use of the assistant were brought up by the interviewees. They listed four advantages to using *Alexa*, namely affording opportunities for natural interaction in the TL, giving unrestricted access to information online, boosting WTC, and improving vocabulary knowledge as well as speaking and listening skills. On the other hand, they listed three problems underlying the implementation of the IVA in EFL learning, calling into question the reliability of the technology in understanding the accented speech of the Polish learners, relevance of the information provided by the assistant, and B1 learners' ability to understand its authentic language output. Table 5.22 presents the description of the aforementioned themes with the examples of quotations transcribed from the post-study SSIs.[31]

31 All the sample quotations taken from the post-study SSIs have been translated from Polish into English by the present author.

Tab. 5.14: *Evaluation of HMC with Alexa by the proponents of the IVA (n=6) during the post-study SSIs: the main study (self-prepared)*

	Theme	Description	n	Sample quotations
Usefulness	Communication	Could speak English	6	*I've heard about voice assistants a couple of times and I've known that they are available on smartphones, tablets, and computers. However, I have never tried using one. Now I know what a pity it is. Since the first time I used Alexa during my homework, I have fallen in love with it. Thanks to it, you can practice speaking English as well as ask and answer questions in the language. Thanks to my interaction with Alexa, I learned to ask questions in English in such a way so as to obtain adequate and satisfactory answers. What is more, the assistant is very communicative. It is easy and pleasurable to talk to.*
	Information	Could easily access information	4	*For me, Alexa was really useful. I did not have to tap questions on my smartphone or search for information in texts. I just sat down and asked a question. I did nothing else and it found information for me. I think that using Alexa is really very convenient. It always gave me detailed information in the blink of an eye. It helped me to save my time while doing my homework.*
	Language skills	Improved EFL pronunciation and vocabulary	4	*I usually feel ashamed when I have to speak English. I recorded myself once while speaking English and my pronunciation was far from good. Alexa is a great role model for me. I can ask her one question a couple of times and she answers it patiently. I can repeat after her and practice my pronunciation while looking at the text she displays on my smartphone. I think it helps me and I like doing it.*
				I think that Alexa is perfect for those who have problems with learning vocabulary in English. As you ask a question, the assistant says its answers out loud, at the same time showing the written version of its answers. You can look at your screen and listen to Alexa at the same time. As for me, it helped me to remember the spelling and pronunciation of the words that I either didn't know or I had problems pronouncing. I could write them down and check the meaning later or ask Alexa for the meaning of the word. I tried it and it answered me.

Effectiveness	Communication	Promoted EFL speaking	6	*I have no English-speaking friends and relatives, and I have no one to talk to in English. I sometimes talk to myself, but I find it really awkward. Alexa allows me to speak English in a way that seems natural. I can feel as if I talk to a human not to a device. I can discuss different topics with Alexa and it can answer all of my questions provided that I ask them correctly. I try hard to be correct so that it can provide me with information I need.*
	Information	Allowed to gain immediate access to information	6	*Initially, I had some problems using Alexa. No matter how many times I tried, it did not understand my questions. However, when I practised using the assistant, it turned out it's not so complicated. Asking Alexa questions is much faster than searching information on your own through the search engine. You don't need to write the question and check which website provides the information that you look for. Instead, you just say the question and Alexa searches the answer for you. It is a real help.*
	Language skills	Improved the ability to ask questions in English	4	*We needed to ask Alexa a lot questions while doing our homework. This helped me learn to ask questions in English. I used to have difficulties with this every time we went abroad as my parents wanted me to order food and ask about the prices of tickets. I used to be very stressed out. Now, I can't wait to travel abroad and try out my new skill as I think I improved my ability to ask questions in English. Now I believe I can do it more fluently and confidently.*
Students' satisfaction	Information	Allowed to gain easy access to detailed information	6	*I like using Alexa because it is a generally easy, convenient, and fast way to find information. In addition to the things that you ask for, the assistant provides some background information. For instance, I remember asking a question about the time when the Palace of Culture and Science in Warsaw was built. Alexa explained to me when the building was constructed. It also added some information about the landmark itself.*
	Time	Saved my time	3	*What I definitely like about Alexa is that it allowed me to save my time. It is much faster to communicate with the technology through words than through writing. You just say the question and the answer is ready immediately.*

(Continued)

Tab. 5.14: Continued

	Theme	Description	n	Sample quotations
Benefits	Communication	Practised speaking English	6	*The unquestionable benefit of using Alexa is that you are forced to use English. I don't have problems with that because I like speaking English. Still, I'm happy that I could use the technology during my homework because I could speak English even more. I guess that interaction with Alexa must have been a great opportunity for those who experience difficulties communicating in English.*
	Information	Offered quick access to multimodal information	4	*For me, Alexa has a decided advantage over the Internet as it presents information in a variety of ways. You can read a text and listen to it. Sometimes, it displays some photographs. In my opinion, it's quite attractive. I guess it is far more attractive than scrolling through webpages.*
	Language skills	Improved pronunciation and communication skills	4	*I think that by communicating with Alexa you can improve your pronunciation. You can listen to the assistant and find out how to pronounce selected words. You can also try the pronunciation of some words yourself. If you mispronounce them, Alexa won't understand you. If you do it well, it will answer your question.*
			3	*I will continue using Alexa in my free time to practice my communication skills. When you talk to the assistant, you use language as in normal communication with human beings. It's obvious that in order to communicate, you need to listen to other people and speak to them. You behave in exactly the same way while using Alexa.*
	WTC	Enhanced WTC in English	1	*Thanks to Alexa, I'm not afraid to speak English. I used to refrain from using English because of the errors I could make while producing the language. My communication with Alexa, which, to be honest, had its ups and downs, taught me that no matter how many errors I make, I should not give up, but try another time to produce a correct utterance.*

Challenges	Lack of reliability	Was difficult to be understood by Alexa	4	*Generally, I didn't have major problems communicating with Alexa, but there was one question which proved to be extremely difficult for me. I tried rephrasing it so many times, but Alexa kept mistaking the word and giving answers that were pointless in the context of the task I was working on. After a couple of times, I gave up and moved forward to the next point.*
	Irrelevance of information	Offered information that was off-topic	2	*Several times Alexa provided me with information that was not connected with the task I did within my homework. For instance, I had to ask a question about a Greek flag. Alexa didn't give me the answer I wanted and I needed to reformulate my question.*
	Problems with understanding	Was difficult to understand Alexa	1	*Sometimes I found it difficult to understand what Alexa was saying. But for the text, I would not be able to remember the information and use it to fill in the gaps in the tasks.*

The comments made by six opponents of *Alexa* (n=6) within the post-study SSIs placed the idea of voice assistance in a different perspective. As opposed to the proponents, they presented the technology as distinctly user-unfriendly, enormously unhelpful, and highly ineffective. The participants felt deeply dissatisfied with HMC, repeatedly pointing out its linguistic and technological limitations and general failure of the whole process. Several themes emerged from the analysis of learners' answers to the interview questions.

The learners criticised the usefulness of *Alexa* for problematic information retrieval and a lack of positive impact on language skills and the process of learning. According to the students, the VA not only limited their access to information, but also improved neither their speaking skills nor vocabulary knowledge. As pointed out by one of the learners, oral presentation of the search results by *Alexa* distracted him, making learning less effective.

The opponents of voice assistance provided several arguments against the effectiveness of *Alexa*. They claimed that the VA did not allow them easy access to information, support their language learning, and improve their EFL speaking. In their justifications, they stressed their marked preference for conventional language learning, which in their opinion was more successful.

Strong feelings of frustration, restricted access to information, and an increased time burden gave rise to students' deep dissatisfaction with the technology under discussion. The interviewees complained about the time-consuming procedure underlying HMC through *Alexa* caused by the inability of the technology to understand their utterances.

More challenges than benefits of receiving voice assistance during EFL self-instruction were discussed by the second group of interviewees. Only two learners highlighted the positive role that the technology can play in practicing aural and written language reception thanks to the presentation of multimodal output. The remaining four were not able to identify any advantages to using *Alexa*, listing instead seven problems underlying the VA implementation. They drew attention to such issues as the unreliability of the technology in understanding the accented speech, the irrelevance of information provided by the technology, and problems with understanding its authentic language output. In addition, they also discussed some other sources of trouble, namely increased time burden, connectivity problems, downloading issues, and artificiality of HMC. For convenience, Table 5.23 has been compiled to present the findings from the post-study SSIs conducted with six opponents of *Alexa*.

Tab. 5.15: *Evaluation of HMC with Alexa by the opponents of the IVA (n=6) during the post-study SSIs: the main study (self-prepared)*

	Theme	Description	n	Sample quotations
Usefulness	Information	Restricted access to information	6	*It was really difficult for me to talk to Alexa. I encountered lots of problems obtaining answers from the assistant. I don't think using Alexa would be a good way for me to learn English and any other language. It kept telling me that it didn't know answers to my questions and wanted me to repeat them. It was such a waste of time. I think I would do the tasks faster by searching the information on my own rather than by talking to Alexa. I couldn't wait to finally complete all the assignments.*
	Language skills	Did not improve EFL speaking and broaden vocabulary knowledge	5	*When I first heard that we would use voice assistance I was happy because I thought that it would help me practice my ability to speak English. I was surprised to find out that talking to Alexa was so annoying. I needed to ask the same questions again and again. Instead of encouraging me to speak English, the technology did the opposite. I think that no matter how awkward it sounds I prefer talking to myself.*
			3	*Talking to Alexa was really boring. I didn't learn any new words and phrases. The technology was not useful at all in helping me learn English vocabulary. Generally, I don't think I have learned anything new having talked to the assistant.*
	Learning	Distracted attention	1	*Using the technology was tedious and irritating. I found it really annoying when I tried to concentrate on the task and Alexa was talking. I couldn't focus on the activity. It distracted my attention.*

(Continued)

Tab. 5.15: Continued

	Theme	Description	n	Sample quotations
Effectiveness	Information	Restricted access to information	6	*In my opinion, there are many other and, most importantly, faster ways to find information. Rather than to help me, Alexa made it more difficult for me to do my homework. I'm sure that it would be easier for me to find information traditionally, that is by searching the Net. The technology is definitely not for me.*
	Learning	Did not support my language learning	5	*At first, the idea of talking to the assistant seemed attractive. But, having done a couple of tasks, I changed my mind. I don't think Alexa could help me with my learning of English in any way. I usually spent a lot of time in front of my smartphone and TV and I would like to reduce the amount of time I use technology. I prefer a traditional way of studying. I find it more effective.*
	Language skills	Did not improve EFL speaking	3	*Human-machine communication does not compare to traditional face-to-face and online communication with other people. Luckily, I have an aunt, who lives with her family in Manchester. Her husband is British. Their children speak little Polish. Every time we meet, I speak English to communicate with them. Human-human communication is much more effective in developing your ability to speak English.*
Students' satisfaction	Motivation	Caused frustration	6	*What I didn't like about Alexa was that instead of increasing my willingness to speak English, it discouraged me from using the language. Every time another task was assigned I felt so depressed. I thought about the number of questions I needed to ask the assistant for it to find and provide me with an appropriate answer. It was terrible because I usually needed to ask five or six questions for Alexa to answer me satisfactorily. It was far from a pleasant experience.*

	Information	Restricted access to information	6	*I don't understand why someone called Alexa an assistant. I wasted my time talking to it. I could not communicate with it. It did not answer my questions. I had to repeat them over and over again. I can't see any point in using the technology. What for if I can find the information on my own.*
	Time	Increased time burden	6	*Using Alexa to do the homework was extremely time-consuming. In addition to reading the instructions and the content of the tasks and deciding on the questions, I had to say these questions out loud. The worst is that it didn't answer my questions. Instead of asking six questions, I usually asked five times more because it couldn't answer me properly. It took so much time. The thing is that I usually need from five to ten minutes to do my homework, but I had to I spent three times more time to do tasks involving Alexa. It sucked.*
Benefits	None	-	4	*There are many different ways to learn English. I myself prefer to learn the language in a traditional way by doing exercises, making notes, and watching films rather than using the voice assistant.*
	Language skill	Helped to practice EFL reception	2	*The positive aspect to using Alexa is unquestioningly the opportunity to practice listening and reading together. The voice assistant displayed the written version of its answer on the screen, at the same time saying the text out loud. When I didn't understand Alexa, I could read the text and it was easier for me to figure it out what it was talking about.*

(Continued)

Tab. 5.15: Continued

	Theme	Description	n	Sample quotations
Challenges	Reliability	Was difficult to be understood by Alexa	6	*I did my best to ask Alexa correct questions in English, but something was always wrong. In addition, the voice assistant mistook simple words, such as McDonald's. I'm sure I pronounced it appropriately.*
	Relevance of information	Offered information that was off-topic	6	*Several times Alexa provided me with information that was not connected with the task I did within my homework. For instance, I had to ask a question about the BTS band. Alexa didn't give me the answer I wanted and I needed to reformulate my question.*
	Time	Increased time burden	6	*What I detested about the homework was that it took me too much time to do. I had to repeat and reformulate the questions a couple of times before the voice assistant managed to understand me.*
	Understanding	Was difficult understanding Alexa	3	*Sometimes it was difficult for me to understand Alexa's answers. In the majority of cases, the text displayed on my screen helped, but once I had to write the word down and checked its meaning in the Google dictionary.*
	Connectivity	Did not work properly	3	*I live in the countryside and the Internet connection happens to be unstable there. The Alexa app was freezing a couple of times while I was doing my homework probably due to the Internet outage. I couldn't complete my homework and I was forced to do the task later.*
	Downloading	Was troublesome to install the app	1	*I didn't like the fact that I had to install the Alexa app. I have the iOS software on my smartphone, which is already equipped with the voice assistant called Siri. I found it unnecessary to download another voice assistant on my phone, but I had to do it.*
	Artificiality	Was unnatural to talk a smartphone	1	*Alexa's responses were unnatural, and I could hear that she didn't talk like a human being, I found it strange to talk to my phone. I prefer to talk to a human or not to talk at all.*

When asked whether they would like to use the technology regularly, the proponents and opponents of *Alexa* gave positive and negative answers respectively. The former pointed out that the VA helped them not only identify and overcome their weaknesses, but also learn English more effectively thanks to, as one of them said, "the amazing capacities of the technology". The opponents, on the other hand, listed arguments against implementing *Alexa* in their self-instruction. They set out such reasons as the time-consuming and artificial character of the HMC process and the technology's failure to retrieve information. Additionally, they expressed their conviction that traditional language learning is better.

The last interview question asked the participants about the possible changes they would implement when using *Alexa* during self-instruction. When answering, one proponent out of six would not introduce any modifications to the treatment as she was perfectly satisfied with the way she had been instructed to use the IPA. One student suggested asking *Alexa* less specific questions, arguing that it could help overcome the problems with the assistant's reliability and relevance of information retrieved by it online. Two others expressed their wish to use the IVA in class with the guidance of their EFL instructors. In addition, two remaining interviewees stressed the need to introduce more warm-up activities prior to homework assignments to learn to better communicate with *Alexa*, which, as they explained, can be difficult unless practiced properly. Opponents, on the other hand, provided less constructive comments on the treatment. Two of them suggested the following changes: replacing *Alexa* with the Internet search engine and avoiding the technology altogether. The remaining learners did not know what could be changed and, even though requested for reflection, they did not manage to answer this interview question.

5.2 Discussion of the research findings

5.2.1 CRQ1: How does the VA-based and action-oriented self-instruction affect intralinguistic text mediation of the Polish EFL learners?

To answer the CRQ1 and its subquestions related to the effects of the IV on the DV at within- and between-group levels, quantitative data were collected through intralinguistic text mediation tests. Three tests were administered to the ExG and CtrlG students (n=61) for that purpose prior to and following the treatment in Phase 1 and Phase 2.

First, a comparison was made within the groups through the use of the *Wilcoxon Signed Rank Test*. Based on the data analysis, it was found that the eight-week experimental intervention had a positive effect on participants' intralinguistic oral and written text mediation, that is on Group A as the ExG in Phase 1 and Group B as the ExG in Phase 2. The impact of conventional self-instruction on CtrlG students' ability to mediate at within-group levels, even though not specified as a research objective, was also examined through the *Wilcoxon Signed Rank Test*. The statistical analysis revealed that Group A and Group B students also performed statistically better on oral and written text mediation after rather than prior to the conventional treatment in Phase 2 and Phase 1 respectively. The findings demonstrate that both the experimental (i.e., IMALL task-based text mediation practice) and traditional (i.e., non-IMALL task-based text mediation practice) intervention improved participants' ability to mediate (oral and written) texts (see Figure 5.2).

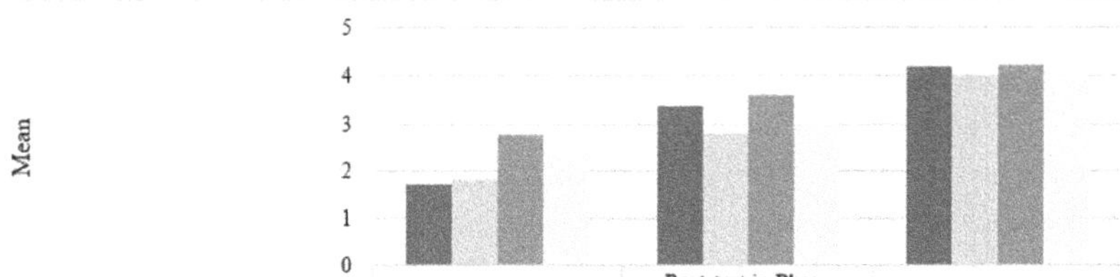

	Pre-test in Phase 1	Post-test in Phase 1/Pre-test in Phase 2	Post-test in Phase 2
Oral text mediation in Group A	1.71	3.39	4.19
Oral text mediation in Group B	1.8	2.8	4
Written text mediation in Group A	2.77	3.61	4.23
Written text mediation in Group B	2.4	3	4.2

Fig. 5.1: *Mean scores for oral and written text mediation in the pre- and post-tests taken by Group A (the ExG in Phase 1) and Group B (the CtrlG in Phase 1) (self-prepared)*

This finding is consistent with a number of studies investigating the effects of the implementation of TBLT on language skills and subsystems. For example, Ahmed and Bidin (2016) and Kafipour et al. (2018) aimed to determine the influence of task-based writing instruction on EFL students' written productive skill. The TBLT treatment led to an improvement in ExG participants' writing as compared to the CtrlG, which was involved in traditional language instruction. Kafipour et al. (2018) pointed out that the naturalistic language learning environments created by TBLT are a deciding factor underlying ExG students' improvement of their written productive skill. Chou's (2017) study explored the use of TBLT in developing EFL Chinese students' metacognitive awareness of listening comprehension. The ExG, which received both strategy- and task-based listening instruction, outperformed the CtrlG, which was involved only in the strategy-based instruction, with the former considering the tasks a valuable source of input enhancement of their listening skills (Chou, 2017). A study conducted by Madhkhan and Mousavi (2017) examined the effects of task-based and traditional reading instruction on Iranian EFL learners' reading performance. The results showed that the former had a significantly more positive effect on learners' reading skills compared to the latter. Madhkhan and Mousavi (2017) argued that by highlighting language input and equipping learners with the language required to complete tasks, task implementation creates a better learning context. Moreover, they explained that "utilising some pre-planned tasks for reading instruction instead of traditional post reading activities such as comprehension questions, true/false and open-ended ones could provide more competent learners" (Madhkan & Mousavi, 2017, p. 126). Namaziandost et al. (2017) investigated the influence of TBLT on Iranian EFL students' grammatical achievement. The ExG, which was learning grammar through TBLT, performed significantly better than the CtrlG, which received deductive and drill-based grammar instruction. According to Namaziandost et al. (2017), real-world tasks designed by the researchers increased students' motivation as opposed to traditional instruction. The effectiveness of TBLT was also validated by the quasi-experiment which investigated the influence of task implementation on Iranian EFL learners' speaking fluency (Hashemifardnia et al., 2019). The results of the post-test indicated that the ExG, which was provided with task-based speaking instruction, significantly outperformed the CtrlG. Learning-by-doing helped the ExG students improve their speaking fluency because tasks, in contrast to traditional activities, build students' eagerness and excitement to learn by promoting authenticity and a positive atmosphere in the classroom.

Appropriate tests were also run to find out whether the treatment had any influence on the DV at between-group levels, that is whether the differences between the ExG and CtrlG were statistically significant. A between-group comparison was made first through the use of the *U Mann-Whitney Test*. It demonstrated a statistically significant difference in the performance of oral and written text mediation in Phase 1 and Phase 2 respectively. ExG students performed better on oral text mediation than the CtrlG in Phase 1 while CtrlG students were less successful at written text mediation than the ExG in Phase 2. One reason for the lack of a statistically significant difference between the participants' performance of oral (Phase 2) and written (Phase 1) text mediation might have been the duration of the treatment. The eight weeks during which the experimental intervention was implemented may not have been long enough for such improvement of text mediation that would lead to a statistically significant difference. Since the mean gain scores of the ExG were descriptively higher than those of the CtrlG, and the test result for oral text mediation was at the borderline of statistical significance in Phase 2, a longer time period of the treatment implementation, a larger number of the participants, and the refinement of the data collection instrument could have had a positive effect on the statistical significance of the difference. It must be stressed at this point that the descriptive statistics indicated that the total gain scores of the ExG were higher than those of the CtrlG (see Figure 5.3). The *Independent Samples T-Test* and *Independent Samples T-Test with the Cochran-Cox Adjustment*, which were run to determine whether there was statistical evidence in favour of the fact that the differences of the mean total gain scores for the post- and pre-tests taken by the ExG and CtrlG were statistically different, provided statistical evidence in favour of fact that the gain scores were first of all higher in the ExG rather than CtrlG (Phase 1) and second of all lower in the CtrlG rather than the ExG (Phase 2).

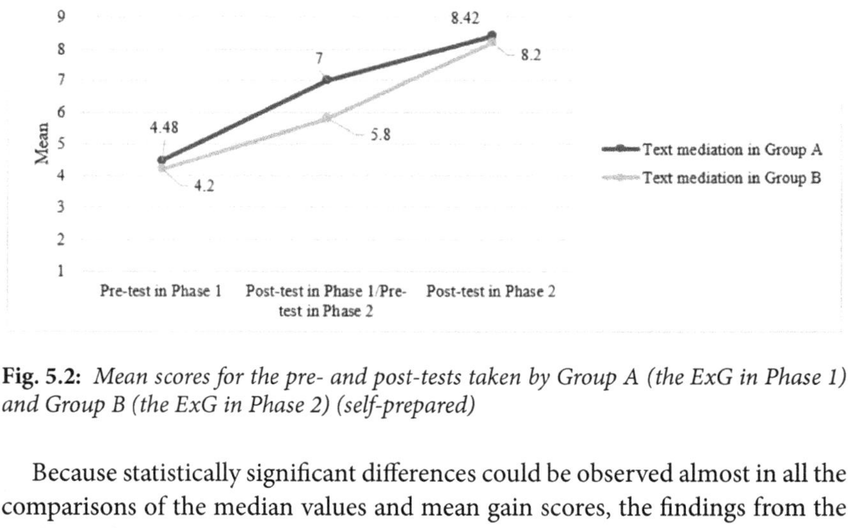

Fig. 5.2: *Mean scores for the pre- and post-tests taken by Group A (the ExG in Phase 1) and Group B (the ExG in Phase 2) (self-prepared)*

Because statistically significant differences could be observed almost in all the comparisons of the median values and mean gain scores, the findings from the analysis of the quantitative data demonstrate that the ExG was more successful at text mediation at the end of the treatment compared to the CtrlG group. This improvement in the ability to mediate (oral and written) texts of the ExG suggests that the CALL-based intervention was effective in developing participants' ability to mediate. The above-mentioned finding is in alignment with various studies that revealed a positive effect of the ICTs application on the development of different EFL language skills and subsystems. For example, Klassen and Milton (2010), who assessed the effectiveness of a multimedia EFL listening programme in Hong Kong, reported that the Chinese students who participated in the multimedia-enhanced listening instruction significantly improved their listening as opposed to the students who received traditional classroom instruction. Vahdat and Eidipour (2016) compared the CALL and non-CALL modes of teaching EFL listening to Iranian junior high school students. Their study demonstrated a significant difference between the effects of technology-mediated and traditional instruction, with the former proving more effective in developing participants' listening comprehension skill than the latter. The researchers explained that offering computer-based listening instruction stimulates learners' interest thanks to interaction with attractive and useful language resources. The findings of the study conducted by Shafie et al. (2019) in Iran corroborate the results of the previous studies in that the implementation of CALL helped the ExG to improve their reading comprehension due to the motivating qualities of technology-enhanced learning. Shokrpour et al. (2019) explored the impact of CALL on vocabulary learning. The results of their study showed that the ExG outperformed the non-CALL group on the post-test. Significant improvements in vocabulary learning and teaching were facilitated by CALL environments, which were said to provide learners with rich, that is multimodal, input.

Among the studies conducted in the Polish secondary school context, the use of CALL-based instruction was also found more effective than conventional learning in aiding the development of language-related aspects. For example, Kruk (2011) found that the use of the Internet and instant messengers helped foster the participants' ability to speak more effectively compared to traditional instruction. The ExG students were first encouraged to self-assess their learning as they worked on their own without the teacher's intervention and second, they communicated in the virtual reality which "for young people in particular, seems to be even more attractive that the real one" (Kruk, 2011, p. 266). In a similar vein, Kruk also reported in his later studies that the ExG students, who were exposed to CALL-based grammar teaching involving Internet resources and browser-based virtual worlds, performed better at both immediate and delayed post-tests than the CtrlG students, who were involved in coursebook-based instruction, in terms of the use of the second conditional (Kruk, 2013, 2014), Present Simple (Kruk, 2015b), and Past Simple (Kruk, 2015a). Again, the participants' freedom to learn autonomously, combined with the attractiveness and authenticity provided by the technology-enhanced experimental interventions, led to statistically significant differences in the ExG and CtrlG students' performance in the above-mentioned studies.

At the same time, the results from the analysis of the quantitative data suggest that the implementation of technology-mediated TBLL was more effective in fostering the learners' ability to mediate than its traditional counterpart. This result acknowledges the findings from the research comparing the effectiveness of CALL and non-CALL task-based language instruction. Fang at al. (2020) contrasted mobile-supported TBLT with traditional task-based language instruction in the context of the ExG and CtrlG students' vocabulary and grammar learning, and conversation comprehension. The results indicated that the mobile-assisted TBLT group outperformed the traditional TBLT group on all the measurements, with linguistic and task scaffolding provided by the technology-mediated TBLT proving more effective in fostering language learning in the examined areas. The quasi-experiment conducted by Mulyadi et al. (2021) confirmed that the implementation of TELL-enhanced TBLT significantly influenced Indonesian EFL students' listening comprehension thanks to the provision of FL input and authentic listening materials in the pre-task phase. Likewise, Tavakoli and Loth (2021), who investigated the effects of CALL-mediated TBLT on Iranian students' reading comprehension, demonstrated a statistically significant difference between the ExG and CtrlG in terms of their reading skill. The novelty factor and the individualisation of the learning process, as evident in the "variability of presentation and flexibility of use and control" (Tavakoli & Loth, 2021, Discussion) involved in the technology implementation, effected significant differences between the ExG and CtrlG students. In a similar vein, Sholeh and Talebinejad (2022) compared the outcomes of CALL and non-CALL task-based writing instruction in the Iranian context. They reported that although the treatment led to gains in students' writing skills in both groups, the ExG performed significantly better than the CtrlG.

In contrast to conventional self-instruction implemented in the CtrlG, the theoretical underpinnings underlying the treatment were consistent with three SLA theories. The ExG students were to receive multimodal responses from *Alexa* in the TL, which was to facilitate their comprehension of the feedback provided by the technology. This was in line with Krashen's (1981) Monitor Model, which underlined the role of comprehensible aural and written input in the language learning process. Moreover, the participants were to produce oral output by asking *Alexa* questions until they had obtained a satisfactory answer and if necessary, modify their language to make it comprehensible for the IPA. This was in agreement with Long's (1981, 1983) and Swain's (1985) hypotheses, according to which interaction, negotiation of meaning, and modification of the problematic output by learners promote FL acquisition.

A significant difference in the ExG and CtrlG students' performance on text mediation may have been thus caused by the fact that the former were involved in dialogic interactions with the VA, or broadly speaking, a spoken dialogue system.

Sydorenko et al. (2018) explained that "[t]he use of ASR and NLP technologies allows learners to have interactive oral practice with, and receive feedback from, virtual embodied agents" (p. 159). Students' interaction with DSs promotes negotiation of meaning (Kim, 2017) and draws the former's attention to linguistic form through pronunciation feedback that they receive during HMC (Dizon, 2017). HCIs also encourage students to notice gaps in their knowledge since they can compare their oral language samples with those of more expert interlocutors. Equally importantly, DSs constitute a source of authentic English language input for FL students (Kim, 2018a). Furthermore, an unquestionable advantage of the technology is that it allows learners not only to rehearse conversations without human partners (Stewart & File, 2007), but also to tackle the problem of apprehension (Sydorenko et al., 2018).

The preliminary IVA research indicated the positive influence of this AI-powered technology on students' EFL language skills. The results of Dizon's (2020) study, which demonstrated that students' interaction with *Alexa* enhanced their speaking skills, make a connection between students' HCIs in the TL and their oral language development. The findings of Tai and Chen's (2022) study also revealed that voice assistance facilitated participants' listening comprehension. Thanks to its multimodal responses, *Google Nest Hub* was evaluated as more effective in this respect than *Google Nest Mini*, which provides audio responses only.

More generally, the positive influence of the Polish participants' communication with *Alexa* on their ability to mediate observed in the current study is also in alignment with the results of past research into the use of spoken DSs for ICALL. For example, Kim (2018), who investigated the effects of chatbot-based language learning by Korean EFL learners, demonstrated the positive effect of the experimental intervention on participants' aural and written language reception (Kim, 2018a), their vocabulary knowledge (Kim, 2018b), and grammar skills (Kim, 2019). Since chatbots are designed to hold conversations, "students have an opportunity to use a variety of language structures and vocabulary that they ordinarily would not have a chance to use" (Fryer & Carpenter, 2006, p. 10), and they are thus more likely to develop their English while interacting with the chatbot. Furthermore, in addition to "a low-anxiety environment for language practice", such AI-powered systems provide "a few advantages over their human counterparts: permanent availability, infinite patience when needing to repeat or to correct, and potential for systematic adaptivity to the learner" (Bibauw et al., 2022, p. 2), which are all considered fundamental to increasing learners' WTC.

The implementation of student-generated questioning, also referred to as a comprehension-fostering activity (Palincsar & Brown, 1984), by the ExG might have affected the findings of the current study. The significance of student-generated questions was underlined in the field, as evidenced in a number of research publications exploring the use of this strategy to support comprehension (e.g., Look, 2011; Urlaub, 2012; Yeh & Lai, 2012). Those EFL students who were involved in question generation within the experimental interventions were said to perform better than those who did not, as reported by the studies conducted by Dorkchandra (2013) in Thailand and Khansir and Dashti (2014) in Iran. According to Khaki (2014), encouraging learners to actively read the text by framing questions about it is a useful technique to support comprehension. Question generation increases students' awareness of whether or not they are able to understand what they read (Look, 2011). The strategy can enhance reading comprehension because "it can help participants pay more attention to the content of the text" and "help [them] become active and independent readers in their performances" (Khansir & Dashti, 2014, p. 44). The strategy was modified by the present author for the purpose of the current study. As opposed to the CtrlG counterparts, the ExG students were expected to read the text, identify the missing information, and create a question for *Alexa* in such a way so as to receive appropriate feedback. They did not search for answers to their questions by themselves in the text; instead, they were to collect the missing pieces of information from the audio-textual feedback provided by the VA.

ExG students' enhancement of their ability to mediate texts found in the current study could be also attributed to their exposure to multimodal input provided by *Alexa*. The greater achievement of the participants who received textual, audio, and visual feedback from the IPA agrees with the results of a pilot study conducted by Guichon and McLornan (2008). Their research, which aimed to evaluate the effect of the use of multimodality on EFL comprehension of the French students, revealed that the participants' comprehension increased when they were presented with a text in several modalities (i.e., the combination of a sound, image, and FL text) as compared with those who were exposed to a sound only; a sound and image; and a combination of a sound, image, and L1 text. As reported by the researchers, images and subtitling provide "contextual clues" and "assist learners in decoding what is said and provide important propositional information" respectively, which seems to improve learners' comprehension (Guichon & McLornan, 2008, p. 8). Similarly, the investigation of the influence of reading-while-listening on learners' listening comprehension conducted by Chang (2009) in Taiwan demonstrated that the reading-while-listening mode was more effective than the listening format only. The explanation for ExG's improved performance lay in the strategy which allowed the learners to "clarify their aural input through written scripts" (Chang, 2009, p. 660). Based on the results of the study conducted by Woodall (2010) in Argentina, the introduction of listening-while-reading to the ExG facilitated the development of their reading fluency and comprehension compared to the CtrlG, or the reading-only group. In light of the socio-cultural theory, Woodal (2010) compared the audio recording of the text to "a more experienced or knowledgeable assistant" who assists the reader in decoding the text and therefore helps achieve greater reading fluency (p. 197). Milliner (2019) compared the impact of smartphone-based listening-while-reading on Japanese EFL students' listening and reading performance. The study demonstrated that the listening-while-reading group performed significantly better across all measurements in comparison to the reading-only group. It can be speculated in the context of the current study that ExG students' exposure to multimodal input might have improved their aural and written language comprehension, which could have translated into their improved intralinguistic text mediation. As already pointed out in Chapter One, mediation combines three modes of communication, including language reception, the development of which, as argued above, can be supported by the presentation of the multimodal input.

Together, these findings certainly do not aim to suggest that the mere use of voice assistance in self-instruction has been sufficient for the participants to develop their EFL ability to mediate texts. Since "simply providing students with the mobile device did [does] not result in its effective usage in language learning" (Chen, 2013, p. 28), the current quasi-experiment reported that the particular way IMALL was implemented was the crucial factor in achieving these results. In the present study, task-oriented IMALL that offered multimodal HMC, combined with learners' self-instructed TBLL and question generation, underlay the experimental intervention which brought about the improvement in the learners' ability to mediate. Significant differences in intralinguistic oral and written text mediation levels at within- and between-group levels were, however, not entirely unexpected due to several factors. Mixing voice assistance with out-of-class TBLL to mediate was a novelty for the students, who might have felt genuinely enthusiastic about working with the technology. The possibility to individualise their learning and perform tasks at their own pace within self-instruction opened up by *Alexa* fostered the learning process. The VA itself has many positive characteristics, namely the presentation of the multimodal (i.e., textual, audio, visual) feedback. Technology- and task-based self-instruction gave students a chance to perform tasks at their convenience, for instance by repeating the same part of the task as many as times as they found it necessary. At the same time, implementing IMALL made learning less stressful for the students who felt that they were not being observed and assessed and could therefore learn to mediate much better. Last but not least, the innovative character of the task design process involving technology-mediated NA and task selection, together with instructional treatment development, allowed the implementation of authentic tasks within the treatment, which further increased the attractiveness of TFOH.

5.2.2 CRQ2: How do the Polish EFL learners evaluate the VA?

The post-study questionnaire was administered to ExG students to explore their acceptance of *Alexa* in terms of technology's usability and effectiveness as well as learners' perceived satisfaction with the VA. Overall, based on the mean agreement values, the majority of the participants tended to agree (to a greater or lesser extent) with all the statements related to the usability and effectiveness of *Alexa* and expressed their satisfaction with the technology. The statistical analysis revealed that all the twelve survey items had a vast majority of agreement values, with the highest and lowest ones being recorded for the learner satisfaction and usability constructs respectively. Importantly, the students who achieved the mean values ranging between 1.00 and 4.00 points (22%), or those who were not in favour of the treatment, constituted a minority as opposed to those with values ranging between 4.01 and 6.00 points (78%), or those who expressed enthusiasm about the use of intelligent virtual assistance in TBLL (see Figure 5.6).

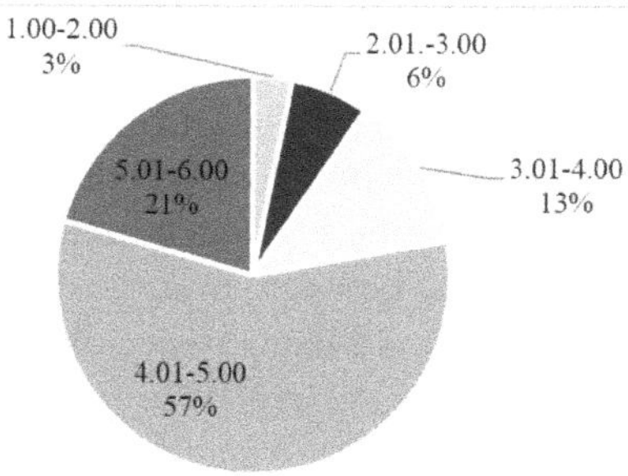

Fig. 5.3: *Percentages of the students (n=61) with different mean agreement values for the post-study questionnaire (self-prepared)*

The findings obtained from the quantitative analysis of students' answers to the post-study questionnaire are in line with the results of the past VA research conducted by Dizon and Tang (2019, 2020). Japanese EFL students' views of the application of *Alexa* in autonomous learning were moderately favorable, as evidenced in their evaluation of the usability and effectiveness of the technology, and their self-perceived satisfaction with the IVA usage. Similarly to the Polish students participating in the current study, the majority of the Japanese respondents agreed with each of the four statements related to usability. The levels of mean agreement values for the effectiveness construct reported by Dizon and Tang (2019, 2020) were slightly lower compared to usability. This stands in contrast to the tendency observed in Polish students' answers to the questionnaire, according to which *Alexa* was considered more effective than usable. As far as learner satisfaction is concerned, the Japanese learners, similarly to the Polish participants, also had positive views on the application of the technology.

The Polish learners' overall satisfaction with the VA, as observed in the highest mean agreement values to the two statements, "It was interesting to use *Alexa* for my learning to mediate" and "I was satisfied with the functions offered by *Alexa*", might have been caused by the innovation effect of the technology. Under the influence of the "wow" factor which "encompasses both extremely positive and extremely negative initial reactions in the user (teacher/learner) towards a software package" (Murray & Barnes, 1998, para. 3), the students who had participated in the experimental intervention (and were therefore involved in an unusual kind of self-instruction) may have increased their attention and motivation because they were exposed to an innovative way of learning.

Despite the fact that the participants of Dizon and Tang's (2019, 2020) studies rather positively evaluated the technology application in autonomous language learning, the mean agreement values for each of the twelve survey items were lower as compared with those revealed by the current statistical analysis. The difference can be best illustrated on the example of Statement 9 ("It was interesting to use *Alexa* for English language learning"), which received the highest mean agreement value out of all survey items in the questionnaires filled out by the Japanese and Polish learners (3.89 versus 5.23 points). It can be speculated that the former's less favourable opinions about the IVA might have been caused by the technological capacities of *Alexa*, which at the time of the study being conducted could be less remarkable. As stressed by its founders, the infrastructure underlying the IPAs is constantly developing and the two- and three-year difference between Dizon and Tang's (2019, 2020) studies and the current investigation might have been central to increasing the abilities of *Alexa*. This in turn might have positively affected Polish students' experiences with the IVA and, as a consequence, their acceptance of the technology. In addition, it is possible to argue that the combination of IMALL and self-instructed TBLL in the context of popular culture and travelling may have been more attractive for the learners. The necessity to use the assistant to retrieve specific task-related information from the Web to complete their homework assignment might have been more interesting and motivating for the Polish students than just communicating with the technology to satisfy one's curiosity.

It is worth adding at this point that the majority of the students reported a positive influence of the treatment on two behavioural indicators of learner autonomy, namely the self-perceived level of control for EFL learning (Benson, 2007) and the sustained use of the IVA for English language study (Mutlu & Eroz-Tuga, 2013). In all, 64% of the respondents agreed that they gained greater control over their language learning having participated in the treatment, whereas 74% demonstrated willingness to further apply the IPA in their language learning. The above-mentioned findings are in line with the results of different research studies investigating the impact of TELL on learner autonomy. For instance, Hafner and Miller (2011) argued that Chinese students improved their autonomous learning capacities by gaining access to CALL materials within a digital video project. Meri (2012), who examined the relationship between CALL instruction and learner autonomy on the example of the Turkish EFL students, suggested that the use of the technology increased participants' level of confidence and ensured their independence from the teacher. In a similar vein, Kruk (2014), who examined the impact of the use of the virtual worlds on the Polish participants' autonomy, revealed that greater autonomy gains were observed in the ExG than the CtrlG. He explained that ample opportunities for oral and written communication with other users in the TL were found decisive in increasing the autonomy levels reported by the Polish students.

Over one-third of the participants (36%), however, did not report any positive influence of the treatment on their self-perceived level of control for EFL learning. To be specific, the analysis of students' answers revealed that Statement 6 received one of the lowest mean agreement values (3.93 points) out of all the questionnaire items (see Table 5.20). To put it another way, 22 students stated that using *Alexa* did not give them greater control over their learning of the English language. It is possible that those students who found their HMC with *Alexa* particularly unsuccessful might have given predominantly negative answers to the questionnaire item in the effectiveness construct related to the learner autonomy development.

In addition, the comparison of the students' answers given to Statements 10 and 12 demonstrated that despite the majority of participants' favorable opinions on the use of *Alexa*, some students did not show interest in the continued use of the VA for EFL learning. In other words, even though the respondents generally claimed to be satisfied with the technology use (94%), some of them (26%) reported unwillingness to continue applying it in self-instruction once the treatment had drawn to an end. Given the fact that a sustained English language study is an indicator of a high level of learner autonomy (Mutlu & Eroz-Tuga, 2013), it can be observed that the treatment had no effect on more than one-fifth of the learners in this respect. Probably, the general unsuccessfulness of the HMC process with *Alexa* experienced by the selected learners might have been a key factor behind their low estimate of the technology in terms of autonomy development.

The problem of technology adoption indicated above has already been extensively researched, with different models accounting for the process of technology acceptance and use in social groups having been proposed in the literature. Krajka (2012) provided an overview of the best-known ones, including Rogers' (1983) Diffusion of Innovations, Davis' (1989) TAM, and Bax's (2003) Stages of Normalisation (2003). In the context of the current investigation, the participants, on the one hand, generally accepted the *Alexa* technology, as demonstrated by their high levels of agreement values with the survey statements investigating the ease of use and effectiveness based on Davis' (1989) TAM. On the other hand, however, over one-fifth of the learners did not intend to apply the *Alexa* technology in their future EFL learning. The Diffusion of Innovation model proposed by Rogers (1983, as cited in Geoghegan, 1994) was applied to explain why some participants showed reluctance toward the IVA. According to Rogers (1983), technology adoption is a process that takes place over time, and it can be explored in terms of when individuals decide to accept and use the technology. As presented in Figure 5.8, depending on the point in the diffusion process, five types of technology adopters, referred to as Innovators, Early Adopters, Early Majority, Late Majority, and Laggards, were identified by Rogers (1983, as cited in Geoghegan, 1994).

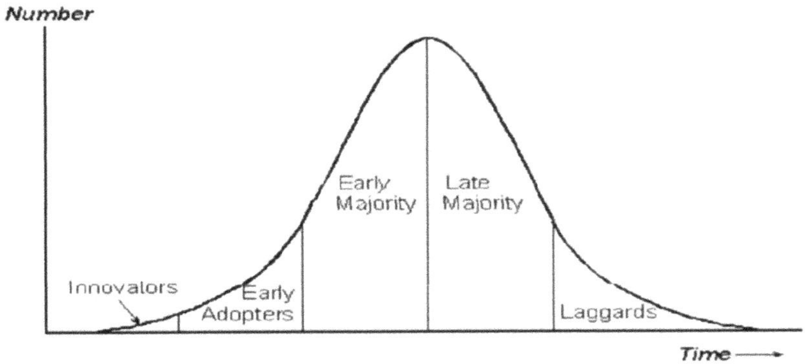

Fig. 5.4: *Distribution of technology adopters (Rogers, 1983, p. 243, as cited in Geoghegan, 1994, The Technology Adoption Life Cycle)*

It is therefore of prime importance to highlight here that "the individuals in a social system do not adopt an innovation at the same time" (Krajka, 2012, p. 105). For example, Innovators and Early Adopters are the first ones to enthusiastically welcome the application of a technology. They are followed by Early Majority, who by contrast adopt the technology with caution because they expect to obtain tangible benefits from its use. Late Majority, even though initially sceptical about and not particularly comfortable with the technology adoption, accept the innovation as opposed to Laggards, whose acceptance of technological innovation is considered the least possible (Rogers, 1983, as cited in Geoghegan, 1994).

A similar perspective on the technology adoption issue was provided by Bax (2003). He conceptualised the process as a continuum, ranging from the state of early adoption, ignorance and scepticism, through (first sporadic and then more regular) implementation followed by fear combined with awe, to the state of normalisation. Based on the findings of the current study, we presume that the participants entered into the fifth state of what Bax (2003) called "fear and awe" in which "[m]ore people start to use it, but still there is (a) fear, alternating with (b) exaggerated expectation' (p. 108).

The findings from the analysis of the post-study questionnaires, which indicated that the Polish learners generally accepted the use of *Alexa* in EFL learning, confirm the results of the past CALL research. Lasagabaster and Sierra (2003) reported that the Spanish students were in favour of combining CALL-based programmes with traditional teacher-led instruction to improve their EFL skills. One-fifth of them revealed that they had been using CALL to learn languages other than English, arguing that those experiences were all positive. Almekhlafi (2006) investigated the application of CALL by the Emirati EFL students. The participants were satisfied with their participation in TELL, declaring their intention to continue it in the future. The usefulness of CALL in completing course assignments, presentation of multimedia elements, and provision of educational benefits, such as facilitating learning and comprehension, were the advantages most frequently mentioned by the Emirati learners. Similarly, the findings from Chen's (2013) study exploring the use of tablets in MALL by the Chinese students indicated that the participants had a favourable attitude towards this mobile technology. Chen (2013) concluded that tablet computers are ideal tools not only to support learner autonomy development, but also to promote ubiquitous learning. In a similar vein, Izadpanah and Alavi (2016) and Jahangard et al. (2020) reported that the Iranian students showed their agreement with the use of CALL. The normalisation of technology, as reflected in the application of different technological tools in people's everyday lives, was found central to encouraging language learners' use of WELL, as speculated by the researchers (Jahangard et al., 2020).

Based on MVS, the students with the highest and lowest mean total scores for the post-study questionnaires (see Figure 5.7) were selected to participate in the post-study SSIs. The examination of the qualitative data revealed that the technology was found useful, effective, and satisfactory by the proponents. They explained that *Alexa* enabled them to communicate in the TL, increased their production of language output, gave them easy and instantaneous access to information, and improved their language skills and ability to ask questions. The opponents, on the other hand, kept referring to *Alexa's* failure to understand their questions as the main cause underlying their self-perceived uselessness and ineffectiveness of the IVA in the context of language development and information retrieval. Time-consuming and troublesome HMC also triggered students' deep dissatisfaction with the technology.

Both the proponents and opponents were able to list the pros and cons of the application of voice assistance in EFL learning. They, however, differed with regard to the aspects that they had found (dis)advantageous about the technology. Opportunities for participating in intensive EFL practice, increasing WTC in the TL, and gaining access to multimodal information were identified as the benefits of the HMC with the VA. Irrelevance of responses, problems with reliability, troublesome understanding and connectivity, increased time burden, downloading issues, and artificiality of interaction were the challenges encountered in the treatment.

Figures 5.9 and 5.10 illustrate the themes related to the self-perceived benefits and challenges of voice assistance in the EFL self-instruction. Code frequencies that emerged from the post-study SSIs with the proponents and opponents of the technology are also included. As demonstrated below, more benefits of using voice assistance during EFL self-instruction were discussed by the proponents and, vice versa, more challenges were identified by the opponents.

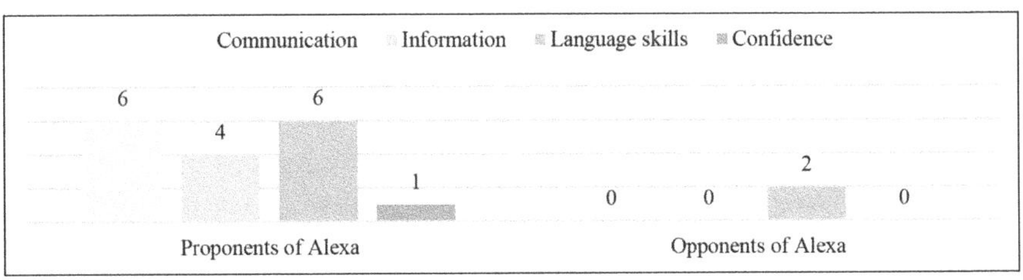

Fig. 5.5: *Self-perceived benefits of using* Alexa *in EFL self-instruction: proponents (n=6) versus opponents (n=6) of the technology (self-prepared)*

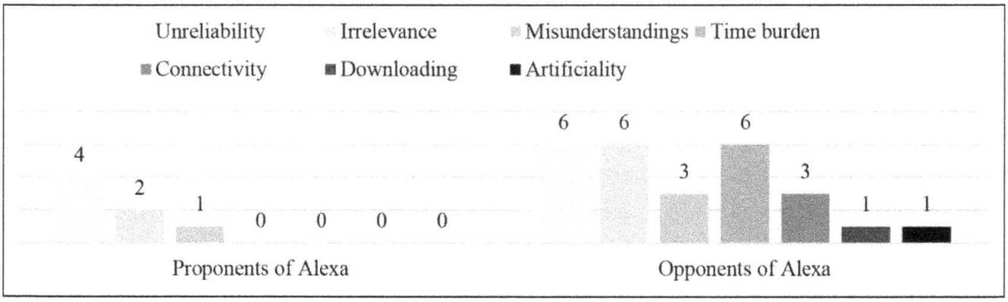

Fig. 5.6: *Self-perceived challenges of using* Alexa *in EFL self-instruction: proponents (n=6) versus opponents (n=6) of the technology (self-prepared)*

Participants' acceptance of and satisfaction with the technology use (or their lack) was also reflected in their answers to the interview questions related to their future application of the IVA and their suggestions to modify the treatment. While the proponents expressed their willingness to use *Alexa*, explaining that the VA helped them learn English more effectively, the opponents listed arguments against implementing the assistant in their self-instruction (i.e., time-consuming, unsuccessful and artificial HMC, preference for traditional learning). Further, as far as potential changes to the treatment suggested by the interviewees are concerned, the proponents called for the implementation of a greater number of preparatory activities and teacher-led in-class training prior to the treatment. The opponents, on the other hand, would prefer to replace *Alexa* with the Internet search engine and avoid using the technology.

The findings of the post-study SSIs are in line with the results of the research into the feasibility of different VAs in formal and informal language learning, according to which the participants were both positive and critical about the technology. Moussalli and Cardoso (2016), who conducted their study with ESL learners in Canada, found that even though their participants considered the *Alexa* application simple, fun, and helpful in the context of their L2 development, they underlined the problem of HMC breakdowns. Likewise, Dizon (2017, 2020) reported that his Japanese students valued *Alexa* for giving opportunities for TL speaking and pronunciation practice in particular. Based on the results of Underwood's (2017) study, the EFL learners in Spain also welcomed voice assistance. Despite their inability to properly respond to all questions and commands, the use of IVAs was said to build up students' excitement, engagement, motivation, and enjoyment. Similarly, in their two studies conducted with Japanese EFL learners, Dizon and Tang (2019, 2020) reported that even though the use of *Alexa* was a pleasant experience, it was problematic in view of frequent speech comprehensibility issues. The findings of the studies administered to Taiwanese EFL students by Chen et al. (2020) corroborate the results of the above-mentioned research by indicating that HMC breakdowns were the major obstacle to voice assistance, as reported by the participants. Likewise, Tai and Chen (2020), who also conducted their study in Taiwan, demonstrated that the learners appreciated the use of the IPA due to the pleasurable and authentic HMC process in the TL.

Moreover, the Polish students' conviction about the beneficial influence of *Alexa* on their attitudes towards English shared by them during the post-study SSIs was in line with the results of the IVA research verifying the impact of voice assistance on the participants' affect. Chen et al. (2020) and Tai and Chen (2020) observed a positive influence of participants' HMC with the IVAs on improving motivation, reducing language anxiety, and increasing WTC in the TL.

From a broader perspective, the tendency displaying the favourable impact of the technology on affective factors in language learning was also documented in CALL research. For example, Fidaoui (2010) reported that the majority of the students learning English in Lebanon found the use of ICTs motivating. Likewise, Anwaruddin (2013), who compared the effect of CALL and non-CALL lessons on students' behaviours in Bangladesh, demonstrated that the use of technology brought about an increase in participants' motivation. A positive effect of CALL-mediated TBLT on ExG students' motivation to learn to write was also documented in an Iranian EFL context. Tavakoli et al. (2019) speculated that "this type of learning is novel, engaging, and, accordingly, motivating to learners. It also accounts for the interactive nature of communication believed to boost learning" (p. 17). In their study administered to Iranian EFL learners, Jahangard et al. (2020) also found that the use of "the CALL program is essentially helpful, especially for introverts, who can undertake the task with increased ease" (p. 8). Similar findings were reported by Hanafiah et al. (2022), who investigated the application of CALL in an Indonesian EFL context. The results of their study demonstrated that the ExG students experienced lower levels of speaking anxiety having been exposed to the treatment compared to the control students. Hanafiah et al. (2022) explained that CALL is found central to decreasing language learning-related anxiety and stress thanks to the combination of fun games and communicative activities.

Technology-enhanced TBLL seemed to offer instruction which, even though highly regarded by the majority of the participants, provoked extremely negative emotions in some learners (see Tables 5.22 and 5.23). Kotuła (2016), who investigated the opinions of the Polish students of French on the use of game-supported language learning, had insights into the application of CALL similar to those from the analysis of the post-study SSIs. As he explained, "[i]n the context of foreign language teaching, techniques going beyond common practices may be the source of both enthusiasm and extreme reluctance expressed by learners" (p. 226). All in all, despite some dissenting voices towards *Alexa* found in the data, the findings of the programme evaluation suggested that the participants in the study evaluated the technology as an easy-to-use, effective, and enjoyable EFL learning tool.

5.3 Pedagogical implications

The current study was designed and administered to fill in the gap in the CALL research. Specifically, it aimed to explore the recent phenomenon of task-oriented IMALL in out-of-class TBLL for text mediation. The findings demonstrate that the treatment involving the use of the *Alexa* IVA by the ExG students during task performance helped increase their ability to mediate texts. Thanks to the combination of IMALL and TBLL, the participants were given a chance to establish HMC with *Alexa* in the context of real-life task performance. Similarly to authentic HHC, they were encouraged to negotiate meanings with the VA to obtain answers to their questions and deal with HMC breakdowns, as reflected in their frequent use of the rephrase and repeat strategies. Despite learner- and technology-related causes for students' communication problems, the participants expressed positive overall opinions on the use of the VA in their learning to mediate, generally evaluating *Alexa* as useable, effective, and satisfactory. These promising findings carry some important implications related to the use of IMALL and self-instructed TBLL to facilitate the development of text mediation. They therefore ought to be considered not only by interested CALL researchers, but also by different stakeholders from the field of FLT, namely EFL instructors, syllabus designers, teacher educators, and policy makers.

The findings of the study demonstrate that the use of the voice-controlled technologies in self-instructed TBLL was effective in aiding the ExG students' improvement of text mediation, with benefits being observable both at within- and between-group levels. Such results not only speak in favour of the effectiveness and usefulness of combining IMALL with TBLL in facilitating the development of learners' ability to mediate texts, but also provide a rationale for the implementation of the two in text mediation instruction. Language educators and programme designers could introduce the treatment offered by the present study, that is to integrate IMALL and TBLL within TFOH in order to promote text mediation practice. The treatment designed and utilised in the current study presents a specific way of applying voice assistance in out-of-class task performance in the context of mediation practice. Technology-mediated TBLL was proposed therein as a pedagogical framework to elucidate the integrative nature of technology and tasks. Students' communication with the IPA during task performance engaged them in simultaneous language reception, production, interaction, and mediation. The treatment was designed to support learners' comprehension of *Alexa*'s responses thanks to multimodal input provided to learners by the technology and the implementation of the question-generation strategy by the participants in the course of their task performance. In view of the above, the study may, hopefully, encourage materials writers to consider including TBLL self-study sections requiring the use of IPAs in coursebook materials.

Involving EFL students in the performance of IVA-based tasks similar to those from the treatment may facilitate the development of language aspects other than the ability to mediate oral and written texts. The use of *Alexa* during task performance was welcomed by the students; they reported that the treatment had increased their TL reception and production and improved their pronunciation and vocabulary knowledge. The technology-mediated and task-based self-instruction for text mediation could therefore offer valuable support to the learners in the aforementioned areas. This finding is of particular significance in the context of Polish learners' preparation for the new 2023 version of the high-stake EFL Matura exam, which, as previously mentioned (see Chapter Two), was seriously hampered by the outbreak of the SARS-CoV-2 pandemic.

The beneficial effect of the treatment on the ExG students' text mediation performance deserves ample attention not only in the context of EFL mediation development and EFL examinations, but also in the realities of FLT contexts, such as Poland. FL instruction in expanding circle countries where students have few FL lessons a week and the TL is not used in out-of-class settings on an everyday basis is very likely to remain clearly inadequate and artificial. Since many learners come from monolingual social backgrounds and rarely come into regular contact with native speakers and speakers of the TL outside school, it is more than justified for language instructors to create opportunities for their students to use the TL in real-life contexts. In so far as controlled language activities pursued in instructed settings usually have little to do with reality, both traditional and technology-mediated TBLL provide authentic contexts for everyday language use and can thus be combined to promote experiential language learning. In the treatment, the participants were given the opportunity to practice mediation on their own within three task phases: pre-mediation, mediation, and post-mediation. It must be stressed here that those tasks which were implemented in conjunction with IMALL could, in contrast to traditional self-instructed TBLL, engage learners in communicative and interactive TL use. Even though the findings of the study point to the effectiveness of both technology-mediated and traditional TBLL, the experimental intervention was more successful than conventional instruction in the context of text mediation improvement. This justifies the implementation of out-of-class IMALL and TBLL to develop text mediation. At the same time, it is not to be suggested that out-of-class CALL-based TBLL should be applied while traditional task-based self-instruction should be forsaken. However, efforts ought to be made to introduce the AI-powered technology whenever it is appropriate, feasible, and profitable.

Based on the findings, the experimental intervention offered an attractive alternative to traditional (i.e., only task-based) self-instruction, let alone coursebook-based homework, in light of the volatile coronavirus pandemic. The uncertain future of traditional on-site learning required adopting urgent measures to foster autonomous and ubiquitous FL learning and tackling the problem of limited teacher-student and student-student interaction underlying online EFL lessons. The self-instruction concept was applied not only in response to the worldwide health crisis, but also the growing importance of the learner autonomy and life-long learning buzzwords. The intervention modified traditional learner and teacher roles, with the learners becoming more active participants and the teachers becoming learning facilitators. Thanks to *Alexa*, which allowed the participants to engage in HCIs, the participants could communicate in the TL without the presence of traditional classroom sine-qua-nons, such as teachers and students, in their home surroundings. In view of the fact that the ExG students reported having gained greater control over their EFL learning after the treatment, language educators who wish to assign their learners with some responsibility for their EFL learning and identify the need to develop their students' communicative competence in an integrative way should find it worthwhile implementing self-instruction similar to the current experimental intervention.

The application of the treatment seemed to offer a viable solution not only to tackling the problem of the students' limited interaction in the TL, but also to reducing the level of language anxiety experienced by some learners. The fact that the participants were given an opportunity to talk to *Alexa* in private in low-stress home environments could contribute to them overcoming inhibitions and freely experimenting in the TL. This in turn might positively affect their overall attitudes to language use and encourage their more willing future language production and interaction, as reported by the proponents of the *Alexa* usage. Those instructors who have identified their learners' problems with the TL use may find it useful to familiarise their learners with the VA application IVA in out-of-class settings.

The amount of attention paid to every student during regular EFL lessons by even the most devoted instructor cannot compare to that provided by *Alexa* during self-instruction. In other words, IVAs, which have been designed to assist human users by responding to their every command and question, have a decided advantage over a human teacher in that a HMC success informs students about the production of correct queries. Given such problems as time limitations and overcrowded classrooms, teachers are not able to focus on an individual student out of a dozen and comment upon every case of their language use. Those teachers who would like to individualise EFL instruction and provide students with the instantaneous feedback on oral language within their homework ought to supply their assignments with IVA-based tasks.

Another implication of the study arises from the data collected in response to CRQ2. The usability construct received the lowest mean agreement value from the respondents, which indicated that probably some students evaluated *Alexa* as difficult to communicate with in the context of their task performance. Moreover, in addition to appreciating the benefits of voice assistance, the learners listed several challenges and proposed different ways to improve the treatment. Based on these, one constructive suggestion would be to include teacher-led training. Namely, a set of preparatory activities conducted with the guidance of the teacher in in-class settings would support the participants in their learning to use the VA and solve HMC breakdowns. This in turn could afford opportunities for more frequent production of modified output by the students in the situations when they abandoned their interaction with the VA under the influence of HMC breakdowns. Furthermore, students' HMC could have been improved by more intensive training, which might have positively influenced their perceived attitudes toward the technology.

The study shows that not only EFL learners who participate in the experimental intervention, but also EFL instructors who utilise the treatment need to have a substantial level of computer expertise. Since the implementation of IMALL and TBLL redefines the traditional roles of classroom actors, teachers are also expected to demonstrate willingness to incorporate the AI-driven technology into their instruction and encourage independence in their students within their out-of-class EFL learning. Those administrators who decide to use CALL in their institutions and apply treatment similar to that from the current study should first and foremost ensure that the teachers who work there possess the essential technical skills and that required training is provided for those who do not comply with this requirement.

Further, the introduction of IMALL and TBLL calls for a careful and meticulous preparation process. As evidenced in the six-stage research procedure underlying the current study, a multimethodological analysis of the learners' needs was conducted in Stage One, in which their necessities, lacks, wants, and their experiences with mobile technology use and the *Alexa* assistant had been considered before the design and development of the treatment. The results of the small-scale research into learners' needs provided the basis for real-life task selection in Stage Two and Stage Three, which both took place prior to the actual implementation and evaluation of voice assistance in TBLL in the pilot testing stage. To be specific, the processes of analysis, design, and development followed by implementation and evaluation underlay the treatment, which is in line with the engineering life cycle model for courseware development proposed by Colpaert (2006, p. 116). An investigation similar in nature to that conducted in the first four stages of the current research procedure is required in any language learning context before the implementation of task-oriented IMALL to guarantee that the tasks FL learners are expected to complete prepare them for their future out-of-class language performance.

5.4 Limitations to the study and suggestions for future research

Based on the literature review stage, which revealed several limitations to the preliminary research into the use of VAs by ESL/EFL learners, we attempted to design such a study which could overcome the weaknesses enumerated therein. In view of students' short-term exposure to the treatment, low number of the participants, and a relatively narrow range of data collection tools used in the studies investigating voice assistance, we decided to extend the duration of our experimental intervention to eight weeks, increase the number of the participants to 30 in the ExG and CtrlG each to ensure statistical significance, and triangulate the sources and methods of data collection.

In addition, the problem of intact grouping was overcome. The study had a quasi-experimental design, that is the ExG and CtrlG had already been formed when the study was planned, and it was not possible to assign individual participants to the two groups randomly. Nevertheless, the factor rotation technique, which increases the internal validity of the study by making it possible for the two groups to undergo the treatment, was employed to control for the group inequality inherent to intact grouping.

It is the belief of the present author that the main strengths of the current investigation lay in its methodological triangulation and factor rotation. Also, the fact that the intervention took place during out-of-class EFL learning offered another advantage in that it allowed the examination of the natural HMC process that took place between the participants and the technology throughout the experimental intervention.

Nonetheless, it is not to be suggested here that the current research study did not have any weaknesses. The fact is that the quasi-experiment and programme evaluation suffered from several design- and application-related limitations that should be addressed in future empirical investigations of the role of voice assistance in TBLL. Taking those limitations into consideration would not only be beneficial in the context of evaluating the findings of the current study, but it would also be helpful in identifying those areas that should be open to further examination.

The findings obtained from the current study should be treated with caution because of its major methodological limitation related to the non-random selection of the sample. To be precise, the convenience sampling strategy decreased the external validity of the results by limiting their representativeness and generalisability only to such cases which are comparable to those in the study. The population investigated within the current study comprised seventeen- and eighteen-year old Polish EFL learners who were enrolled in an English programme in a private secondary school in Lublin. Even though the ExG students participating in this study responded positively to the treatment, it is impossible to guarantee that other Polish EFL secondary school learners would have reacted similarly to the combination of IMALL and TBLL for text mediation within the treatment. Thus, we would like to express a clear need for further VA research to validate the findings from the present study to a different sample. Preferably, other studies should recruit participants based on a probability sampling strategy to obtain more generalisable results.

Equally importantly, the current investigation displayed some degree of selection and sampling bias. In line with the convenience sampling strategy, particular groups of Polish EFL secondary school learners were more likely to be chosen from the population than others. In view of their easy accessibility, intermediate EFL students who at the time of the study attended the private secondary school located in the eastern part of Poland were selected by the author to participate in the current research procedure. There is therefore a pressing need for further studies that explore the use of voice assistance by students of different proficiency levels in their out-of-class text mediation practice in various secondary schools across Poland.

In addition to replicating the current study with Polish EFL students of different proficiency levels and from different parts of Poland, it would be interesting to involve younger, that is grade six, seven, and eight primary school learners, in the investigation. This would allow the exploration of the implementation of voice assistance during self-instruction in this age group to find out how younger learners handle and evaluate their interaction with *Alexa*. As previously mentioned, the eighth-grader exam features text mediation tasks in each of its four sections, which certainly adds further impetus for exploring new possibilities to improve primary school learners' text mediation. Therefore, further studies are recommended to include participants from primary schools in Poland to explore the effects of the IMALL implementation from different perspectives, that is of those of younger learners.

In addition, the analysis of the quantitative data from text mediation tests and post-study questionnaires demonstrated the need for a higher intensity and a longer time period of the IMALL implementation. The current study investigated the effects of the treatment that involved one weekly technology-mediated task over the span of two months. Even though the mean gain scores of the ExG were descriptively higher than those of the CtrlG, the test result for oral text mediation was at the borderline of statistical significance in Phase 2. Further, the introduction of the technology did not have any effect on selected participants' self-perceived level of autonomy, as reported by the students in their answers to the post-study questionnaire. To facilitate a more comprehensive comparison between the ExG and the CtrlG and to examine the effects of the use of VAs on learner autonomy, further studies could either lengthen the duration or increase the intensity of the treatment (or both), for instance by assigning more than one task-based TFOH a week for a time period longer than eight weeks.

Given the aforementioned limitations, further experimental research is called for to verify the effects of voice assistance both on (Polish) EFL learners' text mediation improvement and on other aspects related to language learning. Many research problems, some of which have already been discussed, occurred in the course of the current investigation. Those already mentioned as well as some others are included in the following list in the hope that they will be examined within future empirical exploration:

1. The research study presented in the current dissertation should be replicated with a similar (and more numerous) sample to allow for more generalisation in the event that comparable findings are obtained.
2. A similar research study should be administered to EFL students of different proficiency levels and age groups to check proficiency level and age as variables.
3. A research study which allows for the administration of immediate and delayed post-tests at different time intervals should be designed to evaluate the effectiveness of technology-mediated TBLL in shorter and longer periods.

4. It is recommended that language modes other than mediation ought to be investigated within both cross-sectional and longitudinal studies in the future.
5. Adding a third group of students who would be instructed in text mediation by means of traditional techniques, that is coursebook exercises, could help compare the results of the CtrlG with those of ExG students involved in technology-mediated and traditional TBLL.
6. The research should also take into consideration the cause-effect relationship between the implementation of IVAs in task-based self-instruction and participants' self-perceived autonomy levels.
7. In view of the learning curve theory, the analysis of the number and types of HMC breakdowns occurring over time within the treatment could provide an insight into the dynamics of the student-IVA interaction.

As demonstrated above, the study opened up new possible avenues for future research. It is a deeply-held belief of the present author that only by investigating the above-mentioned research problems and accumulating empirical evidence will it be possible to examine the effects of voice assistance on informal EFL learning, which based on the findings of the current study and the past preliminary research, seems very promising and therefore worthy of further investigation.

5.5 Conclusions

The last century has witnessed the growth of FLT as a field of empirical study. Extensive research in SLA has called into question the method concept and facilitated a shift away from focus on forms and meaning towards a focus on form. In line with the CEFR's AOA conceptual model, which underlined the importance of actions during task performance, FLs have been treated as resources that students will utilise outside instructed settings. Over the last decades, developments taking place in ICTs have further shaped the face of FLT. Smaller yet more sophisticated mobile devices powered by AI technologies revolutionised the face of CALL, which was once limited to the use of bulky and primitive mainframes, fulfilled aspirations for establishing HMC in language education anytime and anywhere.

In the meantime, changes in the Polish education system related to the school structure, FL Core Curricula, and examination principles modernised FLT in Poland. Despite strong pro-Russian tendencies underlying the field of language education in the period after WWII and before the 1989 transformations, English has acquired the status of the most popular FL taught and examined in Poland. Nonetheless, such problems as the neglectful approach towards EFL oracy development and the adoption of the controversial 2017 education reform have been aggravated by the outbreak of the coronavirus pandemic. The Polish governments' decision to close schools and implement e-learning triggered strong criticism in view of the doubtful educational value of those preventive measures.

The current study was designed and administered in response to the latest trends underlying FL education in Europe and the destabilising effect of the COVID-19 pandemic on FLT in EU member states. Cognizant of the significance of mediation in language education, omnipresence of increasingly sophisticated mobile devices, unpredictable nature of FL instruction in Poland in the wake of the health crisis, and fundamental role of learner autonomy in fostering lifelong learning, we combined IMALL with out-of-class TBLL for text mediation.

The study began with the assumption that using both IMALL and TBLL could enhance the Polish intermediate EFL learners' ability to mediate texts. Having administered the pre- and post-tests and performed a specific statistical analysis to answer the CRQ1, the present author found out that the treatment did have a positive effect on the participants' text mediation improvement both at between- and within-group levels. The results of the *Wilcoxon Signed Rank Test*, which was run to determine whether the differences at within-group levels were statistically significant in Phase 1 and Phase 2, challenged the H_0. Even though the conventional treatment also resulted in significant gains in oral and written text mediation, the *U Mann-Whitney Test*, which was used to examine the differences in the performance of oral and written text mediation between the ExG and CtrlG, demonstrated a statistically significant difference in the performance of oral and written text mediation in Phase 1 and Phase 2 respectively. In addition, the *Independent Samples T-Test* and *Independent Samples T-Test with the Cochran-Cox Adjustment*, which were run to determine whether there was statistical evidence in favour of the fact that the mean total gain scores for the ExG and CtrlG were statistically different, provided statistical evidence against the H_0. Generally, the findings demonstrated that the ExG performed significantly better on text mediation activities after the IMALL treatment compared to the performance of the CtrlG and to its performance before the treatment.

The findings to the CRQ2 showed that the learners had positive overall perceptions of the application of voice assistance in EFL learning. They were able to list arguments for and against its usefulness and effectiveness, justify their (dis) satisfaction of using the VA, and to name the benefits and challenges of utilising the technology in TBLL. The majority of the students agreed with all the statements related to acceptance of the technology, with the highest and lowest mean agreement values being reported for the learner satisfaction and usability constructs respectively. Equally importantly, the students who positively assessed the use of the IPA outnumbered those students who expressed the opposite opinion. The technology was found useful by the proponents in the context of facilitating their communication in the TL, allowing them easy access to information, and improving their language skills. When asked about the effectiveness of *Alexa*, they argued that the technology maximised their language output, quickly and easily found information for them, and enhanced their ability to ask questions in English. On the other hand, the opponents drew attention to linguistic and technological limitations of *Alexa* and a generally unsuccessful character of their HMC while arguing for the uselessness and ineffectiveness of the VA. They explained that the VA limited their access to information and turned out to be impractical in improving their EFL speaking and broadening vocabulary knowledge. The opponents were dissatisfied with the technology since their HMC with *Alexa* was, in their opinion, frustrating, time-consuming, and useless in the context of their information retrieval. As argued by both the proponents and opponents, the idea of voice assistance had its pluses and minuses. As far as the benefits are concerned, the participants pointed out the opportunities to practise speaking English, improve pronunciation and communication skills, enhance one's confidence in using English, and gain easier access to multimodal information. Low reliability of the technology, irrelevance of information, problems with understanding and connectivity, increased time burden, downloading issues, and artificiality of HMC were the specific challenges faced by the participants in the context of their task performance.

Based on the findings of the study, several implications ought to be considered by stakeholders in the field of FL education given the character of FL instruction in Poland as an expanding circle country and Polish learners' preparation for the high-stake EFL New Matura examination. First and foremost, the use of IMALL and TBLL was suggested to create a ubiquitous learning environment, which in addition to developing intralinguistic text mediation, was believed to improve pronunciation and vocabulary knowledge by the students. The CALL treatment should be considered a feasible alternative to traditional homework as the former engaged the students in simultaneous language reception, production, interaction, and mediation and supported their comprehension of *Alexa*'s responses thanks to multimodal input and student-generated questions. Technology-mediated TBLL was also said to provide authentic contexts for everyday language use, promoted learning-by-doing environments, and offered individualised feedback on every student' utterance. Equally importantly, the combination of IMALL and TBLL did engage learners in the communicative and interactive TL use in their low-stake home surroundings. It must be stressed at this point that the introduction of the treatment did call for a careful preparation process and in-class training of EFL students and, unless necessary, instructors. Nonetheless, language educators who favour an integrated approach to developing communicative competence and aspire to reduce their learners' language anxiety levels, promote their independence, and assign them with some responsibility for their EFL learning should find it worthwhile considering the implementation of self-instruction similar to the experimental intervention.

References

Abbate, E. (2021). Mediation, multilingual competence, online interaction: Companion Volume descriptors as CLIL activators tasks. *Philologica Jassyensia*, *2*(34), 255–262.

Abdelhalim, S. (2016). An interpretive inquiry into the integration of the information and communication technology tools in TEFL at Egyptian universities. *Journal of Research in Curriculum Instruction and Educational Technology*, *2*(4), 145–173. https://doi.org/10.21608/jrciet.2016.24498

Abdous, M., Camarena, M., & Facer, B. (2009). MALL technology: Use of academic podcasting in the foreign language classroom. *ReCALL*, *21*(1), 76–95. https://doi.org/10.1017/s0958344009000020

About the survey (n.d.). surveylang.org. http://www.surveylang.org/About-SurveyLang/About-the-survey.html

Abraham, R. & Liou, H.-C. (1991). Interaction generated by three computer programs: Analysis of functions of spoken language. In P. Dunkel (Ed.), *Computer-assisted language learning and testing: Research issues and practice* (pp. 85–109). Newbury House.

Abramczyk, A. (2015). Co „gryzie" nauczycieli języków obcych? *Języki Obce w Szkole*, *4*, 126–130.

Abu-Rmaileh, S. (2018). Silent way. In J. Liontas (ed.), *TESOL encyclopaedia of English language teaching* (pp. 1–6). Wiley.

Accenture (2017). *Talk to me.* https://www.accenture.com/_acnmedia/PDF-65/Accenture-Voice-Assistant-Infographic.pdf

Accenture. (2019). *Everyone has a voice. DVAs on the rise*. http://bitly.pl/chlfE

Accenture (2019). *Reshape to relevance.* http://bitly.pl/83jas

Adamopoulou, E., & Moussiades, L. (2020). Chatbots: History, technology and applications. *Machine Learning with Applications*, *2*, 1–18. https://doi.org/10.1016/j.mlwa.2020.100006

Adams, W. (2015). Conducting semi-structured interviews. In K. Newcomer, H. Hatry & S. Wholey (Eds.), *Handbook of practical program evaluation* (pp. 492–505). Jossey-Bass.

Adobe Inc. (2019). *State of voice: Adobe digital insights 2019.* https://www.digitalmarketingcommunity.com/researches/state-of-voice-adobe-digital-insights-2019/

Ahmad, A. (2021, April 13). *Chatbots vs. conversational AI: Is there a difference?* Cognigy. https://www.cognigy.com/blog/chatbots-vs-conversational-ai

Ahmad, K., Greville, C., Rogers, M., & Sussex, R. (1985). *Computers, language learning and language teaching*. Cambridge University Press.

Ahmed, R., & Bidin, S. (2016). The effect of task based language teaching on writing skills of EFL learners in Malaysia. *Open Journal of Modern Linguistics*, *6*(03), 207–218. http://dx.doi.org/10.4236/ojml.2016.63022

Alderson, C. (2007). The CEFR and the need for more research. *The Modern Language Journal*, *91*(4), 659–663. https://doi.org/10.1111/j.1540-4781.2007.00627_4.x

Aleksander, A., & Szarota, Z. (1995). Modernizacja procesu kształcenia pedagogicznego nauczycieli (na przykładzie doświadczeń w Nauczycielskim Kolegium Języka Polskiego w Tarnowie). *Rocznik Naukowo-Dydaktyczny WSP w Krakowie*, 87–95.

Alemi, M., & Daftarifard, P. (2010). Pedagogical innovations in language teaching methodologies. *Journal of Language Teaching & Research*, *1*(6), 765–770. https://doi.org/10.4304/jltr.1.6.765-770

Alemi, M., & Tavakoli, E. (2016, January 28). *Audiolingual method* [Paper presentation]. *3th International Conference on Applied Research in Language Study*, Tehran, Iran.

Alexandru, G. (2020, July 10). *Conversational AI: Intelligent virtual assistants and the road ahead*. towardsdatascience. https://towardsdatascience.com/conversational-ai-intelligent-virtual-assistants-and-the-road-ahead-6345db47d106

Alexiou, T., & Stathopoulou, M. (2021). The pre-A1 level in the companion volume of the Common European Framework of Reference For Languages. *Research Papers in Language Teaching and Learning*, *11*(1), 11–29.

Almekhlafi, A. (2006). The effect of computer assisted language learning (CALL) on United Arab Emirates English as a foreign language (EFL) school students' achievement and attitude. *Journal of Interactive Learning Research*, *17*(2), 121–142.

Amaral, L., & Meurers, D. (2011). On using intelligent computer-assisted language learning in real-life foreign language teaching and learning. *ReCALL*, *23*(1), 4–24. https://doi.org/10.1017/S0958344010000261

Anastasiadou, S., & Tiliakou, C. (2015). The Greek state certificate in English language proficiency (KPG) level A: Item difficulty, learning ability and cultural background through regression analysis. *Procedia: Social and Behavioral Sciences*, *197*, 1501–1506. https://doi.org/10.1016/j.sbspro.2015.07.101

Anderson, J., Boyle, F., & Reiser, B. (1985). Intelligent tutoring systems. *Science*, *228*, 456–462. https://doi.org/10.1126/science.228.4698.456

Andrzejewska, E. (2011). Autonomia a zadania mediacyjne na lekcjach języka obcego. In M. Pawlak (Ed.), *Autonomia w nauce języka obcego. Uczeń a nauczyciel* (pp. 247–259). Wydział Pedagogiczno-Artystyczny UAM w Poznaniu/PWSZ w Koninie.

Anwaruddin, S. (2013). Web 2.0 and language learners' motivation: An action research study. *The Canadian Journal of Action Research*, *14*(1), 51–68.

Arif, S. (2018, January 4). *Chatbots past & future*. The Startup. https://medium.com/swlh/chatbots-past-future-8df2076192e5

Aron, J. (2011, October 26). *How innovative is Apple's new voice assistant, Siri?* New Scientist. https://www.newscientist.com/article/mg21228365-300-how-innovative-is-apples-new-voice-assistant-siri/

Arora, S., Batra, K., & Singh, S. (2013) *Dialogue system: A brief review*. arXiv. https://doi.org/10.48550/arXiv.1306.4134

Arvanitis, P., & Krystalli, P. (2020). Mobile assisted language learning (MALL): Trends from 2010 to 2020 using text analysis techniques. *European Journal of Education*, *4*(1), 13–22. https://doi.org/10.26417/461iaw87u

Asher, J. (1965). The strategy of the total physical response: An application to learning Russian. *International Review of Applied Linguistics*, *3*, 291–300. https://doi.org/10.1515/iral.1965.3.4.291

Azlan, N., Zakaria, S., & Yunus, M. (2019). Integrative task-based learning: Developing speaking skill and increase motivation via Instagram. *International Journal of Academic Research in Business and Social Sciences*, *9*(1), 620–636. https://doi.org/10.6007/ijarbss/v9-i1/5463

Baccalaureate exam in Romania (n.d.). Romaniaeducation.info. https://www.romaniaeducation.info/Tests/The-Baccalaureate-Exam.html

Bachman, L. (1990) *Fundamental considerations in language testing*. Oxford University Press.

Bączkowska, A. (2021). An overview of popular website platforms and mobile apps for language learning. *Forum Filologiczne Ateneum*, *1*(9), 9–35.

Baker, T., Smith, L., & Anissa, N. (2019). *Educ-ai-tion rebooted? Exploring the future of artificial intelligence in schools and colleges*. https://media.nesta.org.uk/documents/Future_of_AI_and_education_v5_WEB.pdf

Bancheri, S. (2006). A language teacher's perspective on effective courseware. In R. Donaldson & M. Haggstrom (Eds.), *Changing language education through CALL* (pp. 31–47). Routledge.

Baran, M. (2015). Dydaktyka kultury a podejście ukierunkowane na działanie w nauczaniu języka polskiego jako obcego. *Postscriptum Polonistyczne*, *16*(2), 185–194.

Bartosik, (2020). Nauczanie mediacji a rzeczywistość zawodowa. *Języki Obce w Szkole*, *2*, 25–30.

Bax, S. (2003). CALL: Past, present and future. *System*, *31*(1), 13–28.

BBC (2019, March 1). *Cheating in exams: Smartphones blamed for rise in incidents.* https://www.bbc.com/news/uk-northern-ireland-47406500

BBC (2021, December 28). *Alexa tells 10-year-old girl to touch live plug with penny.* https://www.bbc.com/news/technology-59810383

Beal, V. (1996, September 1). *PDA.* Webopedia. https://www.webopedia.com/definitions/pda/

Beamon, A. (2021, May 7). *3 ways intelligent virtual assistants will drive citizen services delivery.* GCN. https://gcn.com/articles/2021/05/07/intelligent-virtual-assistants.aspx

Beatty, K. (2003). *Teaching and researching computer-assisted language learning.* Pearson Education.

Belz, J. (2001). Institutional and individual dimensions of transatlantic group work in network-based language teaching. *ReCALL*, *13*(2), 213–231. https://doi.org/10.1017/s0958344001000726a

Benko, A., & Lanyi, C. (2009). History of artificial intelligence. In M. Khosrow-Pour (Ed.), *Encyclopaedia of information science and technology* (pp. 1759–1762). IGI Global.

Bennett, S., Maton, K., & Kervin, L. (2008). The 'digital natives' debate: A critical review of the evidence. *British Journal of Educational Technology*, *39*(5), 775–786.

Benson, P. (2010). Measuring autonomy: Should we put our ability to the test? In A. Paran & L. Sercu (Eds.), *Testing the untestable in language education* (pp. 77–97). Multilingual Matters.

Berdasco, A., Lopez, G., Diaz, I., Quesada, L., & Guerrero, L. (2019). User experience comparison of intelligent personal assistants: Alexa, Google Assistant, Siri and Cortana. *Multidisciplinary Digital Publishing Institute Proceedings*, *31*(1), 1–8. https://doi.org/10.3390/proceedings2019031051

Bhattacharya, S., Bashar, M., Srivastava, A., & Singh, A. (2019). Nomophobia: No mobile phone phobia. *Journal of Family Medicine and Primary Care*, *8*(4), 1297–1300. https://doi.org/10.4103/jfmpc.jfmpc_71_19

Bibauw, S., Françoisn, T., & Desmet, P. (2019). Discussing with a computer to practice a foreign language: Research synthesis and conceptual framework of dialogue-based CALL. *Computer Assisted Language Learning*, *31*(8), 827–877. https://doi.org/10.1080/09588221.2018.1535508

Bibauw, S., Van den Noortgate, W., François, T., & Desmet, P. (2022). Dialogue systems for language learning: A meta-analysis. *Language Learning & Technology*, *26*(1), 1–25.

Blin, F. (2016). Towards an 'ecological' CALL theory: Theoretical perspectives and their instantiation in CALL research and practice. In F. Farr & L. Murray (Eds.), *The Routledge handbook of language learning and technology* (pp. 39–54). Routledge.

Bogucka, M. (2009). Wczesne nauczanie języka obcego: dylematy, fakty i mity. *Języki Obce w Szkole, 4*, 5–10.

Bohle, F. (2012). *Sprachmittlung im Fremdsprachenunterricht*. Diplomica Verlag.

Bonett, D., & Wright, T. (2014). Cronbach's alpha reliability: Interval estimation, hypothesis testing and sample size planning. *Journal of Organizational Behavior, 36*(1), 3–15. https://doi.org/10.1002/job.1960

Borger, J. (2011, April 6). English words fail to take root in Polish vernacular. *The Guardian*. http://www.guardian.co.uk/world/2011/apr/06/english-language-poland-vernacular

Bourguignon C. (2006). De l'approche communicative à l'approche communic'actionnelle: Une rupture épistémologique en didactique des languescultures. *Synergie Europe, 1*, 58–73.

Box, D. (2022, February 10). *Healthcare virtual assistants and the voice tech: Insights from Star's healthtech practice*. Star. https://star.global/posts/healthcare-applications-for-digital-voice-assistants/

Bozkurt, A., & Goksel, N. (2018, July 2–4). *Technology renovates itself: Key concepts on intelligent personal assistants (IPAs)* [Paper presentation]. 10th International Conference on Education and New Learning Technology, Palma, Mallorca, Spain.

Bradburn, N., Sudman, S., Blair, E., Locander, W., Miles, C., Singer, E., & Stocking, C. (1979). *Improving interview method and questionnaire design: Response effects to threatening questions in survey research*. Jossey-Bass.

Braga, J., Silva, L., & Correa, R. (2017). CALL & MALL: Using technology to achieve educational objectives in the language classroom. In A. Oliveira & J. Braga (Eds), *Inspiring insights from an English teaching scene* (pp. 121–141). UFMG.

Breen, M., & Candlin, C. (1980). The essentials of communicative curriculum in language teaching. *Applied Linguistics, 1*, 89–112. https://doi.org/10.1093/applin/1.2.89

Brown, G., & Yule, G. (1983). *Teaching the spoken language*. Cambridge University Press.

Brown, H. (2000). *Principles of language learning and teaching*. Longman.

Brown, H. (2001). *Teaching by principles. An interactive approach to language pedagogy*. Longman.

Brown, H. (2002). English language teaching in the post-method era: Toward better diagnosis, treatment and assessment. In J. Richards & W. Renandya (Eds.), *Methodology in language teaching: An anthology of current practice* (pp. 9–18). Cambridge University Press.

Brown, H. (2004). *Language assessment. Principles and classroom practices*. Pearson Education.

Brown, J. (1995). *Elements of language curriculum: A systematic approach to program development*. Heinle & Heinle Publishers.

Brown, J. (2009). Foreign and second language needs analysis. In M. Long & C. Doughty (Eds.), *The handbook of language teaching* (pp. 269–293). John Wiley & Sons Ltd.

Buchner, A., & Wierzbicka, M. (2020). *Edukacja zdalna w czasie pandemii*. Centrum Cyfrowe. Retrieved May 13, 2022, from https://centrumcyfrowe.pl/wp-content/uploads/sites/16/2020/11/Raport_Edukacja-zdalna-w-czasie-pandemii.-Edycja-II.pdf

Budiharto, A. (2018). The role of silent way method to English teaching in a private Islamic middle school. *Jurnal Solma*, *7*(2), 161–167. https://doi.org/10.29405/solma.v7i2.1396

Buendia, E. (2019, May 7). *Insomnia? Insomnobot will keep you company!* TechAcute. https://techacute.com/insomnobot-will-keep-you-company/

Burbach, L., Halbach, P., Plettenberg, N., Nakayama, J., Ziefle, M., & Valdez, A. (2019, July 23–26). *"Hey, Siri", "Ok, Google", "Alexa". Acceptance-relevant factors of virtual voice-assistants* [Paper presentation]. 2019 IEEE International Professional Communication Conference, Aachen, Germany.

Burston, J. (2013). Mobile-assisted language learning: A selected annotated bibliography of implementation studies 1994–2012. *Language Learning & Technology*, *17*(3), 157–225.

Bush, M., & Terry, R. (Eds.) (1997). *Technology-enhanced language learning*. National Textbook Company.

Bushnell, M. (2021, November 8). *AI faceoff: Siri vs. Cortana vs. Google Assistant vs. Alexa*. Business News Daily. https://www.businessnewsdaily.com/10315-siri-cortana-google-assistant-amazon-alexa-face-off.html

Butler-Pascoe, M. (2011). The history of CALL: The intertwining paths of technology and second/foreign language teaching. *International Journal of Computer-Assisted Language Learning and Teaching*, *1*(1), 16–32.

Cakmak, F. (2019). Mobile learning and mobile assisted language learning in focus. *Language and Technology*, *1*(1), 30–48.

Cambridge dictionary. (n.d.). Mediation. In *Cambridge dictionary*. https://dictionary.cambridge.org/pl/dictionary/english/mediation

Cambridge dictionary. (n.d.). Robot. In *Cambridge dictionary*. https://dictionary.cambridge.org/dictionary/english/robot

Cambridge dictionary. (n.d.). Smartphone. In *Cambridge dictionary*. https://dictionary.cambridge.org/pl/dictionary/english/smartphone

Campbell D., & Stanley, J. (1963). *Experimental and quasi-experimental designs for research*. Rand McNally & Company.

Campbell, M., & Third, A. (2020, December 10). *No, Education Minister, We don't have enough evidence to support banning mobile phones in schools*. The Conversation. https://theconversation.com/no-education-minister-we-dont-have-enough-evidence-to-support-banning-mobile-phones-in-schools-151574

Campo, C. (2022, May 25). *Ultimate knowledge, what is a chatbot? Everything you need to know*. Ultimate. https://www.ultimate.ai/blog/ultimate-knowledge/what-is-a-chatbot

Canale, M., & Swain, M. (1980). Theoretical bases of communicative approaches to second language teaching and testing. *Applied Linguistics*, *1*(1), 1–47. https://doi.org/10.1093/applin/i.1.1

Canale, M. (1983). From communicative competence to communicative language pedagogy. In J. Richards & R. Schmidt (Eds.), *Language and Communication* (pp. 2–14). Longman.

Capgemini Research Institute (2019). *Smart talk: How organizations and consumers are embracing voice and chat assistants*. https://www.capgemini.com/wp-content/uploads/2019/09/Infographic_Conversational-Interfaces_Final.pdf

Carbonell, J. (1970). AI in CAI: An artificial intelligence approach to computer aided instruction. *IEEE Transactions on Man-Machine Systems*, *11*(4), 190–202.

Carroll, J. (1966). The contribution of psychological theory and educational research to the teaching of foreign languages. In A. Valdman (Ed.), *Trends in language teaching* (pp. 93–106). McGraw-Hill.

Carter, R. (2019, December 23). *Is there a difference between bots and chatbots?* CX Today. https://www.cxtoday.com/contact-centre/is-there-a-difference-between-bots-and-chatbots/

Caspari, D. (2013). Sprachmittlung als kommunikative Situation: Eine Aufgabentypologie als Anstoß zur Weiterentwicklung eines Sprachmittlungsmodells. In D. Reimann & A. Rössler (Eds.), *Sprachmittlung im Fremdsprachenunterricht* (pp. 27–43). Narr Verlag.

CBOS (2018). *(Nad)używanie smartfonów*. Fundacja Centrum Badania Opinii Społecznej. https://www.cbos.pl/SPISKOM.POL/2018/K_157_18.PDF

Celce-Murcia, M. (2007). Rethinking the role of communicative competence in language teaching. In E. Soler & M. Jorda (Eds.), *Intercultural language use and language learning* (pp. 41–57). Springer.

Celce-Murcia, M., Brinton, D., & Goodwin, J. (1996). *Teaching pronunciation. A reference for teachers of English to speakers of other languages.* Cambridge University Press.

Celce-Murcia, M., Dörnyei, Z., & Thurrell, S. (1993). A pedagogical framework for communicative competence: Content specifications and guidelines for communicative language teaching. *Deseret Language and Linguistic Society Symposium, 19*(1), 13–29.

Chamberlain, L. (2017, May 3). Geo *101: What are intelligent assistants? Alexa, explain why everyone is talking to their devices.* GeoMarketing. https://geo-marketing.com/geo-101-what-are-intelligent-assistants

Chan, C., & Chan, Y. (2011). Students' views of collaboration and online participation in knowledge forum. *Computers & Education, 57*(1), 1445–1457.

Chang, A. C.-S. (2009). Gains to L2 listeners from reading while listening vs. listening only in comprehending short stories. *System, 37*(4), 652–663. https://doi.org/10.1016/j.system.2009.09.009

Chapelle, C. (1997). CALL in the year 2000: Still in search of research paradigms? *Language Learning & Technology, 1*(1), 19–43.

Chapelle, C. (2001). *Computer applications in second language acquisition.* Cambridge University Press.

Chapelle, C. (2006). Foreword. In P. Hubbard & M. Levy (Eds.), *Teacher education in CALL* (pp. vii-viii). John Benjamins Publishing Company.

Charmaz, K. (1996). The search for meanings: Grounded theory. In J. Smith, R. Harre & L. van Langenhove (Eds.), *Rethinking methods in psychology* (pp. 27–49). Sage Publications.

Chastain, K. (1971). *The development of modern language skills: Theory to practice.* The Center for Curriculum Development.

Chatbot (n.d.). IT Gartner Glossary. https://www.gartner.com/en/information-technology/glossary/chatbot

Chatterbot (2019). Techopedia. https://www.techopedia.com/definition/16366/chatterbot

Chen, H., Yang, C., & Kuo-Wei Lai, K. (2020). Investigating college EFL learners' perceptions toward the use of Google Assistant for foreign language learning. *Interactive Learning Environments*, 1–16. https://doi.org/10.1080/10494820.2020.1833043

Chen, X. (2013). Tablets for informal language learning: Student usage and attitudes. *Language Learning & Technology, 17*(1), 20–36.

Chiappini, R., & Mansur, E. (2020, July 9). *Mediating a text: A practical guide to task creation*. Macmillan Education.

Childnet (2018). *Youth perspectives on voice assisted technology*.

Chinnery, G. (2006). Going to the MALL: Mobile assisted language learning. *Language Learning & Technology*, *10*(1), 9–16.

Chłoń-Domińczak, A. (2017). Changes in the education system in Poland (ESPN Flash Report 2017/38). European Social Policy Network. https://ec.europa.eu/social/BlobServlet?docId=17891&langId=en

Chłopicki, W. (2005). Polish under siege? In G. Anderman & M. Rogers (Eds.), *In and out of English: For better, for worse* (pp. 108–122). Multilingual Matters.

Chomsky, N. (1965). *Aspects of the theory of syntax*. M.I.T. Press.

Chopra, A., Prashar, A., & Sain, C. (2013). Natural language processing. *International Journal of Technology Enhancements and Emerging Engineering Research*, *1*(4), 131–134.

Chou, M.-H. (2017). A task-based language teaching approach to developing metacognitive strategies for listening comprehension. *International Journal of Listening*, *31*(1), 51–70. https://doi.org/10.1080/10904018.2015.1098542

Chowdhury, G. (2003) Natural language processing. *Annual Review of Information Science and Technology*, *37*, 51–89. https://doi.org/10.1002/aris.1440370103

Chun, D. (2016). The role of technology in SLA research. *Language Learning & Technology*, *20*(2), 98–115.

Chun, D. (2019). Current and future directions in TELL. *Educational Technology & Society*, *22*(2), 14–25.

Cichowska, Z., Danielewicz, M., Gmaj, I., Koterwas, A., Urbanik, A., & Wilk, W. (2020). *Smartfony w szkole. Ustalamy reguły gry*. Instytut Badań Edukacyjnych. Retrieved February 13, 2022, from http://bitly.pl/WKzyn

Cichmińska, M. (2015). Sprawdzian szóstoklasisty: Wyniki i komentarze. *Języki Obce w Szkole*, *3*, 17–20.

Cilliers, E. (2017). The challenge of teaching generation Z. *PEOPLE: International Journal of Social Sciences*, *3*, 188–198.

CKE (2005). *Matura 2005. Podstawowe informacje* [PowerPoint presentation]. https://cke.gov.pl/images/_EGZAMIN_MATURALNY_OD_2015/Informacje_o_wynikach/2005/matura_2005.ppt

CKE (2009). *Osiągnięcia maturzystów w 2009 roku. Sprawozdanie z egzaminu maturalnego w 2009 roku.*
https://cke.gov.pl/images/_EGZAMIN_MATURALNY_OD_2015/Informacje_o_wynikach/2009/raport_matura_2009.pdf

CKE (2010). *Informator o egzaminie gimnazjalnym od roku szkolnego 2011/2012.* http://www.oke.krakow.pl/inf/filedata/files/Informator%20gimnazjalny%20od%202011-2012.pdf

CKE (2013). *Informator o sprawdzianie od roku szkolnego 2014/2015.* http://www.oke.krakow.pl/inf/filedata/files/Informator_S1%201.1.pdf

CKE (2015). *Sprawozdanie z egzaminu maturalnego 2015. Język angielski.* https://cke.gov.pl/images/_EGZAMIN_MATURALNY_OD_2015/Informacje_o_wynikach/2015/sprawozdanie/raport_2015_angielski_c.pdf

CKE (2016). *Osiągnięcia uczniów kończących szkołę podstawową w roku 2016. Sprawozdanie ze sprawdzianu 2016.* https://cke.gov.pl/images/_SPRAWDZIAN/OD_2014/Informacje_o_wynikach/2016/Sprawozdanie%20ze%20sprawdzianu_2016.pdf

CKE (2017a). *Informator o egzaminie ósmoklasisty z języka angielskiego od roku szkolnego 2018/2019.* https://cke.gov.pl/images/_EGZAMIN_OSMOKLASISTY/Informatory/Informator_P1_angielski.pdf

CKE (2017b). *Sprawozdanie z egzaminu maturalnego 2017. Język angielski.* https://cke.gov.pl/images/_EGZAMIN_MATURALNY_OD_2015/Informacje_o_wynikach/2017/sprawozdanie/matura_sprawozdanie_2017_angielski.pdf

CKE (2019a). *Osiągnięcia uczniów kończących VIII klasę szkoły podstawowej. Sprawozdanie za rok 2019.* https://cke.gov.pl/images/_EGZAMIN_OSMOKLASISTY/Informacje_o_wynikach/2019/sprawozdania/egzamin%20osmoklasisty_jezyki%20obce_sprawozdanie_2019.pdf

CKE (2019b). *Osiągnięcia uczniów kończących gimnazjum w roku 2019. Sprawozdanie z egzaminu gimnazjalnego 2019.* https://cke.gov.pl/images/_KOMUNIKATY/Sprawozdanie_egzamin%20gimnazjalny%202019.pdf.pdf

CKE (2020a). *Sprawozdanie za rok 2020. Egzamin maturalny. Język angielski.* https://cke.gov.pl/images/_EGZAMIN_MATURALNY_OD_2015/Informacje_o_wynikach/2020/sprawozdanie/sprawozdanie_matura_2020_angielski.pdf

CKE (2020b). *Sprawozdanie za rok 2020. Egzamin ósmoklasisty. Języki obce nowożytne.* https://cke.gov.pl/images/_EGZAMIN_OSMOKLASISTY/Informacje_o_wynikach/2020/sprawozdania/E8_J%C4%99zyki_obce_sprawozdanie_.pdf

CKE (2021). *Informator o egzaminie maturalnym z języka angielskiego od roku szkolnego 2022/2023.* https://cke.gov.pl/images/_EGZAMIN_MATURALNY_OD_2023/Informatory/Informator_EM2023_jezyk_angielski.pdf

CoE (1981). *Recommendation No. R (81) 7 of the Committee of Ministers to Member States on measures facilitating access to justice.* Council of Europe.

CoE (1997). *Modern languages: Learning, teaching, assessment. A Common European Framework of Reference. Draft 2 of a framework proposal.* Council for Cultural Cooperation.

CoE (1998). *Recommendation No. R (98) 1 of the Committee of Ministers to Member States on family mediation*. Council of Europe.

CoE (2001). *Common European Framework of Reference for Languages: Learning, teaching and assessment*. Cambridge University Press.

CoE (2008). *Recommendation No. R (08) 7 of the Committee of Ministers to Member States on the use of the Council of Europe's Common European Framework of Reference for Languages (CEFR) and the promotion of plurilingualism*. Council of Europe.

CoE (2014). *Recommendation No. R (08) 7 of the Committee of Ministers to Member States on the importance of competences in the language(s) of schooling for equity and quality in education and for educational success*. Council of Europe.

CoE (2018). *Common European Framework of Reference for Languages: Learning, teaching, assessment. Companion volume with new descriptors*. Council of Europe.

CoE (2020). *Common European Framework of Reference for Languages: Learning, teaching, assessment. Companion volume*. Council of Europe Publishing.

CoE (n.d.). *Language education policy profile. Poland: 2005–2007*. Language Policy Division/ Poland's Ministry of National Education. https://rm.coe.int/language-education-policy-profile-poland/16807b3c35

Cohen, L., Manion, L., & Morrison, K. (2000). *Research methods in education*. Routledge.

Collin, S. (2009). *Dictionary of computing: Over 10,000 terms clearly defined*. A&C Black Business Information and Development.

Colman, A., & Norris, C. (1997). Comparing rating scales of different lengths: Equivalence of scores from 5-point and 7-point scales. *Psychological Reports*, *80*(2), 355–362.

Colpaert, J. (2006). Toward an ontological approach in goal-oriented language courseware design and its implications for technology-independent content structuring. *Computer Assisted Language Learning*, *19*(2–3), 109–127. https://doi.org/10.1080/09588220600821461

Commission of the European Communities (2005). *A new framework strategy for multilingualism*. http://bitly.pl/5dvSj

Commission Regulation (EC) 962/2006 of 18 December 2002 on key competences for lifelong learning (2002). *Official Journal of the European Union*, L 349/10.

Common European Framework of Reference for Languages: Learning, teaching, assessment. Companion volume (n.d.). Council of Europe. https://www.coe.int/en/web/common-european-framework-reference-languages

Conde Gonzalez, A., Miguel, M., & Penalvo, F. (2008). Mlearning, the first step in the learning process revolution. *International Journal of Interactive Mobile Technologies, 2*(4), 61–63. https://doi.org/10.3991/ijim.v2i4.531

Connolly, K. (2000, August 4). Poland's language police wage war on 'Polglish.' *The Guardian*. http://www.guardian.co.uk/world/2000/sep/04/poland.

Copeland, J. (2000). The modern history of computing. In E. Zalta (Ed.), *Stanford encyclopaedia of philosophy.* Stanford University. https://plato.stanford.edu/entries/computing-history/

Copeland, J. (2022). Artificial intelligence. In *Encyclopaedia Britannica*. https://www.britannica.com/technology/artificial-intelligence

Corbin, J., & Strauss, A. (1990). Grounded theory research: Procedures, canons and evaluative criteria. *Qualitative Sociology, 13*(1), 3–21.

Corder, S. (1967). The significance of learners' errors. *International Review of Applied Linguistics*, 5, 161–169.

Cost, D. (2021, December 28). *Mom claims Alexa encouraged kid to try deadly TikTok challenge*. New York Post. https://nypost.com/2021/12/28/mom-claims-alexa-encouraged-deadly-tiktok-challenge-to-kid/

Coste D., & Cavalli M. (2015). *Education, mobility, otherness. The mediation functions of schools*. Council of Europe.

Couldry, N. (2008). Mediatization or mediation? Alternative understandings of the emergent space of digital storytelling. *New Media & Society, 10*(3), 373–391.

Crackanthorpe, M. (1911). Mediation. In *Encyclopaedia Britannica*. https://en.wikisource.org/wiki/1911_Encyclop%C3%A6dia_Britannica/Mediation

Craig, W. (2021, July 21). *The history of computers in a nutshell.* Web FX. https://www.webfx.com/blog/web-design/the-history-of-computers-in-a-nutshell/

Creanga, O. (2020). Mediation in English language teaching. *Studia Universitatis Moldaviae, 9*(139), 81–88. https://doi.org/10.5281/zenodo.4277393

Creswell, J. (2014). *Research design: Qualitative, quantitative and mixed methods approaches*. Sage.

Crookes, G. (1986). *Task classification: A cross-disciplinary review* (Technical report no. 4). The Centre for Second Language Classroom Research Social Science Research Institute, University of Hawaii at Manoa. http://bitly.pl/VY4t7

Cruz, F., & Díaz, M. (2016). Generation Z's teachers and their digital skills. *Comunicar: Media Education Research Journal, 24*(1), 97–105.

Cuban, L. (1986). *Teachers and machines: The classroom use of technology since 1920*. Teachers College Press.

Cummins, J. (2000). *Language, power and pedagogy: Bilingual children in the crossfire*. Multilingual Matters.

Czerska-Andrzejewska, D. (2016). Mobile assisted language learning. *Zeszyty Glottodydaktyczne*, *6*, 43–52.

Daniels, P., & Iwago, K. (2017) The suitability of cloud-based speech recognition engines for language learning. *The JALT CALL Journal*, *13*(3), 211–221.

Dara, R. (2019, December 15). *The dark side of Alexa, Siri and other personal digital assistants.* The Conversation. https://theconversation.com/the-dark-side-of-alexa-siri-and-other-personal-digital-assistants-126277

Darmi, R. (2014). The effects of the application of Cummins' model on learners' language use. *International Journal of Language Education and Applied Linguistics*, *1*, 1–8. https://doi.org/10.15282/ijleal.v1.235

Davie, N., & Hilber, T. (2015, March 14–16). *Mobile-assisted language learning: Student attitudes to using smartphones to learn English vocabulary* [Paper presentation]. 11th International Conference on Mobile Learning, Madeira, Portugal, 70–78. https://files.eric.ed.gov/fulltext/ED562454.pdf

Davies, G., & Steel, D. (1981, April 8–10). *First steps in computer-assisted language learning at Ealing College of Higher Education* [Paper presentation]. CAL 81 Symposium, Leeds, West Yorkshire, England.

Davies, G. (2006). Language education, computer-assisted. In K. Brown (Ed.), *Encyclopaedia of language and linguistics* (pp. 460–470). Elsevier Science.

Davies, G., Walker, R., Rendall, H., & Hewer, S. (2012). Introduction to computer assisted language learning (CALL). Module 1.4. In G. Davies (Ed.). *Information and communications technology for language teachers (ICT4LT).* Thames Valley University. http://www.ict4lt.org/en/en_mod1-4.htm

Davies, G., Otto, S., & Ruschoff, B. (2013). Historical perspectives on CALL. In M. Thomas, H. Reinders & M. Warschauer (Eds.), *Contemporary computer-assisted language learning* (pp. 19–38). Bloomsbury.

Davies, G., & Hewer, S. (2012) Introduction to new technologies and how they can contribute to language learning and teaching. Module 1.1. In G. Davies (Ed.). *Information and communications technology for language teachers (ICT-4LT).* Thames Valley University. http://www.ict4lt.org/en/en_mod1-1.htm

Davis, F. (1989). Perceived usefulness, perceived ease of use and user acceptance of information technology. *MIS Quarterly*, *13*, 318–341. https://doi.org/10.2307/249008

Debecker, A. (2017, August 11). *Chatbot ELIZA: Deconstructing your friendly therapist.* Ubisend. https://blog.ubisend.com/discover-chatbots/chatbot-eliza

Decoo, W. (2001). *On the mortality of language learning methods.* Retrieved January 27, 2022, from https://csclub.uwaterloo.ca/~rfburger/On-the-mortality-of-language-learning-methods-wilfried-decoo-2001.pdf

Delibas, M., & Gunday, R. (2016). Action-oriented approach in foreign language teaching. *Participatory Educational Research, 4,* 144–153.

Dendrinos, B. (2006). Mediation in communication, language teaching and testing. *Journal of Applied Linguistics, 22*(1), 9–35.

Dendrinos, B. (2013). Testing and teaching mediation. *Directions in English Language Teaching and Testing, 1.*

Dewey, J. (1938). *Experience and education.* Macmillan/Collier.

Deygers, B. (2021). The CEFR companion volume: Between research-based policy and policy-based research. *Applied Linguistics, 42*(1), 186–191. https://doi.org/10.1093/applin/amz024

Dębski, R., & Gruba, P. (1999). A qualitative survey of tertiary instructor attitudes towards project-based CALL. *Computer Assisted Language Learning, 12*(3), 219–239. https://doi.org/10.1076/call.12.3.219.5715

Dębski, R. (1993). Computer assisted language learning (CALL) and a method of foreign language teaching. *Glottodidactica. An International Journal of Applied Linguistics, 21*, 53–62.

Deczewska, J. (2020). Interakcje między uczestnikami nauczania zdalnego: Wyzwania, oczekiwania, możliwe rozwiązania. *Języki Obce w Szkole, 3*, 13–18.

Description of tests (2021). Ylioppilastutkinto. http://bitly.pl/dDZG6

Dickinson, L. (1979). Self-instruction in commonly-taught languages. *System, 7*(3), 181–186. https://doi.org/10.1016/0346-251X(79)90001-0

Dickinson, L. (1987). *Self-instruction in language learning.* Cambridge University Press.

Dizon, G. (2017). Using intelligent personal assistants for L2 learning: A case study. *TESOL Journal, 8*(4), 29–42. https://doi.org/10.1002/tesj.353

Dizon, G. (2020). Evaluating intelligent personal assistants for L2 listening and speaking development. *Language Learning & Technology, 24*(1), 16–26.

Dizon, G. (2021). Affordances and constraints of intelligent personal assistants for second-language learning. *RELC Journal*, 1–8. https://doi.org/10.1177/00336882211020548

Dizon, G., & Tang, D. (2019). A pilot study of Alexa for autonomous second language learning. In F. Meunier, J. Van de Vyver, L. Bradley & S. Thouesny (Eds.), *CALL and Complexity. Short Papers from EUROCALL 2019* (pp. 107–112). Research-publishing.net.

Dizon G., & Tang, D. (2020). Intelligent personal assistants for autonomous second language learning. *The JALT CALL Journal, 16*(2), 117–130. https://doi.org/10.29140/jaltcall.v16n2.273

Do mobile phones, 4G or 5G cause cancer? (2022). Cancer Research UK. https://www.cancerresearchuk.org/about-cancer/causes-of-cancer/cancer-myths/do-mobile-phones-cause-cancer

Dooly, M., Moore, E., & Vallejo, C. (2017). Research ethics. In E. Moore & M. Dooly (Eds.), *Qualitative approaches to research on plurilingual education* (pp. 351–362). Research-publishing.net.

Dorkchandra, D. (2013). The effects of question generating strategy instruction on EFL freshmen's reading comprehension and use of English tenses. *Journal of Liberal Arts Prince of Songkla University*, *5*(2), 32–45.

Dörnyei, Z. (2007). *Research methods in applied linguistics*. Oxford University Press.

Doughty, C., & Long, M. (2003). Optimal psycholinguistic environments for distance foreign language learning. *Language Learning & Technology*, *7*(3), 50–80.

Dudley, D. (2018, November 27). *The evolution of mobile phones: 1973 to 2019*. Flaunt Digital. https://flauntdigital.com/blog/evolution-mobile-phones/

Dudley-Evans, T., & St John, M. (1998). *Developments in English for specific purposes: A multi-disciplinary approach*. Cambridge University Press.

Dwużnik, P. (2020). Objaśnianie pojęć. Zadanie mediacyjne w języku prawniczym. *Języki Obce w Szkole*, *2*, 31–38.

Eckes, T., Ellis M., Kalnberzina, V., Pizorn, K., Springer C., Szollas, K., & Tsagari, C. (2005) Progress and problems in reforming public language examinations in Europe: Cameos from the Baltic States, Greece, Hungary, Poland, Slovenia, France and Germany. *Language Testing*, *22*(3), 355–377.

Egbert, J. (2005). *CALL essentials: Principles and practice in CALL classrooms*. TESOL.

Ehrenhalt, E. (1990, March 27–30). *New tasks for teachers of English in Poland in light of social, economic, and political changes* [Paper presentation]. International Association of Teachers of English as a Foreign Language 24th Annual Meeting, Dublin, Ireland.

Electromagnetic fields and public health: Mobile phones (2014). WHO. https://www.who.int/en/news-room/fact-sheets/detail/electromagnetic-fields-and-public-health-mobile-phones

El-Hussein, M., &. Cronje, J. (2010). Defining mobile learning in the higher education landscape. *Journal of Educational Technology & Society*, *13*(3), 12–21.

Ellis, R. (2003a). Designing a task-based syllabus. *RELC*, *34*(1), 64–81. https://doi.org/10.1177/003368820303400105

Ellis, R. (2003b). *Task-based language learning and teaching*. Oxford University Press.

Enge, E. (2019). *31 must know voice usage trends for 2019*. Perficient. https://blogs.perficient.com/2019/03/05/31-must-know-voice-usage-trends-for-2019/

Engeström, Y. (1987). *Learning by expanding: An activity theoretical approach to developmental research*. Orienta-Konsultit.

Etikan, I., Musa, S., & Alkassim, R. (2015). Comparison of convenience sampling and purposive sampling. *American Journal of Theoretical and Applied Statistics*, *5*(1), 1–4. https://doi.org/10.11648/j.ajtas.20160501.11

European Commission (2002). *Candidate countries Eurobarometer* 2001. https://ec.europa.eu/commfrontoffice/publicopinion/archives/cceb/2001/cceb20011_en.pdf

European Commission (2002). *Presidency conclusions. Barcelona European Council*. https://ec.europa.eu/commission/presscorner/detail/en/PRES_02_930

European Commission (2003). *Eurobarometer 2003.1: Public opinion in the candidate countries*. https://ec.europa.eu/commfrontoffice/publicopinion/archives/cceb/2003/2003.1_youth_analytical_report_en.pdf

European Commission (2006). *Special Eurobarometer 243. Europeans and their languages*. https://ec.europa.eu/commfrontoffice/publicopinion/archives/ebs/ebs_243_en.pdf

European Commission (2012). *First European survey on language competences: Final report*. https://op.europa.eu/en/publication-detail/-/publication/42ea89dc-373a-4d4f-aa27-9903852cd2e4

European Commission (2020). *Digital education action plan 2021–2027. Resetting education and training for the digital age*. https://education.ec.europa.eu/sites/default/files/document-library-docs/deap-factsheet-sept2020_en.pdf

European Parliament (2014). *Higher education entrance qualifications and exams in Europe: A Comparison*. https://www.europarl.europa.eu/thinktank/en/document/IPOL-CULT_ET(2014)529057

Eurydice (2009). *National testing of pupils in Europe: Objectives, organisation and use of results*. https://op.europa.eu/en/publication-detail/-/publication/9bcde655-ddc6-4861-ad99-813b9f738dd0

Eurydice (2015). *Languages in secondary education: An overview of national tests in Europe – 2014/15*. https://eacea.ec.europa.eu/national-policies/eurydice/content/languages-secondary-education-overview-national-tests-europe-%E2%80%93-201415_en

Eurydice (2012). *Key data on teaching languages at school in Europe*. https://eacea.ec.europa.eu/national-policies/eurydice/content/key-data-teaching-languages-school-europe-2012_en

Eurydice (2017). *Key data on teaching languages at school in Europe*. https://eacea.ec.europa.eu/national-policies/eurydice/content/key-data-teaching-languages-school-europe-%E2%80%93-2017-edition_en

Fang, W., Yeh, H., Luo, B., & Chen, N. (2021). Effects of mobile-supported task-based language teaching on EFL students' linguistic achievement and conversational interaction. *ReCALL*, *33*(1), 71–87. https://doi.org/10.1017/S0958344020000208

Fellows, R., Ihshaisha, H., Battlea, S., Hainesa, C., Mayhewa, P., & Deza, I. (2021). *Task-oriented dialogue systems: Performance vs. quality-optima. A review*. arXiv. https://doi.org/10.48550/arXiv.2112.11176

Fernandes, A. (2017, November 15). *NLP, NLU, NLG and how chatbots work*. Chatbots Life. https://chatbotslife.com/nlp-nlu-nlg-and-how-chatbots-work-dd7861dfc9df

Fidaoui, D., Bahous, R., & Bacha, N. (2010). CALL in Lebanese elementary ESL writing classrooms. *Computer Assisted Language Learning*, *23*(2), 151–168. https://doi.org/10.1080/09588221003666248

Figarski, W. (1995). O zainteresowaniu językiem rosyjskim wśród uczniów szkół podstawowych i średnich. *Języki Obce w Szkole*, *5*, 452, 453, 455.

Figueras, N. (2012). The impact of the CEFR. *ELT Journal*, *66*(4), 477–485. https://doi.org/10.1093/elt/ccs037

Fischer, G. (2001). User modeling in human-computer interaction. *User Modeling and User-Adapted Interaction*, *11*, 65–86.

Fischer, R. (2007). How do we know what students are actually doing? Monitoring students' behaviour in CALL. *Computer Assisted Language Learning*, *20*(5), 409–442. https://doi.org/10.1080/09588220701746013

Fisher, T., Denning, T., Higgins, C., & Loveless, A. (2012). Teachers knowing how to use technology: Exploring a conceptual framework for purposeful learning activity. *Curriculum Journal*, *23*(3), 307–325. https://doi.org/10.1080/09585176.2012.703492

Folse, K. (2010). Communicative competence and grammar classes revisited: 1980 and 2010. *Contact*, *36*(2), 7–19.

Fraenkel, J., Wallen, N., & Hyun, H. (2012). *How to design and evaluate research in education*. The McGraw-Hill Companies, Inc.

Frankenfield, J. (2022, May 18). *Chatbot*. Investopedia. https://www.investopedia.com/terms/c/chatbot.asp

Freeman, D., & Richards, J. (1993). Conceptions of teaching and the education of second language teachers. *TESOL Quarterly*, *27*(2), 193–216. https://doi.org/10.2307/3587143

Frith, M. (1978). Interlanguage theory: Implications for the classroom. *McGill Journal of Education, 13*(2), 155–165.

Froese, A., Carpenter, C., Inman, D., Schooley, J., Barnes, R., Brecht, P., & Chacon, J. (2012). Effects of classroom cell phone use on expected and actual learning. *College Student Journal, 46*(2), 323–332.

Fryer, L., & Carpenter, R. (2006). Emerging technologies bots as language learning tools. *Language Learning & Technology, 10*(3), 8–14.

Gabbatt, A. (2011, February 17). *IBM computer Watson wins Jeopardy clash.* The Guardian. https://www.theguardian.com/technology/2011/feb/17/ibm-computer-watson-wins-jeopardy

Gadomska A., (2019). Applying the CEFR descriptors for online interaction and mediation for the design of Moodle based TEFL materials. In E. Smyrnova-Trybulska (Ed.), *E-learning and STEM education* (pp. 473–481). Studio Noa for University of Silesia.

Gajewska-Dyszkiewicz, A., Grudniewska, M., Kulon, F., Kutyłowska, K., Paczuska, K., Rycielska, L., & Szpotowicz, M. (2013). *Europejskie badanie kompetencji językowych ESLC. Raport krajowy 2011.* Instytut Badań Edukacyjnych. http://produkty.ibe.edu.pl/docs/raporty/ibe-ee-1-7-raport-eslc.pdf

Gajewska-Dyszkiewicz, A., & Paczuska, K. (2015). Bilans zmian w edukacji językowej po 2000 roku. In M. Bogucka & A. Grabowska (Eds.), *Rozważania o jakości programu edukacyjnego English Teaching. Profil pełnomocnego nauczyciela* (pp. 42–53). Nidzicka Fundacja Rozwoju NIDA.

Gamper, J., & Knapp, J. (2002). A review of intelligent CALL systems. *Computer Assisted Language Learning, 15*(4), 329–342. https://doi.org/10.1076/call.15.4.329.8270

Garcia Botero, G., Questier, F., & Zhu, C. (2019). Self-directed language learning in a mobile-assisted, out-of-class context: Do students walk the talk? *Computer Assisted Language Learning, 32*(1–2), 71–97. https://doi.org/10.1080/09588221.2018.1485707

Garrett, N. (2009). Computer-assisted language learning trends and issues revisited: Integrating innovation. *The Modern Language Journal, 93*(1), 719–740. https://doi.org/10.1111/j.1540-4781.2009.00969.x

Gattegno, C. (1963). *Teaching foreign languages in schools: The silent way.* Educational Solutions World.

Geoghegan, W. (1994, July 17–20). *Whatever happened to instructional technology?* [Paper presentation]. 22nd Annual Conference of the International Business Schools Computing Association, Baltimore, Maryland.

Gerencer, T. (2019, July 29). *Top 10 ways to use voice assistants.* HP. https://www.hp.com/us-en/shop/tech-takes/top-10-ways-to-use-voice-assistants

Gębal, P. (2010) *Dydaktyka kultury polskiej w kształceniu językowym cudzoziemców. Podejście porównawcze.* Universitas.

Giacaglia, G. (2019, January 22). *How IBM Watson works.* Medium. https://medium.com/@giacaglia/how-ibm-watson-works-40d8d5185ac8

Gillett, F. (2020, March 2). *Getting consumers beyond simple tasks on smart speakers is challenging.* Forrester. https://www.forrester.com/blogs/getting-consumers-beyond-simple-tasks-on-smart-speakers-is-challenging/

Gitsaki, C., & Taylor, R. (1999). Bridging the WWW into the ESL classroom. In K. Cameron (Ed.), *CALL and the Learning Community* (pp. 143–160). Elm Bank Publications.

Glass, A., & Kang, M. (2019). Dividing attention in the classroom reduces exam performance. *Educational Psychology, 39*(3), 395–408.

Godwin-Jones, R. (2011). Emerging technologies: Mobile apps for language learning. *Language Learning & Technology, 15*(2), 2–11.

Goksel-Canbek, N., & Mutlu, M. (2016). On the track of artificial intelligence: Learning with intelligent personal assistants. *International Journal of Human Sciences, 13*(1), 592–601. https://doi.org/10.14687/ijhs.v13i1.3549

Gonzalez-Lloret, M. (2007). Implementing task-based language teaching on the web. In K. van den Branden, K. van Gorp & M. Verhelst (Eds.), *Tasks in action: Task-based language education from a classroom-based perspective* (pp. 265–284). Cambridge Scholars Publishing.

Gonzalez-Lloret, M. (2014). The need for needs analysis in technology-mediated TBLT. In M. Gonzalez-Lloret & L. Ortega (Eds.), *Technology and tasks: Exploring technology-mediated TBLT* (pp. 23–50). John Benjamins Publishing Company.

Gonzalez-Lloret, M. (2017). Technology for task-based language teaching. In C. Chapelle & S. Sauro (Eds.), *The handbook of technology and second language teaching and learning* (pp. 234–247). Wiley-Blackwell.

Goodier, T. (2020, March 2020). *Focus on mediation in English language teaching.* Pearson. https://www.english.com/blog/teaching-mediation/

Gouin, F. (1892). *The art of teaching and studying languages.* George Philip & Son.

Gower, R., Walters, S., & Phillips, D. (1983). *Teaching practice handbook.* Heinemann.

Gray, P. (2016, June 1). *The rise of intelligent virtual assistants.* Interactions. https://www.interactions.com/blog/intelligent-virtual-assistant/rise-intelligent-virtual-assistants/

Greene J., Caracelli V., & Graham W. (1989). Toward a conceptual framework for mixed-method evaluation designs. *Educational Evaluation and Policy Analysis, 11*(3), 255–274. https://doi.org/10.3102/01623737011003255

Grewiński, M. (2017). Polska polityka społeczna w latach 1989–2016: Sukcesy i niepowodzenia. *Studia BAS*, *2*(50), 59–92.

Grodecka, M. (2020, February 4). *Smartfony zakazywane w polskich szkołach. Dzieci same nie nauczą się z nich korzystać*. Spider'sWeb. https://spidersweb.pl/2020/02/zakaz-korzystania-ze-smartfonow-w-szkole.html

Gruba, P. (2004). Computer assisted language learning (CALL). In A. Davies & C. Elder (Eds.), *The handbook of applied linguistics* (pp. 623–648). Blackwell Publishing Ltd.

Grzegorczyk, M. (2021, December 8). *Estonia launches Bürokratt, The Siri of digital public services*. Emerging Europe. https://emerging-europe.com/news/estonia-launches-burokratt-the-siri-of-digital-public-services/

Grzeszkiewicz-Radulska, K. (2012). Metody badań pilotażowych. *Acta Universitatis Lodziensis. Folia Sociologica*, *42*, 113–141.

Guichon, N., & McLornan, S. (2008). The effects of multimodality on L2 learners: Implications for CALL resource design. *System*, *36*(1), 85–93.

Gupta, P., & Schulze, M. (2012). Human language technologies (HLT). Module 3.5. In G. Davies (Ed.), *Information and communications technology for language teachers (ICT4LT)*. Thames Valley University. http://www.ict4lt.org/en/en_mod3-5.htm

GUS (2018). *Oświata i wychowanie w roku szkolnym 2017/18*. https://stat.gov.pl/files/gfx/portalinformacyjny/pl/defaultaktualnosci/5488/1/13/1/oswiata_i_wychowanie_w_roku_szkolnym_2017_18.pdf

GUS (2019). *Rocznik statystyczny Rzeczypospolitej Polskiej*. https://stat.gov.pl/en/topics/statistical-yearbooks/statistical-yearbooks/statistical-yearbook-of-the-republic-of-poland-2019,2,21.html

GUS (2020). *Średnie wyniki egzaminu maturalnego*. https://stat.gov.pl/obszary-tematyczne/edukacja/edukacja/srednie-wyniki-egzaminu-maturalnego,17,1.html

Guzman, A., & Lewis, S. (2020). Artificial intelligence and communication: A human-machine communication research agenda. *New Media & Society*, *22*(1), 70–86. https://doi.org/10.1177%2F1461444819858691

Hafner, C., & Miller, L. (2011). Fostering learner autonomy in English for science: A collaborative digital video project in a technological learning environment. *Language Learning & Technology*, *15*(3), 68–86.

Hajjar, A. (2021, March 21). *Top 6 use cases & examples of chatbots in healthcare*. AI Multiple. https://research.aimultiple.com/chatbot-healthcare/

Hallet, W. (2008). Zwischen Sprachenund Kulturen vermitteln. Interlinguale Kommunikation als Aufgabe. *Der fremdsprachliche Unterricht Englisch*, *42*(93), 2–7.

Hamburger, H. (2014). Tutorial tools for language learning by two-medium dialogue. In M. Holland, M. Sams & J. Kaplan (Eds.), *Intelligent language tutors: Theory shaping technology* (pp. 183–200). Lawrence Erlbaum.

Hanafiah, W., Aswad, M., Sahib, H., Yassi, A. & Mousavi, M. (2022). The impact of CALL on vocabulary learning, speaking skill and foreign language speaking anxiety: The case study of Indonesian EFL learners. *Education Research International*, 1–3. https://doi.org/10.1155/2022/5500077

Haristiani, N. (2019). Artificial intelligence (AI) chatbot as language learning medium: An inquiry. *Journal of Physics: Conference Series, 1387*(1), 1–6. https://doi.org/10.1088/1742-6596/1387/1/012020

Harmer, J. (1996). Is PPP dead? *Modern English Teacher*, *5*, 7–14.

Harmer, J. (2007) *The practice of English language teaching*. Pearson Education Limited.

Hashemifardnia, A., Rasooyar, H., & Sepehri, M. (2019). Enhancing Iranian EFL learners' speaking fluency through using task-based activities. *Global Journal of Foreign Language Teaching*, *9*(1), 24–32. https://doi.org/10.18844/gjflt.v9i1.3998

Hatch, E., & Farhady, H. (1982). *Research design and statistics for applied linguistics.* New Bury House Production, Inc.

Hawking, S., Russel, S., Tegmark, M., & Wilczek, F. (2014, May 1). *Transcendence looks at the implications of artificial intelligence, But are we taking AI seriously enough?* Independent. http://bitly.pl/cUrxT

Heift, T. (2010). Developing an intelligent language tutor. *CALICO Journal*, *27*(3), 443–459. https://doi.org/10.11139/cj.27.3.443-459

Higgins, J. (1983). Computer assisted language learning. *Language Teaching*, *16*(2), 102–114. https://doi.org/10.1017/S0261444800009988

Higgins, A. (2021, August 4). *What is a chatbot? How is it changing customer experience?* Salesforce. https://www.salesforce.com/blog/what-is-a-chatbot/

Hinkel, E. (2006). Current perspectives on teaching the four skills. *TESOL Quaterly*, *40*(1), 109–131.

Hinkel, E. (2012). Cognitive-code learning. In N. Seel (Ed.), *Encyclopaedia of the sciences of learning*. Springer. https://link.springer.com/referenceworkentry/10.1007/978-1-4419-1428-6_737

Historical overview of the development of the CEFR (n.d.). Council of Europe. https://www.coe.int/en/web/common-european-framework-reference-languages/history

Howell, P. (2017). Cross-language mediation in foreign language teaching. *Hiroshima Studies in Language and Language Education*, *20*, 147–155. https://doi.org/10.15027/42619

Hoy, M. (2018). Alexa, Siri, Cortana, and more: An introduction to voice assistants. *Medical Reference Services Quarterly*, *37*(1), 81–88. https://doi.org/10.1080/02763869.2018.1404391

Hrehovcik, T. (2003). The Callan method or "English in a quarter of the time". *Studia Minora Facultatis Philosophicae Universitatis Brunensis*, *9*, 109–116.

Hsieh, H. F., & Shannon, S. E. (2005). Three approaches to qualitative content analysis. *Qualitative Health Research*, *15*(9), 1277–1288. https://doi.org/10.1177/1049732305276687

Hubbard, P. (2008). CALL and the future of language teacher education. *CALICO Journal*, *25*(2), 175–188. https://doi.org/10.1558/cj.v25i2.175-188

Hubbard, P., & Levy, M. (2016). Theory in computer-assisted language learning research and practice. In F. Farr & L. Murray (Eds), *The Routledge handbook of language learning and technology* (pp. 24–38). Routledge.

Hubbard, P. (2021, September 10). *An invitation to CALL. Foundations of computer-assisted language learning.* Stanford University. https://web.stanford.edu/~efs/callcourse2/

Hudson, R. & Self, J. (1982). A dialogue system to teach database concepts. *The Computer Journal*, *25*(1), 135–139.

Hue, A. (2019, September 27). *French Ministry of Education to bring voice assistants into the classroom.* Voicebot.ai. https://voicebot.ai/2019/09/27/french-ministry-of-education-to-bring-voice-assistants-into-the-classroom/

Hulstijn, J. (2007). The shaky ground beneath the CEFR: Quantitative and qualitative dimensions of language proficiency. *The Modern Language Journal*, *91*(4), 663–667. https://doi.org/10.1111/j.1540-4781.2007.00627_5.x

Hutchinson, T., & Waters, A. (1987). *English for specific purposes.* Cambridge University Press.

Hwang, K., Yoo, Y., & Cho, O. (2012). Smartphone overuse and upper extremity pain, anxiety, depression and interpersonal relationships among college students. *The Journal of the Korea Contents Association*, *12*(10), 365–375. https://doi.org/10.5392/JKCA.2012.12.10.365

Hymes, D. (1967). Models of the interaction of language and social setting. *Journal of Social Issues*, *23*(2), 8–28. https://doi.org/10.1111/j.1540-4560.1967.tb00572.x

Hymes, D. (1972) On communicative competence. In J. Pride & J. Holmes (Eds.), *Sociolinguistics. Selected readings* (pp. 269–293). Penguin.

Igielska, B. (2021). *Kanclerz: Wiele rozwiązań z czasu pandemii pozostanie na uczelni.* Prawo. https://www.prawo.pl/student/informatyzacja-uczelni-wiele-rozwiazan-z-pandemii-pozostanie,510807.html

Igira, F., & Gregory, J. (2009). Cultural historical activity theory. In Y. Dwivedi, B. Lal, M. Williams, S. Schneberger & M. Wade (Eds.), *Handbook of research on contemporary theoretical models in information systems* (pp. 434–454). IGI Global.

Iluk, J. (2009). Nauczanie mediacji językowej w kontekście nowej podstawy programowej dla języków obcych. *Języki Obce w Szkole*, *6*, 113–121.

InterNations (2018). *Digital expat havens around the world.* https://www.internations.org/expat-insider/2018/digital-life-39587

Ismail, N. (2019, February 11). *The history of the chatbot: Where it was and where it's going.* Information Age. https://www.information-age.com/history-of-the-chatbot-123479024/

ISTE (2017). *ISTE standards for educators.* International Society for Technology in Education. https://www.iste.org/standards/iste-standards-for-teachers

Izadpanah, S., & Alavi, M. (2016). The perception of EFL high school students in using of computer technology in the process of learning: Merits and demerits. *Advances in Language and Literary Studies*, *7*(3), 146–156.

Jackson, K. (2018, July 25). *A brief history of the smartphone.* Sciencenode. https://sciencenode.org/feature/How%20did%20smartphones%20evolve.php

Jahangard, A., Rahimi, A., & Norouzizadeh, M. (2020). Student attitudes towards computer-assisted language learning and its effect on their EFL writing. *International Journal of New Trends in Social Sciences*, *4*(1), 01–09.

Jakubowski, M. (2015). *Opening up opportunities: Education reforms in Poland.* Instytut Badań Strukturalnych. https://ibs.org.pl/app/uploads/2015/02/IBS_Policy_Paper_01_2015.pdf

Jakubowski, M., Patrinos, H., Porta, E., & Wiśniewski, J. (2016). The effects of delaying tracking in secondary school: Evidence from the 1999 Education Reform in Poland. *Education Economics*, *24* (6), 1–16. https://doi.org/10.1080/09645292.2016.1149548

Jakubowski, M., Konarzewski, K., Muszyński, M., Smulczyk, M., & Walicki, P. (2017). *Szkolne talenty Europy u progu zmian. Polscy uczniowie w najnowszych badaniach międzynarodowych. Raport Fundacji Evidence Institute i Związku Nauczycielstwa Polskiego.* Evidence Institute. https://www.scdn.pl/images/stories/RAPORTY2017/07.pdf

Janowska, I. (2008). Zadaniowy scenariusz jednostki metodycznej. *Języki Obce w Szkole*, *3*, 43–51.

Janowska, I. (2009). Zadanie, ćwiczenie, działanie językowe: Wzajemne relacje i implikacje w dydaktyce językowej. In M. Pawlak, M. Derenowski & B. Wolski (Eds.), *Problemy współczesnej dydaktyki języków obcych* (pp. 117–127).

Wydział Pedagogiczno-Artystyczny UAM w Kaliszu/Uniwersytet im. Adama Mickiewicza w Poznaniu.

Janowska, I. (2011). *Podejście zadaniowe do nauczania i uczenia się języków obcych*. Universitas.

Janowska, I. (2012). Proces przystosowania materiałów dydaktycznych z języka polskiego jako obcego do zasad podejścia zadaniowego. *Postscriptum Polonistyczne*, *2*(10), 177–198.

Janowska, I. (2014). Zadaniowa koncepcja planowania w glottodydaktyce: Problemy i wyzwania. In M. Cichoń, M. Krzemińska-Adamek, A. Pado, H. Rycyk-Sztajdel, B. Sadownik & J. Sękowska (Eds.), *Przez praktyki do praktyki. W stronę innowacyjności w kształceniu nauczycieli* (pp. 43–52). Uniwersytet Marii Curie-Skłodowskiej w Lublinie.

Janowska, I. (2015). Kompetencja komunikacyjna a glottodydaktyka. *LingVaria*, *20*, 41–56.

Janowska, I. (2017). Mediacja i działanie mediacyjne w dydaktyce języków obcych. *Języki Obce w Szkole*, *3*, 8–86.

Janowska, I., & Plak, M. (2021). *Działania mediacyjne w uczeniu się i nauczaniu języków obcych. Od teorii do praktyki*. Księgarnia Akademicka.

Jarvis, H., & Krashen, S. (2014). Is CALL obsolete? Language acquisition and language learning revisited in a digital age. *TESL-EJ*, *17*(4), 1–6.

Johnson, K. (1982). *Communicative syllabus design and methodology*. Pergamon.

Joshi, N. (2018, December 23). *Yes, chatbots and virtual assistants are different!*. Forbes. https://www.forbes.com/sites/cognitiveworld/2018/12/23/yes-chatbots-and-virtual-assistants-are-different/?sh=459209a46d7d

Jurafsky, D., & Martin, J. (2021). *Speech and language processing. An introduction to natural language processing, computational linguistics and speech recognition. Third edition draft*. https://web.stanford.edu/~jurafsky/slp3/ed3book.pdf

Kafipour, R., Mahmoudi, E., & Khojasteh, L. (2018). The effect of task-based language teaching on analytic writing in EFL classrooms. *Cogent Education*, *5*(1), 1–16.

Kang, Y., & Maciejewski, A. (2000). A student model of technical Japanese reading proficiency for an intelligent tutoring system. *CALICO Journal*, *18*(1), 9–40. https://doi.org/10.1558/cj.v18i1.9-40

Kaptelinin, V., & Nardi, B. (2006). *Acting with technology: Activity theory and interaction design*. The MIT Press.

Karolczuk, M. (2020). Zdalnie realnie. Jak uczymy (się) języków w czasie pandemii. *Języki Obce w Szkole*, *2*, 39–43.

Kasztalska, A. (2014). English in contemporary Poland. *World Englishes*, *33*(2), 242–262.

Kaźmierczak, J., & Bulkowski, Z. (2024). *Polscy piętnastolatkowie w perspektywie międzynarodowej. Wyniki badania PISA 2022*. Instytut Badań Edukacyjnych.

Kelly, L. (1969). *25 centuries of language teaching*. Newbury House Publishers, Inc.

Kenton, W. (2022, March 20). *What is a virtual assistant?* Investopedia. https://www.investopedia.com/terms/v/virtual-assistant.asp

Kern, R. (2006). Perspectives on technology in learning and teaching languages. *TESOL Quarterly, 40*(1), 183–210. https://doi.org/10.2307/40264516

Kern, R., & Warschauer, M. (2000). Introduction: Theory and practice of network-based language teaching concepts and practice. In M. Warschauer & R. Kern (Eds.), *Network-based language teaching. Concepts and practice* (pp. 1–19). Cambridge University Press.

Kępczyński, Ł. (2015). Direct method as an alternative to "coursebook teaching" in a contemporary language classroom. *Ateneum Philological Forum, 1*(3), 79–89.

Khaki, N. (2014). Improving reading comprehension in a foreign language: Strategic reader. *The Reading Matrix, 14*(2), 186–200.

Khanna, S., Kaushik, A., & Barnela, M. (2010, March 19–20). *Expert systems advances in education* [Paper presentation]. National Conference on Computational Instrumentation, Chandigarh, India.

Khansir, A., & Dashti, J. (2014). The effect of question-generation strategy on Iranian EFL learners' reading comprehension development. *English Language Teaching, 7*(4), 38–45. https://doi.org/10.5539/elt.v7n4p38

Kiernan, P., & Aizawa, K. (2004). Cell phones in task based learning. Are cell phones useful language learning tools? *ReCALL, 16*(1), 71–84. https://doi.org/10.1017/S0958344004000618

Kim, H., & Kwon, Y. (2012). Exploring smartphone applications for effective mobile-assisted language learning. *Multimedia-Assisted Language Learning, 15*(1), 31–57.

Kim, L., & Albers, M. (2001, October 21–24). *Web design issues when searching for information in a small screen display* [Paper presentation]. 19th Annual International Conference on Computer Documentation, Santa Fe, New Mexico, USA.

Kim, N. (2017). Effects of types of voice-based chat on EFL students' negotiation of meaning according to proficiency levels. *English Teaching, 72*(1), 159–181.

Kim, N. (2018a). A study on chatbots for developing Korean college students' English listening and reading skills. *Journal of Digital Convergence, 16*(8), 19–26. https://doi.org/10.14400/JDC.2018.16.8.019

Kim, N. (2018b). Chatbots and Korean EFL students' English vocabulary learning. *Journal of Digital Convergence, 16*(2), 1–7. https://doi.org/10.14400/JDC.2018.16.2.001

Kim, N. (2019). A study on the use of artificial intelligence chatbots for improving English grammar skills. *Journal of Digital Convergence, 17*(8), 37–46. https://doi.org/10.14400/JDC.2019.17.8.037

Klassen, J., & Milton, P. (1999). Enhancing English language skills using multimedia: Tried and tested. *Computer Assisted Language Learning*, 12(4), 281–294. https://doi.org/10.1076/call.12.4.281.5706

Klinger, K., & Otto-Duszczyk, P. (2019, February 27). *Zakaz używania komórki albo jedynka za jej brak. W szkołach brakuje spójnych przepisów.* Dziennik Gazeta Prawna. https://serwisy.gazetaprawna.pl/edukacja/artykuly/1400034,przepisy-w-szkolach-dotyczace-uzywania-komorki.html

Klopfer, E., Squire, K., & Jenkins, H. (2002, August 29–30). *Environmental detectives: PDAs as a window into a virtual simulated world* [Paper presentation]. IEEE International Workshop on Wireless and Mobile Technologies in Education, Tokushima, Japan.

Kluwer, T. (2011). From chatbots to dialog systems. In D. Perez-Marin & I. Pascual-Nieto (Eds.), *Conversational agents and natural language interaction: Techniques and effective practices* (pp. 1–22). IGI Global.

Kok, N., & Aziz, A. (2019). English language teachers' perceptions on the implementation of CEFR-aligned curriculum among primary schools in Malaysia. *Seminar Wacana Pendidikan*, 212–222.

Kolb, E. (2009). Finite resources – infinite communication: Sprachmittlung im Englischunterricht der Unterstufe. *ForumSprache, 1*, 69–86.

Kołakowska, J. (2015). Test jako narzędzie rozwijania kompetencji komunikacyjnych. *Języki Obce w Szkole, 3*, 84.

Komorowska, H. (1986). Programy i podręczniki a reforma szkolnictwa ponadpodstawowego. *Języki Obce w Szkole, 2*, 103–105.

Komorowska, H. (2007). *Metodyka nauczania języków obcych w Polsce (1957–2007). Z wyborem tekstów z lat 1957-2007.* Centralny Ośrodek Doskonalenia Nauczycieli.

Komorowska, H. (2015a). Rola nauczyciela: Mity i slogany a rzeczywistość. *Neofilolog, 45*(2), 143–155.

Komorowska, H. (2015b). Rozwój glottodydaktyki a kształcenie nauczycieli języków obcych. *Postscriptum Polonistyczne, 2*(16), 11–29.

Komorowska, H. (2016). Zmienne losy innowacji edukacyjnych na przykładzie CEFR. In D. Gabryś-Barker & R. Kalamarz (Eds.), *Ocenianie i pomiar biegłości językowej: Wybrane aspekty teoretyczne i praktyczne* (pp. 13–24). Wydawnictwo Uniwersytetu Śląskiego.

Komorowska, H. (2017). *Kształcenie językowe w Polsce. 60 lat czasopisma Języki Obce w Szkole*. Fundacja Rozwoju Systemu Edukacji.

Komorowska, H., & Krajka, J. (2020). *The culture of language education. Foreign language teaching in diverse instructional contexts*. Peter Lang.

Konarzewski K. (2000) *Jak uprawiać badania oświatowe: Metodologia praktyczna*. Wydawnictwa Szkolne i Pedagogiczne.

Kondracki, N., Wellman, N., & Amundson, D. (2002) Content analysis: Review of methods and their applications in nutrition education. *Journal of Nutrition Education and Behaviour, 34*, 224–230. https://doi.org/10.1016/s1499-4046(06)60097-3

Koole, M. (2009). A model for framing mobile learning. In M. Ally (Ed.), *Mobile learning: Transforming the delivery of education and training* (pp. 25–47). AU Press.

Koper, D. (2017). *Analiza nowej podstawy programowej kształcenia ogólnego w zakresie języka obcego nowożytnego dla języka obcego nauczanego w szkole podstawowej jako drugi*. Wydawnictwa Szkolne i Pedagogiczne.

Kordasiewicz, S. (2018). Historyczna i międzynarodowa perspektywa mediacji. In E. Gmurzyńska & R. Morek (Eds.), *Mediacje. Teoria i praktyka* (pp. 39–55). Wolters Kluwer.

Kordus, M. (2020). Komunikacja przez prezentację. O wykorzystaniu narzędzi TIK w zdalnym nauczaniu języków obcych. *Języki Obce w Szkole, 2*, 49–54.

Kotuła, K. (2016). New technologies and the "wow" factor: Investigating the relationship between time of exposure to new media and students' opinions on game-supported language learning. In M. Pawlak (Ed.), *Classroom-oriented research* (pp. 213–228). Springer.

Kozińska, M. (2021). *Poradnik ucznia: Egzamin wstępny do liceum*. Nowa Era. https://www.nowaera.pl/szkola-srednia-bez-tajemnic/egzamin-wstepny-do-liceum

Krajewska, A. (1995). Education in Poland. *Eastern European Economics, 33*(4), 38–54.

Krajewska, M. (2010). *Nauczyciel ogrodnikiem, czyli nowa ustna matura z języka angielskiego 2012 w praktyce*. Macmillan Polska.

Krajka, J. (2012). *The language teacher in the digital age*. Wydawnictwo Uniwersytetu Marii Curie-Skłodowskiej.

Kramsch, C., & Whiteside, A. (2008). Language ecology in multilingual settings. Towards a theory of symbolic competence. *Applied Linguistics, 29*(4), 645–671. https://doi.org/10.1093/applin/amn022

Krashen, S. (1981). *Second language acquisition and second language learning*. Pergamon.

Krashen, S. (1985). *The input hypothesis*. Longman.

Krashen, S., & T. Terrell (1983). *The natural approach: Language acquisition in the classroom*. Pergamon.

Krippendorff, K. (2018). *Content analysis: An introduction to its methodology*. Sage Publications.

Kristianto, D. (2020, July 23). *Mobile app usage surged 40% during COVID-19 pandemic*. Data.ai. https://www.data.ai/de/insights/market-data/mobile-app-usage-surged-40-during-covid-19-pandemic/

Kruk, M. (2011). The use of the internet and instant messengers in assisting the acquisition of speaking skills in English lessons. In M. Pawlak, E. Waniek-Klimczak & J. Majer (Eds.), *Speaking and instructed foreign language acquisition* (pp. 258–267). Multilingual Matters.

Kruk, M. (2012). Using online resources in the development of learner autonomy and English pronunciation: The case of individual learners. *Journal of Second Language Teaching and Research, 1*(2), 113–142.

Kruk, M. (2013). Helping students to learn the English second conditional by blending Internet resources with virtual worlds: The results of a study. *JALT CALL Journal, 9*(3), 241–257.

Kruk, M. (2014). The use of internet resources and browser-based virtual worlds in teaching grammar. *Teaching English with Technology, 14*(2), 52–67.

Kruk, M. (2015a). CALL vs. traditional grammar instruction. The case of the past simple tense. In A. Turula & M. Chojnacka (Eds.), *CALL for bridges between school and academia* (pp. 129–142). Peter Lang.

Kruk, M. (2015b). Practicing the English present simple tense in Active Worlds. *International Journal of Computer-Assisted Language Learning and Teaching, 5*(4), 52–65. https://doi.org/10.4018/IJCALLT.2015100104

Krumm, H. J. (2007). Profiles instead of levels: The CEFR and its (ab)uses in the context of migration. *The Modern Language Journal, 91*(4), 667–669.

Krzyżanowski, P. (2013). *Odpowiedź podsekretarza stanu w Ministerstwie Edukacji Narodowej z upoważnienia ministra na zapytanie nr 4408 w sprawie wygaśnięcia dotychczasowych umów patronackich z uczelniami wyższymi*. https://www.sejm.gov.pl/Sejm7.nsf/InterpelacjaTresc.xsp?key=7BAEF672&view=null

Kucharczyk, R. (2013). Normy europejskie w polskiej edukacji językowej. *Języki Obce w Szkole, 1*, 64–69.

Kucharczyk, R. (2014). Egzamin maturalny z języka obcego nowożytnego od 2015 r.: Poziom podstawowy i rozszerzony. *Języki Obce w Szkole, 1*, 77–80.

Kucharczyk, R. (2015). Jak definiować poprawność językową w epoce wielojęzyczności? Kryteria oceny wypowiedzi ustnej na egzaminie z języka obcego nowożytnego (na przykładzie egzaminów maturalnych). In J. Sujecka-Zając

(Ed.), *Ewaluacja biegłości językowej. Od pomiaru do sztuki pomiaru* (pp. 11–132). Rada Koordynacyjna ds. Certyfikacji Biegłości Językowej UW.

Kucharczyk, R. (2016). Kontekst nauczania języków obcych w Polsce. Glottodydaktyczne implikacje dla drugich języków obcych. *Linguodidactica, 20,* 195–212.

Kucharczyk, R. (2020). Językowe działania mediacyjne na lekcjach języka obcego. Od teorii do praktyki. *Języki Obce w Szkole, 2,* 5–14.

Kukulska-Hulme, A. (2009). Will mobile learning change language learning? *RECALL, 21,* 157–165. https://doi.org/10.1017/s0958344009000202

Kukulska-Hulme, A. (2013). Mobile-assisted language learning. In C. Chapelle (Ed.), *Encyclopaedia of applied linguistics* (pp. 3701–3709). Wiley.

Kukulska-Hulme, A. (2016). Mobile assistance in language learning: A critical appraisal. In A. Palalas & M. Ally (Eds.), *The international handbook of mobile-assisted language learning* (pp. 138–160). China Central Radio & TV University Press.

Kukulska-Hulme, A. (2017, November 27–28). *Mobile and intelligent assistants in education* [Paper presentation]. MEC 2017 Conference, Rovaniemi, Finland.

Kukulska-Hulme, A. (2018). Mobile assistance for personal learning on a massive scale. In M. Orsini-Jones & S. Smith (Eds), *Flipping the blend through MOOCs, MALL and OIL: New directions in CALL* (pp. 1–7). Research-publishing.net.

Kukulska-Hulme, A. (2019). Assistance for mobile language learners. In B. Trebinjac & S. Jovanovic (Eds), *Proceedings of 10th international conference of e-learning* (pp. 9–11). Belgrade Metropolitan University.

Kukulska-Hulme, A. (2019). Intelligent assistants in language learning: Friends or foes? In C. Glahn, R. Power & E. Tan (Eds.), *Proceedings of world conference on mobile and contextual learning* (pp. 127–131). LearnTechLib.

Kukulska-Hulme, A., Traxler, J., & Pettit, J. (2007). Designed and user-generated activity in the mobile age. *Journal of Learning Design, 2*(1), 52–65. https://doi.org/10.5204/jld.v2i1.28

Kukulska-Hulme, A., & Shield, L. (2008). An overview of mobile assisted language learning: From content delivery to supported collaboration and interaction. *ReCALL, 20*(3), 271–289. https://doi.org/10.1017/s0958344008000335

Kukulska-Hulme, A., Norris, L., & Donohue, J. (2015). *Mobile pedagogy for English language teaching: A guide for teachers.* The British Council. https://www.teachingenglish.org.uk/sites/teacheng/files/E485%20Mobile%20pedagogy%20for%20ELT_v6.pdf

Kukulska-Hulme, A., Lee, H., & Norris, L. (2017). Mobile learning revolution: Implications for language pedagogy. In C. Chapelle & S. Sauro (Eds), *The handbook of technology and second language teaching and learning* (pp. 217–233). Wiley & Sons.

Kukulska-Hulme, A., & Viberg, O. (2018). Mobile collaborative language learning: State of the art. *British Journal of Educational Technology*, *49*(2), 207–218. https://doi.org/10.1111/bjet.12580

Kukulska-Hulme, A., & Lee, H. (2020). Intelligent assistants in language learning: An analysis of features and limitations. In K. Frederiksen, S. Larsen, L. Bradley & S. Thouesny (Eds.), *CALL for widening participation: Short papers from EUROCALL 2020* (pp. 172–176). Researchpublishing.net.

Kukulska-Hulme, A., Gaved, M., Paletta, L., Scanlon, E., Jones, A., & Brasher, A. (2015). Mobile incidental learning to support the inclusion of recent immigrants. *Ubiquitous Learning: An International Journal*, *7*(2), 9–21. https://doi.org/10.18848/1835-9795/cgp/v07i02/58070

Kuliniak, R. (2010). Badanie predyspozycji językowych. In S. Urbański & J. Mulawa (Eds.), *Wokół diagnostyki edukacyjnej* (pp. 13–18). Wałbrzyska Wyższa Szkoła Zarządzania i Przedsiębiorczości.

Kuliniak, R. (2013). *Testy predyspozycji językowych*. Instytut Badań Kompetencji.

Kumaravadivelu, B. (1994). The post-method condition: Emerging strategies for second/foreign language teaching. *TESOL Quarterly*, *28*(1), 27–48. https://doi.org/10.2307/3587197

Kumaravadivelu, B. (2006). *Understanding language teaching: From method to postmethod*. Lawrence Erlbaum Associates.

Kuznekoff, J., & Titsworth, S. (2013). The impact of mobile phone usage on student learning. *Communication Education*, *62*(3), 233–252. https://doi.org/10.1080/03634523.2013.767917

Lafford, B. (2009). Toward an ecological CALL: Update to Garrett (1991). *The Modern Language Journal*, *93*, 673–696. https://doi.org/10.1111/j.1540-4781.2009.00966.x

Lam, Y., & Lawrence, G. (2002). Teacher-student role redefinition during a computer-based second language project: Are computers catalysts for empowering change? *Computer Assisted Language Learning*, *15*(3), 295–315. https://doi.org/10.1076/call.15.3.295.8185

Lancaster, L., & Stillman, D. (2002). *When generations collide: Who they are. Why they clash. How to solve the generational puzzle at work*. Collins Business.

Lange, R., Bochenek, M., Wrońska, A., & Niedzielska-Barczyk, D. (2018). *Raport. Dziecko w krainie smartfonów*. NASK Państwowy Instytut Badawczy.

Laricchia, F. (2022). *Number of digital voice assistants in use worldwide from 2019 to 2024 (in billions).* Statista. https://www.statista.com/statistics/973815/worldwide-digital-voice-assistant-in-use/

Larsen-Freeman, D. (1991). Research on language teaching methodologies: A review of the past and an agenda for the future. In K. de Bot, R. Ginsberg & C. Kramsch (Eds.), *Foreign language research in cross-cultural perspective* (pp. 119–132). John Benjamins Publishing Company.

Larsen-Freeman, D., & Long, M. (1991). *An introduction to second language research.* Longman.

Lee, K. (2000). English teachers' barriers to the use of computer-assisted language learning. *The Internet TESL Journal, 6*(12), 1–8.

Lee, L. (2016). Autonomous learning through task-based instruction in fully online language courses. *Language Learning and Technology, 20*(2), 81–97.

Lee, U., Lee, J., Ko, M., Lee, C., Kim, Y., Yang, S., Gweon, G., Chung, K. & Song, J. (2014, April 26-May 1). Hooked on smartphones: An exploratory study on smartphone overuse among college students. *SIGCHI Conference on Human Factors in Computing Systems*, Toronto, Ontario, Canada.

Leek, J. (2015). Ewolucja podstaw programowych kształcenia ogólnego w Polsce. Ku zmianie edukacyjnej. In M. Kamińska (Ed.), *Wybrane problemy nauczania i wychowania. Z doświadczeń okresu transformacji* (pp. 23–35). NOVUM: Oficyna Wydawnicza Szkoły Wyższej im. Pawła Włodkowica.

Lenox, T., & Woratschek, C. (2018). Personal digital assistants. In *Encyclopedia.com.* Retrieved June 2, 2022, from https://www.encyclopedia.com/science-and-technology/computers-and-electrical-engineering/computers-and-computing/personal-digital-assistant

Levitas, A., & Herczyński, J. (2012). Decentralizacja w Polsce w latach 1990–1999: Tworzenie systemu. In M. Herbst (Ed.), *Decentralizacja oświaty* (pp. 55-117). Wydawnictwo ICM.

Levonius, D. (2015). *Generational differences in the classroom.* Association for Talent Development. https://www.td.org/newsletters/atd-links/generational-differences-in-the-classroom

Levy, M. (1997). *Computer-assisted language learning: Context and conceptualization.* Oxford University Press.

Levy, M. (2009). A tutor-tool framework. In P. Hubbard (Ed.), *Computer assisted language learning: Critical concepts in linguistics* (pp. 45–78). Routledge.

Levy, M., & Hubbard, P. (2005). Why call CALL "CALL"? *Computer Assisted Language Learning, 18*(3), 143–149. https://doi.org/10.1080/09588220500208884

Lewoc, A. (1994). Computer aided language learning in Poland. Is it worth trying? *Anglica Wratislavensia, 27*, 13–25.

Liaw, S.-S., Huang, H.-M., & Chen, G.-D. (2007). Surveying instructor and learner attitudes toward e-learning. *Computers & Education*, *49*(4), 1066–1080. https://doi.org/10.1016/j.compedu.2006.01.001

Lin, K. (2020, June 24). *Evolution of chatbots*. Posh AI. https://poshai.medium.com/evolution-of-chatbots-dcb679bf6ca0

Lindaman, D., & Nolan, D. (2015). Mobile-assisted language learning: Application development projects within reach for language teachers. *The IALLT Journal, 45*(1), 1–22. https://doi.org/10.17161/iallt.v45i1.8547

Lipska, A. (1995). To już 50 lat… *Języki Obce w Szkole, 2*, 101-102.

Little, D. (1991). *Learner autonomy. Definition, issues and problems*. Authentik Language Learning Resources Ltd.

Little, D. (2006). The Common European Framework of Reference for Languages: Content, purpose, origin, reception and impact. *Language Teaching, 39*(3), 167–190. https://doi.org/10.1017/S0261444806003557

Little, D. (2007). The Common European Framework of Reference for Languages: Perspectives on the making of supranational language education policy. *Modern Language Journal, 91*(4), 645–653.

Littlewood, W. (1981). *Communicative language teaching: An introduction*. Cambridge University Press.

Liu, Q., Diao, L., & Tu, G. (2010, November 12–14). *The application of artificial intelligence in mobile learning* [Paper presentation]. International Conference on System Science, Engineering Design and Manufacturing Informatization, Yichang, China.

Liu, Q., & Shi, J. (2007). An analysis of language teaching approaches and methods: Effectiveness and weakness. *US-China Education Review*, *4*(1), 69–71.

Liu, Y., Theodore, P., & Lavelle, E. (2004). Experimental effects of online instruction on teachers' concerns about technology integration. *International Journal of Instructional Technology and Distance Learning, 1*(1), 27–59.

Lohnes, S., & Kinzer, C. (2007). Questioning assumptions about students' expectations for technology in college classrooms. *Innovate: Journal of Online Education*, *3*(5), 1–6.

Long, M. (1981). Input, interaction and second language acquisition. In H. Winitz (Ed.), *Native language and foreign language acquisition* (pp. 259–278). New York Academy of Sciences.

Long, M. (1983). Native speaker/non-native speaker conversation in the second language classroom. In M. Clarke & J. Handscombe (Eds.), *On TESOL '82: Pacific perspectives on language and teaching* (pp. 94–120). TESOL.

Long, M. (1985). A role for instruction in second language acquisition: Task-based language training. In K. Hyltenstam & M. Pienemann (Eds.), *Modelling and assessing second language acquisition* (pp. 77–99). Multilingual Matters.

Long, M. (1996). The role of the linguistic environment in second language acquisition. In W. Ritchie & T. Bhatia (Eds), *Handbook of second language acquisition* (pp. 413–468). Academic Press.

Long, M. (2005). *Second language needs analysis.* Cambridge University Press.

Long, M. (2015). *Second language acquisition and task-based language teaching.* John Wiley & Sons Ltd.

Long, M. (2016). In defence of tasks and TBLT: Nonissues and real issues. *Annual Review of Applied Linguistics, 36*, 5–33. https://doi.org/10.1017/S0267190515000057

Long, M., & Crookes, G. (1991). Three approaches to task-based syllabus design. *University of Hawaii Working Papers in ESL, 10*(1), 1–36.

Look, S. M. (2011). *Question generation. Effective instructional strategies series.* Pacific Resources for Education and Learning. https://files.eric.ed.gov/fulltext/ED585173.pdf

Lopes, A., & Ruiz-Cecilia, R. (2017). Designing technology-mediated tasks for language teaching: A methodological framework. *Hacettepe University Journal of Education, 32*(2), 265–279. https://doi.org/10.16986/huje.2017025101

Lopez, G., Quesada, L., & Guerrero, L. (2017, July 17–21). *Alexa vs. Siri vs. Cortana vs. Google Assistant: A comparison of speech-based natural user interfaces* [Paper presentation]. International Conference on Applied Human Factors and Ergonomics, Los Angeles, USA.

Luckin, R., Holmes, W., Griffiths, M., & Forcier, L. (2016). *Intelligence unleashed: An argument for AI in education.* Pearson Education.

Łobocki, M. (2003). Minimum wiedzy o eksperymencie pedagogicznym. *Annales Universitatis Mariae Curie-Skłodowska. Sectio J, Paedagogia-Psychologia, 16*, 19–30.

Łockiewicz, M., & Pietras, I. (2018). Polska szkoła w multijęzykowej Europie. Analiza przebiegu edukacji językowej w odniesieniu do nauczania języków obcych. *Prace Językoznawcze, 20*(1), 101–118.

Maciaszczyk, S. (2020). Mediacja, inteligencja i NVC: W poszukiwaniu rozwiązań. *Języki Obce w Szkole, 2*, 21–24.

Madhkhan, M., & Mousavi, S. (2017). The effect of implementation of TBLT in reading comprehension classes of Iranian EFL learners. *English Language Teaching, 10*(11), 119–128. https://doi.org/10.5539/elt.v10n11p119

Makrakis, V. (2005, October 7–9). *Training teachers for new roles in the new era: Experiences from the United Arab Emirates ICT programme* [Paper presentation]. 3rd Pan-Hellenic Conference on Didactics of Informatics, Korinthos, Greece.

Marczak, M., Muszyński, M., Campfield, D., Gajewska-Dyszkiewicz, A., Paczuska, K., Pitura, J., & Szpotowicz, M. (2015). Realizacja podstawy programowej dla języka obcego nowożytnego. In J. Choińska-Mika & M. Sitek (Eds.), *Realizacja podstawy programowej kształcenia ogólnego. Wnioski z badań przeprowadzonych przez Zespół Dydaktyk Szczegółowych* (pp. 69–85). Instytut Badań Edukacyjnych.

Margaryan, A. & Littlejohn, A. (2008). *Are digital natives a myth or a reality? Students' use of technologies for learning.* Glasgow Caledonian University Insight Paper. http://oro.open.ac.uk/53083/1/Digital%20Natives%202008.pdf

Mart, C. (2013). The audio-lingual method: An easy way of achieving speech. *International Journal of Academic Research in Business and Social Sciences, 3*(12), 63–65.

Martin, C. (1996). *"Designer" approaches: Which ones will fit the 21st century?* [Paper presentation]. 16th Annual Conference of MATE, Mohammedia, Morocco.

Martin, C., & Tulgan, B. (2002). *Managing the generational mix.* HRD Press.

Martynenko, O. (2019, November 21). *What is speech recognition used for?* Verbit. https://verbit.ai/what-is-speech-recognition-used-for/

Martyniuk, W. (2021). ESOKJ 2020: Nowy, zmodernizowany europejski system opisu kształcenia językowego. *Postscriptum Polonistyczne, 28*(2), 1–18.

Martyniuk, W., & Noijons, J. (2007). *Executive summary of results of a survey on the use of the CEFR at national level in the Council of Europe member states.* Council of Europe. https://rm.coe.int/CoERMPublicCommonSearchServices/DisplayDCTMContent?documentId=090000168069b7ad

Maturita exam in Slovakia (n.d.). Slovakiaeducation.info. https://www.slovakiaeducation.info/tests/matura-exam-in-slovakia.html

Mauldin, M. (1994, October 5). *Chatterbots, Tinymuds and the Turing test: Entering the Loebner prize competition* [Paper presentation]. 12th National Conference on Artificial Intelligence, Seattle, Washington, USA.

McCarthy, J. (2007). *What is artificial intelligence?* Formal Reasoning Group. http://faculty.otterbein.edu/dstucki/inst4200/whatisai.pdf

McCracken, H. (2012, June 1). *Newton, reconsidered. A hands-on assessment of Apple's pioneering, ill-fated personal digital assistant, twenty years after its original unveiling.* Time. https://techland.time.com/2012/06/01/newton-reconsidered/

McDonald, D. (1986). *Natural language generation: Complexities and techniques.* Department of Computer and Information Science, University of Massachusetts. https://apps.dtic.mil/sti/pdfs/ADA175122.pdf

McNamara, T. 2014. 30 years on evolution or revolution? *Language Assessment Quarterly*, *11*(2), 226–232. https://doi.org/10.1080/15434303.2014.895830

McTear, M. (1993). User modelling for adaptive computer systems: A survey of recent developments. *Artificial Intelligence Review*, *7*(3), 157–184.

MEN (2009). *Podstawa programowa z komentarzami. Tom 3. Języki obce w szkole podstawowej, gimnazjum i liceum.*

MEN (2020). *Wymagania na egzaminach ósmoklasisty i maturalnym. Rozporządzenie podpisane.* https://www.gov.pl/web/edukacja-i-nauka/wymagania-na-egzaminach-osmoklasisty-i-maturalnym

MEN (2021). *Informatory o egzaminie maturalnym w formule 2023.* https://www.gov.pl/web/edukacja-i-nauka/informatory-o-egzaminie-maturalnym-w-formule-2023

Meri, S. (2012, November 15–16). *Autonomous computer-assisted language learning: Turkish primary school students' perceptions of DynEd software* [Paper presentation]. 5th International Conference on ICT for Language Learning, Florence, Italy.

Milliner, B. (2019). Comparing extensive reading to extensive reading-while-listening on smartphones: Impacts on listening and reading performance for beginning students. *The Reading Matrix: An International Online Journal*, *19*(1), 1–19.

Miangah, T., & Nezarat, A. (2012). Mobile-assisted language learning. *International Journal of Distributed and Parallel Systems*, *3*(1), 309–319. https://doi.org/10.5121/ijdps.2012.3126

Milan-Gee, E., & Gee, P. (2020). Mediation: Classroom activities for the skills needed for the 21st century workplace. *Języki Obce w Szkole*, *2*, 15–19.

Milbrath, Y.,& Kinzie, M. (2000). Computer technology training for prospective teachers: Computer attitudes and perceived self-efficacy. *Journal of Technology and Teacher Education*, *8*(4), 373–396.

Miles, M., & Huberman, A. (1984). *Qualitative data analysis.* Sage.

Miller, G. (2012). The smartphone psychology manifesto. *Perspectives on Psychological Science*, *7*(3), 221–237. https://doi.org/10.1177%2F1745691612441215

Ministry of Education, Science, and Sport (n.d.). *Matura examinations.* https://smsm.lrv.lt/en/sector-activities/education_1/matura-examinations

Miodunka, W. (2013). Podejście zorientowane na działanie w nauczaniu języków obcych: Od (małych) zadań do (dużych) projektów. *Języki Obce w Szkole*, *2*, 80–85.

Miśkowiec, A. (2020). Zdalne nauczanie 2020: O edukacyjnej rewolucji czasu pandemii z perspektywy nauczycielki LO. In A. Kania, K. Mucha-Iwaniczko & M. Szumal (Eds.), *Nauczanie zdalne w dobie pandemii. Wyzwania i doświadczenia edukacji polonistycznej* (pp. 65–77). Stowarzyszenie Twórczej Edukacji Polonistycznej.

Molnar, G., & Szüts, Z. (2018, September 13–15). *The role of chatbots in formal education* [Paper presentation]. 16th International Symposium on Intelligent Systems and Informatics, Subotica, Serbia.

Moras, S. (2001). Computer-assisted language learning (CALL) and the Internet. Karen's Linguistics Issues. https://silo.tips/download/computer-assisted-language-learning-call-and-the-internet

Moskvitch, K. (2017, February 15) *The machines that learned to listen.* BBC. https://www.bbc.com/future/article/20170214-the-machines-that-learned-to-listen

Motivalla, L. (2007). Mobile learning: A framework and evaluation. *Computers & Education*, *49*, 581–596. https://doi.org/10.1016/j.compedu.2005.10.011

Moulton, W. (1963). Linguistics and language teaching in the United States 1940–1960. *International Review of Applied Linguistics in Language Teaching*, *1*, 21–41. https://doi.org/10.1515/iral.1963.1.1.21

Moundridou, M., & Virvou. M., (2003). Analysis and design of a web-based authoring tool generating intelligent tutoring systems. *Computers & Education*, *40*(2), 157–181. https://doi.org/10.1016/s0360-1315(02)00119-7

Moussalli, S., & Cardoso, W. (2016). Are commercial "personal robots" ready for language learning? Focus on second language speech. In S. Papadima-Sophocleous, L. Bradley & S. Thouesny (Eds), *CALL communities and culture: Short Papers from EUROCALL 2016* (pp. 325–329). Research-publishing.net.

Moussalli, S., & Cardoso, W. (2017). Can you understand me? Speaking robots and accented speech. In K. Borthwick, L. Bradley & S. Thouesny (Eds.), *CALL in a climate of change: Adapting to turbulent global conditions. Short papers from EUROCALL 2017* (pp. 217–221). Research-publishing.net.

Moussalli, S., & Cardoso, W. (2019). Intelligent personal assistants: Can they understand and be understood by accented L2 learners? *Computer Assisted Language Learning*, *33*(8), 865–890. https://doi.org/10.1080/09588221.2019.1595664

Muchisky, D. (1985). *The unnatural approach: Language learning in Poland* (Report 264728). ERIC Document. https://files.eric.ed.gov/fulltext/ED264728.pdf

Mugenda, O., & Mugenda, A. (2003). *Research methods, quantitative and qualitative approaches.* Act Press.

Murray, L., & Barnes, A. (1998). Beyond the "wow" factor: Evaluating multimedia language learning software from a pedagogical viewpoint. *System*, *26*(2), 249–259. https://doi.org/10.1016/S0346-251X(98)00008-6

Musoeva, A. (2019). What do Uzbekistani EFL teachers know and believe about the usefulness of the CEFR? *International Journal of Academic Research and Reflection*, *7*(6), 5–18.

Muszyński, M., Campfield, D., & Szpotowicz, M. (2015). *Język angielski w szkole podstawowej: Proces i efekty nauczania. Wyniki podłużnego badania efektywności nauczania języka angielskiego (2011–2014)*. Instytut Badań Edukacyjnych.

Muszyński, M., Gajewska-Dyszkiewicz, A., Paczuska, K., & Szpotowicz, M. (2016). Jak maturzyści poradzili sobie z egzaminem z języka angielskiego? Omówienie wyników matury z języka angielskiego 2015 r. *Języki Obce w Szkole*, *1*, 75–85.

Mutchler, A. (2019, October 5). *What are virtual assistants?* Voicebot.ai. https://voicebot.ai/2019/10/05/what-are-virtual-assistants/

Mutlu, A., & Eroz-Tuga, B. (2013). The role of computer-assisted language learning (CALL) in promoting learner autonomy. *Eurasian Journal of Educational Research*, *51*, 107–122.

Nah, K., White, P., & Sussex, R. (2008). The potential of using a mobile phone to access the internet for learning EFL listening skills within a Korean context. *ReCALL*, *20*(3), 331–347. https://doi.org/10.1017/S0958344008000633

Nagata, N. (1996). Computer vs. workbook instruction in second language acquisition. *CALICO* Journal, *14*(1), 53–75. https://doi.org/10.1558/cj.v14i1.53-75

Nagata, N. (2009). Robo-Sensei's NLP-based error detection and feedback generation. *CALICO Journal*, *26*(3), 562–579. https://doi.org/10.1558/cj.v26i3.562-579

Namaziandost, I., Bohloulzadeh, G., & Pazhakh, A. (2017). The effect of task-based language teaching on motivation and grammatical achievement of EFL junior high school students. *Advances in Language and Literary Studies*, *8*(2), 243–259. https://doi.org/10.7575/aiac.alls.v.8n.2p.243

Nanda, T., Gupta, H., Kharub, M., & Singh N. (2013). Diagnostics for pretesting questionnaires: A comparative analysis. *International Journal of Technology Policy and Management*, *13*(1), 67–79. https://doi.org/10.1504/ijtpm.2013.051008

Negishi, M., Takada, T., & Tono, Y. (2013). A progress report on the development of the CEFR-J. In E. Galaczi & C. Weir (Eds.), *Exploring language frameworks: Proceedings of the ALTE Kraków Conference* (pp. 135–163). Cambridge University Press.

Neiterman, E., & Zaza, C. (2019). A mixed blessing? Students' and instructors' perspectives about off-task technology use in the academic classroom. *The Canadian Journal for the Scholarship of Teaching and Learning*, *10*(1), 1–16. https://doi.org/10.5206/cjsotl-rcacea.2019.1.8002

Newby, D., Alle, R., Brit, A., Jones, B., Komorowska, H., & Soghikyan, K. (n.d.). *European portfolio for student teachers of languages* (EPOSTL). European Centre for Modern Languages.

Nhung, P. (2019). Implementing the CEFR at a Vietnamese university: General English language teachers' perceptions. *CEFR Journal – Research and Practice*, *41*, 41–67.

Nielsen (2018). *(Smart)Speaking my language: Despite their vast capabilities, smart speakers are all about the music.*

Niemiec-Knaś, M. (2011). *Metoda projektów w nauczaniu języków obcych.* Impuls.

Niemierko, B. (2002). *Ocenianie szkolne bez tajemnic.* Wydawnictwa Szkolne i Pedagogiczne.

NIK (2014). *System egzaminów zewnętrznych w oświacie. Informacja o wynikach kontroli.* https://www.nik.gov.pl/kontrole/P/14/022/LWA/

NIK (2021). *Funkcjonowanie szkół w sytuacji zagrożenia COVID-19. Informacja o wynikach kontroli.* https://www.nik.gov.pl/plik/id,25380,vp,28141.pdf

Nobles, A., Leas, E., Caputi, T., Zhu, S., Strathdee, S., & Ayers, J. (2020). Responses to addiction help-seeking from Alexa, Siri, Google Assistant, Cortana, and Bixby intelligent virtual assistants. *NPJ Digital Medicine*, *3*(1), 1–3. https://doi.org/10.1038/s41746-019-0215-9

Norris, J. (2009). Task-based teaching and testing. In M. Long & C. Doughty (Eds.), *The handbook of language teaching* (pp. 578–594). John Wiley & Sons.

North, B. (1997). Perspectives on language proficiency and aspects of competence. *Language Teaching*, *30*, 92–100. https://doi.org/10.1017/s0261444800012829

North, B. (2007). The CEFR illustrative descriptor scales. *The Modern Language Journal*, *91*(4), 656–659. https://doi.org/10.1111/j.1540-4781.2007.00627_3.x

North, B. (2014). Putting the Common European Framework of Reference to good use. *Language Teaching*, *47*(2), 228–249. https://doi.org/10.1017/S0261444811000206

North, B. (2020). The CEFR renewed: Inspiring the future of language education. *Italiano LinguaDue*, *12*(1), 549–560. https://doi.org/10.13130/2037-3597/13945

North, B. (2021). The CEFR companion volume: What's new and what might it imply for teaching/learning and for assessment? *CEFR Journal*, *4*(5), 5–24.

North, B. (2022). Plurilingual mediation in the classroom. Examples from practice. In E. Piccardo, A. Germain-Rutherford & G. Lawrence (Eds.), *The Routledge handbook of plurilingual language education* (pp. 319–336). Routledge.

North, B., & Piccardo, E. (2016). Developing illustrative descriptors of aspects of mediation for the Common European Framework of Reference (CEFR): A Council of Europe project. *Language Teaching, 49*(3), 455–459. https://doi.org/10.1017/S0261444816000100

NUCEM (n.d.). *Maturita*. https://www2.nucem.sk/en/measurements/maturita

Nunan, D. (1989). *Designing tasks for the communicative classroom*. Cambridge University Press.

Nunan, D. (2004). *Task-based language teaching*. Cambridge University Press.

Nussbaum-Beach, S., & Hall, L. (2012). *The connected educator: Learning and leading in a digital age*. Solution Tree Press.

Oblinger, D., & Oblinger, J. (2005). Is it age or IT: First steps toward understanding the net generation. In D. Oblinger & J. Oblinger (Eds.), *Educating the net generation* (pp. 2.1–2.20). Educause.

OECD (2021). *OECD digital education outlook 2021: Pushing the frontiers with artificial intelligence, blockchain and robots*. https://read.oecd-ilibrary.org/education/oecd-digital-education-outlook-2021_589b283f-en#page1

OKE (2020). *Rozkłady wyników i parametry statystyczne. Egzamin ósmoklasisty. Język polski, matematyka, języki obce nowożytne.*

Okonkwo, C., & Ade-Ibijola, A. (2021). Chatbots applications in education: A systematic review. *Computers and Education: Artificial Intelligence, 2*, 1–10.

Olsen, S. (2003, January 30). *Instant chat bot comes back to life*. CNET. https://www.cnet.com/tech/services-and-software/instant-chat-bot-comes-back-to-life/

O'Malley, C., Vavoula, G., Glew, J., Taylor, J., Sharples, M., Lefrere, P., Lonsdale, P., Naismith, L., & Waycott, J. (2005). *Guidelines for learning/teaching/tutoring in a mobile environment*. MOBIlearn. https://hal.archives-ouvertes.fr/hal-00696244/document

Opólska-Danecka O. (1954). Nauczanie języka rosyjskiego w szkołach polskich od r. 1945 do chwili obecnej. *Język Rosyjski, 6*(34), 7–11.

ORE (2011). *Powszechność nauczania języków obcych w roku szkolnym 2009/2010.* http://bc.ore.edu.pl/Content/200/Powszechnosc+nauczania+jezykow+obcych+2009-2010.pdf

Otwinowska-Kasztelanic, A. (2007). Programy i materiały nauczania w szkolnictwie podstawowym Polski i innych krajów UE a rekomendacje Rady Europy i Unii Europejskie. In H. Komorowska (Ed.), *Nauczanie języków obcych: Polska a Europa* (pp. 117–134). Academica.

Pachler, N., Bachmair, B., & Cook, J. (2010). *Mobile learning. Structures, agency, practices*. Springer.

Paczuska, K., Kutyłowska, K., Gajewska-Dyszkiewicz, A., Ellis, M., & Szpotowicz, M. (2014). *Język angielski w gimnazjum. Raport cząstkowy z I etapu Badania uczenia się i nauczania języków obcych w gimnazjum.* Instytut Badań Edukacyjnych.

Palacios-Hidalgo, F. (2020). TELL, CALL and MALL: Approaches to bridge the language gap. In C. Huertas-Abril & M. Gomez-Parr (Eds.), *International approaches to bridging the language gap* (pp. 118–134). IGI Global.

Pałczyńska, A. (2021). Godne polecenia narzędzia internetowe do nauczania słownictwa, gramatyki i tworzenia wypowiedzi ustnych. *Języki Obce w Szkole, 1*, 31–36.

Pamuła-Behrens, M. (2015). Wszystko zaczyna się w przedszkolu: Nauka języka obcego dla dzieci. *Języki Obce w Szkole, 1*, 8–12.

Pandemia a problemy ze zdalnym nauczaniem. (2021, January 11). DW. https://www.dw.com/pl/pandemia-a-problemy-ze-zdalnym-nauczaniem/a-56195496

PAP (2019a, September 2). *Piontkowski dla PAP: na pewno w przyszłym roku będzie podwyżka wynagrodzeń dla nauczycieli.* https://www.pap.pl/aktualnosci/news%2C504847%2Cpiontkowski-dla-pap-na-pewno-w-przyszlym-roku-bedzie-podwyzka-wynagrodzen

PAP (2019b, April 15). *Rozpoczął się egzamin ósmoklasisty.* https://www.pap.pl/aktualnosci/news%2C437222%2Crozpoczal-sie-egzamin-osmoklasisty.html.

PAP (2021, April 21). *Czarnek: egzamin maturalny i ósmoklasisty zgodnie z zaplanowanymi terminami.* https://www.pap.pl/aktualnosci/news%2C856848%2Cczarnek-egzamin-maturalny-i-osmoklasisty-zgodnie-z-zaplanowanymi-terminami

Papert, S. (1980). *Mindstorms: Children, computers and powerful ideas.* Basic Books.

Park, M., & Slater, T. (2014). A typology of tasks for mobile-assisted language learning: Recommendations from a small-scale needs analysis. *TESL Canada Journal, 31*(8), 93–115.

Patel, M., & Jain, P. (2008). *English language teaching. Methods, tools and techniques.* Sunrise Publishers & Distributors.

Pater, M. (2018). Komunikacja, czyli co jest najważniejsze na egzaminie ósmoklasisty. *Języki Obce w Szkole, 4*, 115–119.

Paulston, C. (1974). Linguistic and communicative competence. *TESOL Quarterly, 8*(4), 347–362. https://doi.org/10.2307/3585467

Paulston, C. (1992). *Linguistic and communicative competence: Topics in ESL.* Multilingual Matters.

Pawlak, M. (2006). *The place of form-focused instruction in the foreign language classroom*. Wydział Pedagogiczno-Artystyczny w Kaliszu/Uniwersytet im. Adama Mickiewicza w Poznaniu.

Pawlak, M., & Kruk, M. (2012). The development of learner autonomy through internet resources and its impact on English language attainment. *Studia Anglica Posnaniensia*, *47*, 2–3.

Pennycook, A. (1989). The concept of method, interested knowledge, and the politics of language teaching. *TESOL Quaterly*, *23*(4), 589–618. https://doi.org/10.2307/3587534

Pericherla, S. (2016, April 22). *History of computers*. Startertutorials. https://www.startertutorials.com/blog/history-of-computers.html

Personal digital assistant (PDA) (2016). Techopedia. https://www.techopedia.com/definition/4619/personal-digital-assistant-pda

Peters, M. (2006) Developing computer competencies for pre-service language teachers: Is one course enough? In P. Hubbard & M. Levy (Eds.), *Teacher education in CALL* (pp. 153–165). John Benjamins Publishing Company.

Petr Naske, Matura po czesku (n.d.). Unia Europejska: Polska i czeska perspektywa. https://forum-pl-cz.com/index.php/polityki-publiczne/39-petr-naske-matura-po-czesku#

Petrescu, S. (n.d.). *Validity issues of the German Abitur: Linking the test design to the assessment purpose and to the results.*

Petrock, V. (2019, August 15). *Voice assistant use reaches critical mass*. eMarketer. https://www.emarketer.com/content/voice-assistant-use-reaches-critical-mass

Pham, X., Pham, T., Nguyen, Q., Nguyen, T., & Cao, T. (2018, November 5–7). *Chatbot as an intelligent personal assistant for mobile language learning* [Paper presentation]. 2nd International Conference on Education and E-Learning, Bali, Indonesia.

Piaget, J., & Inhelder, B. (1967). *The child's concept of space*. Norton Library.

Piccardo, E. (2010). From communicative to action-oriented: New perspectives for a new millennium. *Contact*, *36*(2), 20–35.

Piccardo, E. (2014). *From communicative to action-oriented: A research pathway.* Curriculum Services Canada.

Piccardo, E., Berchoud, M., Cignatta, T., Mentz, O., & Pamuła, M. (2011). *ECEP project guide. Pathways through assessing, learning and teaching in the CEFR.* Council of Europe.

Piccardo, E., & North, B. (2019). *The action-oriented approach. A dynamic vision of language education*. Multilingual Matters.

Piccardo, E., North, B., & Goodier, T. (2019). Broadening the scope of language education: Mediation, plurilingualism, and collaborative learning. The CEFR companion volume. *Journal of e-Learning and Knowledge Society*, *15*(1), 17–36. https://doi.org/10.20368/1971-8829/1612

Piper, A. (1986). Conversation and the computer: A study of the conversational spin-off generated among learners of English as a foreign language working in groups. *System*, *14*(2), 187–198. https://doi.org/10.1016/0346-251X(86)90008-4

PISA (2006). *Program międzynarodowej oceny umiejętności uczniów. Wyniki badania 2006 w Polsce*. Instytut Badań Edukacyjnych. https://www.ibe.edu.pl/images/download/pisa_raport_2006.pdf

Pizorn, K. & Huhta, A. (2016). Assessment in educational settings. In D. Tsagari & J. Banerjee (Eds.), *Handbook of second language assessment* (pp. 239–255). De Gruyter Mouton.

Platform of resources and references for plurilingual and intercultural education (n.d.). Council of Europe. https://www.coe.int/en/web/platform-plurilingual-intercultural-language-education/home

Plebańska, M. (2017). Stan cyfryzacji polskich szkół na podstawie badania „Polska szkoła w dobie cyfryzacji. Diagnoza 2017" w kontekście potrzeby wdrożenia nauczania w modelu STEAM. *Interdyscyplinarne Konteksty Pedagogiki Specjalnej*, *23*, 53–70.

Plebańska, M., Szyller, A., & Sieńczewska, M. (2020). *Edukacja zdalna w czasach COVID-19. Raport z badania*. Wydział Pedagogiczny Uniwersytetu Warszawskiego.

Pokrivcakova, S. (2019). Preparing teachers for the application of AI-powered technologies in foreign language education. *Journal of Language and Cultural Education*, *7*(3), 135–153. https://doi.org/10.2478/jolace-2019-0025

Polakova, P. & Klimova, B. (2019). Mobile technology and generation Z in the English language classroom: A preliminary study. *Education Sciences*, *9*(3), 203–213. https://doi.org/10.3390/educsci9030203

Popescu, A. (2018, January 25). *Keep your head up: How smartphone addiction kills manners and moods*. The New York Times. https://www.nytimes.com/2018/01/25/smarter-living/bad-text-posture-neckpain-mood.html

Prabhu, N. (1987). *Second language pedagogy*. Oxford University Press.

Prejbisz, A. (1961). Próba nakreślenia modelu nauczania języków obcych w naszym kraju. *Języki Obce w Szkole*, *4*, 223, 225–226.

Prejbisz, A. (1966). Nowe programy języków obcych dla szkół średnich ogólnokształcących. *Języki Obce w Szkole*, *4*, 223, 225–226.

Prejbisz, A. (1969). Programy nauczania języków obcych w dwudziestopięcioleciu (1944–1969). *Języki Obce w Szkole, 4*, 190-191.

Prensky, M. (2001). Digital natives, digital immigrants. *On the Horizon, 9*, 1–6.

Presser, S., Couper, M., Lessler J. Martin E., Martin J., Rothgeb J., & Singer, E. (2004). Methods for pretesting and evaluating survey questions. *Public Opinion Quarterly, 68*(1), 109–130. https://doi.org/10.1093/poq/nfh008

Psion organiser 1. (n.d.). Centre for Computing History http://www.computing-history.org.uk/det/28549/Psion-Organiser-1/#

PWC (2018). *Consumer intelligence series: Prepare for the voice revolution.* https://www.pwc.com/us/en/advisory-services/publications/consumer-intelligence-series/voice-assistants.pdf

Pyae, A., & Joelsson, T. (2018, September 3–6). *Investigating the usability and user experiences of voice user interface: A case of Google home smart speaker* [Paper presentation]. 20th International Conference on Human-Computer Interaction with Mobile Devices and Services Adjunct, Barcelona, Spain.

Pyter, M. (2015). Prawne zasady funkcjonowania oświaty w Polsce Ludowej. *Studia Iuridica Lublinensia, 24*(4), 105–122.

Pyne, H. (2020, September 7). *What is a smart speaker and how do they work?* RadioTimes. https://www.radiotimes.com/technology/what-is-a-smart-speaker/

Pyżalski, J., Zdrodowska, A., Tomczyk, Ł., & Abramczuk, K. (2019). *Polskie badanie EU kids online 2018. Najważniejsze wyniki i wnioski.* Wydawnictwo Naukowe UAM.

Rahimi, A., & Bigdeli, R. (2014). ICT and EFL students' self-regulation mastery: Educational meat or poison? *AsiaCALL Online Journal, 8*(1), 1–10.

Ramos, D. (2018, April 16). *Voice assistants: How artificial intelligence assistants are changing our lives every day.* Smartsheet. https://www.smartsheet.com/voice-assistants-artificial-intelligence

Randell, B. (1982). Introduction. In R. Brian (Ed), *The origins of digital computers: Selected papers* (pp. 1–7). Springer-Verlag.

Reaburn, C. (2019, November 13). *What is conversational AI? Get started with fundamentals.* Nextiva. https://www.nextiva.com/blog/what-is-conversational-ai.html

Reber, A. (1985). Aptitude test. In *The Penguin dictionary of psychology* (p. 6). Penguin Books.

Reichelt, M. (2005a). English in Poland. *World Englishes, 24*(2), 217–225.

Reichelt, M. (2005b). English-language writing instruction in Poland. *Journal of Second Language Writing, 14*, 215–232.

Reinders, H., & Hubbard, P. (2013). CALL and learner autonomy: Affordances and constraints. In M. Thomas, H. Reinders & M. Warschauer (Eds.), *Contemporary computer-assisted language learning* (pp. 359–376). Bloomsbury.

Reinders, H. & Benson, P. (2017). Research agenda: Language learning beyond the classroom. *Language Teaching, 50*(4), 561–578. https://doi.org/10.1017/S0261444817000192

Resnik, D. (2015). *What is ethics in research and why is it important?* National Institute of Environmental Health Sciences.

Richards, J., & Rodgers, T. (1986). *Approaches and methods in language teaching: A description and analysis.* Cambridge University Press.

Richards, J., & Rodgers, T. (2001). *Approaches and methods in language teaching. Second edition.* Cambridge University Press.

Richards, J., & Rodgers, T. (2014). *Approaches and methods in language teaching. Third edition.* Cambridge University Press.

Rivers, D. (2009). Utilizing the quick response (QR) code within a Japanese EFL environment. *The JALT CALL Journal, 5*(2), 15–28.

Roberts, J., Yaya, L., & Manolis, C. (2014). The invisible addiction: Cell-phone activities and addiction among male and female college students. *Journal of Behavioural Addictions, 3*(4), 254–265. https://doi.org/10.1556%2FJBA.3.2014.015

Robinson, P. (2001). Task complexity, task difficulty and task production: Exploring interactions in a componential framework. *Applied Linguistics, 22*(1), 27–57. https://doi.org/10.1093/applin/22.1.27

Robinson, P. (2007). Criteria for classifying and sequencing pedagogic tasks. In M. Garcia-Mayo (Ed.), *Investigating tasks in formal language learning* (pp. 7–27). Multilingual Matters.

Rodgers, T. (2001). *Language teaching methodology.* Online Resources: Digests. http://bitly.pl/JgkEo

Rogers, E. (1983). *Diffusion of innovations.* The Free Press.

Roschelle, J. (2003). Keynote paper: Unlocking the learning value of wireless mobile devices. *Journal of Computer Assisted Learning, 19*, 260–272. https://doi.org/10.1046/j.0266-4909.2003.00028.x

Rothman, D. (2016). *A tsunami of learners called generation Z.* https://mdle.net/journal/A_Tsunami_of_Learners_Called_Generation_Z.pdf

Roulet, E. (1972). *Linguistic theory, linguistic description and language teaching.* Longman.

RPO (2018). *RPO kolejny raz wskazuje MEN negatywne skutki reformy oświaty.* https://bip.brpo.gov.pl/pl/content/rpo-o-reformie-oswiaty

RPO (2019). *Reforma edukacji. Działania rzecznika praw obywatelskich w sprawie likwidacji gimnazjów.*

Rubin, A., & Peltier, E. (2018, September 20). *France bans smartphones in schools through 9th grade. Will it help students?* The New York Times. https://www.nytimes.com/2018/09/20/world/europe/france-smartphones-schools.html

Runnels, J., & Runnels, V. (2017). Impact of the Common European Framework of Reference. A bibliometric analysis of research from 1990–2017. *CEFR Journal, 1*, 18–32.

Russell, S., & Norvig, P. (2010). *Artificial intelligence: A modern approach.* Prentice Hall.

Rustipa, K. (2011). Suggestopedia: How does it accelerate language learning? *LITE: Jurnal Bahasa, Sastra, dan Budaya, 7*(1), 1–7.

Ruzkova, I., Kolinska, K., & Drahna, U. (n.d.). *Nowy egzamin maturalny w Republice Czeskiej.* Polskie Towarzystwo Diagnostyki Edukacyjnej. Retrieved March, 14, 2021, from http://www.ptde.org/pluginfile.php/11/mod_page/content/19/59.pdf

Rysak, D. (2010). Jakie typy tekstów rozwijają sprawność komunikacyjną uczących się języka polskiego jako obcego? *Acta Universitatis Lodziensis. Kształcenie Polonistyczne Cudzoziemców, 17*, 285–292.

Rysiewicz, J. (2008). Measuring foreign language learning aptitude. Polish adaptation of the modern language aptitude test by Carroll and Sapon. *Poznan Studies in Contemporary Linguistics, 44*(4), 569–595.

Sabharwal, A. (2020). *The world's first human centric AI.* CoRover. https://query.prod.cms.rt.microsoft.com/cms/api/am/binary/RWF8eT

Sabzian, F., & Gilakjani, A. (2013). Teachers' attitudes about computer technology training, professional development, integration, experience, anxiety and literacy in English language teaching and learning. *International Journal of Applied Science and Technology, 3*(1), 67–75.

Salaberry, M. (2001). The use of technology for second language learning and teaching: A retrospective. *The Modern Language Journal, 85*(1), 39–56. https://doi.org/10.1111/0026-7902.00096

Salmani-Nodoushan, M. (2006). Language teaching: State of the art. *The Reading Matrix, 6*(2), 125–140.

Sauro, S., & Zourou, K. (2017). Call for papers for CALL in the digital wilds. Special Issue. *Language Learning & Technology, 21*(1), 186.

Savignon, S. (1972). *Communicative competence: An experiment in foreign language teaching.* The Centre for Curriculum Development

Savignon, S. (2018). Communicative competence. In J. Liontas (Ed.), *TESOL encyclopaedia of English language teaching* (pp. 1–7). Wiley.

Schetzer, H., & Warschauer, M. (2000). An electronic literacy approach to networked-based language teaching. In M. Warschauer & R. Kern (Eds.), *Networked-based language teaching: Concepts and practice* (pp. 171–185). Cambridge University Press.

School cell phone ban causes uproar (2006, May 12). CBS News. https://www.cbsnews.com/news/school-cell-phone-ban-causes-uproar/

Schroer, W. (2008). Defining, managing and marketing to generations X, Y and Z. *Portal*, *40*, 9.

Schulze, M. (2008). AI in CALL: Artificially inflated or almost imminent? *CALICO Journal*, *25*(3), 510–527.

Schulze, M. (2010). Taking intelligent CALL to task. In M. Thomas & H. Reinders (Eds.), *Task-based language learning and teaching with technology* (pp. 63–82). Continuum International Publishing Group.

Schulze, M., & Heift, T. (2012). Intelligent CALL. In M. Thomas, H. Reinders & M. Warschauer (Eds.), *Contemporary computer-assisted language learning* (pp. 249–266). Bloomsbury.

Schwartz, E. (2021, December 8). *Estonia will launch Bürokratt voice assistant for government services in 2022.* Voicebot.ai. https://voicebot.ai/2021/12/08/estonia-will-launch-burokratt-voice-assistant-for-government-services-in-2022 /

Science: Shoebox is listening (1961). Time. http://content.time.com/time/subscriber/article/0,33009,828878,00.html

Segal, E. (2021, December 28). *A crisis is averted after Amazon's Alexa tells child about lethal viral challenge.* Forbes. https://www.forbes.com/sites/edwardsegal/2021/12/28/a-crisis-is-averted-after-amazons-alexa-tells-child-about-lethal-viral-challenge/

Self, J. (1994). The role of student models in learning environments. *IEICE Transactions on Information and Systems*, *77*(1), 3–8.

Selinker, L. (1972). Interlanguage. *IRAL: International Review of Applied Linguistics in Language Teaching*, *10*(1), 209–232. https://doi.org/10.1515/iral.1972.10.1-4.209

Sewastianowicz, M. (2021). *Raport: Pandemia przyspieszyła cyfryzację uczelni.* Prawo. https://www.prawo.pl/student/szkolnictwo-wyzsze-a-technologie-2021-raport-wolters-kluwer-i,510537.html

Shadwell, T. (2021, July 5). *Mobile phones could be banned from schools in England as early as January.* Mirror. https://www.mirror.co.uk/news/politics/mobile-phones-could-banned-schools-24459075

Shafiee, S., Akbari, S., & Hajijalili, M. (2019). Comparing the impact of CALL-based versus non-CALL-based methods of instruction on reading comprehension among Iranian upper-intermediate EFL learners. *Language in India*, *19*(5), 33–49.

Shanks, D. (2021). Technology-facilitated oral homework: Leveraging technology to get students speaking outside the classroom. In T. Beaven & F. Rosell-Aguilar (Eds), *Innovative language pedagogy report* (pp. 69–75). Researchpublishing.net.

Sheen, R. (1994). A critical analysis of the advocacy of the task-based syllabus. *TESOL Quarterly*, *28*(1), 127–151. https://doi.org/10.2307/3587202

Shewan, D. (2022, April 22). *10 of the most innovative chatbots on the Web*. WordStream. https://www.wordstream.com/blog/ws/2017/10/04/chatbots

Shokrpour, N., Mirshekari, Z., & Moslehi, S. (2019). Learning vocabulary electronically: Does computer assisted language learning (CALL) instruction have any impacts on Iranian EFL learners? *Cogent Education*, *6*(1), 1–20. https://doi.org/10.1080/2331186X.2019.1702827

Sholeh, M., & Talebinejad, M. (2022). ESP via TBLT in an online environment: Focus on Iranian university students' writing skill and self-efficacy. *International Journal of Language Studies*, *16*(1), 1–10.

Sienicki, W. (1957). W sprawie nauczania języków zachodnioeuropejskich. *Języki Obce w Szkole*, *3*, 130–131.

Sierra, F. (1995). Foreign language teaching methods. Some issues and new moves. *Encuentro: Revista de investigación e innovación en la clase de idiomas*, *13*(8), 110–132.

Silverstone, R. (2002). Complicity and collusion in the mediation of everyday life. *New Literary History*, *33*(4), 761–780.

Simensen, A. (1999). Shifts of paradigm: A dilemma in foreign language didactics as a major component in the education of teachers. *TNTEE Publications*, *2*, 187–194.

Singh, A., & Dangmei, J. (2016). Understanding the generation Z: The future workforce. *South-Asian Journal of Multidisciplinary Studies*, *3*(3), 1–5.

Singh, M., & Samah, N. (2018). Impact of smartphone: A review on positive and negative effects on students. *Asian Social Science*, *14*(11), 83–89. https://doi.org/10.5539/ass.v14n11p83

Sirotova, M., Michvocikowa, V., & Rubacha, K. (2021). Quasi-experiment in the educational reality. *Journal of Education, Culture and Society*, *1*, 189–201. https://doi.org/10.15503/jecs2021.1.189.201

Sitek, M. (2015). Miejsce egzaminów zewnętrznych w systemach edukacyjnych i polityce edukacyjne. In D. Roman & M. Sitek (Eds.), *Egzaminy zewnętrzne w polityce i praktyce edukacyjnej. Raport o stanie edukacji* (pp. 11–29). Instytut Badań Edukacyjnych.

Skehan, P. (1996a). A framework for the implementation of task-based instruction. *Applied Linguistics, 17*(1), 38–62. https://doi.org/10.1093/applin/17.1.38

Skehan, P. (1996b). Second language acquisition research and task based instruction. In J. Willis & D. Willis (Eds.), *Challenge and change in language teaching* (pp. 17–30). Heinemann.

Skehan, P. (1998). *A cognitive approach to language learning.* Oxford University Press.

Skinner, B. (1957). *Verbal behaviour*. Appleton-Century-Crofts.

Skolverket (2005). *National assessment and grading in the Swedish school system.* http://bitly.pl/uLTde

SKVC (n.d.). *Education in Lithuania. General education.* https://www.skvc.lt/default/en/education-in-lithuania/general

Słomczyński, K., Andrejuk, K., Wysieńska, K., Kołczyńska, M., Baczko-Dombi, A., Jarosz, E., Wysmułek, E., Franczak, A., Życzyńska-Ciołek, D., Sztabiński, P., Sztabiński, F., Mikucka, M., Kunovich, S., & Marquart-Pyatt, S. (2014). *Podstawowe informacje o polskim badaniu panelowym POLPAN 1988–2013.* POLPAN. https://polpan.org/wp-content/uploads/2014/05/Podstawowe-informacje.pdf

Smith, A., & Wempen, F. (2011). *CompTIA strata study guide.* John Wiley.

Smolik, M., & Trzcińska, B. (2011) *Zmiany w systemie egzaminów* (2012–2015) *a europejski system opisu kształcenia językowego* [PowerPoint presentation]. http://beta.eduentuzjasci.pl/images/stories/newsy/01.pdf

Smolik, M., (2012). Języki obce na egzaminach zewnętrznych: Innowacje w latach 2012–2015. *Języki Obce w Szkole, 1*, 22–33.

Smolik, M., & Poszytek, P. (2017). Podstawa programowa kształcenia ogólnego w zakresie języka obcego nowożytnego w wychowaniu przedszkolnym i ośmioletniej szkole podstawowej: Słowo komentarza. *Języki Obce w Szkole, 1*, 70–82.

Social Lens Research (2018). *Voice commands: Current state.* http://bitly.pl/R5j3E

Son, J., Thomas R., & Charismiadji, I. (2011). Computer literacy and competency: A survey of Indonesian teachers of English as a foreign language. *Computer-Assisted Language Learning Electronic Journal, 12*(1), 26–42.

Squire, K. (2009). Mobile media learning: Multiplicities of place. *On the Horizon, 17*(1), 70–80. https://doi.org/10.1108/10748120910936162

Srikanth, A. (2020, November 5). *Virtual assistants vs chatbots: What's the difference and how to choose the right one?* Freshdesk Blog. https://freshdesk.com/customer-engagement/virtual-assistant-chatbot-blog/

Stathopoulou, M. (2011, December 22). *Written mediation task description and analysis* [Paper presentation]. 3rd Postgraduate Student Conference in Applied Linguistics, Athens, Greece.

Stathopoulou, M. (2014). The linguistic characteristics of KPG written mediation tasks across proficiency levels. In N. Lavidas, T. Alexiou & A. Sougari (Eds.), *Major trends in theoretical and applied linguistics* (pp. 349–366). Versita.

Stathopoulou, M. (2015). *Cross-language mediation in foreign language teaching and testing*. Multilingual Matters.

Stathopoulou, M. (2021). Language education for students from migrant and refugee backgrounds: Exploiting the new CEFR descriptor scales for mediation. In M. Mattheoudakis, E. Griva & M. Moumtzi (Eds.), *Migration and language education in southern Europe: Practices And challenges* (pp. 37–53). Cambridge Scholars Publishing.

Stern, H. (1983). *Fundamental concepts of language teaching*. Oxford University Press.

Stewart, I., & File, P. (2007). Let's chat: A conversational dialogue system for second language practice. *Computer Assisted Language Learning, 20*(2), 97–116. https://doi.org/10.1080/09588220701331386

Stevens, V. (1989). A direction for CALL: From behavioristic to humanistic courseware. In M. Pennington (Ed.), *Teaching languages with computers: The state of the art* (pp. 31–43). Athelstan.

Stockwell, G. (2007). Vocabulary on the move: Investigating an intelligent mobile phone-based vocabulary tutor. *Computer Assisted Language Learning, 20*(4), 365–383. https://doi.org/10.1080/09588220701745817

Stockwell, G. (2009). Teacher education in CALL: Teaching teachers to educate themselves. *International Journal of Innovation in Language Learning and Teaching, 3*(1), 99–112. https://doi.org/10.1080/17501220802655524

Stockwell, G. (2012). *Computer assisted language learning*. Cambridge University Press.

Stockwell, G. (2022). *Mobile assisted language learning: Concepts, contexts and challenges*. Cambridge University Press.

Stockwell, G., & Hubbard, P. (2013). *Some emerging principles for mobile-assisted language learning*. The International Research Foundation for English Language Education.

Stone, J. (2017, October 26). *Companion robot helping patients with Alzheimer's*. University of Denver. https://www.du.edu/news/companion-robot-helping-patients-alzheimers

Strauss, M. (2016, October 4). *Demanded by Alexa, Cortana and Siri: Why Chatbots will be the new apps!* Linkedin. https://www.linkedin.com/pulse/demanded-alexa-cortana-siri-why-chatbots-new-apps-michael-strauss

Stufflebeam, D., McCormick, C., Brinkerhoff, R., & Nelson, C. (1985). *Conducting educational needs assessments*. Kluwer Academic Publishers.

Strzałkowski, M. (2019, August, 2). *Niemcy: Asystenci głosowi Google już nie mogą podsłuchiwać*. Euractiv.pl. https://www.euractiv.pl/section/gospodarka/news/niemcy-komisarz-ds-ochrony-danych-zabronil-google-podsluchiwania-przez-asystentow-glosowych/

Suarez, B. (2021). The ethics of digital voice assistants. *Viterbi Conversations in Ethics*, *5*(1).

Sujecka-Zając, J. (2016). *Kompetentny uczeń na lekcji języka obcego: wyzwania dla glottodydaktyki mediacyjnej*. Wydawnictwo Werset.

Surface, E., & Dierdorff, E. (2003). Reliability and the ACTFL oral proficiency interview: Reporting indices of interrater consistency and agreement for 19 languages. *Foreign Language Annals*, *36*(4), 507–519. https://doi.org/10.1111/j.1944-9720.2003.tb02140.x

SurveyLang (n.d.). *About the survey*. http://www.surveylang.org/About-SurveyLang/About-the-survey.html

Swain, M. (1985). Communicative competence: Some roles of comprehensible input and comprehensible output in its development. In S. Gass & C. Madden (Eds.), *Input in second language acquisition* (pp. 235–253). Newbury House.

Swain, M. (2005). The output hypothesis: Theory and research. In E. Hinkel (Ed.), *Handbook of research in second language teaching and learning* (pp. 471–483). Routledge.

Swain, M. (2006). Languaging, agency and collaboration in advanced second language proficiency. In Byrnes H. (Ed.), *Advanced language learning: The Contribution of Halliday and Vygotsky* (pp. 95–108). Continuum.

Sydorenko, T., Daurio, P., & L. Thorne, S. (2018). Refining pragmatically-appropriate oral communication via computer-simulated conversations. *Computer Assisted Language Learning*, *31*(1–2), 157–180. https://doi.org/10.1080/09588221.2017.1394326

Szczepanek, M. (2018). Przemiany polskiego systemu edukacji podstawowej od lat 80. XX wieku. *Edukacja – Technika – Informatyka*, *4*(26), 524–528.

Szpotowicz, M. (2011). *Nowa podstawa programowa a europejski system opisu kształcenia językowego* [PowerPoint presentation]. http://bitly.pl/kqn0f

Szostek, A. (2020). Raczej przyspieszenie niż rewolucja. In J. Lubacz (Ed.), *Nauczanie po pandemii. Nowe pytania czy nowe odpowiedzi na stare pytania?* (pp. 147–148). Wydawnictwo SGGW.

Śliwa, M. (2010). Catching up with civilization: Reflections on language spread in Poland. *Journal of Organizational Change Management*, *23*(6), 689–709.

Śliwerski, B. (1999). Remanent reformowania oświaty w III RP. *Edukacja i Dialog, 3*, 30–36.

Tafazoli, D., & Golshan, N. (2014). Review of computer-assisted language learning: History, merits and barriers. *International Journal of Language and Linguistics, 2*(5-1), 32–38.

Taher, A., & Hussein, J. (2019). A review of intelligent mobile assisted language learning (IMALL) system. *International Journal of English Language Literature in Humanities, 7*(4), 879–892.

Taherdoost, H. (2019). What is the best response scale for survey and questionnaire design: Review of different lengths of rating scale/attitude scale/ Likert scale. *International Journal of Academic Research in Management, 8*(1), 1–10.

Tai, T., & Chen, H. (2020). The impact of Google Assistant on adolescent EFL learners' willingness to communicate. *Interactive Learning Environments*, 1–18. https://doi.org/10.1080/10494820.2020.1841801

Tai, T., & Chen, H. (2022). The impact of intelligent personal assistants on adolescent EFL learners' listening comprehension. *Computer Assisted Language Learning*, 1–28. https://doi.org/10.1080/09588221.2022.2040536

Talley, P., & Tu, H. (2016). A relative comparison made of two teaching methodologies: The examples of suggestopedia vs. total physical response. *International Journal of Humanities and Social Science, 6*(4), 40–46.

Tarone, E. (2014). Enduring questions from the interlanguage hypothesis. In Z. Han & E. Tarone (Eds.), *Interlanguage. Forty years later* (pp. 7–26). John Benjamins.

Tavakoli, H., Lotfi, A., & Biria, R. (2019). Effects of CALL-mediated TBLT on motivation for L2 reading. *Cogent Education, 6*(1), 1–21.

Tavakoli, H., & Loth, A. (2021). The impact of CALL-mediated TBLT on L2 reading comprehension. *Journal of Educators Online, 18*(2), 142–157.

Taylor, J. (2006). Evaluating mobile learning: What are appropriate methods for evaluating learning in mobile environments. *Big Issues in Mobile Learning, 1*(3), 25–27.

Taylor, L. (2005). Washback and impact. *ELT Journal, 59*(2), 154–155.

Taylor, P. (2023). *Number of smartphone mobile network subscriptions worldwide from 2016 to 2022, with forecasts from 2023 to 2028*. Statista. https://www.statista.com/statistics/330695/number-of-smartphone-users-worldwide/

Taylor, R. (1980). *The computer in the school: Tutor, tool, tutee*. Teachers College Press.

Taylor, R., & Gitsaki, C. (2004). Teaching WELL and loving IT. In S. Fotos & C. Browne (Eds.), *New perspectives on CALL for second language classrooms* (pp. 143–160). Routledge.

Terell, S. (2012). Mixed-methods research methodologies. *The Qualitative Report, 17*(1), 254–280. https://doi.org/10.46743/2160-3715/2012.1819

Terzopoulos, G., & Satratzemi, M. (2019, September 26–28). *Voice assistants and artificial intelligence in education* [Paper presentation]. 9th Balkan Conference on Informatics, Sofia, Bulgaria.

TESOL International Association (2014). *Research agenda 2014.* https://www.tesol.org/media/z22pn2hw/2014_tesol-research-agenda.pdf

Thompson, C. (2018). *The case for the six-point Likert scale.* Quantum Workplace. https://www.quantumworkplace.com/future-of-work/the-case-for-the-six-point-likert-scale

Thornton, P., & Houser, C. (2003). Using mobile web and video phones in English language teaching: Projects with Japanese college students. In B. Morrison, C. Green & G. Motteram (Eds.), *Directions in CALL: Experience, experiments and evaluation* (pp. 207–224). English Language Centre/Hong Kong Polytechnic University.

Thuy, N., & Yukawa, T. (2021). Mobile devices applied in self-studying English as a foreign language among non-native students in Vietnam and Japan. *International Journal of Interactive Mobile Technologies, 16*(9), 70–87. https://doi.org/10.3991/ijim.v15i09.19993

Toland, S., Mills, D., & Kohyama, M. (2016). Enhancing Japanese university students' English-language presentation skills with mobile-video recordings. *JALT CALL Journal, 12*(3), 179–201. https://doi.org/10.29140/jaltcall.v12n3.207

Tosun, F., & Glover, P. (2020). How do school teachers in Turkey perceive and use the CEFR? *International Online Journal of Education and Teaching, 7*(4), 1731–1739.

Toyoda, E., & Harrison, R. (2002). Categorization of text chat communication between learners and native speakers of Japanese. *Language Learning and Technology, 6*(1), 82–99.

Traxler, J. (2005). Defining mobile learning. In P. Isaias, C. Borg, P. Kommers & P. Bonanno (Eds.), *Proceedings of the IADIS international conference mobile learning 2005* (pp. 261–266). International Association for Development of the Information Society.

Traxler, J. (2009). Current state of mobile learning. In M. Ally (Ed.), *Mobile learning: Transforming the delivery of education and training* (pp. 9–24). Marquis Book Printing.

Trifonova, A., Knapp, J., Ronchetti, M., & Gamper, J. (2004). *Mobile ELDIT: Challenges in the transition from an e-learning to an m-learning system* (Report No. DIT-04–009). Universa di Trento. http://eprints.biblio.unitn.it/532/

Trim, J. (2001). *The work of the Council of Europe in the field of modern languages, 1957–2001*. European Centre for Modern Languages. http://bitly.pl/p9pvu

Trim, J. (2010). The modern languages programme of the Council of Europe as a background to the English profile programme. *English Profile Journal, 1(1)*, 1–12. https://doi.org/10.1017/s2041536210000097

Trinder, J. (2005). Mobile technologies and systems. In J. Traxler & A. Kukulska-Hulme (Eds.), *Mobile learning: A handbook for educators and trainers* (pp. 7–24). Routledge.

Turkle, S. (2015). *Reclaiming conversation: The power of talk in a digital age*. Penguin Press.

Twarog, L., & Pereszlenyi-Pinter, M. (1988). Telephone-assisted language study at Ohio State University: A report. *Modern Language Journal*, *72*(4), 426–434. https://doi.org/10.1111/j.1540-4781.1988.tb04204.x

UCAS (2016). *Germany: Zeugnis der Allgemeinen Hochschulreife*. https://qips.ucas.com/qip/germany-zeugnis-der-allgemeinen-hochschulreife-abitur

UCAS (2017). *Hungary: Érettségi bizonyítvány*. https://qips.ucas.com/qip/hungary-erettsegi-bizonyitvany

Uchwat-Zaród, D. (2020). Czy doświadczenie edukacji zdalnej zmieni polską szkołę? *Języki Obce w Szkole*, *4*, 7–10.

Uchwat-Zaród, D. (2020). Edukacja zdalna: Od mądrej dydaktyki do narzędzi cyfrowych. *Języki Obce w Szkole*, *2*, 45–48.

Underwood, J. (1984), *Linguistics, computers and the language teacher: A communicative approach*. Newbury House Publishers.

Underwood, J. (2017). Exploring AI language assistants with primary EFL students. In K. Borthwick, L. Bradley & S. Thouesny (Eds.), *CALL in a climate of change: Adapting to turbulent global conditions. Short Papers from EUROCALL 2017* (pp. 317–321). Research-publishing.net.

Underwood, J. (2021). Speaking to machines: Motivating speaking through oral interaction with intelligent assistants. In T. Beaven & F. Rosell-Aguilar (Eds.), *Innovative language pedagogy report* (pp. 127–132). Researchpublishing.net.

UNESCO (2018). *UNESCO ICT competency framework for teachers*. https://unesdoc.unesco.org/ark:/48223/pf0000265721

UNESCO (2013). *UNESCO policy guidelines for mobile learning*. https://unesdoc.unesco.org/ark:/48223/pf0000219641

Urlaub, P. (2012). Reading strategies and literature instruction: Teaching learners to generate questions to foster literary reading in the second language. *System*, *40*(2), 296–304. https://doi.org/10.1016/j.system.2012.05.002

Using the Gouin series in the foreign language classroom. (2012, February 10). World Language Classroom. https://wlclassroom.com/2012/02/10/using-the-gouin-series-is-the-foreign-language-classroom/

Vahdat, S., & Eidipour, M. (2016). Adopting CALL to improve listening comprehension of Iranian junior high school students. *Theory and practice in language studies, 6*(8), 1609–1617. https://doi.org/10.17507/tpls.0608.13

Vainu, I. (2021, February 16). What is an intelligent virtual assistant? Alpha chat. https://www.alphachat.ai/blog/what-is-an-intelligent-virtual-assistant

van Avermaet, P., & Gysen, S. (2009). From needs to tasks. Language learning needs in a task-based approach. In K. Van den Branden, M. Bygate & J. M. Norris (Eds.), *Task-based language teaching. A reader* (pp. 144–170). John Benjamins.

van Ek, J. (1975). *Systems development in adult language learning: The threshold level in a European unit credit system for modern language learning by adults.* Council of Europe. https://files.eric.ed.gov/fulltext/ED108482.pdf

van Lier, L. (2007). Action-based teaching, autonomy and identity. *International Journal of Innovation in Language Learning and Teaching, 1*(1), 46–65.

van Lier, L. (2008). Ecological-semiotic perspectives on educational linguistics. In B. Spolsky & F. Hult (Eds.), *The handbook of educational linguistics* (pp. 596–605). Blackwell Publishing.

Verspoor, K., & Cohen, K. (2013). Natural language processing. In W. Dubitzky, O. Wolkenhauer, K.-H. Cho & H. Yokota (Eds.), *Encyclopaedia of systems biology* (pp. 1495–1498). Springer.

Viberg, O., & Gronlund, A. (2013). Systematising the field of mobile assisted language learning. *International Journal of Mobile and Blended Learning, 5*(4), 72–90. https://doi.org/10.4018/ijmbl.2013100105

Viken, A. (2009, April 10). *The history of personal digital assistants 1980–2000.* Agile Mobility. https://web.archive.org/web/20131030153659/http://agilemobility.net/2009/04/the-history-of-personal-digital-assistants1/

Vishnoi, L. (2020, June 30*). Conversational agent: A more assertive form of chatbots.* Towards Data Science. https://towardsdatascience.com/conversational-agent-a-more-assertive-form-of-chatbots-de6f1c8da8dd

Vourdoumpa, A. (2018, June 26). *Greece bans mobile phones in schools.* SBS Greek. https://www.sbs.com.au/language/english/greece-bans-mobile-phones-in-schools

Vygotsky, L. (1978). *Mind in society: The development of higher psychological processes.* Harvard University Press.

Walczak, M. (2015). Kompetencje Polaków w zakresie języków obcych i ich wpływ na działalność przedsiębiorstw. *Polskie Towarzystwo Profesjologiczne, 2*, 127–137.

Walker, R., Davies, G., & Hewer, S. (2012). Introduction to the Internet. Module 1.5. In G. Davies (Ed.), *Information and communications technology for language teachers (ICT4LT)*. Thames Valley University. http://www.ict4lt.org/en/en_mod1-4.htm

Walker, T. (2017, September 15). *Technology makes it easier, but what do we really know about why students cheat?* National Educational Association. https://www.nea.org/advocating-for-change/new-from-nea/technology-makes-it-easier-what-do-we-really-know-about-why

Wang, B. (2017). Designing mobile apps for English vocabulary learning. *International Journal of Information and Education Technology*, *7*, 279–283. https://doi.org/10.18178/ijiet.2017.7.4.881

Wang, H. (2012, July 9). *Father of the cellphone "unleashed" world's callers from copper wires*. Npr.

Warschauer, M. (1996). Computer assisted language learning: An introduction. In S. Fotos (Ed.), *Multimedia language teaching* (pp. 3–20). Logos International.

Warschauer, M., & Healey, D. (1998). Computers and language learning: An overview. *Language Teaching*, *31*(2), 57–71. https://doi.org/10.1017/S0261444800012970

Warschauer, M. (2000). The death of cyberspace and the rebirth of CALL. *English Teachers' Journal*, *53*, 61–67.

Warschauer, M. (2004). Technological change and the future of CALL. In S. Fotos & C. Brown (Eds.), *New perspectives on CALL for second language classrooms* (pp. 15–25). Lawrence Erlbaum.

Warschauer, M., Turbee, L., & Roberts, B. (1996). Computer learning networks and student empowerment. *System*, *24*(1), 1–14. https://doi.org/10.1016/0346-251X(95)00049-P

Watanabe, Y. (2006). A needs analysis for a Japanese high school EFL general education curriculum. *Second Language Studies*, *25*(1), 83–163.

Weischedel, R., Voge, W., & James, M. (1978). An artificial intelligence approach to language instruction. *Artificial Intelligence*, *10*, 225–240. https://doi.org/10.1016/S0004-3702(78)80015-0

West, R. (1994). Needs analysis in language teaching. *Language Teaching*, *27*(1), 1–19. https://doi.org/10.1017/s0261444800007527

What is the Callan method? (n.d.). callanschool.info. https://www.callanschool.info/en/callan-method

White, R. (1988) *The ELT curriculum*. Blackwell Publishers.

Wickstrom, G., & Bendix, T. (2000). The Hawthorne effect: What did the original Hawthorne studies actually show? *Scandinavian Journal of Work, Environment and Health*, *26*(4), 363–367. https://doi.org/10.5271/sjweh.555

Wieluniecka, A. (2010). Ekspansja anglicyzmów w języku reklamy prasowej. *Linguistica Copernicana, 2*(4). 263–272.

Wiggins III, R. (2004). Personal digital assistants. *Journal of Digital Imaging, 17*(1), 5–17. https://doi.org/10.1007/s10278-003-1665-8

Wilczyńska, W., & Michońska-Stadnik, A. (2010). *Metodologia badań w glottodydaktyce Wprowadzenie*. Avalon.

Wilkins, D. (1974). Notional syllabuses and the concept of a minimum adequate grammar. In S. Corder & E. Roulet (Eds), *Linguistic insights in applied linguistics* (pp. 119–128). Didier.

Williams, R. (1983 [1976]). *Keywords: A vocabulary of culture and society*. Fontana Press.

Willis, J. (1994). Task-based language learning as an alternative to PPP. *The Teacher Trainer, 8*(1), 17–20.

Willis, J. (1996). *A framework for task-based learning*. Longman.

Willis, J. (2004). Perspectives on task-based instruction: Understanding our practices, acknowledging different practitioners. In B. Leaver & J. Willis (Eds.), *Task-based instruction in foreign language education: Practices and programs* (pp. 3–44). Georgetown University Press.

Wirtualni asystenci AI a chatboty (2019, May 9). IBM Cloud Education. https://www.ibm.com/pl-pl/cloud/learn/chatbots-explained

Wise, D. (2021, December 28). *Amazon responds after Alexa encourages dangerous penny challenge*. 9to5Mac. https://9to5mac.com/2021/12/28/amazon-responds-after-alexa-encourages-dangerous-penny-challenge/

Wiśniewski, J., & Zahorska, M. (2020). Reforming education in Poland. In F. Reimers (Ed.), *Audacious education purposes. How governments transform the goals of education systems* (pp. 181–208). Springer Open.

Wojtaszek, B. (1998a). *Tematy i zagadnienia maturalne. Język angielski. Część 1. Matura '99*. Wydawnictwo Szkolne Omega.

Wojtaszek, B. (1998b). *Tematy maturalne. Język angielski. Część 2. Matura '99*. Wydawnictwo Szkolne Omega.

Woodall, B. (2010). Simultaneous listening and reading in ESL: Helping second language learners read (and enjoy reading) more efficiently. *TESOL Journal, 1*(2), 186–205. https://doi.org/10.5054/tj.2010.220151

Wróblewska-Pawlak, K., & Strachanowska, I. (2000). Preferencje językowe młodzieży polskiej w okresie transformacji: 1990–1999. *Studia Europejskie, 1*, 99–114.

Wysmułek, I., & Oleksiyenko, O. (2015). *Strukturalne zróżnicowanie znajomości języków obcych*. POLPAN.

Yamaguchi. T., (2005, August 2–4). *Vocabulary learning with a mobile phone* [Paper presentation]. 10th Anniversary Conference of Pan-Pacific Association of Applied Linguistics, Edinburgh, UK.

Yaman, I., & Ekmekci, E. (2016). A shift from CALL to MALL? *Participatory Educational Research. Special Issue*, *4*, 25–32.

Yang, J. (2013). Mobile assisted language learning: Review of the recent applications of emerging mobile technologies. *English Language Teaching*, *6*(7), 19–25. https://doi.org/10.5539/elt.v6n7p19

Yang, Y. (2010). Computer-assisted foreign language teaching: Theory and practice. *Journal of Language Teaching and Research*, *1*(6), 909–912. https://doi.org/10.4304/jltr.1.6.909-912

Yang, X., Aurisicchio, M., & Baxter, W. (2019, May 4–9). *Understanding affective experiences with conversational agents* [Paper presentation]. CHI '19: CHI Conference on Human Factors in Computing Systems, Glasgow, Scotland.

Yedla, S. (2013). MALL (Mobile assisted language learning): A paradise for English language learners. *Journal of English Language & Translation Studies*, *1*(2), 91–99.

Yeh, H., & Lai, P. (2012). Implementing online question generation to foster reading comprehension. *Australasian Journal of Educational Technology*, *28*(7), 1152–1175. https://doi.org/10.14742/ajet.794

Zając, H. (2007). *Ewolucja teorii nauczania języka rosyjskiego w szkole polskiej w latach 1950–2000*. Wydawnictwo Naukowe Akademii Pedagogicznej.

Zając, T. (2016). Wartość prognostyczna wyników rekrutacyjnych dla powodzenia w studiowaniu. *Edukacja*, *1*(136), 114–128.

Zakolska, K. (n.d.). *Analiza porównawcza egzaminu ósmoklasisty z egzaminem w klasie trzeciej gimnazjum na poziomie podstawowym oraz rozszerzonym*. Macmillan Polska. https://www.macmillan.pl/files/Analiza_Egzamin8kl_vs_EgzGimn.pdf

Zaranis, N., Kalogiannakis, M., & Papadakis, S. (2013). Using mobile devices for teaching realistic mathematics in kindergarten education. *Creative Education*, *4*(7A1), 1–10. https://doi.org/10.4236/ce.2013.47a1001

Zawadowska-Kittel, E. (2017). Matura z języków obcych w świetle zmian edukacyjnych. *Języki Obce w Szkole*, *4*, 65–70.

Zemcik, T. (2019, June 23–24). *A brief history of chatbots* [Paper presentation]. AICAE 2019: 2019 International Conference on Artificial Intelligence, Control and Automation Engineering, Wuhan, China.

Legal sources:

Act of December 14, 2016 on the education law, *Journal of Laws*, Item 59, Article 99.

Act of January 8, 1999 on the provisions introducing the reform of the education system, *Journal of Laws*, No. 12, Item 96 (1999).

Act of July 15, 1961 on the development of the education and pedagogical system, *Journal of Laws*, No. 32, Item 160 (1965).

Act of July 25, 1998 on the change in the education system, *Journal of Laws*, No. 117, Item 759 (1998).

Act of November 5, 2009 on the change of the act – law on higher education, *Journal of Laws*, No. 202, Item 1553 (2009).

Act of October 7, 1999 on the Polish language, *Journal of Laws*, No. 90, Item 999 (1999).

Act of September 7, 1991 on the education system, *Journal of Laws*, No. 95, Item 425 (1991).

Announcement of the Marshal of the Sejm of the Republic of Poland on May 7, 2020 regarding the consolidated text of the aAct – education law, *Journal of Laws*, Item 910 (2020).

Announcement of the Marshal of the Sejm of the Republic of Poland on May 22, 2020 regarding the consolidated Act – education law, *Journal of Laws*, Item 910 (2020).

Announcement of the Minister of Education on May 16, 1996 regarding the consolidated text of the Act on the education system, *Journal of Laws*, No. 67, Item 329 (1996).

Ordinance No. 55 of the Minister of Education on September 4, 1989 regarding the administration of the Matura exam, *Official Journal of the Ministry of Education*, No. 6, Item 56 (1989).

Ordinance of the Minister of Education on May 4, 1948, regarding the organisation of the 1948/49 school year in secondary school education, *Official Journal of the Ministry of Education*, No. 5, Item 86 (1948). http://mbc.cyfrowemazowsze.pl/dlibra/plain-content?id=25951

Ordinance of the Minister of Education on June, 15 1991 regarding teacher training and foreign language teacher training colleges, *Official Journal of the Ministry of Education*, No. 3, Item 15 (1991).

Ordinance of the Minister of Education on September 25, 1965, regarding the adaptation of secondary and vocational schools to the changes introduced by the act on the education and pedagogical system, *Official Journal of the Republic of Poland*, No. 54, Item 282 (1965).

Regulation No. 5 of the Minister of Education on February 2, 1990 regarding teaching frameworks for comprehensive schools and changes to teaching framework for vocational schools, *Official Journal of the Ministry of Education*, No. 2, Item 8 (1990).

Regulation of the Minister of Education on January 30, 2018 regarding the Core Curriculum for general education in secondary, technical, and vocational schools (level 1), *Journal of Laws*, Item 467 (2018).

Regulation of the Minister of Education on May 30, 2014 changing the regulation regarding the Core Curriculum for pre-primary school education and general education in particular types of schools, *Journal of Laws*, Item 803 (2014).

Regulation of the Minister of Education on December 23, 2008 regarding the Core Curriculum for pre-primary school education and general education in particular types of schools, *Journal of Laws*, No. 4, Item 17 (2008).

Regulation of the Minister of Education on February 15, 1999 regarding the adaptation of primary schools to the requirements of the new educational system and the creation of middle schools, *Journal of Laws*, No. 14, Item 124 (1999).

Republic of Poland (2017). Regulation of the Minister of Education on February 24, 2017 regarding the Core Curriculum for pre-primary school education and the Core Curriculum for general education in primary schools, including students with moderate and significant intellectual disabilities, general education for vocational schools (level 1), general education for special vocational training schools, and general education for post-secondary schools, *Journal of Laws*, Item 356.

Regulation of the Minister of Education on February 15, 1999 regarding the Core Curriculum for general education. *Journal of Laws*, No 14, Item 129 (1999).

Appendices

A. List of the selected bilingual schools in Poland

Warsaw	Stefan Żeromski Secondary School Nicolaus Copernicus Bilingual School Stefan Batory Secondary School Księżna Izabela Czartoryska Secondary School Robert Schuman Secondary School
Lublin	Nauczyciele Tajnego Nauczania Secondary School Paderewski Secondary School
Poznań	38 Bilingual School Dąbrówka Secondary School
Katowice	Maria Konopnicka Secondary School Harcerzy Obrońców Secondary School
Gdańsk	Lech Bądkowski Secondary School Zbigniew Herbert Secondary School
Białystok	Księżna Anna z Sapiehów Jabłonowska Secondary School
Rzeszów	Stanisław Baranczak Bilingual School 9 Secondary School with Bilingual Classes
Łódź	Emilia Sczaniecka Secondary School 11 Secondary School Adam Asnyk Secondary School
Kraków	Młoda Polska Secondary School Leopold Staff Secondary School Adam Mickiewicz Secondary School
Wrocław	Bolesław Krzywousty Bilingual School EKOLA Bilingual School
Opole	Maria Skłodowska-Curie Secondary School
Szczecin	11 Secondary School with Bilingual Classes Adam Asnyk Secondary School
Kielce	Stefan Żeromski Secondary School

B. Background questionnaire

Kwestionariusz dotyczący doświadczeń uczniów związanych z nauką języka angielskiego

1. Jak długo uczysz się języka angielskiego? Swoją odpowiedź zaokrąglij do liczby całkowitej. ________________ lat
2. Jak bardzo lubisz uczyć się języka angielskiego? Wybierz jedną z opcji, która jest najbardziej prawdziwa dla Ciebie.
   bardzo nie lubię nie lubię raczej nie lubię raczej lubię lubię bardzo lubię
3. Dlaczego lubisz/nie lubisz uczyć się języka angielskiego? Uzasadnij wybór, którego dokonałeś/łaś w punkcie 2.

   ____
   ____
   ____

4. Czy w przeszłości brałeś/łaś udział w dodatkowych pozaszkolnych zajęciach z języka angielskiego? Tak/Nie. Jeśli tak, to w jakich? ________________
5. Czy obecnie uczestniczysz w dodatkowych pozaszkolnych zajęciach z języka angielskiego?
   Tak/Nie. Jeśli tak, to w jakich?________________________
6. Czy posiadasz certyfikat z języka angielskiego? Tak/Nie
   Jeśli tak, to jaki?________________________
7. Jak często używasz języka angielskiego poza szkołą? Wybierz jedną z opcji, która jest najbardziej prawdziwa dla Ciebie.
   w ogóle bardzo rzadko czasami raczej często bardzo często zawsze
8. W jakich okolicznościach używasz języka poza szkołą? Wymień te sytuacje.

   ____
   ____
   ____

9. Jak zwykle uczysz się języka angielskiego? Podaj jeden najczęściej wykorzystywany sposób. ________________________
10. Jak dużo czasu poświęcasz dziennie na naukę języka angielskiego? Wybierz jedną z opcji, która jest najbardziej prawdziwa dla Ciebie.
    w ogóle mniej niż 5 minut 5–15 minut 15–30 minut 30–60 minut więcej niż 1h
11. Dlaczego poświęcasz tyle czasu na naukę języka angielskiego? Zapisz swoje uzasadnienie poniżej.

    ____
    ____
    ____

C. Needs questionnaire (Learner version)

Kwestionariusz ankiety dotyczący nauki języka angielskiego - Część 1 (Moje potrzeby)

Używając skali od 1 (w ogóle nie ważne) do 6 (bardzo ważne), oceń, jak ważne są dla Ciebie poniższe potrzeby wykorzystania znajomości języka angielskiego.

	1	2	3	4	5	6
1. porozumiewanie się z anglojęzycznymi członkami rodziny						
2. porozumiewanie się z anglojęzycznymi przyjaciółmi/ znajomymi						
3. dostęp do anglojęzycznej popkultury (filmów, seriali, muzyki, książek, gier, itp.)						
4. dostęp do wiadomości i artykułów online w j. angielskim						
5. możliwość podróżowania i zwiedzania						
6. osiągnięcie bardzo dobrego wyniku z części pisemnej egzaminu maturalnego						
7. osiągnięcie bardzo dobrego wyniku z części ustnej egzaminu maturalnego						
8. uczestnictwo w zajęciach w języku angielskim podczas studiów w Polsce						
9. uczestnictwo w zajęciach na studiach za granicą						
10. przyszła praca zawodowa						
11. pobyt stały za granicą						

Kwestionariusz ankiety dotyczący nauki języka angielskiego - Część 2 (Moje problemy)

Używając skali od 1 (w ogóle nie sprawiają mi problemów) do 6 (mam z nimi duże problemy), określ, jak bardzo wykonanie poniższych czynności w języku angielskim sprawia Ci problemy.

	1	2	3	4	5	6
1. czynności wymagające umiejętności słuchania w języku angielskim						
2. czynności wymagające umiejętności czytania w języku angielskim						
3. czynności wymagające umiejętności tworzenia wypowiedzi pisemnych w języku angielskim						
4. czynności wymagające umiejętności tworzenia wypowiedzi ustnych w języku angielskim						
5. czynności wymagające umiejętności reagowania pisemnego w języku angielskim						
6. czynności wymagające umiejętności reagowania ustnego w języku angielskim						
7. czynności wymagające umiejętności przetwarzania tekstu pisanego (np.: poprzez tłumaczenie, parafrazę, przekazywanie przeczytanych informacji innym osobom) w języku angielskim						
8. czynności wymagające umiejętności przetwarzania tekstu mówionego (np.: poprzez tłumaczenie, parafrazę, przekazywanie usłyszanych informacji innym osobom) w języku angielskim						

Kwestionariusz ankiety dotyczący nauki języka angielskiego - Część 3 (Moje preferencje)

Używając skali od 1 (w ogóle nie chciałbym/chciałabym) do 6 (bardzo chciałbym/chciałabym), określ, jak bardzo chciałbyś/chciałabyś rozwijać umiejętność wykonania poniższych czynności w języku angielskim.

	1	2	3	4	5	6
1. umiejętność wykonania czynności opartych na słuchaniu w języku angielskim						
2. umiejętność wykonania czynności opartych na czytaniu w języku angielskim						
3. umiejętność wykonania czynności opartych na tworzeniu wypowiedzi pisemnych w języku angielskim						
4. umiejętność wykonania czynności opartych na tworzeniu wypowiedzi ustnych w języku angielskim						
5. umiejętność wykonania czynności opartych na reagowaniu pisemnym w języku angielskim						
6. umiejętność wykonania czynności opartych na reagowaniu ustnym w języku angielskim						
7. umiejętności wykonania czynności opartych na przetwarzaniu tekstu pisanego (np.: poprzez tłumaczenie, parafrazę, przekazywanie przeczytanych informacji innym osobom) w języku angielskim						
8. umiejętności wykonania czynności opartych na przetwarzaniu tekstu mówionego (np.: poprzez tłumaczenie, parafrazę, przekazywanie usłyszanych informacji innym osobom) w języku angielskim						

Kwestionariusz ankiety dotyczący nauki języka angielskiego - Część 4 (Urządzenia mobilne)

Jaką rolę pełnią w Twoim życiu urządzenia mobilne, takie jak smartfon czy tablet? Używając skali od 1 (w ogóle się nie zgadzam) do 6 (całkowicie się zgadzam), określ, w jakim stopniu zgadzasz się z podanymi poniżej twierdzeniami.

	1	2	3	4	5	6
1. Korzystam ze smartfona bądź tabletu każdego dnia.						
2. Swoją umiejętność korzystania z urządzeń mobilnych oceniam na bardzo dobrą.						
3. Mam nieograniczony dostęp do Internetu na swoich urządzeniach mobilnych w domu.						
4. Moim zdaniem urządzenia mobilne, tj. smartfon i tablet, to narzędzia, które są pomocne w nauce.						
5. Często korzystam z pomocy inteligentnego asystenta głosowego (np.: *Google Assistant*, *Alexa*, *Siri*) w j. polskim.						
6. Często korzystam z pomocy inteligentnego asystenta głosowego (np.: *Google Assistant*, *Alexa*, *Siri*) w j. angielskim.						
7. Uważam, że inteligentny asystent głosowy (np.: *Google Assistant*, *Alexa*, *Siri*) może mi pomóc w samodzielnej nauce j. angielskiego.						
8. Wierzę, że dzięki interakcji z inteligentnym asystentem głosowym (np.: *Google Assistant*, *Alexa*, *Siri*) w j. angielskim rozwinę swoje sprawności językowe.						

E. Sample tasks for the ExG and the CtrlG

The ExG tasks

ZADANIE 1
KROK 2

- **Wykonaj zadanie, uzupełniając luki w mailu brakującymi informacji.**

Tekst A: *Hi, I've heard from Kate that you are in Greece on holidays. Lucky you! I would like to be there with you, but I have to study for my entrance exams. Tell me at least a few things about this beautiful country. I've heard once that there is some other name for Greece. Is it true? Is Greece a big country – how many people live there? What countries does Greece border? I am pretty certain that one of the neighbouring countries must be Turkey. I remember the information from my Geography class. LOL! Are there many mountain ranges in Greece? I know that the Greek flag is white and blue, but I have no idea why it is so. Do you know anything about it? In addition to Acropolis of Athens, what else Greece is famous for? By the way, have you seen it already? I know that Greece founded democracy and philosophy. Is there anything else that the Greeks created? Tell me what the weather is like in Athens this time of the year. Best, George*

Tekst B: *Hi George, Thanks for your e-mail. I feel wonderful here in Athens. I hope you are fine there in Glasgow too! Let me tell you a few facts about Greece. Greece is a small country in Southeastern Europe. It is also officially known as* **(1)**……………………. *Its capital city is Athens. The population of Greece is estimated to be* **(2)**…………………. *You are right that Greece borders Turkey. It also borders* **(3)**……………………. *Eighty percent of the country is mountainous, with* **(4)**……………………. *being the highest peak. The Greek flag with a white cross on a blue field was used as a land flag from 1828 until 1969 and from 1975 to 1978. In 1978, the flag became a national flag. There are many theories about the origins of the colour of the flag. One says that blue and white represent the* **(5)**……………………….. *In addition to Acropolis of Athens that you've mentioned, some other popular attractions in Greece include* **(6)**……………………….. *Greece is considered a birthplace not only of democracy and philosophy, but also* **(7)** ……………………… *It has been really hot in Athens recently, but I hope I will manage to see all the sights planned for today. This evening I will upload some photos on WhatsApp! I must go now. XOXO*

ZADANIE 1
KROK 1

- **Przeczytaj uważnie treść polecenia znajdującego się poniżej.**

Jesteś na tygodniowych wakacjach w Atenach. Twój anglojęzyczny znajomy ze Szkocji jest zaintrygowany tą wiadomością i prosi Cię o przedstawienie szczegółów dotyczących Grecji. Ty jednak nie jesteś w stanie podać mu wszystkich informacji, o które Cię prosi w swoim e-mailu (Tekst A). Nie chcąc robić mu przykrości, konsultujesz się z *Alexą*, aby uzyskać odpowiedzi na jego pytania. Na podstawie odpowiedzi zaproponowanych przez asystenta, uzupełnij e-mail do swojego kolegi (Tekst B).

- **Zanim zaczniesz wykonywać zadanie, zastanów się, jakich informacji na temat Grecji może od Ciebie oczekiwać Twój znajomy?**

ZADANIE 1
KROK 3

- **Aby upewnić się, że przekazujesz swojemu koledze właściwe informacje, wykonaj zadanie ponownie.**
- **Czy jesteś zadowolony/a z odpowiedzi, jakie zaproponowała Ci *Alexa* na Twoje pytania? Czy uważasz, że Twój szkocki kolega uzna przesłane przez Ciebie informacje za satysfakcjonujące?**

ZADANIE 2
KROK 3

- Aby upewnić się, że przekazujesz swojej koleżance właściwe informacje, wykonaj zadanie ponownie.
- Czy jesteś zadowolony/a z odpowiedzi, jakie zaproponowała Ci *Alexa* na Twoje pytania? Czy uważasz, że Twoja austriacka koleżanka uzna przesłane przez Ciebie informacje za satysfakcjonujące?

ZADANIE 2
KROK 2

- Wykonaj zadanie, uzupełniając luki w mailu brakującymi informacji.

INGRID: Hi, it's Ingrid here. We met during the Austrian-Polish student exchange three months ago. I hope you remember me. I'm really sorry to disturb you, but I badly need your help. I'm preparing a project about the most intriguing tourist attraction to visit in Poland. Guess what? I've chosen the Palace of Culture and Science, about which you told me during one of our trips around Vienna. As I got down to the project yesterday evening, it turned out that my Internet connection is terribly slow. It took me three minutes to load the Google search engine. I can't work like that! The deadline for the presentation is tomorrow. Please help me! Ingrid

YOU: Hi Ingrid, of course I remember you. Don't worry! I'll help you. What information do you need?

INGRID: Awesome! You're great! Thank you a lot! In my presentation, I would like to include basic facts about the Palace of Culture and Science. Firstly, I would like to tell how tall it is. Secondly, I would like to inform the class when it was constructed and who its designer was. Next, I would like to make it clear that originally there was a different name used with reference to the Palace of Culture and Science. Also, I would like to mention some of the innovations made to the building. Finally, I would like to explain why it has been considered controversial by Poles.

YOU: Ingrid, here is what I found for you. The Palace of Culture and Science is a skyscraper located in central Warsaw, Poland. It is (1)............................, which makes it one of the tallest buildings in Europe. The tower was constructed between (2)........................ by 3,500 to 5,000 Soviet workers and 4,000 Polish workers. It was designed by a Soviet Russian architect (3)............................The building was originally known as (4) .... (5)........................ were added to the top of the building in 2000. In 2010, high-power LED lights were installed, allowing the Palace to take various colours at night. The building currently serves as an exhibition centre and office complex. The Palace of Culture and Science is a highly controversial building as it is reminds Poles of (6).................. Others, however, disagree, arguing that over the years it became the symbol of Warsaw.

ZADANIE 2
KROK 1

- Przeczytaj uważnie treść polecenia znajdującego się poniżej.

Wróciłeś ze szkoły do domu i masz zamiar odrabiać swoją pracę domową. Jednak w chwili, kiedy otwierasz jeden z podręczników, otrzymujesz powiadomienie na WhatsAppie. Okazuje się, że skontaktowała się z Tobą Twoja koleżanki z Austrii, Ingrid, którą poznałeś/łaś podczas wymiany studenckiej. W swojej wiadomości błaga Cię ona o pomoc w dokończeniu szkolnego projektu na temat Pałacu Kultury i Nauki w Warszawie. Zapoznaj się z jej prośbą i pomóż jej przygotować się na zajęcia. Wykorzystaj do tego celu asystenta głosowego *Alexę*. Na podstawie odpowiedzi zaproponowanych przez asystenta, uzupełnij luki w wiadomości znajdującej się poniżej

- Zanim zaczniesz wykonywać zadanie, zastanów się, jakich informacji na temat Pałacu Kultury i Nauki może oczekiwać od Ciebie Ingrid.

The CtrlG tasks

ZADANIE 1
KROK 1

- **Przeczytaj uważnie treść polecenia znajdującego się poniżej.**

Jesteś na dwutygodniowych wakacjach na hiszpańskiej Gran Canarii. Anglojęzyczni animatorzy, Jake i Sasha, z hotelu, w którym się zatrzymałeś/aś, zorganizowali tego wieczoru warsztaty kulturowe, podczas których każda para uczestników ma za zadanie przygotować krótką prezentację na temat wylosowanej atrakcji turystycznej. Ty i twój partner wylosowaliście Muzeum Figur Woskowych Madame Tussaud w Londynie. Wykorzystując informacje zawarte w nagraniu (Tekst A), które przekazali Wam Jake i Sasha, uzupełnij Waszą prezentację brakującymi informacjami (Tekst B).

- **Zanim zaczniesz wykonywać zadanie, zastanów się, jakich informacji na temat Muzeum Figur Woskowych Madame Tussaud mogą od Was oczekiwać Jake i Sasha.**

ZADANIE 1
KROK 2A

Tekst A:

Posłuchaj Rebecci Holmes, która opowiada o Muzeum Figur Woskowych w Londynie.

Adapted from https://www.youtube.com/watch?v=...

ZADANIE 1
KROK 2B

Tekst B:

The Madame Tussauds Wax Museum is one of the most famous paid tourist attractions in London. The museum has been functioning since the first half of the 19th century. Its history dates back to the time of **(1)** .... when the founder of the museum, Mary Tussaud, came to London from France. This London landmark survived the fire in **(2)**........................... as well as the bombing during World War II. What is extraordinary about this place is that **(3)**...................... now. For instance, the hairs of the figures are inserted one by one individually in the wax figures' heads. The visit to the museum is interactive as visitors **(4)**........................ One of the most popular attraction is the One Directions exhibition. Another one is unquestioningly **(5)**............................ Over the last decades, there have been **(6)**.................... figures made of her in different periods of her lifetime.

ZADANIE 1
KROK 3

- Aby upewnić się, że przekazujecie właściwe informacje, odsłuchaj nagranie jeszcze raz i wykonaj zadanie ponownie.
- Czy nagranie zaproponowane Ci przez animatorów umożliwiło Ci wykonanie zadania, jakim było przygotowanie prezentacji? Czy uważasz, że Wasza widownia uzna przedstawione przez Was informacje za satysfakcjonujące?

ZADANIE 2
KROK 1

- Przeczytaj uważnie treść polecenia znajdującego się poniżej.

  Twoje tygodniowe wakacje w Valletcie, stolicy Malty, dobiegają końca. Twój anglojęzyczny znajomy z Warszawy, Sam, jest bardzo podekscytowany tą informacją, gdyż również planuje wycieczkę na Maltę. W związku z tym, w swojej wiadomości mailowej prosi Cię o przedstawienie mu kilku szczegółów dotyczących tego kraju. Wykorzystując dane przedstawione poniżej (Tekst A, B, C, D), uzupełnij swoją wiadomość zwrotną do Sama (Tekst E).

- Zanim zaczniesz wykonywać zadanie, zastanów się, jakich informacji na temat Malty może od Ciebie oczekiwać Sam.

ZADANIE 2
KROK 2A

Tekst A:

The Maltese archipelago lies 93 km south of Sicily and 288 km north of Africa. It consists of three islands: Malta, Gozo and Comino with a total population of over 500,000 inhabitants. Malta is the largest island and the cultural, commercial, and administrative centre. Gozo is the second largest island and is more rural, characterised by fishing, tourism, and agriculture. The smallest, Comino, is largely uninhabited.

Adapted from https://www.visitmalta.com/en/a/about-malta/

Tekst B:

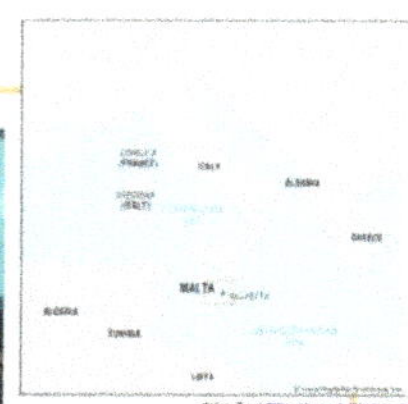

Taken from https://www.britannica.com/place/Malta

Tekst C:

AROUND THE WORLD BLOG

In my post today, I want to share with you guys my experiences from my recent trip to Malta. I've visited the majority of the countries in Europe, but none of them has made such a huge impression on me. Believe me! Megaliths, medieval towers and dungeons as well as Calypso's Cave are just a handful of things that has made my visit to Malta so unique. The narrow meandering streets of Maltese towns and villages which lead to the main square and huge baroque churches are more than spellbinding. Follow me on Instagram to see the photos from the most charming corners of Malta. Who else has been there? What do you think about this place? Leave your comments below.

Self-prepared

Tekst D:

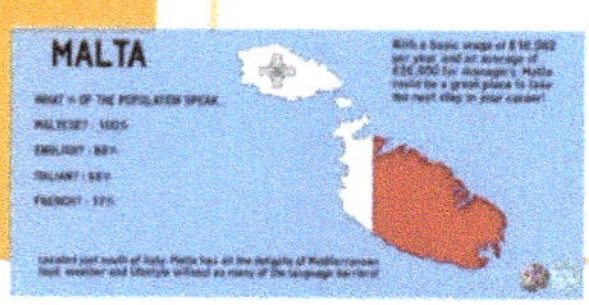

Taken from https://www.europeanlanguagejobs.com/blog/English-Speaking-Countries-Europe

ZADANIE 2
KROK 2B

Tekst E:

Hi Sam,

Thanks for your e-mail. It's been amazing here in Valletta. I hope you are fine there in Warsaw too! I remember you mentioning that your dream would be to go to Malta. I can see that you're making it come true now. Let me tell you a few facts about Malta. It is the largest island and the cultural heart of **(1)** .... *It is located close to Italy, Tunisia, and* **(2)** .... *Malta together with the remaining islands,* **(3)** ...., *are inhabited by over 500,000 people. The Maltese landscape is particularly spectacular. The centre of each town and village is* **(4)** .... *where you can always find a charming baroque church. It is really comfortable to travel around Malta because the majority of people (almost ninety percent of the population)* **(5)**...................... *so you'll have no problems communicating with the locals. I've also heard that in addition to travelling, Malta is also a top destination for due to* **(6)**........................ *per year. This evening I will upload some photos that I have taken in Valetta and the surroundings on WhatsApp! Bye for now.*

XYZ

ZADANIE 2
KROK 3

- Aby upewnić się, że przekazujesz Samowi właściwe informacje, zapoznaj się jeszcze raz z treścią tekstów A-D i wykonaj zadanie ponownie.
- Czy zaproponowane teksty umożliwiły Ci wykonanie zadania, jakim było uzupełnienia maila do Sama? Czy uważasz, że uzna on przedstawione przez Ciebie informacje za satysfakcjonujące?

F. Screenshots of multimodal responses provided by *Alexa*

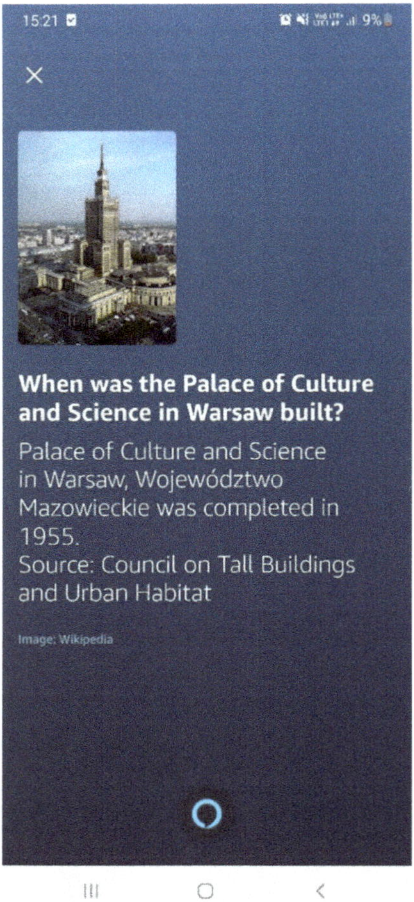

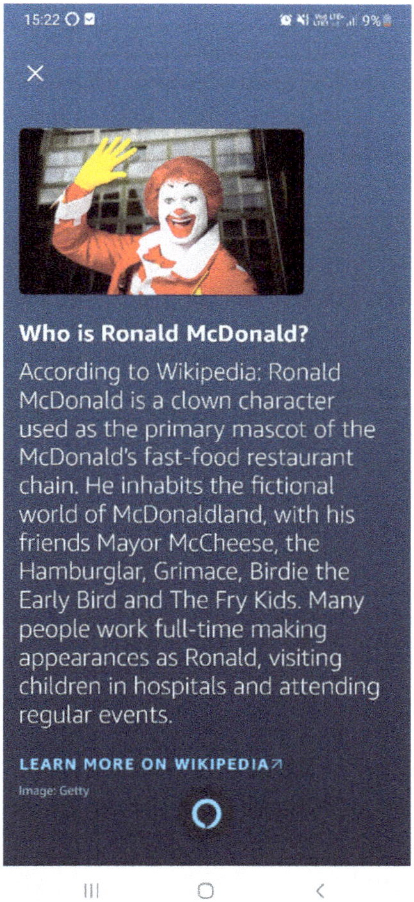
15:22
9%
Who is Ronald McDonald?
According to Wikipedia: Ronald McDonald is a clown character used as the primary mascot of the McDonald's fast-food restaurant chain. He inhabits the fictional world of McDonaldland, with his friends Mayor McCheese, the Hamburglar, Grimace, Birdie the Early Bird and The Fry Kids. Many people work full-time making appearances as Ronald, visiting children in hospitals and attending regular events.
LEARN MORE ON WIKIPEDIA
Image: Getty

G. Sample intralinguistic text mediation test

Version A

ROZUMIENIE ZE SŁUCHU

1. Usłyszysz dwukrotnie fragment wywiadu radiowego. Na podstawie informacji zawartych w nagraniu uzupełnij luki 1-5 w poniższej notatce. Luki należy uzupełnić w języku angielskim.

Jobcentre Plus

- *Jobcentre Plus* is a government-funded (1) ________________ that helps people to find work. Its offices are located in most cities across the UK.
- It provides resources such as up-to-date job vacancy listings. People can access these resources via the *Jobcentre Plus* website and (2) ________________ called *Jobcentre Direct*.
- *Jobpoints*, that is (3) ________________ computer terminals, can be used by people who do not have access to computers to search for jobs for free.
- For people who don't have the right qualifications, *Jobcentre Plus* provides information about (4) ________________ .
- Benefits such as Income Support and Jobseeker's Allowance help people to cover their (5) ________________ while they're out of work.

ROZUMIENIE TEKSTÓW PISANYCH

2. Zapoznaj się z zawartością Tekstów 1-3, a następnie uzupełnij luki w tekście 4. Luki należy uzupełnić w języku angielskim.

Tekst 1

https://www.dreamstime.com/camping-checklist-flat-color-vector-informational-infographic-template-essentials-poster-booklet-ppt-page-concept-design-image189654967

Tekst 2

https://www.flickr.com/photos/jkgroove/3511097779

Tekst 3

CAMPING IN THE WILD FORUM

at_a_loss: Hello, it'll be my first time at a campsite next week. Share with me some do's and don'ts of camping, please☺

diana_22: I think, there's nothing more irritating than an itchy mosquito bite. I take some insect repellent with me every time I go camping.

at_a_loss: Thanks @diana_22. Is there anything else that I should remember about, guys?

handyman_jake: Dear @at_a_loss, even in the summer, temperatures may drop sharply once it gets dark. Bear in mind to pack a sleeping bag to stay warm in the tent at night. Also, don't forget how dangerous the sun can be in the summer time. Sunburn is not only painful, but it is also dangerous. A bottle of sunscreen is a must for all campers.

at_a_loss: Thank you handyman_jake!

pablo_06: Hi! diana_22 and handyman_jake are absolutely right, but I think that you should also remember that there is no electricity in the wild. Pack a flashlight in order to see in the dark. You'll also need a lighter so that you can start fires.

(self-prepared)

Tekst 4

Hey, Jude!
Are you ready for our summer camp this year? I can't wait to meet you there! I've just made some Internet research and here is what I've found. We all know how terrible insect bites are. I will never forget how badly I was bitten by mosquitos a couple of years ago during my holidays at the lake. We should ***(1)*** ____________________ *with us to avoid them. Also, don't forget to pack a/an* ***(2)*** ____________________ *because it is usually gets colder after dark. What else? We shouldn't get lost with a map, but, who knows. Just in case, remember to use your* ***(3)*** ____________________ *to go in the right direction. Pack* ***(4)*** ________________ *as there will be no electricity available. Finally, we can't forget that we will spend those two weeks surrounded by nature so we have to learn to respect it. We should recycle our rubbish and remember not to* ***(5)*** ________________________ *See you the day after tomorrow!*

XOXO,
Julie

Summary

Over the last century, foreign language teaching has grown into a field of theoretical and empirical research, calling the concept of a method into question and effecting the transition away from focus on forms and focus on meaning to focus on form. The 2001 publication of the *Common European Framework of Reference for Languages: Learning, teaching, assessment* by the Council of Europe was an essential step forward in the evolution of the field. Considered a direct continuation of previous methodological and second language acquisition traditions, the framework's conceptual model promoted the action-oriented vision of language use and language learning by underlining the importance of social actions during task performance.

At the same time, continuous technological advancements have exerted their profound influence on foreign language teaching practices. The scope of computer-assisted language learning, once limited to primitive room-size mainframes and drill-and-kill courseware, has expanded significantly with the arrival of increasingly smaller yet more powerful mobile devices. The use of artificial intelligence algorithms in language learning and teaching created intelligent computer-assisted language learning and made it possible for the once impossible dream of human-machine communication to be realised anytime and anywhere in language education.

The idea of voice assistance easily accessible on mainstream smartphones and dedicated appliances came into greater public attention fairly recently. Voice-based artificially intelligent technologies (i.e., *Siri*, *Google Assistant*, *Alexa*, *Cortana*, *Celia*) have been designed to support human users in everyday digital task and service performance. An increase in the research interest in the application of these technologies in in-class and out-of-class English as a second/foreign language instruction has taken place over the last several years. In so far as using voice assistants has been reported to have a positive influence on both linguistic and affective aspects of language learning, the research has suffered from serious limitations related to the short duration of the treatment, low number of the participants, and a narrow range of data collection tools.

The present research study was designed and conducted in response to the latest educational European trends underlying foreign language teaching, developments in the field of computer-assisted language learning, and the adverse effect of the COVID-19 pandemic on language instruction in European Union member states. Given the buzzword status of the action, mediation, and lifelong learning concepts in language education and the ubiquity of increasingly sophisticated portable devices, self-instructed task-based language learning was combined with intelligent mobile-assisted language learning within the treatment to verify the effects of this experimental intervention on the participants' ability to mediate a text.

The book was divided into five main chapters, each of which played an equally important role in the presentation of the theory and methodology underlying the current research project. A list of appendices was also attached to demonstrate sample materials developed and used by the present author.

Chapter One provided an overview of the trends in European policies and practices for developing foreign language learners' communicative competence. It began with the presentation of the communicative competence construct and its prominence in the field of foreign language teaching. Next, it discussed the action-oriented approach, the conceptual model developed within the Council of Europe's seminal documents. Lastly, it defined mediation in the context of language education (and beyond) and explored practical aspects of the concept in instructed settings.

Chapter Two addressed the problem of foreign language learning, teaching, and assessment in post-war Poland. First, it discussed the selected education reforms implemented by the Polish government and examined their impact on the state of language instruction in the country. Later, it looked at English as a foreign language secondary school examinations in both European and Polish secondary school contexts. Finally, it listed the challenges related to the development of communicative competence by foreign language learners in Poland.

Chapter Three gave background to the application of voice assistants in language education. It stressed the increasing mobility of computer technologies and assessed implications involved in their application to language education. Also, it presented an overview of technological developments that led to the emergence of intelligent mobile-assisted language learning. Next, it elaborated upon the novel concept task-oriented intelligent mobile-assisted language learning, which was developed for the purpose of the current discussion. Finally, it identified the research trends and sources of limitations of the selected studies on the use of voice assistants in in-class and autonomous English as a second/foreign language learning.

Chapter Four shifted the focus onto the methodology underlying the current research project. It began with the presentation of the research problem, aims, questions, and hypotheses. Next, it described a mixed-methods approach to the research design adopted in the study. Once basic information about the sample selected for the purpose of the current investigation was provided, the six-stage research procedure consisting of the needs analysis, target task selection, instructional treatment design, pilot testing, study proper, and programme evaluation was presented. The final subchapter was devoted to the discussion of ethical considerations in the context of the current research procedure.

Chapter Five presented the results of the quantitative and qualitative analyses of the data obtained from the current quasi-experiment and programme evaluation. Next, it discussed the findings in the context of the three research questions and the relevant literature. Additionally, the chapter listed pedagogical implications for foreign language learning (to mediate) and several conclusions based on the data presented in the preceding subchapters. Finally, it identified and discussed limitations to the study and put forward recommendations for potential future research.

A six-stage task-based language learning programme was designed to fill the gap in the computer-assisted language learning research, that is to examine the effects of task-oriented and intelligent mobile-assisted language learning on intralinguistic mediation of oral and written texts by Polish teenage learners of English as a foreign language. It started with the multimethodological research on participants' needs (i.e., needs analysis, Stage One), whose results laid the basis for the selection of the target tasks (Stage Two) and the development of the intervention (Stage Three). Next, the instruments of data collection, analysis methods, and selected tasks were piloted within the pilot-testing stage one month before the study proper began (Stage Four). Once the necessary changes had been introduced to the main study, the quasi-experiment with the factor rotation technique took place (Stage Five) followed by the evaluation of the technology-mediated task-based programme (Stage Six).

Six intact groups of Polish teenage EFL secondary school students were selected to participate in the study based on non-probability sampling. In total, 61 graduates of eight-year primary schools were assigned to Group A and Group B and took part in the quasi-experiment and programme evaluation. To increase the validity of the study, factor rotation was implemented, which means that both groups took on the status of the experimental group in either Phase One or Phase Two of the study.

Three data collection instruments (i.e., text mediation tests, post-study questionnaires, and semi-structured interviews) were used in the current research study. A mixed-methods approach to research design was adopted to conduct the product and process evaluation of the programme. The quasi-experiment was undertaken to answer the first research question, that is to examine the effects of the treatment on the Polish EFL students' intralinguistic text mediation both at within- and between-group levels. The results of the experimental groups were compared with those from the pre-tests as well as with those of the control students who had followed a conventional task-based programme. To answer the second central research questions, which investigated the participants' perceptions of voice assistance, quantitative and qualitative data were collected within the descriptive research. Quantitative and qualitative analyses of the data collected in the quasi-experiment and programme evaluation were conducted in view of the requirements of the specific research questions.

The findings demonstrated that the treatment did have a positive effect on the participants' text mediation improvement both at between- and within-group levels. Generally, the experimental groups performed significantly better on text mediation activities having received the experimental intervention compared to their performance before the treatment and to the performance of the control groups.

Thanks to the combination of intelligent mobile-assisted language learning and task-based self-instruction, the participants could communicate with *Alexa* to perform real-life tasks on their own in their private home surroundings. The participants positively assessed their interaction with *Alexa* and expressed positive opinions on the use of voice assistance in learning to mediate texts. They generally evaluated the technology as useable, effective, and satisfactory. As far as its benefits are concerned, the participants underlined their opportunity to practise speaking English, enhance pronunciation, broaden vocabulary knowledge, increase confidence in using the language, and gain easy access to multimodal information. Unreliability of the technology, irrelevance of its feedback, problems with understanding and connectivity, increased time burden, downloading issues, and artificiality of communication were the challenges listed by the participants.

Despite strengths of the research procedure, such as the use of factor rotation and methodological triangulation, the study suffered from some limitations. Most importantly, the findings were far from generalisable because the sample was not selected randomly, thus, it was not representative of the entire population of Polish EFL secondary school students. Furthermore, the current investigation displayed selection and sampling bias because particular groups of Polish EFL learners were more likely to be selected from the population than others.

Even though several weaknesses related to the design and application of the study could be identified, it must be emphasised that the treatment implemented in the current investigation was well worth replicating. First and foremost, it offered an attractive alternative to traditional task-based self-instruction because it provided a ubiquitous learning environment, which in addition to improving participants' intralinguistic text mediation, promoted their target language reception and production as well as pronunciation and vocabulary practice. Moreover, it not only involved the students in simultaneous language reception, production, interaction, and mediation, but also supported their comprehension of *Alexa*'s responses through the presentation of multimodal input by the voice assistant. Equally importantly, technology-mediated task-based language learning created authentic contexts for everyday target language use, promoted experiential learning, and offered individualised feedback. Last but not least, it involved learners in communicative and interactive English as a foreign language use which could take place in students' low-stake home surroundings.

In view of the above, it is justified to argue that important implications of the use of *Alexa* (and other voice assistants) in self-instructed and task-based language learning arose from the findings not only for interested researchers, but also for different stakeholders in the field of foreign language teaching. First, the study opened up promising avenues for future research within computer-assisted language learning because a positive relationship between the implementation of voice assistance in task-based language learning and participants' improvement in the ability to mediate texts was discovered. Second, language educators who intend to develop their students' communicative competence in an integrative way as well as to lower their learners' language anxiety and promote their independence in learning English as a foreign language should find it worthwhile considering assigning homework similar to the experimental intervention.

ŁÓDŹ STUDIES IN LANGUAGE
Edited by
Barbara Lewandowska-Tomaszczyk and Łukasz Bogucki

Vol. 1 Barbara Lewandowska-Tomaszczyk / Patrick James Melia (eds.): PALC'99: Practical Applications in Language Corpora. Papers from the International Conference at the University of Łódź, 15-18 April 1999. 2000.

Vol. 2 Lou Burnard / Tony McEnery (eds.): Rethinking Language Pedagogy from a Corpus Perspective. Papers from the Third International Conference on Teaching and Language Corpora. 2000.

Vol. 3 Barbara Lewandowska-Tomaszczyk / John Osborne / Frits Schulte: Foreign Language Teaching and Information and Communication Technology. 2001.

Vol. 4 Piotr Cap: Explorations in Political Discourse. Methodological and Critical Perspectives. 2002.

Vol. 5 Ewa Waniek-Klimczak / Patrick James Melia (eds.): Accents and Speech in Teaching English Phonetics and Phonology. EFL perspective. 2002.

Vol. 6 Barbara Lewandowska-Tomaszczyk / Kamila Turewicz (eds.): Cognitive Linguistics Today. 2002.

Vol. 7 Barbara Lewandowska-Tomaszczyk (ed.): PALC 2001: Practical Applications in Language Corpora. 2003.

Vol. 8 Corpus Linguistics by the Lune. A Festschrift for Geoffrey Leech. Edited by Andrew Wilson, Paul Rayson and Tony McEnery. 2003.

Vol. 9 Barbara Lewandowska-Tomaszczyk (ed.): Practical Applications in Language and Computers. PALC 2003. 2004.

Vol. 10 Imagery in Language. Festschrift in Honour of Professor Ronald W. Langacker. Edited by Barbara Lewandowska-Tomaszczyk and Alina Kwiatkowska. 2004.

Vol. 11 Seana Coulson / Barbara Lewandowska-Tomaszczyk (eds.): The Literal and Nonliteral in Language and Thought. 2005.

Vol. 12 Piotr Cap (ed.): Pragmatics Today. 2005.

Vol. 13 Jacek Waliński / Krzysztof Kredens / Stanisław Goźdź-Roszkowski (eds.): Corpora and ICT in Language Studies. PALC 2005. 2007.

Vol. 14 Krzysztof Kosecki (ed.): Perspectives on Metonymy. Proceedings of the International Conference "Perspectives on Metonymy", held in Łódź, Poland, May 6-7, 2005. 2007.

Vol. 15 Barbara Lewandowska-Tomaszczyk / Tomasz Płudowski / Dolores Valencia Tanno (eds.): The Media and International Communication. 2007.

Vol. 16 Krzysztof Kredens / Stanisław Goźdź-Roszkowski (eds.): Language and the Law: International Outlooks. 2007.

Vol. 17 Barbara Lewandowska-Tomaszczyk (ed.): Corpus Linguistics, Computer Tools, and Applications - State of the Art. PALC 2007. 2008.

Vol. 18 Barbara Lewandowska-Tomaszczyk / Katarzyna Dziwirek (eds.): Studies in Cognitive Corpus Linguistics. 2009.

Vol. 19 Barbara Lewandowska-Tomaszczyk / Marcel Thelen (eds.): Meaning in Translation. 2010.

Vol. 20 Łukasz Bogucki / Krzysztof Kredens (eds.): Perspectives on Audiovisual Translation. 2010.

Vol. 21 Piotr Stalmaszczyk (ed.): Turning Points in the Philosophy of Language and Linguistics. 2011.

Vol. 22 Stanisław Goźdź-Roszkowski: Patterns of Linguistic Variation in American Legal English. A Corpus-Based Study. 2011.

Vol. 23 Kamila Ciepiela (ed.): Identity through a Language Lens. 2011.

Vol. 24 Stanisław Goźdź-Roszkowski (ed.): Explorations across Languages and Corpora. PALC 2009. 2011.

Vol. 25 Krzysztof Kosecki / Janusz Badio (eds.): Cognitive Processes in Language. 2012.

Vol. 26 Alina Kwiatkowska (ed.): Texts and Minds. Papers in Cognitive Poetics and Rhetoric. 2012.

Vol. 27 Paul A. Wilson (ed.): Dynamicity in Emotion Concepts. 2012.

Vol. 28 Piotr Pęzik (ed.): Corpus Data across Languages and Disciplines. 2012.

Vol. 29 Mikołaj Deckert: Meaning in Subtitling. Toward a Contrastive Cognitive Semantic Model. 2013.

Vol. 30 Łukasz Bogucki: Areas and Methods of Audiovisual Translation Research. 3rd Revised Edition. 2019.

Vol. 31 Janusz Badio / Kamila Ciepiela (eds.): Language, Action, Interaction. 2013.

Vol. 32 Barbara Lewandowska-Tomaszczyk / Krzysztof Kosecki (eds.): Time and Temporality in Language and Human Experience. 2014.

Vol. 33 Iwona Witczak-Plisiecka (ed.): Cognitive and Pragmatic Aspects of Speech Actions. 2014.

Vol. 34 Małgorzata Anna Kamińska: A History of the Concise Oxford *Dictionary*. 2014.

Vol. 35 Łukasz Bogucki / Mikołaj Deckert (eds.): Accessing Audiovisual Translation. 2015.

Vol. 36 Joanna Jabłońska-Hood: A Conceptual Blending Theory of Humour. Selected British Comedy Productions in Focus. 2015.

Vol. 37 Krzysztof Kosecki / Janusz Badio (eds.): Empirical Methods in Language Studies. 2015.

Vol. 38 Katarzyna Stadnik: Chaucer's Choices. Through the looking-glass of medieval imagery. 2015.

Vol. 39 Paulina Pietrzak / Mikołaj Deckert (eds.): Constructing Translation Competence. 2015.

Vol. 40 Małgorzata Fabiszak / Karolina Krawczak / Katarzyna Rokoszewska (eds.): Categorization in Discourse and Grammar. 2016.

Vol. 41 Marcel Thelen / Gys-Walt van Egdom / Dirk Verbeeck / Łukasz Bogucki / Barbara Lewandowska-Tomaszczyk (eds.): Translation and Meaning. New Series, Vol. 1. 2016.

Vol. 42 Łukasz Bogucki / Barbara Lewandowska-Tomaszczyk / Marcel Thelen (eds.): Translation and Meaning. New Series, Vol. 2, Pt. 1. 2016.

Vol. 43 Łukasz Bogucki / Barbara Lewandowska-Tomaszczyk / Marcel Thelen (eds.): Translation and Meaning. New Series, Vol. 2, Pt. 2. 2016.

Vol. 44 Przemysław Łozowski / Katarzyna Stadnik (eds.): Visions and Revisions. Studies in Theoretical and Applied Linguistics. 2016.

Vol. 45 Marek Kuźniak / Bożena Rozwadowska / Michał Szawerna (eds.): From Motion to Emotion. Aspects of Physical and Cultural Embodiment in Language. 2016.

Vol. 46 Anna Rędzioch-Korkuz: Opera Surtitling as a Special Case of Audiovisual Translation. Towards a Semiotic and Translation Based Framework for Opera Surtitling. 2016.

Vol. 47 Mateusz Sajna: Video Game Translation and Cognitive Semantics. 2016.

Vol. 48 Kamila Ciepiela (ed.): Identity in Communicative Contexts. 2016.

Vol. 49 Mikołaj Nkollo: The Entrenchment of the 'unus alterum' Pattern. Four Essays on Latin and Old Romance Reciprocal Constructions. 2016.

Vol. 50 Paweł Rydzewski: Backness Distinction in Phonology. A Polish Perspective on the Phonemic Status of *y*. 2016.

Vol. 51 Piotr Pęzik / Jacek Tadeusz Waliński (eds.): Language, Corpora and Cognition. 2017.

Vol. 52 Janusz Badio (ed.): Events and Narratives in Language. 2016.

Vol. 53 Mikołaj Deckert (ed.): Audiovisual Translation – Research and Use. 2017. 2nd Expanded Edition 2019.

Vol. 54 Michał Szawerna: Metaphoricity of Conventionalized Diegetic Images in Comics. A Study in Multimodal Cognitive Linguistics. 2017.

Vol. 55 Artur Gałkowski / Monika Kopytowska (eds.): Current Perspectives in Semiotics. Signs, Signification, and Communication. 2018.

Vol. 56 Artur Gałkowski / Monika Kopytowska (eds.): Current Perspectives in Semiotics. Text, Genres, and Representations. 2018.

Vol. 57 Łukasz Bogucki / Piotr Cap (eds.): Exploration in Language and Linguistics. For Professor Piotr Stalmaszczyk on the Occasion of His 60th Birthday. 2018.

Vol. 58 Michał Kornacki: Computer-assisted Translation (CAT) Tools in the Translator Training Process. 2018.

Vol. 59 Marcin Walczyński / Piotr Czajka / Michał Szawerna (eds.): On the Verge between Language and Translation. 2018.

Vol. 60 Łukasz Bogucki / Paulina Pietrzak / Michał Kornacki (eds.): Understanding Translator Education. 2018.

Vol. 61 Marcin Walczyński: Psycho-Affective Factors in Consecutive Interpreting. 2019.

Vol. 62 Kamila Ciepiela (ed.): Language, Identity and Community. 2019.

Vol. 63 Olga Łabendowicz: Audiovisual Translation in Poland. Changing Audiences. 2019.

Vol. 64 Enrique Bernárdez / Joanna Jabłońska-Hood / Katarzyna Stadnik (eds.): Cognition in context. New insights into language, culture and the mind. 2019.

Vol. 65 Montse Corrius / Eva Espasa / Patrick Zabalbeascoa (eds.): Translating Audiovisuals in a Kaleidoscope of Languages. 2019.

Vol. 66 Barbara Lewandowska-Tomaszczyk / Valeria Monello / Marco Venuti (eds.): Language, Heart, and Mind. Studies at the intersection of emotion and cogni-tion. 2020.

Vol. 67 Marta Chodkiewicz: Understanding the Development of Translation Competence. 2020.

Vol. 68 Urszula Paradowska: Developing Information Competence in Translator Training. 2021.

Vol. 69 Luca Valleriani: Upper-class English in Natural and Audiovisual Dialogue. 2021.

Vol. 70 Michał Kornacki and Gary Massey (eds.): Contextuality in Translation and Interpreting. Selected Papers from the Łódź-ZHAW Duo Colloquium on Translation and Meaning 2020–2021. 2022.

Vol. 71 Monika Kopytowska / Artur Gałkowski / Massimo Leone (eds.): Thought-Sign-Symbol. Cross-Cultural Representations of Religion. 2022.

Vol. 72 Bartosz Pietrzak: The Concept of Honor in the Language of Early Arabic Poetry. A Cultural Linguistic Study. 2022.

Vol. 73 Aleksandra Beata Makowska: Terminology and phraseology in research papers in the domains of new technologies. A cognitive corpus-based perspective. 2024.

Vol. 74 Marco Venuti / Emanuela Campisi / Ester Di Silvestro (eds.): Strategies of Inclusion and Exclusion in online and offline Interaction. 2024.

Vol. 75 Łukasz Dutka: The Quality of Live Subtitling. Technology, User Expectations and Quality Metrics. 2024.

Vol. 76 Klaudia Gajewska: Voice Assistants in Action-oriented Mediation Practice. Insights from Polish Learners of English as a Foreign Language. 2025.

www.peterlang.com

www.ingramcontent.com/pod-product-compliance
Ingram Content Group UK Ltd.
Pitfield, Milton Keynes, MK11 3LW, UK
UKHW021829100926
8556IPUK00004B/232

9 783631 907917